MOTHER TOWN

Episodes in the history of BURSLEM

By

Fred Hughes

GENERAL EDITION

Published by Burslem Community Development Trust, October 2000

Printed and bound by **Sherwin Rivers Ltd.**, Waterloo Road, Cobridge,
Stoke-on-Trent, Staffordshire, ST6 3HR.

© Fred Hughes 2000

First Published 2000

All rights reserved. No part of this publication may be reproduced, stored in a retrieval system, or transmitted, in any form or by any means, electronic, mechanical, photocopying, recording or otherwise without the prior written permission of the copyright holder.

ISBN 0-9539355-0-7

Contents

Introduction

Chapter One	**Arrival and Departure**	Page 1
Chapter Two	**Methody and Reason**	Page 23
Chapter Three	**Reform and Riot**	Page 43
Chapter Four	**Hucksters and Eremites**	Page 83
Chapter Five	**Murder and Martyrdom**	Page 109
Chapter Six	**Music and Mystery**	Page 137
Chapter Seven	**Art and Artists**	Page 177
Chapter Eight	**Drunkenness and Sobriety**	Page 207
Chapter Nine	**A Death a Day**	Page 239
Endpiece		Page 265

Photographs can be found between pages 69-82 and 161-176

(Water sustains life on this world. Because of it we have died. Without it we will die. It will be there at the end, you'll see! Meanwhile....

"Ahem!" said the Mouse with an important air, "are you ready? This is the driest thing I know. Silence all around, if you please!")

Foreword

As producer and presenter of BBC Radio Stoke's history based afternoon show, I have been involved over a number of years with the recording of the oral history of the fascinating district known throughout the world as 'The Potteries'. During this time I have interviewed many acknowledged experts as well as thousands of local people all who have made wonderful and fresh contributions to the ongoing record of history. I have also had the great pleasure of reading and reviewing many new books written about North Staffordshire, many of which have become standard reference works in their subject. This latest book, Mother Town, is no exception.

In this dedicated book of the Mother Town of the Potteries, Fred Hughes has thoroughly researched his subject and has proved that he is well qualified to report the history of a town he clearly knows intimately with pride and with passion. Among a variety of themes there is a wealth of new information that will surprise us all. But it is in its style of presentation that this book brings freshness to the subject of 'boring history'. It may well be that new benchmarks have been set here.

Together, the author and I have spent many long hours sitting on rooftops, climbing through dusty cellars and exploring lofts and attics last visited 200 years previously. Our conversations have always centred on how the old potters would have viewed the same scenes in their own times. And this is how this book is told as we go on a pub crawl with Fred Horry the night before he kills his wife. We are privy to final hours shared between Madame Reymond and her pupil, John Cope; witness to the introduction of new music forms in the Potteries. We are in the front line at the 1842 'battle of Burslem' and hear the terrible consequences threatened by the reading of the Riot Act. We join Arthur Berry as he talks to us from the dark rooms of a gloomy, smoky pub during an afternoon 'lock-in'. But most of all we meet the many anonymous men and women who have made their own contributions in previously unrecorded events that are brought to life on each page. The horror of war is given humility as we find two men spawned in Burslem fighting side by side in Flanders - two men who couldn't have come from more different backgrounds. Page after page of oral history that absorbs the reader in its telling.

Fred Hughes is a writer who can tell a good story. His popular walks and talks are always presented with something which is excitingly different. And, like a good story-teller, he makes you feel that you are part of it, and indeed, that you actually discovered it.

History seems to inhabit every street corner in Burslem whispering through the streets and lanes reminding us of pleasant ghosts. This is a provocative and sometimes controversial book in which everyone will find something to relate to. If you love Burslem and pottery, you will enjoy reading this book.

Barbara Adams.

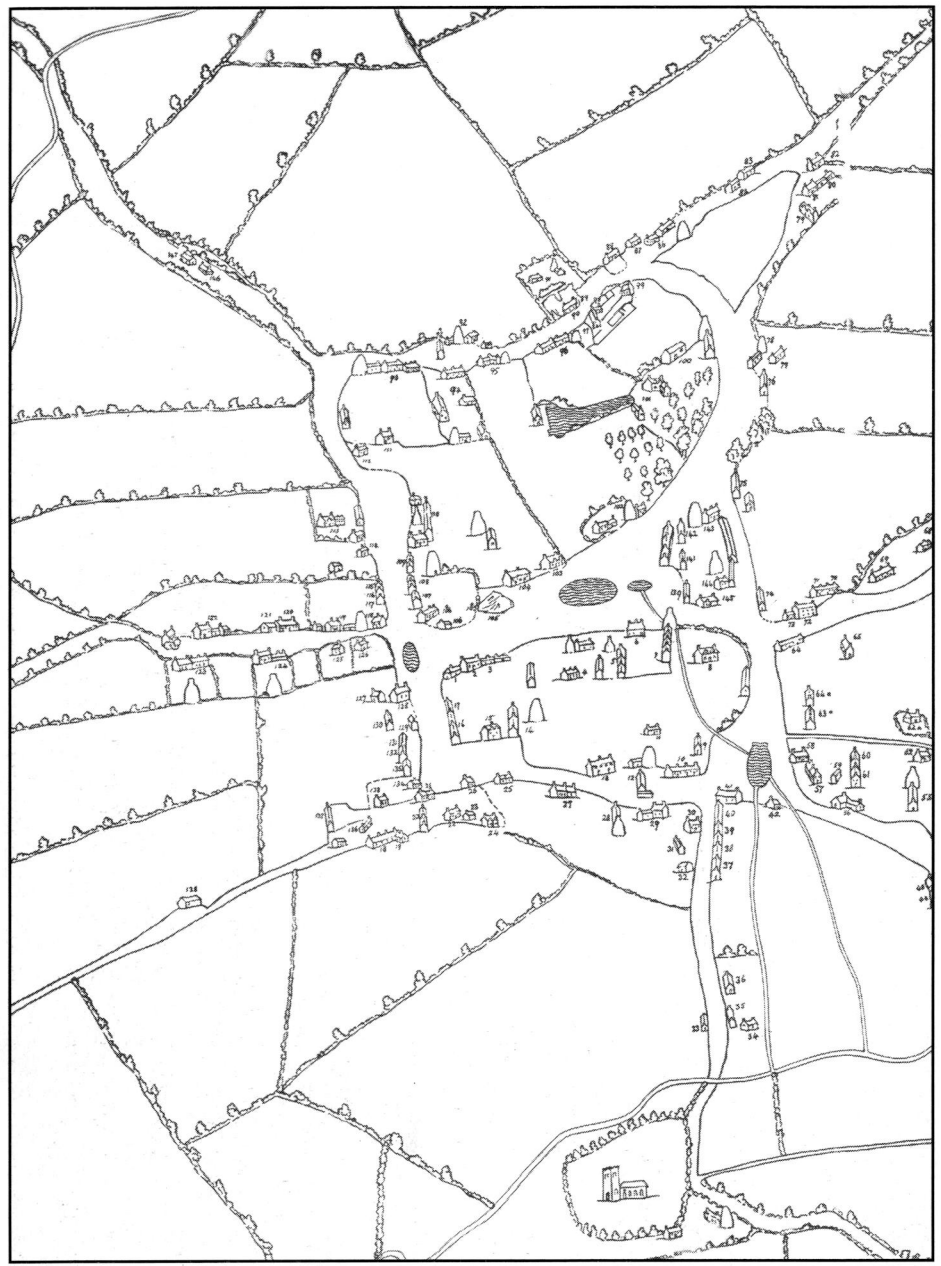

Ryles' Map

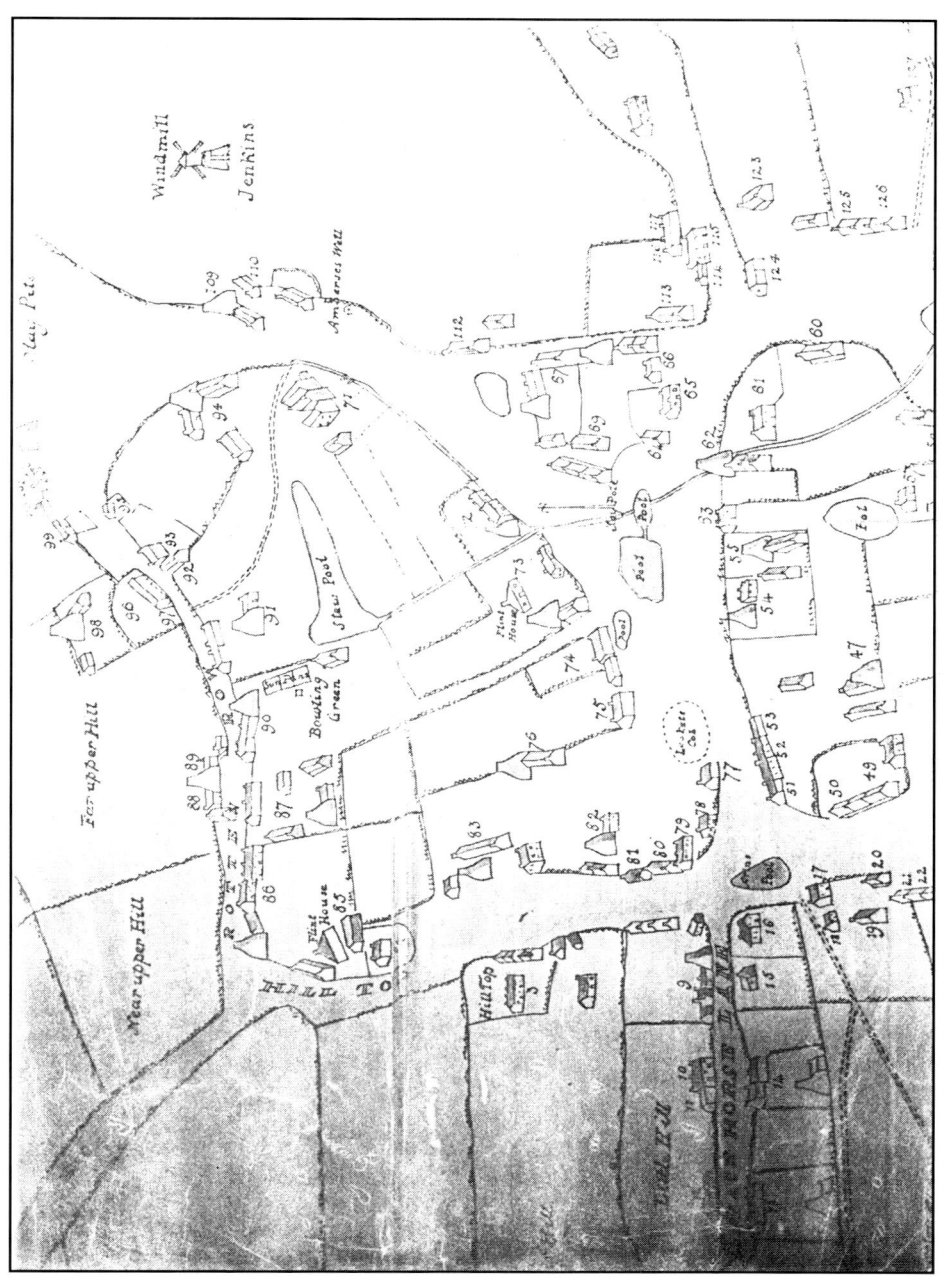

Burslem 1768

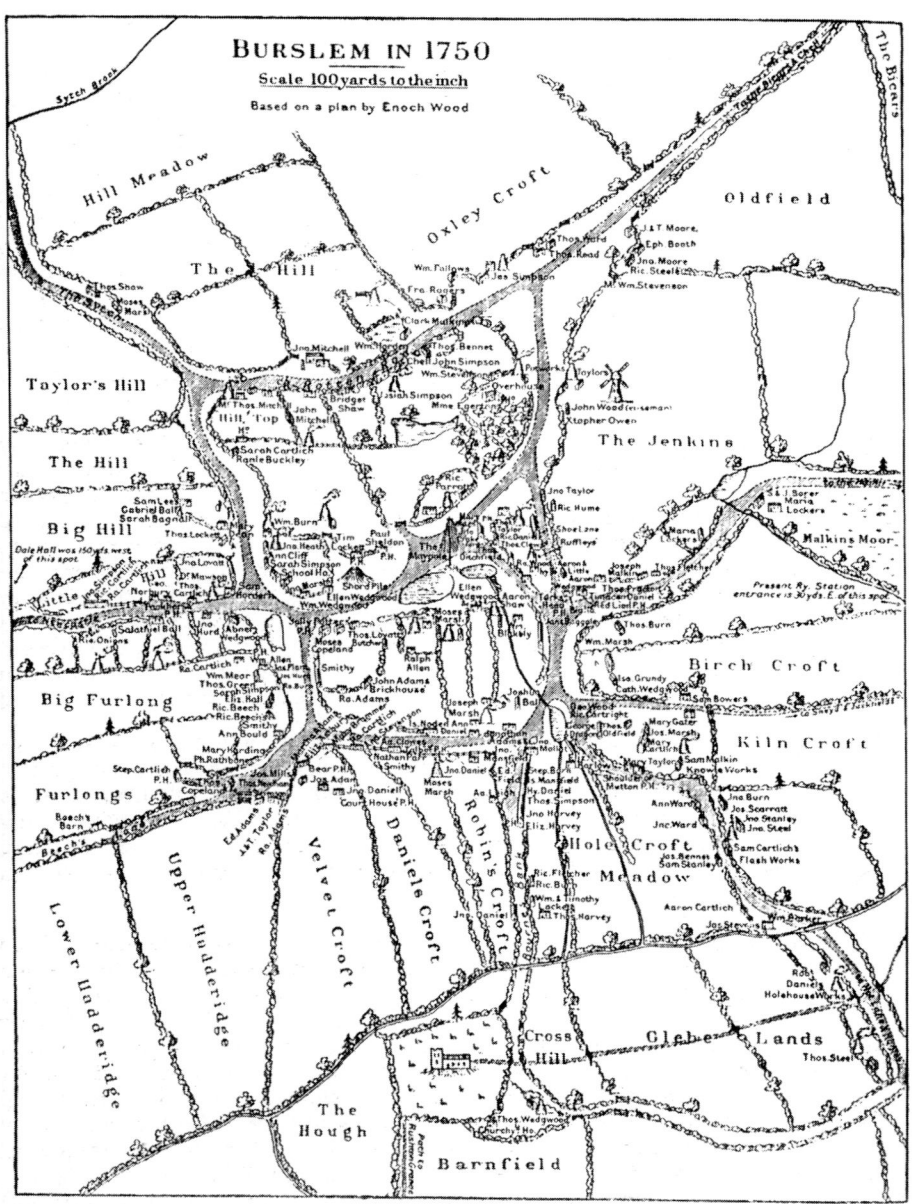

Enoch Wood's Map

Introduction

This history of Burslem could not have been written without a full study of **History of the Borough of Stoke on Trent** by John Ward published in 1843. The six-hundred page volume, together with a comprehensive appendix, remains the seminal work on the history of North Staffordshire containing the research and study of documents prior to 1840. Like others who have followed, Ward strikes-out with an account of previous archeological finds and land formation. The patent precursor then engages his chronology in Celtic England with remarks on the Druid Bridestones at Biddulph, after which he steers his story through the benefits left by the culture and civic order of the Romans before he negotiates the Anglo-Saxons' disregard for permanency. Finally, as with all English historians, his pace gathers with the arrival of the influential Normans, and reaches cruising speed in his coverage and the implications of the reform of parliamentary and local government legislation which were the big issues of his times.

Ward was a solicitor who, like many others then entering into the fast developing service industry behind the crest of the surging Industrial Revolution, saw advantages in setting-up in a new town and starting a family dynasty. He came to Burslem to do just that in 1809. But, while he himself achieved more than he perhaps might have expected, his only son and his grandson added nothing to Ward's dynastical hopes. The Wedgwood's, who formerly held complete authority in Burslem for the hundred previous years, had already withdrawn to the luxury of the Georgian estates of the Gentry. Great Britain was the richest country in the world and there was, on the surface, a great optimism gathering all around for those who could afford it. The lower Gentry, having earned their wealth with opportunity and enterprise, lived only for the pursuit of happiness.

Born in Leicestershire, John Ward was twenty-nine when he opened his chambers in Market Place Burslem ingratiating himself upon the young set of manufacturers who had poured into the spaces that the Wedgwood's, Adams's and the Daniel's had left in transition It was a town that was filled with young men at the cutting-edge of industry, the second generation of those who had hitched-up to the unstoppable carriage of science and mercantilism begun a mere fifty years before.

Ward immediately saw openings in the exertion to reform representation. This called for a free-handed style of civic litigation in new towns which had grown from villages all over the midlands and the north-west and were now controlled by energetic and autocratic men from money-making families who, in their independence, still had to turn to the shire capitals for a parliamentary voice. A rapid growth in foreign trade in manufactured goods saw factories fighting for space with the houses of the masses of workers who were needed to make the factories function. Towns within towns around which were woven community structures. Even in the year of his arrival, eleven new potworks were erected in Burslem as Ward immediately secured work from Enoch Wood, the most important potter and largest employer in the town. As clerk to the **Burslem, Longport and Cobridge Association For The Prosecution Of Felons**, Ward had the intimate ear of Wood, its president, that is until they fell-out over a personal case of defamation of character, which Ward won.

It is likely that John Ward, solicitor, would have passed un-remembered into history as did so many of those late Georgian comptrollers and notaries; remaining as silent names under letter-headed waxed documents of authentication and reputation. But he had a great passion for antiquity and applied the lawyer's care for detail as he collated documents and other materials particular and effective to the purpose of his researches. Ward was able to see what others could not. His experiences elsewhere told him that one day these dust-attracting parchments would be indispensable to future historians. Furthermore, rather than leaving his name as a minor researcher or as an antiquarian, Ward was determined that his name would be perpetuated in book form in a volume that would never be challenged as an authoritative force of its times.

His early ventures into the archives brought him in contact with a local schoolteacher named Simeon Shaw, an ex-patriot like Ward, although Shaw came from Salford. Shaw was an intellectual who variously worked as a printer for local newspapers until he came of note as the master of an academy for young gentlemen in Northwood, Stoke on Trent, on the eastern slopes of Hanley Green.

Over a short period of time, Shaw, a linguist and writer in a variety of subjects, became an established member of the academia in the Potteries, and in 1829 published what was then the only book of its kind on the rise of the Potteries, under the convoluted title - **History of the Staffordshire Potteries and the Rise and Progress of the Manufacture of Pottery and Porcelain; With References to Genuine Specimens, and Notices of Eminent Potters**. Although there were some errors in the work, many students of history saw that it was a book that had taken up a great deal of time in research and included references to documents and sources that had not been used hitherto.

Shaw's research into pottery processes had brought him to the attention of Enoch Wood, himself an ardent collector of antique and ancient documents and pottery. It was Wood that provided Burslem with its first museum, although not for the curious eyes of the general public. The exhibits of the works of the Elers' brothers and Thomas Toft were of valued interest to fellow manufacturers, and the museum's collection of the pots and medallions of Josiah Wedgwood formed the permanent exhibition of Burslem Museum which was situated in the town hall and in the subsequent hall that took its place in 1856.

Enoch Wood and Simeon Shaw became friends bound by their common interests in Methodism and collecting. To assist in the researches for his book, Wood allowed Shaw to examine his own historic document collection and agreed to engrave a town plan of Burslem as it would have appeared in 1720 through to 1750. This plan was composed from a list produced by Josiah Wedgwood detailing the locations of practising potters in 1717 and of memories of older workmen interviewed by Wood himself. Because of high costs of publication, the plan of the town did not appear in Shaw's book but was deferred for publication in a second book that Enoch Wood encouraged Shaw to commence.

This second volume of Shaw's history began to appear in monthly parts entitled; **The Borough of Stoke Upon Trent in 1838**, and was to deal with the Parliamentary union of towns and political emancipation of the electorate introduced by the Reform Acts commencing in 1832 and the Municipal Corporations Act of 1835. Eight parts of Shaw's new book had been duly published when Shaw ran into financial difficulties over the recuperation of the sales money resulting in the refusal of his printer, W Lewis and Son of London, to publish any further editions. Efforts to raise more money brought him into communication with John Ward who arranged to underwrite Shaw's non-published work but in his own name. Over the ensuing twelve months Ward continued with the monthly publications which came to an end at the beginning of 1842. At this point, both Ward and Shaw had become involved in bitter dispute of ownership of the primary documents and material sources. Indeed Ward goes to some length in the introduction of his own book to explain how it came that he was able to have the alleged unsanctioned rights to the sources. Sadly contributions which Shaw undoubtably made are belittled and many of his facts are contradicted by Ward.

It may seem now that Ward should be re-judged in the light of the implied plagiarism of Shaw's work. Many researchers today believe that the record should be set straight and that Ward should be indicted for the unscrupulous use of his colleague's copyright. The circumstances of the literary collaboration are of no doubt; Shaw was broke and he came to Ward for help bringing with him his collections. Ward needed Shaw's material and the other needed Ward's backing. But let there be no doubt that both men contributed equally in evidence though it has to be reflected that Ward, in his eagerness to promote his own contributions, takes more of the credit. We need only to compare the styles of Shaw's earlier book to see that the editorial of the collaborated history is very much in the style of the lawyer Ward. It should also be considered that during the period of the collaboration, Shaw was involved in poor domestic relationships, in particular the breaking up of his marriage to his second wife, which gave him no comfort from his financial strife and which brought ever pressing demands from his creditors. During the time he worked with Ward he became morose, undependable and overworked. His increasing difficulties led to a mental breakdown from which he never recovered, and he died in the County Asylum in 1859. Ward published the great book but sadly did not fully acknowledge the unique contribution of his collaborator, a fact which would have brought the powerful anger of Enoch Wood to bear upon his shoulders. It is perhaps as well that Wood died in his eighty-third year some fourteen months before the introductory criticism of Shaw was made public.

The book was not an immediate success among his peers. A single issue of a thousand saw many remainders returned. But it was at once saluted for its seminal sources and research by the National Library and by the numerous students of pottery research. Much later it became valued by the Victoria History Society, by the North Staffordshire Field Club, the Universities of Keele and of Staffordshire, and by all independent historians down to the present. The book was reprinted in 1969 by S.R. Publishers Ltd of Wakefield, and again in 1996. It remains the first choice as a book of early reference of the Potteries.

Though much has occurred in the district in the hundred years between 1842 and 1942, no single work has been commended that incorporates the events through that period with the notable exceptions of **The Romance of Staffordshire** by Henry Wedgwood and **Staffordshire Pottery and its History** by Josiah Clement Wedgwood (1922), who also wrote for **Collections for A Parliamentary History of Staffordshire** published between 1917 and 1933. Another exception were the recollections of William Scarratt in a privately published work (1906), based on articles he had published in the Sentinel and entitled, **Old Times in The Potteries**. Mr Scarratt notes in his own preface the absence of a continuous work following on from Ward and Shaw which needed to, *'systematically follow up the work'* of the early historians. Another biography of personal experience to which Scarratt did not refer appeared in 1903. Published by Methuen, **'When I Was A Child' (An Old Potter)** by Christopher Shaw, which gives dramatic and truthful accounts of detention in the town's workhouse and the appaling conditions in the workplace of children in the nineteenth century potteries. A description of a boy's first day at work features as a corner-piece in Arnold Bennett's autobiographical novel **'Clayhanger'**, and was admitted by the author to have been appropriated in text and tone from 'When I was A Child'.

An interesting book depicting the times of social breakdown and in criminal activity appeared as an independently published document in 1887 called **Stafford Gaol And Its Associations** by William Payne, but certainly the 'systematic follow up' that Scarratt desired did not appear; that is until 1960.

Describing his massive work as a *'labour of love'*, Ernest J D Warrillow, preferring his middle names to remain as initials, produced the book that Scarratt called for. A big blue book, **'weighing 4 lbs and 280,000 words... thudded like a sack of potatoes'** on the desks of literary newspaper editors. Published by Etruscan Publications, part financed by the writer, its dust jacket depicts a montage of local photographs taken personally by the author showing a street of workers' cottages among which the corner shop is identified by the brass balls of a pawn broker. Beneath a gas-lit street lamp stand a group of Edwardian men, women and their children, while overlooking the street scene are the huge smoking bottle ovens and colliery winding wheels that were so much a feature of the district that outsiders over the years have come to instantly recognise buried beneath great palls of chimney smoke.

Daily Mail reviewer H R Jeans, insisted that he would eventually read it all but its very size prevented a full review. And yet here is the respected reviewer instantly able to praise the book: already: **'...it becomes plain that he (Warrillow) has achieved something big in more senses than one. Unfolding before me is a vast Hogarthian panorama of human struggle for betterment... a real saga of a great city and its growing pains from infancy to maturity'.**

Warrillow was a photographer for the Staffordshire Sentinel. His daily work took him into all the unobserved and forgotten corners of Stoke on Trent. And he made use of it all, taking pictures, collecting and preparing vast files for future use. He first wrote about Etruria, the village where was born, the village that Josiah Wedgwood had created. He respected those who had gone before him relating his photographs to their deeds. Wedgwood and Arnold Bennett were high in his ratings and published interpretations. But it is in the publication of his 'labour of love' that Warrillow gives us in his time all that Ward and Shaw had bequeathed as chroniclers in theirs - a magnificent comprehension and compendium of the history of the Potteries from where they had left off. He gives us more. He presents pictorial evidence that has set a pattern and a standard of history-telling that has reached far outside this district; pictorial recording which has become a benchmark often emulated but rarely equalled and certainly never in the Potteries since. Remarkably, Warrillow reprinted his book in the jubilee year of Queen Elizabeth II when he added three extra chapters and many more unique photographs. The book was published in a limited edition with gilt edges to the top pages and a leather bound hard cover. It now weighed eight lbs!

The means that set these great un-academic historians apart from the rest of us lay in their possession and their instant accessibility of personal collections and treasures. Surely, as the Internet becomes more a part of our lives, there will never again be a history of the Potteries in book form to compare with these three?

For no other reason, and to express my personal salute to these committed historians, I have, with some boldness, introduced each of my sections with an appropriate quote from Ward's History - his work has been the most used by those who followed. Ward's treatise on the merits of local history on page one of his book, says as much as I would wish to say on a subject which continues to uphold the traditions of recording local events and social subjects down through the ages to the present time.

So much for the greats, for this now allows to me to pay tribute to those they have influenced. The self-taught men and women who have taken it upon themselves to research the stories of their own towns and villages, the lives of their own relations, and the many and diverse sociological aspects of the communities in which they live. Qualified or not, their hard work and human interest and endeavours warrants them the title, local and oral historian, and all the prestige that goes with it. These people and groups are too numerous to name, but in the course of this work, I shall identify many of them. Their energies have made them indispensable to everyone interested in local history.

Having briefly mentioned Arnold Bennett as a recorder of Potteries history, albeit coloured by fictional characters, no writer who turns to the Potteries for his or her subject, would be able to proceed without reference to the novelist's work. This 'Man From The North' has left much more than a library of exemplary stories of the place of his birth, so much more that it is impossible to review his canon without resorting to wonder at the concentration of his own historical knowledge. Bennett certainly knew Burslem through and through; what he didn't know he employed his friends as researchers to chase the background studies. Given any of Bennett's 'Five Town's' novels, the first time visitor to the Potteries would, even today, be able to find their way around the streets simply by following Bennett's themes and directions. AB, as he became affectionately known, became the ultimate social historian of his times. And because of his ubiquitous influence, it is inevitable that I am deposed to liberally quote from his books, for, in the majority of cases, his characters were real persons of note and others were real characters of anonymity. His device of fictionalising local events is as fresh and interesting today as it was in Edwardian England. I can do no other than to admit to his pull in certain elements of my own narrative style when dealing with his subjects.

History and its relevance to our communities, in particular to the towns of the Industrial Revolution, is perpetually in vogue simply because it is reachable. The passions these times hold for us today are widely distributed across all fields of learning. Mine is the story of one of those industrial towns. No more than a backwater of the Midlands, it finds its historical niche in being the '...greatest pottery around...' To the people of North Staffordshire, it is known as Mother Town.

Before Moorcroft, Doulton, Cooper and Cliffe, more distant in time than the **Tellwrigytt** and **Danyell** families (those two old rogues!); long before Turner,

Adams, Wood and Wedgwood; earlier than the Staffordshire Norman ancestry, and even prior to the Saxons, Romans, and Celts, there was to be found in North Staffordshire, a rough undulating stretch of land at the southern tip of the Pennine Chain of hills that form the backbone of Great Britain. From these outcrops, within a variety of accompanying higher lands, the whole of the western flats of the Cheshire Plain could, then as now, be seen in panoramic imagery; while in the opposite direction, towards the south east, extensive views over the fertile soils of Staffordshire reached out in accord to touch the deeper lying moist Midlands, thence to the fruit laden southern shires of England's real and honest gardens. Today, standing on the highest northern ridge at Lask Edge, it can be visually understood just why this geographic situation attracted early settlement. Its defensive contours and rhythmic undulations provide natural fortress elevations over the lower flat-lands at the head of the River Trent. While all around were more desirable agricultural resources, these northern plots were left to the occupation of only the hardiest and flintiest folk. Here was a descending valley in the heart of the country. The River Trent brought most of its people this way from the east lands; the rest trickled down from the high moorlands in search of ready communications.

The clayey soils of North Staffordshire did not at first arouse the interest of the few sturdy farmers willing to diversify. Here the land probably encouraged more the growing numbers of wandering shepherds from the nearby peaks rather than the travelling itinerants looking for a place to settle and to cultivate both land and community. Later, miners came and passed through the district stopping to retrieve the outcrops of coal and ironstone that lay about in abundance. A few stayed. In the accessibility of raw minerals these few did not comprehend the initial fabrication of English pottery as a future industry, but there were still the tile makers. Arriving early hereabouts in their rush to occupy the land after the Romans had retreated, the Mercian Anglo/Saxons were no doubt encouraged by the availability of forests of supple wood and the clay with which to build their huts and fashion their weapons and utensils. Dishes and tiles had already become memorials and forgotten Roman souvenirs

The ancient name of 'Tilewright' has been known in Burslem for several centuries to which John Ward asserts that there were **'Several individuals of the name on the rolls of Tunstall Court, of remote date.'** These authorisations, Court Rolls, are the earliest social documents relating to this district - the first being published here in 1326 and the last in 1719. They provide much information relating to the leasing of land, permission to engender private enterprise, the punishment of discourtesy, trespass and encroachment. The Tunstall Rolls precede Burslem's parish records by at least two-hundred years but include many diversities and misdemeanours that happened in all the land around with Burslem being a prominent entry.

Although Henry VIII instructed the keeping of parish registers in 1538, it wasn't until 1578 that the first lists in the records of Burslem Parish were made, which may indicate there was little to record, management being in the hands of the Hulton Abbey monks. However, this first register was burned in a fire at St John's Church in 1717 so that written history of the parish is relatively sketchy compared to other document sources.

It is generally accepted that the first transcribed documented church registers date from 1636. Of the name Tellwright, Ward continues, **'In the earliest parish** *register the name is written promiscuously, Terrick and Telwright.'* The first noted family reference in the Tunstall Court Rolls to the **Tellwrights of Burslem** appears in 1553 when we find that **Thomas Tyright** is granted a piece of land in Burslem - he was probably himself a land-guardian in the employ of the Lord of the Manor, who at the time were the Sneyd family. The rolls tell us that in 1616 **Samuel Tellwright**, a constable of the Tunstall Manor and tenant farmer working for Ralph Sneyd of Keele Hall, owned twenty-eight acres of land on which stood a large house and three cottages for his workers. The Tellwright family held this property which was situated in the Stanfield district up until 1828 when the estate passed to the absent owner, one **William Tellwright** of Biddulph. Up to this time all the cases where this surname appears locally, each reference describes the title of the ancient trade name - tile-wright - a man who makes tiles.

The parish church of St John has been dated from as early as the late 12th century to the early 15th century, although unrecorded historical architects favour the 14th century. Its parent church dating from the Stoke Rectory Act of 1807 is St Peter's at Stoke. The first incumbent rector of St John's took office in 1532, one Thos. Heath, when the parish was divided into its parochial responsibility for four hamlets of which Burslem was the principal because of its stewardship of the church building. The other hamlets were Rushton, (Cobridge) Sneyd, (Sneyd Green) and Brownhills (Sytch).

In 1580 the land containing Burslem was acquired by Thomas Burslem whose lineage cannot be dated further than his grandfather John Burslem who died in 1596 while in residence in the house he built, Dale Hall, formerly situated on a plot of land occupied today by houses at the north of Ellgreave Street. For the earliest family names in connection with Burslem however, we turn once again to the Tunstall Court Rolls beginning in 1416 with the name Thomas Burwardeslym - the etymology seeming to have risen from reference to the land which he owned - his name would be grammatically interpreted today as Thomas of Burslem. This is interesting in that it follows the phonetics of the Anglo-Saxon in preference to the Norman pronunciation - Barcardeslim - a French interpretation of the Saxon used in the Domesday Book.

The Burslem family was undoubtedly related to the Lords of Stafford straying somewhere within this Norman hierarchy but probably clouded without by the Audley's and Sneyd's. Generating through the marriage of Gilbert Wedgwood to Margaret Burslem in 1610, much of Burslem was by this time developed and acquired by family consanguinity running through the Burslem's, while thereafter it was owned by Wedgwood's and later dispersed by sale or long-lease to various pottery manufacturers some of whose names appear in the Wood map of Burslem of 1750.

By 1830 though, the principal landowners lay within the two branches of the Wood family, connected by marriage to the Wedgwood's, of which Enoch Wood had emerged the most important and most illustrious pottery manufacturer in the district due in the main to his involvement in public affairs and his acceptance of numerous roles of office. Second to Enoch Wood in manufacturing prominence and land ownership was John Davenport, (Longport and Dalehall) followed by John Wood's family, (Brownhills) Samuel Alcock, (the Sytch) and the Riley family of Hadderidge. These were important people who demonstrated their self-earned wealth in spending their money on large houses and expensive furniture. The Misses Riley held the largest portion of private land of the south side of the

Hill as it was called, facing west and overlooking the Furlongs to the side of Beeches Row, then the main south-west travelling thoroughfare. Part of the Riley property, the family home of Portland House, still stands in Newcastle Street used as offices for Stoke on Trent Social Services Department.

Enoch Wood owned the expanse of land on the north-west facing side which included a mansion built inside his pottery on Spens Fields. So majestic was the spaciousness of Wood's land that the drive to the mansion began at the former gates of Dale Hall and ran along a line now occupied by Hall Street. Surrounding the house and factory were high brick walls topped with castle-like battlements indicating the strength of the owner.

The Haywood brothers, Richard and Howard, together with Henry Williamson, Thomas Goodfellow and John Meir, were the main clay and marl producers and tile manufacturers with houses in the north-western reaches of Brown Hills in what now lies within the Tunstall district. And the John Wood family, cousin to Enoch, owned Brownhills Hall where today Brownhills High School stands.

During the rise of the Victorian potteries, fierce competition inspired the emergence of family controlled businesses. But added to these were new men who came from far and wide, attracted to the magnet of industry and wealth, and stayed to build their own empires - Burgess, Hulme, Macintyre, Malkin, Maddock, Wilkinson, Wade, Woodall and many others, while the giant pot works of Royal Doulton began life as a shared company passing from James Courmie of Queen Street into the hands of Thomas Pinder and his partner John Bourne and then Shadwell Pinder and Henry Doulton during the passage of the 19th century. But from the middle of the twentieth-century, most family companies had begun to transfer into public ownership where amalgamations and takeovers controlled the market. Most of the land in Burslem today is owned by absent landowning corporates many of whom are descended from the early potting and commercial families.

Although the innovative institutions of the Industrial Revolution and the great manufacturing enterprises of the Victorian potter have almost totally disappeared today, Burslem still has a proportionate number of internationally renowned pottery manufacturers dating back to Victorian times: the names of Barratt, Doulton, late of Sadler, Price, Wade and Wood are still prominent in today's business world, along with other familiar company trading names such as Steelite International and Royal Stafford Potteries, even though all of them have taken a battering from cheap imitative imports, outsourcing, and the fluctuations of European, national and regional economy. The whole district and its manufacturers however, still refer to Burslem as the Mother Town irrespective that its importance has been lost to history many years since during which time the wealth and fame of these famous potters remains only in their names. Their houses have been replaced by commercial units, semi-detached housing estates or wasting as un-filled spaces. All of these famous ceramic names, remembered by collectors more outside the district than inside, have past into the great expanse of history. We who live in their abandoned intervals in an economically changing world are able to claim nothing of their antecedents. What then, is the use of history to tell the story of this town, and how important is Burslem in the big picture of the region and in the Big History of the ages?

The essence we wear today becomes yesterday's incense tomorrow; a fugitive perfume that remains an endless stink.

This is a definition that I own, and I can see at once how it confuses reality. History is exclusive to mankind because of mankind's understanding of time and its ability to communicate and to remember. History is our fingerprint. We try to put it into language and by remembering we believe we will become the better off. And as we stretch our words into sentences they become more than just utterances. The words and their letters are our early symbols. Unshackled as he took to his feet and wandered, man used his symbols to provoke, and to warn and to welcome. And so sentences became paragraphs, then pages became chapters. History began with the cave pictures of the wanderer, his symbols of language remain our structures to meld into the compositions that we wish to remember. The future is full of the past. Stretched out before us are millennia of history; behind lie only the scrappy remains of the beginning. And yet the future is running out of time - but the past is full of it! As a definition, I suspect my motto is as good as the best that can be reached. A potpourri of timelessness.

History will deter those who are among the youngest - a musty thing that is owned by grandparents; that reminds us of grandparents and slow-moving objects, afraid of flight, afraid of immobility. The many are the young, the few are the old - history at each end of the scale in a lifetime that belongs to both.

> ***When you are old and grey full of sleep,***
> ***And nodding by the fire, take down this book,***
> ***And slowly read, and dream of the soft look***
> ***Your eyes had once, and of their shadows deep;***
>
> ***How many loved your moments of glad grace,***
> ***And loved your beauty with love false or true,***
> ***But one man loved the pilgrim soul in you,***
> ***And loved the sorrows of your changing face;***
>
> ***And bending down beside the glowing bars,***
> ***Murmur, a little sadly, how Love fled***
> ***And paced upon the mountains overhead***
> ***And hid his face amid a crowd of stars.***

At an age when long-term recollection changes to the short-term memory loss, it is then that the young can reach out able to touch history, encompass it with the affection of affiliation and familiarity - forgetful of the present, the old become young again. Then they are able to find the true form of its intangible essence; when they from another plane touch the dust of an unlocked bureau or, a wardrobe or a dressing table. In dark corners of condemned houses they will see that history is nothing more than an event unthinkingly created by those who think least about it. **'Who we are is what we were.'** It may be as simple as that.

The inspirations of the young were once the aspirations of the old. It is just that when we are old and feel the glance of the dying sun off the sickle above our shoulders, we shall see our history, not written in books, but in those facial lines and twisted joints. And we may say, 'But for me, the history of the world would be different;' and it will be true. Isn't it also true that those without influence were never born? That uncountable gamete intended to make billions of lives. The unborn ovules - people - that are periodically evacuated in streams of coagula after a pairing: what of they? And what of the babies who die in the first seconds of life, the first hours or in a few weeks or months? Will the world be different because of their appearance or non-appearance? How do *they* sit among the world's records?

History, as defined by academics is, **'the written record of human societies'**. Are people who die within twelve months of their birth part of human society? History belongs to no other species on Earth; the rest have only to be content with age-aching evolution - it is as though the Earth belongs to them, for they are going nowhere: and for man, it is a transit camp in which we carelessly and neglectfully use its facilities and hospitality. Accordingly the history of animals and all other properties of natural living and of fixed substances are not related. And so we categorise them into other subjects for our own benefit. They are as detached from sociological anthropology as a man's horse, or his dog - a falcon say or a goose - in their relationship to the man. Is it a falsehood or a dupe that these beasts do not affect the historical patrol of their human owners and yet remain our best friends? In these relationships we find that it is impermissible to record retrospective development of interrelated life, even of warm blooded life with sad eyes, hunting brains and supple backbones. Intelligence is the word and the word is the symbol that completes the record, that fills the gaps in which our evolution continues. We tell it to happen and we record it when it has. So, are we special on Earth?

In the future will there be other life forms that will create their own history and will it be so different to ours? Are we that life? It seems that we have governed our future to link with extraterrestrial life, life that may not exist, rather than the life which we know we have evolved from. That should tell us much about ourselves. Already mankind is deciding its own fate and preparing its own history. Man believes that his destiny lies in the stars, out there in the Universe in the soup of creation. Is he saying that Earth is the starting point on his journey 'Home'? If so then his history has already been decided.

My grandfather, in philosophical mood, told me that he often used a religious assurance heard in a popular statement throughout the unsettled decades of the 1920's and 1930's, in order to steam-off his despair. He carried this with him into the 1940's when he passed it on to me in order to explain why we were surviving the war. **"Many now living will never die"** - he would shake his head with owlish insight, after which he would sit and whistle an old music hall tune, a reminder to him perhaps that the world keeps on turning whatever - stoic comforts from which he hoped I would gain my future as he had his. My grandfather was a promoter, though not a disciple, of **'Gypsy Smith'**, a former Salvation Army warrior and local evangelist; a radical preacher who emerged out of the late Edwardian Potteries. Grandfather would follow the crowds into the fields and sing along with the ranting choruses. **'Many of us who live today will pass over into the kingdom of heaven'**, Smith would shout. It was his war cry, a threat to the non-believer, a reminder that each should fear the ultimate judgement. For me, a wide-eyed learning boy, my grandfather's version of the religious threat bore no mental coalition with Smith's transient subject. And yet my grandfather's paraphrased annunciation has become the best definition of history that I know.

People remember history as a taught educational subject, churned out in hoary numbers from the spoils and the dust of the fields of glory; or lying tearfully on the pillows of mistake and dishonour beneath the shrouds of cursed dates. Grandeur and Empire are typical history terms. The mere eulogy in parrot-fashion of those dates of wars and the reasons why nations rose to them, is to cast history in its most corruptible form. In this mode we abide in the fashion of 'important' dates. And so the dating of 'important' events fires dignity into the classical formula; a dignity that carries with it a quality borne aloft out of the world's great learning universities and those class-divided invented English public schools; and from Italian and French and German academies and salons. Out of the countries of Romance and the lands of eastern mystery come the numbers. On the cricket fields of the English lords where tactical battles have been re-played; and in gentlemen's clubs where once deserve and honour was given to rank, the numbers pour. In the richness of Samarkand and surrounding the mosques and churches of Constantinople and the golden temples of Beijing: the golden domes of Muscovy. Along the silk-roads and the sea-routes of African slavery. Such is history, the history of empire: Greek, Roman, Chinese and English spoken in the same native tongue of numbers; measured by how many millions were killed, how many tons of gold were stolen.

My grandfather was a good individual historian. By this I mean that he fed me with all the knowledge that he himself acquired. He provided me with detail of his kin and their lineage, numbers and dates particular to his own grandparents who were born at the close of Georgian England - he himself at the end of the Victorian age - and I, born just before the world entered its second awesome conflict of numbers of the 20th century. From him I learned authentic lullabies sung into the cradles of Hanoverian babies; farming rondolet and carols of village apologue; risque Turkish folk-songs from the mosquito-plagued hills overlooking the Bospherus at Gallipoli. From him I knew the crafts of the earth studied by my great-great grandfather, and learned that we each pass-on our own inherited references as we skip through the generations, dwelling only at the beginning and the end, accepting that the very old and the very young are tied together much more intellectually than the bonds that lock mother to daughter and father to son. Only the grandparent's memories can look back in detail along this transitional journey in order for them to become of deeper interest to the grand-child; and it is only upon the death of the grandparent that chronology begins to fade into diminishing links to be taken up by the next-but-one generation in timeless erosion. It is at these times that memory becomes myth.

My own grandchildren will spare me pity as I recall for them my stealing coal from a colliery waste tip to provide a meagre domestic heat - they will not smirk at the petty theft, but they will snigger that *my* parent's generation found it necessary to use fossil fuel for heat and power as they gathered in fumy light-flickering parlours listening to disembodied voices coming from a 'wireless'; urgent sounds - words - symbols of communication - from the far-flung world crackling, as though those foreigners were only next door, through rooms of inter-terraced houses while families ate the cooked meat of animals cut into chops, fillets and steaks; and going to chapel to sing to the praise of 'all things bright and beautiful, the Lord God made them all'. And *my* grandchildren in turn will nod in family surety to *their* grandchildren as they pass-on reports about the irksomeness of digital computers, and the morbid pleasures of recreational drugs and their prurient interest in pornography.

Shakespeare has Hamlet saying of his anticipated death: **"No man knows ought** *of what he leaves"*. Hamlet weeps at the resounding truth. We know by experience those signals of emptiness and hollowness wrung-out in truth at the end - **'what was it all for?'** we weep in the death rooms of our relatives and loved ones. We remember the last words spoken by Burslem's novelist, Arnold Bennett, crying-out to his marital companion Dorothy Cheston, **'It's all gone wrong my girl'**. What did he mean? What history did they berate? These men of words!

But Shakespeare knew of history - he filled his works with historical deeds; ethnic camps and folklore-ish strains. Thus, in romantic words, we know of Denmark's gothic tragedies, Plantagenet crusades, scenes of romance in Padua and courtly deceit in Scotland and Windsor, not from history books but from the prose of plays. Of this we may say that Shakespeare may have truly been a historian, *but what a poet!*. And was Bennett less a historian as he chronicled the lives of people he knew, leaving for us descriptions of how his home town once looked? All those lives so tentatively strung, mistily obscured, and frailly positioned? Neither Shakespeare nor Bennett were historians in the academic sense. They wrote only of other people in causal research. They wrote for money and fame, though in differing ways and for different reasons. They told us also of rank and file as well as general and judge. Today a similar genre is oral history.

My grandfather was an oral historian. He was also a polymath. He taught me to recite the titles of the Books of the Old Testament for no other reason than that he himself had been disciplined to use his power of recall in that same manner when he was a child. A waste of time? The recitation of this useless toneless monologue nevertheless earned me sixpence from a religious over-enthusiastic headmaster on my first day at infant's church school. The lesson I learned best was, that practice of a parlour piece often resulted in a rewarded performance. As a child I loved the sounds of words but importantly the vocal articulation of them even though their representations then meant little to me - the feel in my mouth of the word 'cuneiform' - the Sumerian style of writing on clay tablets - was a thrilling and modulated vocal treat that I enjoyed ejaculating when called upon by an RI teacher. **'Cuneiform, Sir, Cuneiform!'**, I'd say it twice out of joy. A word - just a word - which earned me house-marks - parlour pieces that later made it easier to stimulate pictures at examination tables.

What then is history? Emerging out of the 19th century, we are taught that there are three basic categories: ancient, middle and modern. To the 19th century scholar this roughly meant, a) any order before the Romans (ancient), b) the period until 1850 (middle), and c) from that period to date (modern). In which future time then does Modern become Middle and Middle become Ancient?

The recording of ancient history, and all written history for that matter, is said to have begun with Herodotus 484-425 BC. From this point in time sprang an age in which the first Greek and Roman historians introduced literacy, science and political philosophy as its guiding media. Middle history is essentially found to be controlled by dogmatic religious philosophy. But it is only since the middle of the 19th century that it became popular, with the arrival of popular journalism and its coincidental relationship with mass education transmitting a competency of reading and writing for all, a magnificent combination that enabled the historian to release the straight-jackets of theology and philosophy, once the property of a few, now to the interest of the many. And now to express, and yes to tamper with, sociological developments even to the benchmark of applied theory and inference.

In this entanglement of communication it is easy for factual history to become blurred, surrounded as it always has been by episodes of exaggeration, invention and deception.

For some this is disconcerting, but I see nothing altogether wrong with the introduction of made up characters fitting into factual events, just so long as the facts remain untainted. I would argue that it is a form of roll-playing which detracts from actuality, and I would always hold the line that a dramatised story is better than no story at all - what historical biographer does not employ some form of theatre to influence the storyline? On the other hand, the real Robin Hood and King Arthur may not have lived, but those two invented icons, and the deeds of some others like them, and, the historical settings, seem to me to be acceptable to accuracy not merely because of style and contemporary romantic writing, but to illuminate the shadows of the times in coded narrative. As in Shakespeare's history plays, the reader accepts the prose in order to see the picture, notwithstanding that the prose is exceptional. The life of King Arthur of Camelot, and all the sensuality and illicit and tragic sexual deception among honourable knights, is far more entertaining than the unknown epic of the real Arthur, the Briton, Ambrosius Aurelianus, who won a legendary victory over the invading Anglo-Saxons at Mons Badonicus, somewhere in England at an unknown date in the fifth century. And who really was the outlaw Robin Hood, first introduced in the 14th century poem Piers Plowman - an invented character of William Langland? Was he from Yorkshire, or Leicester or Nottingham?

History or historical fiction? Will we one day say that the late 20th century writers, among whom are included Pat Barker and Peter Ackroyd and many others beside, were particularly adept at a style of novel writing that involved the invention of a principal character in whom to surround their fiction with endorsed historical fact, so much so as to beguile the reader into believing that fiction is fact. Let us be straight about this, their work is definitely historical fact, and the authors are indeed fiction writers introducing a form of tale-telling. And yet these thematic tools do not detract from the truth of history, rather they flatter the myth of fiction and clearly their work encourages subordinate research, an effect of the interest they created. This fictional style is traceable to the Romantic Poets and the Edwardian Realist novelists in their dynastic volumes, emerging into a comparatively innovative stage in the 1970s with writers of dynastical novels the like of Alex Haley. The American novelist's research of his family's history through kidnap and slavery coined the idiom 'faction'. This seems acceptable to me within in the parameters of my grandfather's assertion which insists that history is made by us all and not confined to the historical few. A grain of sand contributes uniquely to the blanket of desert, as much as one man's spermatozoa creates an infinitesimal list of micro-organisms so that another human being shall live. Is history then human enough to be persuadable, alterable, interchangeable? Are the facts of history best left with the reporter or the myth-maker - constructional or exceptional? The answers surely lie with the chronicler of the now rather than the researcher of the then.

In the last ten years of the twentieth-century the passion for oral history - the telling of local events to reach the masses by conveyance through popular media - progressed in leaps and bounds out of the writings of local history from where it was conceived. Oral history has no defined enclosures or divisions; it makes no preference as to the qualifications of the teller, nor does it select its audience. This form is distinct from the casual publication of factual local history which has, over a period of time in the last quarter of the 20th century, become the standard line in telling history. A large sway in the appreciation of local history has been caused by the advent of photography and film making. The problems that oral history brings arises when publishers, ever searching for sellable material, encourage the committal to paper the ego rather than the industry of the local historian and photographer. In this manner a recherche of available material often brings a distortion of fact, as each author attempts to sharpen his pencil to a finer point, turn his shutter-speed faster, or even to introduce new detail into a story which may have related to an obscure fable in the first place. Exaggeration and invention become the consequence. Let's consider the story of the witch of Burslem.

We first generally come across reference to this lady, Margaret Leigh, in 1843 upon the publication of Ward's History. In his description of St John's churchyard the local solicitor and historian pays some disrespect to the quality of the graveyard's lay-out and the un-notableness of the tombs (influenced no doubt in his own superintendency of the recently dedicated St Paul's church in Dalehall). He refers to, **"...an alter tomb standing due north and south, near to the south door, which has now lost its inscription, but is well known to be the tomb of Miss Margaret Leigh of Jackfield who (as appears by the Register) was buried the 1st April 1748. It has been attested as an undoubted fact, by old persons, who well-remembered the occurrence, that after the body had been interred some days, it was taken up, and placed in its present transverse position, for the purposes of pacifying the ghost of the deceased, which found no rest until this fortunate expedient was adopted."**

It is reasonable to assert that had not Ward drawn attention to the woman's grave, passing on this acquired information obtained from oral historians - as he says himself, culled from the memories of **'old persons, who well remember the story'**- and why it was situated north to south instead of the customary east to west, the story of Molly Leigh, the Burslem witch, would have remained in the dust of the 18th century. Contemporary readers of the first edition of Ward's history at once attempted to add-to or out-do the historian's version; from this time it appears the story becomes distorted with 'witnessed' knowledge of an old woman who lived alone with a pet raven (owl, crow, rook, ouzel are some other names given to describe the type of bird) in a remote cottage on the outskirts of the town and who was so ugly that she turned milk sour. Within a generation the poor lady had become a witch performing outrageous tricks and casting spells to affect seasonal expectancies. From the 1840's we find the town's children dancing around her unattended grave engaged in a 'chase and search' game; the 'hare' would run away singing, **'Molly Leigh, Molly Leigh, follow me into all the holes I see!'** At the time of the burial, it is said that the officiating parson returned to Miss Leigh's Hamil cottage where her ghost was seen sitting at a window, and, in an attempt to exorcise its spirit, the cadaver was turned about and her pet bird thrown alive into the newly thwartwise grave in a gesture of resuscitated reunion. It seemed to work, for the ghost, if there ever was one, was never seen again. But it never stopped Burslem locals forever thereafter from claiming sight of it or being haunted by it.

This then is the popular doctrine of the 'witch of Burslem' - it probably says more about a drunken parson who openly criticised Miss Leigh for not attending Sunday church and not giving money to assist his stipend. There have been some eleven exceptional local history books written which have included a chapter on the story of Molly Leigh and rarely a year passes without some reference is made to her ghost story in the local newspapers and on radio. The events surrounding the burial and re-interment of Molly Leigh are as obscure for us today as they were for John Ward. The mystery remains unresolved - and the ghost story is the only answer that fits the riddle as to why the grave was really turned about. This vicar, a man named Spenser, was a regular drinker as were many in his profession in those times. The day of the burial was All Fool's Day 1748! Thus are myths and legends made. It is not history but *of* history. That Margaret Leigh lived in Burslem, and was related to the potting family of Ralph Leigh, who gives a first hand account in Ward's history, is a matter of fact. That she entered the historical chronicles of the town is due to events which occurred after she died. Of her life, nothing is known.

The publican Fred Horry is another example; not of truth manipulation but of social escapism. And this time not through fear or infamy but through the need to embellish a pathetic life, its scandal and notoriety. A simple record of a young man who resided in Burslem for but five years during the 1870s. A rich man who owned the George Hotel; a blackguard and a libellous alcoholic who squandered his wealth on drink and sexual debauchery, who abused his wife and ultimately murdered her in Boston Lincolnshire, a heinous crime for which he was hanged. And yet this man remains in the affectionate folklore of the town, his marble memorial standing in pride of place in the churchyard. How say the use of history, for when the year Horry was hanged two local men of similar ignominious antecedents met the same fate on the Stafford gallows and yet nought of exception is returned of their memories?

How do we group in any category the children of the factories who met their death knowing nothing brighter than the foulness of the workplace and their urine-stinking, bug-ridden hot-beds? The tens of thousands of men and women whose breasts erupted to the tearing claws of silicosis, pneumoconiosis and TB; the insanity of terrors caused by the trade's common illness, lead poisoning? Those masses who shaped the beauty that graced the noble tables of the rich? All gone now, all un-named, all unknown, all un-remembered. And yet it was as much through the industry of this agglomeration of human resource, this mass of forgettable and expendable humanity that created art and beauty enabling the Wood's and Wedgwood's to rise and live among the stars. How do we measure all of this in historical terms?

We are forced to generalize, is the simple answer. We refer to Wedgwood, Watt, Priestly, Boulton, Stephenson and many other prominent captains of industry when we write the history of Capitalism and the political principles of Laissez-faire. We compartmentalise. When we write of poverty we talk of the reformers, of Wilberforce and Shaftesbury, of Elizabeth Fry and Florence Nightingale - education, social and prison reformers. We compartmentalise. But we are unable to talk of the individual poor for there were so many. The voices of Shaftesbury's ragged children who provided the labour to make Capitalism a state of control, sing-out weakly for individual freedom, while the profitability of their endeavours gave range to the upper scales of but a few. The poor people who were condemned at the outset to historical silence, where are their names writ? And so we generalize and compartmentalise. We talk of manpower, combustibles, consumables and refer to the proletariat, the commoners, the masses, the disenfranchised and the dispossessed. We scan Cruikshanks' picture of the **'British Beehive'** to see in which compartment we fit. And yet it is as much from the levels of the universal poor that the heroes of history spring, their ghost's arising out of transverse graves like that of Molly Leigh; and their names pleading for recognition, reverberating wickedly out of crude songs sung in tavern bars and taprooms. So, are these icons best left in history's recycling bin or does the device of oral history take care of them?

A quarter of a century ago, a good friend of mine passed over to the great tavern in the sky. I use the drinking metaphor unreservedly for it was in a pub that I first met him, and I said goodbye to him in a bar during his last night on earth after drinking seven pints of Bass beer. Albert was seventy-three when he died and he looked and behaved like the character from whence he came - from the depressed terraces of the 1930's - the time of the peak of his achievements. He wore a collarless striped flannelette shirt with a knotted white silk scarf amplifying the fact that he wished it not to be known that he dressed without a necktie. A dark greasy suit with a waistcoat, the pockets of which held the spread of a gold double hunter - watch and chain - won in a wager. His feet were shod by polished boots, heel-tipped with metal guards, and on his head he carried a flat cloth cap set at a jaunty angle. The coincidence of his birth date saved him, as well as most other men in his age group, from service in either of the two major wars - too young for one, too old for the other - although he lived through them both when it was as traumatic to be on the Home Front as it was to be in the trenches. At home, while others bled in foreign lands, Albert was condemned to have the time of his life! He and the others who were left at home bore the brunt of the years of unemployment, poverty and slump. He was one of those who learned the crafts of 'the street' in company with the spiv, the loafer, the black marketeer and the under-the-counter merchant. Although he was none of these - perhaps he was a little tempted on occasions - it was difficult not to succumb to opportunity in those hard times. And of course he did!

A loquacious man. When men late of the Western Front kept their own silent counsel, Albert talked to anyone who was prepared to listen about his own troubled times; his youth, old folk, good and bad events, what ever took his fancy to entertain and beguile his audience. He yarned about his relations and friends, characters who appeared not to exist for ordinary people; strange companions, stranger happenings in public houses and in chapels. His world was a faery's land full of drunken imps and pixies, where families tucked into a Sunday lunch of stuffed butterfly's hearts and lettuce; where it was wrong for an unemployed man on the dole to enter a working-men's club; where a keeper of canine pets could escape paying for a dog's licence by owning only bitches. In this odd world secretive meetings would take place on trams as they clattered through the smoky towns; where paper bets and wagers passed from hand to hand to be taken on by boys called 'runners', who would dash off and run from pub to pub and leave coded messages from 'OXO' and 'POW' and 'STYMIED' under a loose brick in the wall of the commission agent's office.

When he was himself a publican in the impoverished 1930s, he would stand on his doorstep calling to neighbours to come in for drinks on the 'slate', an unwritten invoice that he unlawfully carried. And when he'd got a roomful he would undertake the business of a pawnshop proprietor, popping anything of use while the 'slate' steadily mounted in fixed-odds and sweepstakes. And at the age of seventy it was common for him to casually sidle up to some unsuspecting public house patron to whom he would relate his morning meeting with his grandfather whom, he said, was courting a **'damsel some ten miles yonder o'er Longton way'**. The old fly-by-night had wished to borrow Albert's bicycle to meet her - a swain and his damsel! And though the grandson warned him that the bike had only a single working gear, that the brake-blocks were scratching the rims, and to mind the hills, granddad replied that it made no matter as he was **'on a promise'**, hurrahing away precariously along Waterloo Road. At the conclusion of his narrative, Albert would have a sizable group around him, and for the remains of that afternoon, as on many other such afternoons, his drinks would be on them! Those who had the mind to listen; and all did!

> *He wore steel heel-rims on his shoes;*
> *For so, whenever he drew near*
> *They would hear him, clip-clopping, clear*
> *As anything. People knew the tip-tapping clues.*
> *The patrons of the Leopard knew him well -*
> *Ceramic mosaic is conducive to such footfall -*
> *Arthur would chuckle: "Hey-up. Here he is".*
> *And chuckle again. A draught of Bass unless*
> *He was 'going a bundle'. Then mild beer.*
> *Dark rain from a brewer's paradise.*
>
> *At seventy-three, he worshipped his granddad.*
> *And glad to have you listen to the seventy-third*
> *Telling of the family tale. Calling to all in earshot*
> *To regale them with his confidences.*
> *"Owd granddad came dine this mornin'"*
> *And then, more intimately and with a telling nod,*
> *"He wanted borrow me bike, goo Longton on-*
> *he's got a damsel o'er yonder thay knowst!"*
> *Thay knowst - they did - they did,*
> *Thay knowst.*
>
> *They knew owd Albert, they knew him well.*
> *And well are people liked and sought as he.*
> *We are mere mortals who pale against the deeds*
> *And actions of such characters as these;*
> *When they go Solo through such a life,*
> *Jack-Joker declares misère ouverte for them.*
> *And Alb? He'd sing 'Old Pal' for them,*
> *Joking on a hand of whist.*
> *You must never take a trick. He never would...*
> *Thay knowst.*

And he, and Arthur: Frank Beech, Jack Jones,
Would stand their round and talk their riddley tales
On pumps in smoky rooms with smoky friends.
Being there - together - would slow those times
And comfort those companions lovingly.
Longingly to know again those captains of the bars;
Those colonels of drink, generals of song.
Twenty-four carat men whose kind are lost.
And losers we, can only mourn their memory,
Though their images we may still see
Through silent tears.

And when he died, the game of chance died too.
None yet survive the gleanings of an ancient past.
His funeral brought out Burslem's best;
Yet most were so amazed that Albert's grandpa 'd stayed away!
Un-nerved, those past believers saw the lie at last!
But when a tip-tap cracks the tiles at Sunday lunch;
Yes! They all turn round. "Hey-up. He's here!"
Arthur would chuckle, and all about the laughter sings;
And all their love lies
Reflected in their happy tears.

Local artist and playwright Arthur Berry also knew Albert well. And out of the taverns in the town, Berry would commit to paper the old man's stories. In Berry's fiction Albert was the man who insulated himself with beer to escape the daily drudgery of life and to preserve himself against the common illnesses to which others seemed regularly to fall. Albert was the 'toff' who held his head high as he walked past the Labour Exchange and Dole office while singing 'Bless This House'. He was Berry's famous 'Pope of the taverns, Perse' in that glorious **'Lament For The Lost Pubs Of Burslem'** - in a summer of fond reminiscence - a last summer before the beer-drinker's world changed forever.

'Oh Let's have another one, Let's have another one. Let's have another one, before it's time to go. Sing me another song. Sing me another song. Sing me another song, before it's time to go.'

Is this history? These men are part of the fabric of a society that is just reachable, and will these memories stay with us or fade away because their deeds were too workaday; because they themselves were too parochial; or is it simply that they were parochial too?

In their times these same men also feared the threats of imperialism and dictatorship; cowed by class-divisions. And yet they suffered as much as the warriors did, in their case from the epidemics of community depression, encumbered by unemployment and dogged by poverty. They cheered as the Titanic broke the western waves on its maiden voyage, for they were of that kind who built the unsinkable ocean-going palace - the swanky crockery and the flushing toilets were made by them. They felt proud and boasted of affiliation with the class above them, the adventures of Captain Scott and Oates, of George Mallory and Irvine. They puffed again with pride as Jack Hobbs struck an expected century and empathised with working class heroes, Harold Larwood, Dixie Dean, Tom Finney and Stanley Matthews. **'Make 'em have it boys! Up the Potters!'**

They watched with mixed emotions as their fathers and elder brothers queued to fight a common enemy while they remained to tend allotments and keep the home fires burning. Their turn would come in those *not-so-far-off* far-off days when people rarely starved because they ate sensibly well, and yet were hardly ever sober. When common men and women wore black and white, captured on colourless photographic wet plates, drinking at public fountains in cobblestone streets donated and erected by their employers. Or strolling around the Sunday pleasure parks - huge hats and umbrellas covering the most meagre of exposed flesh - the grey faces wearing the grim smiles of 'make-do'.

Of the twentieth-century writers none exposed the grain of history better than its poets. Those young men who faced their troubled times head-on, who saw through the veneer of pretence through the cover of smile; who discovered their subjects in the stuff that stagnated at the bottom of trenches in 'the Pity of War', that skull-grinning ashamed phantom that laughed at the 'breathless grandeur of the Charge'. The yearning for times gone, of hay-fields and long summers; seaside holidays; of trains stopping to let off the hiss of steam amid yellow nature-bursting fields in fantastic sleepy villages named Adelstrop. Competing for the space of sound in the endless happy-blue skies with the skylarks hovering in constant song even as each successive conflict outdid the other in death, leaving only the wispy mists of nostalgia, the memory of something and someone just departed, something nearly stayed - held on to - just missed - now lost to history.

> ***Those long uneven lines***
> ***Standing as patiently***
> ***As if they were stretched outside***
> ***The Oval or Villa Park,***
> ***The crowns of hats, the sun***
> ***On moustached archaic faces***
> ***Grinning as if it were all***
> ***An August Bank Holiday lark;***
>
> **And the shut shops, the bleached**
> **Established names on the sunblinds,**
> **The farthings and sovereigns,**
> **And dark-clothed children at play**
> **Called after kings and queens,**
> **The tin advertisements**
> **For cocoa and twist, and the pubs**
> **Wide open all day;**
>
> **And the countryside not caring:**
> **The place-names all hazed over**
> **With flowering grasses, and fields**
> **Shadowing Domesday lines**
> **Under wheat's restless silence;**
> **The differently-dressed servants**
> **With tiny rooms in huge houses,**
> **The dust behind limousines;**

> *Never such innocence,*
> *Never before or since,*
> *As changed itself to past*
> *Without a word - the men*
> *Leaving the gardens tidy,*
> *The thousands of marriages*
> *Lasting a little while longer:*
> *Never such innocence again.*

This poem, **MCMXIV** by Philip Larkin, evokes the history of the twentieth-century as no other does. It tells of a world that cannot be recovered, an air-brushed snapshot of stuttering decades where common expectations were about to be attained, yet escaped, were snatched away from reaching fingers; time stolen in the last minutes of permanency in the closing seconds of ordinariness and custom. A century of men who always seemed to be leaving home, whether for the battlefields, the pits or the factory; carrying baggage, brown cardboard suitcases or small brown paper parcels tied with string: some leaving their bodies behind; all of them their spirits. Stretched out in their lines, mouths agape, wanting to protest before being stopped mid-sentence by some others telling them it's time to go, disappearing into clouds of steam at railway stations; doing the right thing. Ordinary men leaving home, never to return. Smiling - putting on a brave face to hush ma's tears. But leaving nevertheless.

In every town in this island country, fugitive history has been left. We see it in the frontages of old chapels which have been adapted into cinemas, and cinemas re-used as bingo-halls; bingo-halls changed into warehouses. And in the waste land of post-demolition. A shop has become a public house before becoming a dwelling and then a storeroom. A school where tens of thousand of workers were educated to count their meagre wages and read their redundancy notices; where they were sometimes taught to sing in choirs. A school which has become a tin-pot business centre. Potteries and factories that have been shut-down and partitioned into 'units'. Railway stations that have become trendy offices; parks and cemetery lodges turned into drop-in rooms.

Still, in certain quarters of these towns, communities born out of the Industrial Revolution, there remain no exceptions to satisfy the description of that malignant word invented and so commonly applied and frequently used in the twentieth-century, 'depression'. Successions of local representatives have fought the long losing battle to remove it from the lexicon of local government administration not realising that to obliterate it the whole root and crop must be pulled-out as well; poisoned and scoured and then burned-out. For this is our heritage and we must live among it. Should we smash down the ramparts of the castles, these fortresses we see now as troublesome, and remove them because they are of no use to us, because they stand in our way and are impossible to maintain; the once glorious symbols of achievement of our fathers who repaid the promises to their fathers who, before them, planned their own brave castles in the sky? Father - son, father - son, father? Are we to be, through our young, the preservers of all our heritage? Is this what history has become - an obligation? And in our burden's package - that brown parcel that we leave home with - is there room for our stories: history makers we, as well as those who chronicle our deeds - historians?

Burslem in Stoke on Trent, is an old town. It was given the name 'Mother Town' at the beginning of the 19th century. The town had by then progressed so deep in the international market that the term was used to identify it from the other five important pottery manufacturing towns in the long-lying undulating region which has become commonly known as The Potteries. No one knows who coined the term Mother Town but it is likely that it was inspired by the masters of the trades who had become to form the businesses and self-preserving civic associations in Burslem. They would have passed the term around with the fat cigars and glasses of port at their antediluvian dinners. The name soon caught on with the workers and was used by them as they competitively defended their successes in games like Prison Bars and later football against the other towns - particularly Hanley - whose citizens, they feared, were trying to deny them their named entitlements; for had not many earlier historians and geographers referred to Burslem the most important town? Burslem, as 17th century historian Dr Robert Plott found on his visit states that Burslem was **'the seat of the greatest Pottery then carried on in the county.'**

A visit to the old churchyard of St John's, south of the town centre, immediately tells the visitor that he is standing in a place of history. All about are stone slabs with chiselled inscription of the names of Adams, Allen, Cartlich, Colclough, Daniel, Lees, Lockett, Marsh, Steel, Taylor, Turner, Egerton, Wedgwood and Wood - names counted among the most famous potters who ever moulded clay. In the more modern public cemetery, a mile away, are marble tributes to famous Victorians: here lie the ashes of Arnold Bennett, the bones of the Price family, Swinnerton, Beardmore, Leigh, Norris, Powell; more Wood's and Adams's, continuations of dynasties of families who brought their influence and impress into civic development, industry, the arts. In both cemeteries lie MP's, factory owners, trades unionists, commercial brokers, shopkeepers, publicans and scoundrels.

In a landscape that once emulated Hell on Earth with hundreds upon hundreds of fiery bottle-ovens belching smoke across the skyline, (there are now only seven in Burslem) all is peaceful, silent and still; as still as the graves in St John's. Though the land pattern and contours and geographic layout remains pretty much the same, one new road has been cut across a dereliction of land which once housed a village of terraced houses supporting the largest community of workers in Burslem just on the edge of the town's shopping centre. And all those houses have gone now, and the people with them. But the great Victorian buildings still stand; the town hall bearing its golden angel on top of the clock tower, the Wedgwood Institute with its acclaimed facade of brick and terracottas designed with Etruscan figures of the seasons and depictions of the pottery trades, with individual walled backgrounds stuccoed with cobalt and gold tessellations. And the Edwardian School of Art is still there, its moulded and polished potclay bricks supporting a portico of Ionic columns the passage through which leads to a thrilling lobby overlooked by a studio mezzanine shaded and illuminated by a glass roof. These are the buildings erected in tribute to and in glorification of their ages, commissioned by the civic superintendents for their architectural beauty with afterthoughts that they should be for the use of ordinary people.

> **'We strolled along a quiet street, and came to a large building with many large lighted windows, evidently some result of public effort.**
>
> *"What's that place? I demanded.*

> *"That's the Wedgwood Institution."*
>
> *"Oh! So that's the Wedgwood Institution, is it?"*
>
> *"Yes, commonly called the Wedgwood. Museum, reading-room, public library - dirtiest books in the world, I mean physically - art school, science school. I've never explained to you why I'm chairman of the Management Committee, have I? Well, it's because the Institution is meant to foster the arts, and I happen to know nothing about 'em. I needn't tell you that architecture, literature and music are not within the meaning of the Act. Not much! Like to come in and see the museum for a minute? You'll have to see it in your official capacity tomorrow."*
>
> *We crossed the road, and entered an imposing portico. Just as we did so a thick stream of slouching men began to descend the steps, like a waterfall of treacle. Mr Brindley they appeared to see, but evidently I made no impression on their retinas. They bore down the steps, hands deep in pockets, sweeping over me like Fate. Even when I bounced off one of them to a lower step, he showed by no sign that the fact of my existence had reached his consciousness - simply bore irresistibly downwards. The crowd was absolutely silent. At last I gained the entrance hall.*
>
> *"It's closing-time for the reading-room," said Mr Brindley.*
>
> *"I'm glad I survived it," I said.*
>
> *"The truth is," said he, "that people who can't look after themselves don't flourish in these latitudes. But you'll be acclimatised by tomorrow..."*

These views of the chairman of the Institute's Management Committee, are made in the manner of enlightenment for the benefit of the man from the British Museum in Bennett's perfect short story, **The Death of Simon Fuge**. The councillor's views say much as to how the Victorian/Edwardian trustee applied his preferences to the structure of this fine building in contrast to his disregard for the common townsfolk. In the construction of that other 'fine building', the town hall in Market Place, the trustees here made sure that its entrance and its use were fashioned in such a way so as to debar, prohibit and prevent admittance to those with 'no business' to be there. The imposing double-winding stairs of the town hall that rise to the concert room and ballroom were designed in steepness and contour as much to deter the unwanted individual's progress, the 'cripple', the 'blind beggar', the infirmed and the unwashed, all of whom were actively stopped from entering into the upper echelons of Victorian class. They were forbidden!

Once temporarily situated in the town hall, the reading-room of the library was defenceless to the invasion of the unemployed and the unhoused, the vagrant and idler who needed sanctuary, a place of warmth, an asylum in which to pass monotonous hours of ennui. It was closed at particular times for cleaning; and in winter the windows were fastened open so that any climatic respite for the poor would be curtailed. And yet these moral departures were seen by the benefactors as being born out of the interests of betterment for rather than discrimination against their workers. The lines that separated bad and good, straight and bent, were well defined by the compulsive Victorian legislators. It was a matter of simple reality: *'...people who can't look after themselves don't flourish in these latitudes...'*

For each one Victorian pile in Burslem there are four simple Georgian residences. The best of these stands at the town's main junction and is a good example of a modest mansion built in the middle of the eighteenth-century for members of the Wedgwood family. Named, and still known as 'The Big House' on account of its comparative size with other buildings in the rest of the town. This three storey house with a capacious cellar was built in 1750 by the brothers John and Thomas Wedgwood, bachelors, who, when they had achieved their wealth and success, moved away in the trail of their nephew Josiah to be inside the new traditions of working and living side by side in the countryside away from 'those awful towns'.

After the Wedgwood's moved, their expansive house passed into the hands of their relations, the Wood family, where it overlooked history in the making during the Chartist Riots of 1842. In the 1890s, the Big House was purchased by the rising Conservatives in the wake of the hapless first Liberal Home Rule for Ireland Bill, the collapse of which led to Gladstone's resignation. Gladstone's pursuit of the second Home Rule Bill of 1896 caused the majority of Burslem Liberal Party members to quit, many of whom became Conservative simply by walking across the street to join the other club, in an example of how the Victorian business masters followed their domestic needs by wielding the powers given to them by the 19th century Reform Acts, enabling them to independently control local authorities with national policies. What was formerly the most powerful political party in the Mother Town, overnight became a shambles of a rump. Gladstone had shattered the ardent faith of the mature national Liberal supporters, and so those solid businessmen moved to the Tory Right leaving the socialist-minded young gentlemen to pick up the pieces out of which Left-Wing Liberalism emerged.

In Arnold Bennett's excerpt of the occasion in the novel Clayhanger, the author relates the shamed collapse of Darius Clayhanger's support for the Liberals after hearing of Gladstone's proposals. Of a sudden whim, Darius resigns, leaves the Liberal Club and goes to the Big House to become a Conservative:

> *'...They both entered. In the large room two young men were amusing themselves at the billiard table... on the ledges of the table were two glasses. The steward in an apron watched them... If Edwin with his father had surprised two young men drinking and playing billiards before noon in the Conservative Club, he would have been grimly pleased... the spectacle of a couple of wastrels in the Liberal Club annoyed and shamed him...*
>
> *"Well, Mr Clayhanger," said the steward, in his absurd boniface way, "you're quite a stranger."*
>
> *"I want my name taken off this Club," said Darius shortly. "Ye understand me! And I reckon I'm not the only one these days."*
>
> *The steward did in fact understand. He protested in a low amiable voice, while the billiard-players affected not to hear; but he perfect-*

ly understood. The epidemic of resignations had already set in and there had been talk of a Liberal-Unionist Club. The steward saw that the grand folly of a senile statesman was threatening his own future prospects. He smiled.'

In a few minutes of leaving the Liberal Club, Darius, followed closely by his son Edwin, crossed the road and headed for the Big House.

'...At the top of Duck Bank, Darius silently and without warning mounted the steps of the Conservative Club. Doubtless he knew how to lay his hand instantly on a proposer and seconder. Edwin did not follow him.'

Within forty years, the Conservative Club had itself moved out of the Big House and in the late 1930s the home of Thomas and John Wedgwood had become the local branch of the Midland Bank. The Conservative's own overnight move across the way in Moorland Road, saw the Party take up residence in moderate splendour in an oak-panelled domain of leather chairs that smelled wholesomely of cigars, looked over approvingly by autographed photograph portraits of Winston Churchill, Edward Heath, Margaret Thatcher and of course, an un-signed photo of Her Majesty Queen Elizabeth II, resplendent in her ceremonial equestrian clothes at the Trooping of the Colours.

In 1986 this club itself closed due to lack of money urgently required to repair the building's structure, later undertaken by the next new owners. It is now shops and offices. There is no longer a political club of any calling in Burslem. The former Liberal Club may be seen with its brick facade, erected in the good times before the unexpected demise of the Party. This Gothic styled frontage comes to an overhanging pointed apex with a plaque depicting the name surmounted on a zodiac sign - 'Liberal Club' - it says modestly in blue and gold mosaics, interlaced with the initials of the architect, CAB. And yet, if seen from behind, it rises steeply like an elongated cube used and abused over the years in a variety of commercial enterprises. Now only pigeons live there in their immaculate loft.

In and out of these conspicuous former buildings of brotherhood and affiliation, are small cottages that retreat in modest assemblage. They needn't baulk however for the they are still good examples of mid-Georgian houses though slightly caricatured by revised titivations. The north side of market Place is dotted with them starting at number 38 which has roof beams made from reclaimed Elizabethan ship timbers. This house also can boast of bowed mullioned display windows and outside stone-steps lead to a cellar passage open to the street with a moulded cast-iron street lamp formerly erected to give illumination to the stock provider and deliverer. Once a chemist's shop owned by Thomas Leicester, in the late 1960's it was turned into a fine high-class ladies fashion shop, a boutique, with the 1960's fashionable name, 'Janette'. And on the same row are the tumbling offices of solicitors Boulton's and Ellis Moxon - great Burslem names in trades that reach back to the beginning of the nineteenth-century as they sit either side of a covered alley which connects the High Street of the town with the Market Place dividing the pot works of Hackney's, formerly Steventons, and Sadlers, a company old enough to have provided transfers for Josiah Wedgwood when the great man was at the Ivy House and they were Liverpool printers. The frontages of the main town centre block are almost all of Georgian origin, except where Victorian frontages have been un-necessarily erected to cover and hide their Georgian ancestry in the name of modernisation.

The Leopard Hotel has a curious bowed Victorian double-bay frontage which itself is imitative of a Hanoverian boarding house, hosting a square-shaped taproom reminiscent of a standing gin parlour. It is this amusing deception that hides the actual low ceiling of the house of 1768, although the building was erected much earlier than this. In 1768 it was an inn and it is satisfying for the visitor to note that it is in the main front room that Josiah Wedgwood and James Brindley sat to dine and discuss the cutting of the Trent and Mersey Canal. And as one steps along the lopsided passage of this time capsule, from its three-hundred year old front rooms and into the clearly Victorian hotel at the rear, one is not even aware of the transitional demarcation line as the conundrum turns again into another dog-legged passage which leads to a palatial modernised ballroom and restaurant. Who could possibly imagine that overhead lie some sixty empty and unused bedrooms built in the 1890's and mothballed in the dust of ages? But it is in the cellar of this puzzling cabinet that the true story can be told.

Sunk below the ground are the men's toilets; chambers that the Victorians loved to make privy as gentlemen descended to urinate away from the accidental curiosity of the demure ladies and protected children. At the bottom of the twenty or so one-hundred and eighty degree turning staircase, stand the two doors that lead to the old and the new beer cellars. It is the left hand door that commands attention. Over-painted in tavern-green and permanently locked, the door hides a subterranean capsule of history. Behind this unassertive portal are a number of dungeon rooms, all at some time superceding or complementing each other: six in all.

It can be seen that there were originally three stooping-rooms each one reaching well out under the pavement in the street above. They are of ancient origin and are lined against the earth and clay with Georgian hand-made bricks. The furthest from the cellar entrance is directly beneath the posting box of the town centre post office and was without doubt used by the long-ago owner of the house, Ellen Wedgwood, who converted the private dwelling into a public house sometime around 1765. In this unlit cellar-room a slow trickle of fresh water creeps across the brick floor from the outside wall. This is the culvert of a stream that begins in the falling fields of Stanfields and Bycars, (those that the Tellwight's formerly owned, and where Molly Leigh lived) and is collected within the old disused mine shafts of innumerable coal pits of collieries that were once sunk there. The stream can be seen above ground beginning in the fields at the north of Port Vale's football stadium before it goes deep underground as it progresses through the town. Evidence of it can be found as it tries to surface in the town hall cellars before it passes under Market Place and below the Leopard, beneath the Wedgwood Institute, and under Queen Street as it follows the line of Bournes Bank, finally coming above ground at the bottom of Enoch Street where it passes through the southern drifts of Grange Fields as it pursues the Fowlea Brook to meet the River Trent at Stoke.

Also in this far room of the Leopard's cellars, is the bricked-up entrance of a passage, laid with newer brick emphasising the shape of the opening of the tunnel which once passed under Market Place to connect with the cellars of Norris's Brewery and bottling plant on the other side of the road. The tunnel allowed the passage of barrels of beer and crates of spirits to be towed along a narrow gauge rail from end to end averting the necessity of a hazardous traverse across the traffic-busy main road. Unused since 1957, the weight of heavy vehicles inevitably stopped this underground transit before its collapse could cause serious damage.

The other rooms in the Leopard cellars are whitewashed and painted dark brown and are as dry and cool today as they were intended to be those hundreds of years ago. Discarded stillage chocks, bung pegs, brass taps, corks, sparging tools and fining measures possess dark corners companioned by crouching webby spiders. Stacks of wooden crates - nines - twelves and fifteens with the name James Norris branded on the sides, litter the floor in an abandoned tumble. Wine and champagne racks grip along the unvisited walls of these chambers. It is easy to imagine that pot-boys once lived down here, scurrying in candle-lit darkness across the slippery-damp floor, racing with bottles, boxes, crates and firkins, throwing them into the open hatch of the dumb-waiters as the refreshments were pulled up into the music palaces where dance bands played, amid the confident commands of men in dress suits and the gay squeals of ritzy ladies.

Victorian architects were adept at improvising frontages into whatever style or age they wished, and very often the practice was adopted by later designers. The public house is amenable to this kind of development and alteration, thus the front of the Bulls Head in St John's Square was rebuilt in the 1930s with a Georgian frontage behind which were original flat mullioned windows fixed into the original 17th century town house - modern Georgian architecture covering and hiding the original! The Swan Inn was re-arranged similarly as were the row of shops and offices in Market Place known as the Pearl Assurance buildings - new fronts cladding old interiors. As for change, the former Burgess's confectionery shop in Queen Street is still lightened with an art-deco black Bakelite surround to a frosted-glass display window, the word Burgess's scripted in **Broadway** lettering across and above the glass.

Other architectural styles have visited the town and stayed. The Co-operative Emporium, the first department store, with its huge display windows and slabs of white marble cladding bearing the oval plaque of the blue and gold BCS (Burslem Co-operative Society) high above the main entrance, rushing head-on into the street like the bow of some huge liner breaking the swell. Its opening in 1929 must have been sensational. And the Co-op's main offices at the top of Newcastle Street, once again in that preferred bold decorative Co-op style so typical of all its buildings, an image that associates and links them with the great social institutions of the times. But there were buildings on those sites before, and on plots like the Central in Queen Street, where once stood a Methodist chapel, demonstrating Victorian escapism from the darkness; translated in the 1890's into a specialist multi-purpose commercial building spearheaded by the corporation, and yet ironically unable to escape far enough from the influences of Gothic turrets and narrow shaft windows. The row of 1960's conceptual boxes centred on Boots Chemist. And in Moorland Road, alongside the Big House, the unimposing Red Lion public house, embarrassed to stand on the site where its predecessor stood in Elizabethan grandeur. And the brand new minimalist Ceramica in stone, glass and copper, honest in modern architectural style, sits in impudence between the two town halls, waiting for its turn to make a name. It is, however, this ebb and flow of fashion and style which indicates that the Mother Town is still as willing as she ever was to lend her body to embrace innovation and initiative in order to keep her place at the forefront of parochial history in the Potteries.

Like most industrial towns Burslem still has a mixture of architecture of identifiable styles, age and influences. But the saddest consequence of such assortments is that successive elected authorities never seem able to grasp what should be retained and what should be disposed of. The 1930's saw the first of three programmes of housing slum clearances. The virtue of such programmes cannot be doubted but the imprudence of emptying the town centres and re-settling the communities as far away as in another district, to rely upon the commerce of neighbouring towns, ought to have been questioned at the time. Lessons were not learned, for even after this first tranche, which had caused much concern and loss of business for the town's shops and businesses, the local council persisted blindly. In the first three post-WWII decades, two subsequent programmes of slum housing clearance simply compounded the mistakes of the pre-war planners.

Between 1946 and 1950 there was as great a housing shortage in North Staffordshire as anywhere else in the realm. In an avalanche of delayed marriages and the subsequent baby-boom, many couples were forced to bring up their families in lodgings, even to the sacrifice of husband and wife temporarily living apart, meeting briefly after work in fields or at the cinema. The misery of such arrangements served only to stiffen the resolve of young married couples and it may be considered factual that these pioneering partnerships brought a refreshing determination in order to make marriage as an institution work. That much maligned institution was never before as strong, and never since as blessed.

Housing programmes were hastened and home-efficient prefabricated bungalows, affectionately known as 'prefabs', mushroomed throughout the land. New estates were commissioned, many built temporarily, shoddy with cheap materials, to fill the gap of need. In addition the Potteries district provided accommodation for new ethnic residents as the Mother Town welcomed large sections of eastern European displaced persons whose labouring skills were greatly needed by industry to catch-up with the back-tracking of the missing war years. The majority of these men, Poles, Lithuanians, Czechs, Italians, worked in the North Staffordshire collieries and were provided with campus accommodation, the largest being at Bradeley, some two miles east of Burslem. Eventually, this workforce integrated with the potters and took-over the large houses in the Cobridge district, those high symbols of Victorian middle class business society, whose grandchildren, helped by inherited money, had moved away into the new status stamped estates of Clayton and the Westlands, somewhere in the country in Newcastle under Lyme, out of the view and the stench of the factory.

Burslem also made room to accommodate a community of Caribbean families who had come to seek the available work that their own country could not provide. Here as well, the Cobridge district provided a new home to hundreds of black people, while more families from the depressed and worked-out coalfields of the North East and South Wales, in the wake of industrial nationalisation in 1948, initiated greater mobility and community integration. The Mother Town has never been last in coming forward with welcoming arms to strangers as her own new post war communities looked for new diversions. The houses the immigrants took-up eventually introduced these various British races into a new-town parishioner. But it was the town centre clearance programme of the 1960's and 1970's that became acknowledged as the most ill-advised and poorly planned deal of all, although the indications of the mischief that was to come was already being devised and to some extent implemented ahead in the middle of the 1950's.

The overall design was to provide Burslem with the means to become the equal of Hanley, independent, standing on its own two feet, autonomous in both commerce and new building. But more than that, the idea was for Burslem to become an individual specialist town. The blueprint was simple - by gradual stages the clutter of old buildings were to be removed and made into a spacious garden town where pedestrians could roam free of traffic through a variety and choice of shops. The first task was to take on the scars of industry - cutting out this root entanglement was given priority. The city councillors were given free use of the scalpel.

The premier assignment was to remove the forests of coal-fired bottle ovens. Town planners and councillors refused to confront the obvious question, that of perception - how do others view us? While every town and city in industrial Britain possessed centralised public and industrial buildings, only the Potteries had a skyline of extraordinary architectural geometry. Preference was given to the building of a new Britain in a smokeless environment for which legislation was created. To the old potter, when the ovens were at full fire, smoke hid neighbour from neighbour. Green fields, trees and lakes were rendered black. Windows were impossible to keep clean as smoke concealed the light of day. Turbulent clouds blackened freshly washed clothes on clotheslines; the sticky atmosphere gave human faces a look of smut, sickly, greasy-grey. Daily, eyes were filled with grit and dust, and common ailments were asthma and sties. And yet, for people who saw this huge skittle-alley of bottles from the outside, they saw it as a dark orchestra, its percussion section made of thundering chimneys echoing Mephisthophelean romance, intrigue and fascination. To visit the Potteries was to be at the heart of an industry that the ancients knew - a finger-dip into Hell's historic cauldron.

Because of war, many inventions and much material not previously considered, were introduced onto the factory floors of the nation's workplaces. For the pottery trades, the great step forward was the invention of the tunnel and flat-bed electric kilns. By the end of the 1950's the brick bottle-oven was obsolete. Urged on by the introduction of continuing stages of Clean-Air legislation, these impressive landmarks were bulldozed into the soil of history. Thousands of the town's identifiable architectural features were torn-up like pages from the chronology of working life until just a few dozen remain throughout the Potteries to show how it once was. And, as soon as this wild, wild enterprise was accomplished, the guardians of civic corporation cast their glances at other 'hateful' buildings. It mattered not that the Mother Town's ancient meat market was situated in, architecturally, the finest market hall building in North Staffordshire, health regulations took priority. It did not occur to the planners to find another use for the famed Hopton stone building that imitated the style of a huge grey Roman Forum with a magnificent stone-carved set of bull's horns above the heroic colonnaded entrance. The whole, all of it, the connected brewery as well, was doomed to the whim of progress.

A common anecdote at this time among city planners was, 'It's a pity Hitler didn't target Burslem as it did Coventry - then we could have started afresh.' Can you believe it!

Important buildings started to tumble to the ball-hammers of articulated tractors. The 1950's saw the demolition of the Legs of Man, Burslem's first post office and posting inn. Rows of shops and cottages in Newcastle Street, Bourne's Bank and the Sytch, all of which areas were intended to be replaced with new buildings but nobody ever got round to doing it. But it was the 1960's which witnessed the worst times in the council's desperation to wipe the slate clean and to 'start afresh.'

The slogan Stoke on Trent City Council adopted was 'Modernisation', and was based on a platform of land reclamation which was only partially successful. In order to wipe away the old and stagnant Burslem forever, the authorities even changed the names of many of the main streets: Liverpool Road to Westport Road: Church Street to William Clowes Street: High Street to Greenhead Street, and many others which achieved nothing except confusion among older residents.

The mini-slump in the pottery industry at this time saw the council agreeing with private owners to remove some of their unused buildings in long term projects of land redevelopment. The first of these factories to be demolished was the Alcock pot works in Westport Road. It had stood for many years empty and forsaken and had not produced pottery for a decade before 1960. Commissioned by Samuel Alcock in 1839 and known as Hill Pottery, it was a magnificent piece of architecture of classical mode. Built in three storeys, the brick reception building covered a third of an acre sitting on top of a hill overlooking Brownhills towards the adjacent township of Tunstall. The street-facing wall was treated to intermittent tiers of windows with stone architraves geometrically crafted and fanned. There was a central roof apex, behind which was a large cupola regularly flying the Union Jack. But it was the doorway that drew the eye. Twelve feet by six feet, an oak panelled central opening door which was capped with turned classical Venetian mouldings. Two complimentary doors on each side were paired at a height of eight feet and separated from the master door by flat-faced Doric columns. The whole doorway was covered by a pediment with a rear-set balcony favoured with vase-shaped pillars supported in groups of four by fluted and scrolled Ionic columns with leaved capitals. Five stone-chiselled wide steps led from the pavement while over the doorway was a grand Venetian window echoing the identity of the entrance in size and style. Imagine arriving from America to buy pottery from Alcock's, to be confronted by such an imposing warehouse!

Arnold Bennett thought the front of this building more ornate than any other seen in the Potteries. In his autobiographical masterwork, Clayhanger, Bennett, through the eyes of Osmond Orgreave, the architect, and the would-be architect, Edwin Clayhanger, called it the Sytch Pottery:

> *'...Mr Ogreave stopped an instant in front of the Sytch Pottery, and pointed to a large window at the south end that was being boarded up. "At last!" he murmured with disgust. Then he said, "That's the most beautiful window in Bursley, and perhaps in the Five Towns; and do you see what's happening to it."*
>
> *Edwin had never heard the word 'beautiful' uttered in quite that tone, except by women...*
>
> *Mr Orgreave crossed the road and then stood still to gaze at the facade of the Sytch Pottery. It was a long two storey building, purest*

> *Georgian, of red brick with very elaborate stone facings which contrasted admirably with the austere simplicity of the walls. The porch was lofty, with a majestic flight of steps narrowing to the doors. The ironwork of the basement railing was unusually rich and impressive.*
>
> *"Ever seen another pot-works like that?" demanded Mr Orgreave, enthusiastically musing.*
>
> *"No," said Edwin. Now that the question was put to him, he never had seen another pot-works like that.*
>
> *"There are one or two pretty fine works in the Five Towns", said Mr Orgreave, "But there's nothing else to touch this. I always stop and look at it if I'm passing. Just look at the pointing! The pointing alone...."!*
>
> *Edwin had to readjust his ideas. It had never occurred to him to search for anything fine in Bursley. The fact was, he had never opened his eyes at Bursley....'*

And for many years that's what the majority of Burslem people failed to do as they passed through the town centre on their way to work, heads bent, wondering if the day will be theirs.

It was in the 1960's that a great number of public houses were also demolished to make room for new architectural concepts. Of these were the Black Lion and the Star in Queen Street, the Volunteer in Newcastle Street and the Red Lion in Moorland Road were of distinctive value; the first being of Georgian cottage style, the second and third of imperial Victorian creation, and the fourth, the Red Lion, one of the most important buildings in the Mother Town, had features dating to Jacobean times. Only the Red Lion was replaced by another licenced premises retaining its predecessors footings and curtilages and its name, but ditching its heritage. Today the Red Lion stands as a figure of contempt thumbing its nose at tradition; it represents misguided policy of all that is bad in regeneration

The 1960's also saw the high-alter of Methodist worship being pulled down, the Swan Bank Wesleyan Chapel with its Gothic facade in dark stone. The Sneyd Church in Nile Street went in the 1950's replaced by a private car park, while the 1970's saw the demolition of the unequalled Italian stuccoed architecture of Hill Top Chapel and school, leaving an un-reclaimed bomb site with its portico lying bloodless amid the dereliction, guarded by the insistence of a misguided council by a preservation order. And throughout these twenty years of the 1950's and 60's, pot works simply tumbled to the ground and were buried beneath waste land and car parks, as whole communities of houses were flattened, their families scattered. The Coliseum, a theatre/cinema, the Palace next door; the Palladium around the corner, all victims of the insensitive bulldozer.

Shops closed as a consequence. It was a Rubicon; one day there were Boyce Adams, the Maypole, Cliff's butchers, Cropper's ladies outfitters and Swettenhams. Gentlemen's outfitters and drapers, Cock's, Hepworths, John Collier, Fifty Shilling Tailors. Brace and Flowers for shoes and footwear as were Freeman, Hardy and Willis, K's; and Johnson's tobacconists with branded names of tobaccos from all corners of the world. Music shops, Bew's and Alcock's; three or four chemists, grocers that sold everything and opened all through the day and evening. And there was the grand indoor market where one could buy fish, rabbits, game, poultry - dead or alive - to eat or to keep as pets. Several fish and chip saloons - *saloons* not shops - adorned the byways where grand family meals could be taken, banquets of huge fresh haddock on plates piled with chips and peas, or dishes of tripe, hodge and chitterlings swimming in vinegar, sandwiches of cows udders and cows heals and succulent Wright's Pies. The whole town then was a magical commercial theatre where unique artists performed and great transactions were made. But in the end, when the motley was rubbed away, the stars packed-up their paraphernalia and sadly moved on into the distant ether. This town, and similar industrial towns throughout this great historical country are left as Never-Never lands, arenas of unfinished projects and half-finished demolition - dissolving dreams and fading memories, lost in the shadow of city centre shopping malls, super stores and business parks.

Is this what oral history is, talking out memories, regrets, lost opportunities: yearning for the 'good old days? Am I? What of the melancholy tears of a bent widow sitting alone in a terraced house after a funeral, fingering the spring lid of her husband's broken spectacles' case; a gadget that he always meant to repair? Still warming his worn-out slippers beside the fire, ready for when he comes home from work? All those years ago when together they listened to the Variety Bandbox on the Light Programme; joining in Songs from the Shows, with comedians 'aye-aying' with funny, lurid and cryptic catch-phases. Widows who were once young, rosy, bouncy girls - 'IT Girls', 'Can-I-do-yer-now-Sir? girls', 'Glad Eyes' girls. Girls waiting for their men to come home. Men leaving home. Brown paper parcels tied with string. 'Aye-aye Lady - That's Yer Lot!'

The following chapters are designed to present some facts in the history of Burslem through the stories of its people. Here are people who have lived in the town past and present, and some of those who are planning its future. Their outlines have been deposited in a trace that is of history, constructional history. For no reason other than of their presence here, that they once lived in this town, means that the whole history of the world has been touched - we are all part of the story as we are all part of the stars that have flown away from the first explosion. And there are events here that have taken place which have also provided turning points in that slow erosion of evolution which, when looked back upon, may be seen as allegoric keynotes in the tunes of a great synchronised concerto.

My chapters are not chronological, rather the chapters have been blended to manufacture a studied theme in an overall pot of historical sociology. Here a future reader will discover Potteries people from various walks of life, surprised no doubt, if they were still alive, to find themselves connected and spoken about in the same themes of their counterparts in ways they would not have planned, condoned or admitted to. Thus I have attempted to show how a variety of apparently unrelated factors have influenced the same occurrences, each element in its own way remaining individual to the common result.

Touched with the modern historian's natural passion for photography, I have used my own pictures to illustrate locations and events. This serves to bring substance to a town which visitors may find less familiar when they look at the old photographs, therefore my pictures may incline them to remain awhile to recapture the mysteries of the past paths the early potter walked. Selfishly, and in order to indulge my own preference of narrating history in a readable form, I have succumbed to the improvisation of some episodes which clearly are not factual reports. But the reader may think, after reading this introduction, that my modest inventions are justifiable to the benefit of atmospheric continuity. However, the factual content of these notes have been thoroughly researched to the best of my ability and passed on in my honest belief that its information is all perfectly true.

Is history then an academic subject belonging to others, or is it for all of us in the way once promoted in the grand view of Edward Gibbon: an experience **'that exalts and enlarges the horizon of our intellectual view.'?** Or is it as simple perhaps as the humbling proclamation of John Quincy Adams, **'Who we are is who we were'?** Or is it the complex thing that Arnold Toynbee riddles out of the inevitability of existence? As he embarks to tell the weighty story of the whole of mankind, he begins with a sentence of such simplicity that his words heighten to the shocking state of helplessness: **'After a human being has been conceived and has then been born, the baby may die before it has awakened to consciousness'.** So what of all those dead things? Think not, I urge of those, for in my grandfather's humble declaration there is hope: **'Many now living will never die!'**

Chapter One

ARRIVAL AND DEPARTURE

'...Now that we come to the subject of Railways;- contemplate the future viaduct over the Turnpike Road, and the station adjoining; and again survey the channel of water communication between the Eastern and Western S, which the Father of Engineers, Brindley, planned and mainly executed, - and all this at Longport.....'

(Ward, pg 161)

There once ran a satirical caption on a picture postcard which was produced in the Staffordshire Potteries during the period from 1905 to 1960 - **"The air SOOTS me fine in Burslem"**, it proclaimed. Above this affirmation was a monochrome photograph depicting a landscape of megalithic chimneys shrouded in thick palls of smoke and veiled in an atmosphere of vapid pitch and globs of carbonised steam. **"A good SMOKE in Stoke"**, extolled another postcard, portraying curtains of blackness descending as a Wagnerian backdrop to camouflage forests of fat aching bottle ovens, gasometers, dwarf churches and houses, all set against the grime-curls of an expressionist sky. Scenes from long ago. Picture postcards from the past. Fearsome sights posted home by travellers visiting the theatre of hell. And at the bottom of this scorching cauldron, the inhabitant potters scurry industrially; very small people with pale faces glancing vigilantly out of the collars of white smocks, fixed like dimmed stars against the blackness of night. Is it possible, the recipients of the postcards wondered, that these Lilliputians never saw the sun below the black clouds? Even on Sunday when they went to chapel - did they ever see the light of day?

Despite their environmental retreat, the Potters of Stoke on Trent have always contrived to put on a sunny show for the benefit of travellers who might be passing through. The furnace-flame extinguished, the coals dampened, the ovens cooled; the porcelain inhabitants would place before the visitor a carpet of welcome such as rarely seen even in the bosom of the county towns. And they would reach out with warm artistic hands to extend animated greetings to one and all - *'We're so, so, glad you came...don't hurry away...stay awhile'*. It was as though their long watch beside the fires beneath the smoke gave immense release to their enforced isolation when they were visited. And whenever their most famous visitors came, the dark elements that hid their progenies pain of industry, colluded to create an atmospheric welcome as well in happy, bumper fare, as if in celebration of its own spirit of fellowship - imprisoned nature released - an extension of respect for all the special guests. And the dark clouds would roll away and the sun would race to its zenith amid blue skies above the still sentinel chimneys.

Friday June 5th 1925 was such a day, the day the king of Great Britain and the British Empire arrived at Stoke railway station, carried in his wonderful and ornate train from his castle in Windsor. Mid-morning, and the sun was already pounding upon the dusty cobblestones of Winton Square where the hands of the statue of Josiah Wedgwood carefully held a pottery vase - the great potter inspecting with critical inclination the ageless beauty of the moulded ornament.

The visit that day of King George V and his wife Queen Mary was only the second sojourn they had made to the Potteries - their first being on the eve of the Great War in 1913 when they spent two days observing the manufacture of pottery at the world's centre of ceramics and ceramic trades at Wedgwood's at Etruria and Doulton's at Burslem before taking lunch at fine Elizabethan Moreton Old Hall. But the visit that day in 1925 was to be something of a special occasion in the history of the Potteries. After many years of civic and central administrative negotiation, the title of 'City' was to be conferred on the district by royal consent. Though some say that the king announced the decision on the spur of the moment, there is no doubt that this was the purpose of his visit and that it had been well planned in advance. The king had decided to come and give grace to the occasion personally for he knew that the potters loved him well and had been touched by their honest and open loyalty.

This royal event was to be a culmination of mediation and bargaining begun nearly a century earlier at the time of the Great Reform Act of 1832 when the district first received its own members of Parliament; and this was followed by the Federation of its towns under one civic administration in 1910. This day in 1925 was to end with the Potteries becoming the City of Stoke on Trent with its own civic autonomy, like Manchester and Bristol, Norwich and London.

Though few and far between, royal visits were not new to the Potteries. Even so there never had been a visit by a reigning monarch. Victoria, who was so beloved here, sent only her children as envoys, she herself never came. The last occasion of a royal visit was by the King's father Edward and his wife Alexandra who were, at the time, the Prince and Princess of Wales. That was in 1897. And it was during the visit of 1897 that an elderly Danish expatriate, Fredrik Idon Holst, was asked to make a civic presentation of a hand-carved milk pail to the Queen, his countrywoman, who herself was also living in chosen exile in England. On that occasion the royal party had also visited Fenton where the Prince opened a church bazaar at the invitation of his friend and Queen Victoria's chaplain, the Hon. Reverend Leonard Francis Tyrwhitt. It was Tyrwhitt, a controversial spiritual leader, who, some six years later, caused a great social division throughout the six towns by preaching two disturbing sermons under the title of **'The Devil in The Potteries'** in which he castigated the potter for the obscenities of drunkenness, prostitution and immoral social behaviour. Then, a thirty-seven year old native novelist from the distance of Paris, responded in print to the provocative vicar to proclaim that Tyrwhitt was *'well meaning but ill-informed'* about the people of the Potteries among whose numbers he was proud to be counted. The novelist, Arnold Bennett, had by this time achieved world fame for his 'Five Town's' books, and although he was endured in five of the six 'real' towns, he came to be loathed in Fenton by the people he contrived to 'forget' in a whim of phonetic choice. It was an 'error' for which there is evidential proof of unreasonable resentment to this day.

Tyrwhitt was not minded to let Bennett's inferences and criticism of his sermons pass without response and he publicly replied that, **"I have been making enquiries as to who the gentleman was. I have been informed** (by people in Fenton) **that the gentleman is a commercial traveller, although only, out Burslem way. People have told me that he is a writer of fiction. I am inclined to believe this for the gentleman seems to be a writer of the second**

rate type. " Bennett was not drawn to further comment.

During that week-long visit the Prince and Princess of Wales stayed at Trentham Hall, the home of the Duke and Duchess of Sutherland, an aristocratic seat where they were frequent and popular guests of Cromartie and Millicent Leveson-Gower. The royal party were treated to a concert at the Victoria Hall Hanley at which the Stoke on Trent Philharmonic Orchestra performed Charles Swinnerton Heap's cantata, 'The Fair Maid of Astolat'. Among the guests that evening were Burslem salon musician and teacher Madame Marie Reymond, the daughter of the Danish cooper Holst, the same who had presented the wooden milk pail to Alexandra. And accompanying Madame Reymond was her protégé, a locally born 18 years old lad, John Cope. The potters were so proud of their prince and princess, so honoured by their presence! And so it was at the royal visit in 1925, that the Prince's son, George, now king, had come to give the Potteries its supreme possession, the conference and recognition of the title 'City'.

The King and Queen were met at Stoke railway station by the Mayor, Alderman Harry Leese and other civic representatives. Outside in Winton Square, in front of the graciously styled and ivy-clad North Stafford Hotel, tens of thousands had gathered, cheering and waving flags and coloured banners and streamers as the band of the North Staffordshire Regiment struck up the National Anthem, a rendition hardly heard over the high voices of the squealing holidaying school children lined-up in their school classes. In a Rolls Royce, the royal couple were swept through the people-lined streets to the Council House and the King's Hall where other principal guests were waiting. On behalf of the Corporation, Alderman Leese made his welcome speech and the King rose to respond:

> ***"The development and importance of your town and industry enable me gladly to consent to the request that the title and status of a City shall be conferred upon your County Borough. I pray that the Divine Blessing may rest upon your labours, and that the City of Stoke on Trent may enter upon and enjoy a future of even greater usefulness and prosperity."***

It was twelve noon. The Potteries had become the City of Stoke on Trent. Resounding in the bright daylight from the spires of Christ Church in Tunstall to St Mary's in Longton, church bells rang-out in harmonious celebration and salute. Families gathered in their communities to eat and drink at long tressel-tables in sun-lit narrow streets. All the million bottle ovens stood as stilled escorts, clear, cold and smokeless. The sky, blue and cloudless, held galleries of songbirds hovering in astonished exceptional chorus above the slagheaps and the pits, surprised by the occasion: rabbits ran unhunted among the wooden posts and sleepers at the pit-heads; dogs lay morose in the thousands of empty backyards and cats stretched across the pitched shed-tops glad there was no shade in which to skulk. Yet no bells rang in Burslem, or at least, their cheer and the glee of the people was not of gala cause. And the two giant town halls that it boasted were as empty that day as they would be the tomorrows and the days thereafter. For, in those rejected fifteen years since 1910, Burslem's civic meeting rooms had been symbolically padlocked. No bustling committees wove in and out of their oak-panelled rooms, no sounds in the chambers that lined their deep-reaching corridors, no mayoral dignity graced their parlours. Time's circumstance had passed by. The 'Mother Town' stood alone.

'Where is this Burslem?', the traveller might query, knowing it only by its name given by Arnold Bennett. Bursley, he called it, and Bursley it often remains today to a great many outsiders. 'Why, here it is! Between Manchester and Birmingham. Ha-ha! I was looking for Bursley'. A famous potting town where famous potters lived and live. A place in a region which, even oftener today, all the communities still refer to it as 'Mother Town'. 'But how to get there?'

Physically Burslem lies at the southern tip of the Pennine Chain. It nestles on the flattened south side of a small un-distinguished hill; and, from the sky, it appears very much the same as many other green landlocked former villages that grew into towns born out of the Industrial Revolution across the rich mineral tracts of industrial middle England and the north-west.

In late summer swallows assemble in clouds over Burslem for annual migration. Once galaxies of starlings wheeled over the giant sheds of Sneyd colliery and brickworks, but they moved to other transit stations once new owners knocked down their miles of empty lofts and perches. Birds will know the land best of all lying between the deep wetland vale of Whitfield and Norton in the Moors, where a tributary of the Trent flows, the same that rises at Mow Cop to offer its waters to the southern vales. And in a lower valley to the west where another Trent tributary trickles out of Bathpool meandering pleasantly along the Chatterley valley. All around swallows and starlings know well such secret places, and remember them when summer comes round again.

> *"Established almost precisely on the fifty-third parallel of latitude. A little way to the north.... in the creases of a hill famous for its religious orgies, rose the River Trent, the calm and characteristic stream of middle England. Somewhat further northwards in the near neighbourhood of the highest public house in the realm, rose two lesser rivers, the Dane and the Dove, which, quarrelling in early infancy, turned their backs on each other, and, the one by favour of the Weaver and the other by favour of the Trent, watered between them the whole width of England, and poured themselves out respectively into the Irish sea and the German Ocean."*

Thus, majestically, opens the first page of Arnold Bennett's masterpiece novel, **The Old Wives' Tale**. To begin a visit to the Mother Town with a quote by Bennett is entirely appropriate, for it is merely to pay deserved respect to the Potteries' finest novelist. While so many other local artists have made huge contributions to the world of decorative and ceramic art, it is the great Edwardian novelist who speaks so grandly and honestly of Victorian times in order to use his literary genius to tell the potter's story. This is his invention, the creation of the Five Towns.

Bennett was an addicted traveller who told fellow travellers about his home; the dark potbanks, dark terraces and darker public buildings. Of civic and class discriminations. Dour aldermen who legislated for dourer citizens. He describes with mirrored accuracy locations that, in their realistic interpretation, reflected his reader's own lives within their own drawing rooms and parlours. But above all, as his journals testify, Bennett talked endlessly of Potteries' people, his family relations, their relationships, and of his friends and of his enemies.

The author recalled the narrow cobble-stone lanes of his childhood and youth, the smoke-shrouded roads bearing the weight of the clanging and fizzing trams;

the ugly beauty of the region through which bleakly shone the 'Grim Smile' of the potters in their creation of beauty from the most cavernous and troll-like of worlds. Bennett left at an early age. 'Escaped', it was claimed. But he could never shake the potbank's dusts from his Saville Row shoes. Truth to say, he couldn't had he wanted to.

To bring the traveller to Burslem in a time when a new millennium is about, one needs only to take directions to junction 15 or 16 of the M6 motorway. Or travel along the A34 into the ancient and loyal borough of Newcastle under Lyme - the middle-land's road that reaches from Brighton to Manchester. Or by way of the A50 from Congleton, or even the old winding and creeping road from Leek through Brown Edge and Norton in the Moors. But better still, arrive by train as the King did - come as 'royal' visitors. And take advantage of measuring with the eye the distinctive Victorian stone and brick facade of the entrance to Stoke railway station and look back into the inside of its bowed cavern. Hear the fizz of the railway station, the joyous crying in the breathless expectation of arrival, the tearful whispers of departure as farewells are breathed silently beneath the iron stanchion canopy:

>**Far away, someone muffles an announcement.**
>**A charge of steam enjoins a squeal of metal brakes.**
>**In one last roaring gasp of egress.**
>**Doors thud amid a milieu of rapid shoes on stone.**
>**A discordance of a hundred greetings; a hundred fare-thee-wells.**
>**And then, a sudden alien silence binds.**
>**A full two minutes, until a whistle squeals**
>**Across this temporary termination, as carriages shuffle from the white-edged platform,**
>**Leaving nought but a jacket of ascending vapour**
>**And the shock of it all;**
>**Of being there, but briefly.**

Built on behalf of the North Staffordshire Railway Company in 1849, Stoke railway station boasts a beautiful seven arched structure in the Italian Renaissance style with an enclave of offices attached to the north elevation which today are occupied by the University Bookshop. This Virgin North-West main-line station was well-known by Bennett who used to talk about it often in his stories as he progressed to describing the inter-connecting Potteries Loop Line; a rail route which he helped to immortalise. The 'Knotty'- its engines and carriages emblazoned with the gold Staffordshire Knot symbol on a background of claret livery, winding its way through the Six Potteries' towns. Oh to have been there as engine number one, **'Dragon'** it was accurately and fearsomely named, drew away from Winton's Wood, a name by which the land area of the railway was formerly known; land once historically owned by Algar, a Saxon earl of Mercia before the Norman conquest.

Now take a PMT bus to travel a winding four mile journey along distinctive main roads and minor streets filled with little shops and corner sited pubs. Roll past the lanes and the malls and arcades of Hanley, the city centre, once the unremitting competitor of Burslem for the right to claim the commercial and central privilege of 'main town'. The journey has a feel of company, as though the passenger is being handed-on gently from street to street; exchanged from district to district with romantic names like Havelock, Snow Hill, Shelton, Hanley, Vale Place: travelling uphill all the way.

Suddenly all inner roads converge at a high point in the northern reaches of the city. The road widens and a street sign says that the bus is entering Cobridge. On either side high red-bricked and terra cotta faced dwellings peer grandly across the road at each other. Yes, looking a little weary these days, they have seen better times, but they still capture the atmosphere of horse-drawn carriages, growlers and hansoms, dog carts and high-sided flat-backs laden with straw-padded crates of pottery and vats of liquid slip. And, if the traveller comes at dusk, old times are attendant once again, stealing across the footpaths to haunt with gnome-like shadows under umbrellas of gas-lit incandescence beneath which knotted groups of people dressed in Victorian black gather to share a conversation, shrouded in dark modesty against impudent and imprudent watchers. Young ladies with bonnets, lace-edged petticoats; young men with velvet pantaloons. Girls clutching rag dolls, boys rolling hoops.

The bus will pass the Bennett house, number 205 Waterloo Road. Enoch Bennett, the pater, commissioned its building for eleven hundred pounds in 1882. It was Arnold's last home before he left for London. And, although his father paid for the house, the author looked upon it as being his very own. Every day during its construction the sixteen year old boy would watch from the family's temporary home across the road as the new house went up brick by brick. He wrote about it in Clayhanger, a story of himself and his consciousness.

> *"The house was his father's only in name. In emotional fact it was Edwin's house, because he alone was capable of possessing it and enjoying it. To Darius, to Bursley in general, it was just a nice house, with red brick and terracotta facings and red tiles in the second Victorian style, the style that had broken away from Georgian austerity and the first Victorian stucco and smugness, and wandered off vaguely into nothing in particular. To the plebeian in Darius it was of course grandiose, and vast; to Edwin also, in a less degree. But to Edwin it was not a house, it was a work of art, it was an epic poem, it was an emanation of the soul."*

This is Waterloo Road and it was once full of such houses, some with even deeper and higher 'emanation of the soul'. It was a part of Burslem that was symbolic to arriving and iconic to arrival!

If the traveller decides to alight from the bus at Cobridge in order to walk into the town - a good idea by the way - a clear view is available of the whole of the southern aspect of Burslem. A mere fifty years ago, during a working day, the same view would have been obscured by thick smoke, not only being expelled from the myriad of bottle ovens but also from the hundred and hundreds of chimneys of terraced houses in back-to-back streets. Today, those houses have gone and all of the chimneys and all those bottle-shaped potbanks have doused their fires; and most of the people have left. The arc of the horizon has been changed, now it is bright; the structured composition - that rough mixture of houses, workplaces and places of entertainment - has been modified, straightened a little in places, but the Victorian grace and charm remains in truthful reminiscence.

To the right of Waterloo Road the traveller will see open spaces where once stood the might of Burslem's economic strength. On a stretch of land a few council houses and a newly built community home for older people have replaced the massive potbank of the Washington Works and the heroic 'Bleak Hill Pottery' designed and worked by the Warburtons, a dynasty begun with the marriage of

Ann Daniel, a famous potter in her own right, descended from a famous family, to John Warburton a noted pottery enameller. One might in passing note the street names, Bleak Street and Warburton Street. Indeed, the last known licensees of the Bleak Inn, were Harry and Blanche Warburton who departed the premises when it was demolished in the 1960s. In a little terraced beerhouse called the Washington Stores, William Moorcroft developed his unique artistic creations - connected to his master's works - James Macintyre - by a tunnel under the road. Mind, it was much earlier, in the year 1610, that Thomas Danyell a potter, petitioned Tunstall Court to dig for clay in Brownhills:

> **'Tho. Danyell of Burslem, sen. Potter, a pasture called Brownehills & another pasture called The Hill in Burslem containing three acres, withe liberty to digge claye, ffillinge up the pitts after him, for a term of 21 years, rendering 4s yearly for all services.'**

During this period there were numerous similar petitions made to the Tunstall court indicating that pottery making had already developed and was well established in the district. Conditions and penalties were laid down over trespass, encroachment and refusing to make repairs on and to the common-ways and footpaths. It was commanded to be an offence, derived from the obstruction of a path or high-way, **'on every person which have made any pitt whereby the high-way is annoyed, and for not repaireing any pitt or encroachment'**.

Ann Daniel, born in 1713, was a master potter and enameller in her own right and the eldest daughter of Thomas Daniel (1681-1768) of the Smug Potworks, near to the Adam's Brickhouse. The family's patriarch was the earlier Thomas Danyell who had established a house and hovel below the Hill at the foot of what is presently Westport Road. Ann's husband, John Warburton, was already himself a master potter from a family known in Burslem since 1710, and although she survived him by three decades, the business prospered under Ann, her eldest son, John, and her brother Ralph Daniel, particularly in sales to the Netherlands. By the 1780s, the Warburtons' were executing a substantial amount of Wedgwood's enamelling work for the Etruria Works. Another of Ann's sons, Jacob, (1740-1826) also became an internationally respected potter who was a family friend of Josiah Wedgwood and was always a welcome guest at Etruria Hall.

The Daniel's had set-up important enamelling workshops in eastern reaches of the Out Lane district of Burslem where they owned much of the land that straddled the former boundary between Burslem and Rushton. This district became the early singular centre for their enamelling crafts while other parts of Burslem, belonging to the various branches of the Daniel's family included, Daniel's Croft, which housed a number of potworks. The old town additionally boasted two important family-owned inns - the Court House, (John Daniel) and the Red Lion, (Timacen Daniel). A study of the earliest Burslem map dated 1720 clearly indicates the importance of this pioneering family and its association with the Wedgwoods', and Adams', the two other principal potting landowners at the time, even though none were more powerful than the Wedgwood's.

The connections of this part of Burslem with American trade brought fame and wealth to these potters during the middle period of the 19th century, so much so that a large hotel was built in 1831 on the site of an old un-named inn at the southern end of Commercial Street. The new premises were first named **'Waterloo and American Inn'**, and was deliberately established to accommodate the influx of Burslem's growing American visitors. It was renamed **'The American Hotel'** in 1850, the name by which it was last known until it finally closed in 2000. The most interesting aspect of the hotel is in its comparisons with the present day frontage and the rear yard. Here today it can be clearly seen that the house originally lay in Commercial Street prior to the alterations in 1831. Stabling for 12-15 horses was a feature of the new front-to-back rear yards and arrangements could be made up until 1835 for the London to Liverpool and Manchester coach travelling along the Telford roads to call here for a change of horses and for passengers to alight or take refreshments in the new 'ample accommodation and extensive function room.' It was here in 1833 that Enoch Wood, in his capacity as High Sheriff and Chief Constable, hosted the annual dinner of the Association For The Prosecution Of Felons, and in his address on that occasion remarked that he was, **'pleased to see the splendid inn in which we have sit to dine.'** He told his guests that, **'sixty years previously...'** he had been **'accustomed to travel that road, or rather, to cross the fields through which the road was cut. And night and morning, I could scarcely meet a solitary person.'**

The American Hotel today is at 144 Waterloo Road, de-licensed and soon to be converted into a block of residential apartments. Nearby is the small beerhouse, today the workshop of a dental laboratory - number 136, which was formerly William Moorcroft's workshop, **Washington Stores**, de-licensed in 1903. It has been well attested to that the tunnel which ran from the beer cellar beneath the road, was originally designated for clandestine visits by the potters for ale and spirits. It is likely that William Moorcroft, a sober man, would have strongly refuted this allegation!

This was the road which hosted many a public house, so many that it was said that if a toper took a half pint in the first pub at the north end and doubled it up in each successive pub until he arrived back to his starting point, having travelled the length and back, he would have consumed 32,768 pints of beer! Some session! Some headache! And this, all along the fronts of a single road barely a mile in length! Nearly all of those inns and beerhouses have been closed many years since - only one now remains - and yet it is possible still to see the buildings which held the former pubs standing inconspicuously in their change of use to shops and offices, perhaps a little embarrassed by their past, perhaps a little cowed as they dream of their former importance.

To supply those public houses, and more besides, would have taken the business skills of a great entrepreneur. Such a man was Henry Parker whose brewery lay below the huge Bleak Hill works. Parker had been born in Wales in 1825. From inauspicious beginnings, the young man began his progress to Burslem by enlisting in the Welch Royal Dragoons in which he became a non-commissioned officer. Though this enabled him to travel extensively, Parker saw little military action. At the age of forty he came to the Potteries where he was employed by the Tunstall brewery, Hedges. Taking advantage of the lax licensing legislation, Parker began to buy houses in Burslem which he supplied with a home-brew from a small premises in Nile Street. Almost overnight he had, in 1865, become Burslem's principal common-brewer acquiring land in Regent Street (Zion Street), where his plant brewed three strengths of beer and maintained its own coopering yards. As trade grew, Parker recruited a partner, Manchester hop merchant Matthew Dobson whose eldest son William Warrington, came to Burslem to look after his father's interests in Parker's Burslem Brewery. The young Dobson settled in the Potteries and under his management Parker's Brewery became easily the largest brewery in North Staffordshire owning 56 tied public houses in Burslem and 468 overall.

Henry Parker was a man of leisure and used his wealth in domestic comforts. He built Bleak House at 183 Waterloo Road, later owned by a number of well known Burslem notables including William Woodall MP who lived there until he moved to 'the Potter's Playground', Llandudno in 1900 where he died. Parker himself, had left Burslem to live in the Hollies in the Brampton, Newcastle under Lyme, a sumptuous mansion in which he comfortably retired until he quietly passed away in 1885 leaving a personal wealth of almost one hundred thousand pound. High profit for those times.

The brewery continued to thrive under Dobson who became one of North Staffordshire's leading celebrities. His business skills and social and political undertakings were rewarded by a knighthood in 1933, and he died at Seghford Hall, Stafford in 1941. Under the reluctant management of Dobson's children Burslem Brewery was sold to the Burton on Trent company of Ind Coope and Allsopp, thus ending the connection with the town of Burslem of both the Dobson and the Parker families. In turn the brewery was acquired by monopolisation in succession by the Midland's Ansells Brewery and later Allied Breweries. Parker's Brewery ceased brewing beer in 1963 and finally closed and was pulled down in the 1970s. Part of the office rooms have been preserved under an architectural protection order because of its ceramic mosaic sign on the outside wall and for its stone name carvings.

The little group of streets where the brewery once stood have changed dramatically over the years. Criss-crossing Waterloo Road are still Zion Street and Baptist Street and Pitt Street. But where once stood the great brewery and a huge potworks, the only features today are a supermarket and its car park, and even that has superceded an important 1960's-70's entertainment spot still remembered as the Adulte Ballroom - later owned by Rank and called Cindy's - which was purpose built in the late sixties and demolished in the early 1980's because of mining subsidence. Time treads so swiftly when buildings, like obsessions, are built on feet of clay.

Today's traveller will also see that a new road lay-out has been fashioned across land which formerly housed a large estate of workers' terraced cottages. This town centre bypass has even taken a large slice of earth out of the old churchyard causing the removal of a number of old burial sites and their contents to be re-interred in a corporation cemetery, happily though at Carmountside near to the old Hulton Abbey thus retaining the monastic connection.

This missing slice of consecrated ground has been replaced by a new wall, set back from the road, surrounding the church. Standing in the car park of St John's Church, the location will seem today to the traveller to be as isolated from the main town centre as when the district was little more than a Saxon hamlet. The stubby square-shaped mean Gothic tower is clearly of Norman influence and the stone was probably carried from quarries that lie between Cheadle and Stafford. The tower is extremely well preserved considering the attacks from the wastes of industrial energy and from the generations of the clinging pollution it has had to withstand. The structure of the present nave however, was not settled until 1788 and the vestry was added in 1794. Its final restoration was completed in 1880 when the interiors were extended to accommodate 850 seated worshippers. These days the graveyard and the adjacent houses are well maintained and tidied due entirely to the conditions agreed with Stoke on Trent City Council when highway's engineers cut the bypass through part of the south of the town in 1992. It's all so very different from the way it once looked, for the whole district has witnessed many changes.

The stone chapel of St John the Baptist was probably erected in the late twelfth or early thirteenth century, and certainly by the Lord Barons of Stafford. It is dedicated to the saint whose Patronal Feast Day is the first Sunday after June 24th which was when the 'Burslem Wakes' traditionally commenced. Even now the Potteries' main summer holiday begins from the last week in June, to the irritation of education officials whose pupils are removed from class three weeks before the scheduled national break - such is the quirkiness of the potter whose insistence remains observed to this day.

St John's church was placed at the centre of a community which grew out of misty beginnings. As already stated, the retreat of the last Ice Age some 6000 years ago exposed rich deposits of minerals from the Carboniferous Age 240 - 330 million years back, as well as creating the huge tract of the lime woodlands stretching from Lancashire through North Staffordshire and into Shropshire. Iron, the heroic mineral of civilisation, was found here in two forms, Clayband and Blackband: limonite, a brown oxide, and siderite, a carbonaceous ore. These deposits are to be found clamped between soft-coal seams and huge thicknesses of marl-clays; icons for earnings which first attracted wandering coal-getters out of the north west and up from the midlands. It is very possible that a family of these early travellers set down temporary roots at the edge of a thick forest of alder, yew, lime and other supple woods, properties extremely versatile in the construction of domestic habitat and the weaving of baskets and a host of other pliable and durable utensils.

Ecclesiastic references of Burslem do not appear before those of Stoke or Penkhull where the Right of Presentation (Avowdson) was shared between the Norman earl, Robert of Stafford, and the king himself who personally owned the land at Penkhull. The earl's portion was given to Stone priory in 1155 by agreement with the second Robert of Stafford and his caretaker under-lord, Walter of Caverswall. It has been established that Stoke had a wooden church at the time of a Saxon sovereign-order of 805 at the start of the Viking invasions. This instrument of tribal law instructed that all churches should be built of stone. This much is clear, but historians and archaeologists may only guess at whether there was a wooden church on the site in Burslem before the erection of the Norman tower. What *is* certain is that St John's Church tower is the oldest standing building in use in the Potteries - much older than its 'mother' church of St Peter's in Stoke.

But it is the churchyard that brings enlightenment to the traveller and visitor, even in a mere casual examination of the hundred or so graves here. The oldest stone to be found is undedicated and bears the carved date, 1428, an interment made during the early part of the reign of the last Lancastrian, Henry VI. Close to the south side of the tower is an open stone coffin said to have been used in the burial of a monk from the abbey at nearby Hulton, a couple of miles south east of Hanley, the Potteries city centre. Between 1536 and 1540 Henry Tudor (Henry VIII) dissolved the powers of the monasteries. It is possible that this stone coffin, and maybe others, were carried to the Burslem graveyard from Hulton for preserved interment. It is also possible that it is a burial place of a monk who died in the fields of his Grange - once monastic farmlands which were, in the 16th century, literally in the next field to the church. One well-held theory is that the stone coffin was cut into the shape of Elizabeth the wife of Nicholas, 5th Baron Audley. That being so, the coffin's body-space is but 14 inches wide and 6 ft. 3 ins. Long. So the stone coffin was carved for sideways laying or perhaps just for the bones!

It is because of this connection with St John's church and the abbey at Hulton that the area of St John's is such an oasis of important historical record, for this is where the story of the Mother Town and the Potteries begins.

The abbey was founded in 1219 and endowed in 1223 by Henry of Audley who was the great, great, great grandson of Richard de Toeni, the Norman standard bearer of William the Conqueror, a warrior knight who rode to the right of the Duke of Normandy at the Battle of Hastings. Henry Audley was the son of Petronella Gresley and Adam Audley, a knight who inherited great wealth and land not only from his own family but from the accumulated possessions of the barons who came with the Conqueror in 1066. Because of this wealth, Henry Audley possessed huge royal patronage that brought him importance and power, however temporary. Indeed, his court connections might have seemed impetuous to his household colleagues as he sided with King John in his dispute with the barons, an event that brought about the agreement of Magna Carta. Henry's blood relations extended to Randle de Blundeville, earl of Chester and of Lincoln, an extremely powerful aristocrat. And his marriage to Bertred Meisnelwaring (Mainwaring) the daughter in descent from Saxon earldom, brought Henry even more connections and power.

The monks at Hulton were French Cistercians who were encouraged by Henry to build the monastery near to the meadows left uncultivated by the Anglo Saxon earth miners on the south side of the then fast flowing River Trent. This led to the development of a number of farms called granges, one of the most productive being Rushton Grange below which was erected St John's chapel and tower. The intentions of the monks were primarily to re-establish the diminishing disciplines of St Benedict who had directed them to a life of agriculture and farming. The first abbot of Hulton took the name Adam in tribute to Henry of Audley's father, the Stafford earl who bore the given name. In Burslem the monks grew wheat and reared sheep and, by the time of Henry Audley's death in 1246, a thriving wool trade and self-sufficient agricultural system had been well established.

This was the golden age of the Audley family who went on to become closer than ever to the succeeding monarchs of England having been granted the writ of barony in 1296. But, by 1400, the male line had expired in name and the family lines had become fragmented. Thus weakened, its local powers and holdings and its close affiliation with the royal house waned. By the time of the completion of the dissolution of the monasteries in 1540, the Roman Catholic Audley's authority, along with the presence of the monks in the district, had been removed leaving their local land wealth, such as it was, in abeyance. Before the story of how industry settled here is further considered, the importance of the Audley family and of others who influenced the development of the town must be addressed.

The account begins in the middle of the 14th century when a young boy, James Audley, the fourth baron and later a hero of Poitiers who supported Edward the

Black Prince and eldest son of Edward III, was placed in the parental custody of Roger Mortimer, the Cheshire Earl of March. Mortimer's daughter became James Audley's first wife. His guardian and now father-in-law, stood to richly benefit from his ward through the subsequent issue and male rights of descent. But various misdemeanours committed by Mortimer against monarchical authority, allowed the guardianship to be terminated and the control of the Audley estate was appointed by the Crown to the Lord Ralph Camois. The title of **Lord Camoy** was left unused from 1426 until 1839 when it was resurrected by an appeal made by Thomas Stonor, a senior co-heir descended from the Camois family, who had entered the Biddulph family in marriage by way of the Goring family of Burton on Trent. The Lords Camoy to this day remain hereditary peers. Testament to the family names are bourne in local Cobridge street names: Camoys Road, Camoys Court and Stonor Street. In the lower northern reaches of Cobridge, however, other important names can be seen in carved testimonials of their greatness.

At the east side of St John's church the visitor is able to walk among and examine the inscribed gravestones of Josiah Wedgwood's mother and father, his sisters and brothers and his many uncles and cousins. The great early master potters, John Adams; Ralph Wood, Enoch Wood, John Daniel, John Warburton, lie interwoven with those of the 'witch' Margaret (Molly) Leigh; the 19th century brewer, Henry Parker and his wife. The relations of a former church rector, Alfred Watton (1830-86), a heavy drinker who committed suicide in his Middleport rectory, an irresponsible minister who had commissioned the erection of a monument, near to the front of the tower in tribute to his friend a convicted murderer Frederick William Horry and Horry's victim, his murdered wife, Jane. But possibly the most significant of the graves in St John's churchyard is that of Catherine Egerton who died in 1756.

Madame Egerton, as she was known, inherited the bulk of the riches of two Wedgwood families as well as the additional wealth of her three husbands. She was in direct descent from Gilbert Wedgwood as was her first husband, Richard - Catherine and Richard were second cousins. Catherine's dowry was the Over House and its adjacent manufactory. After the marriage she came to occupy the house which was situated at Burslem's highest point. Richard was much older than Catherine and he died in 1718, their only child, an infant, survived him by just two years.

Widowed Catherine then married an important Burslem potter, Thomas Bourne. Again the union saw a large difference in age and Thomas passed away some eight years later, much of his wealth falling to Catherine. Twice widowed Catherine's third and last husband was the gentleman Rowland Egerton of Manchester who was a nephew of Francis Egerton the Duke of Bridgewater the coal owner and canal financier. Catherine also outlived this third spouse and remained a childless widow without any direct descendants for the rest of her life. Throughout her life, the grande dame of Burslem was an unselfish benefactor to members of the Wedgwood's among whom was a favourite Thomas of the Churchyard potworks. It was to this favoured cousin that she gave or loaned money for the retention and upkeep of his pottery and his house, not a particularly thriving business but a factor of his life which provided a reasonable family income. It was here, at the Churchyard works that Josiah Wedgwood was born on 12th July 1730.

St John's churchyard is a place which truly deserves the calling of 'potter's field'; and the names of Wood, Wedgwood, Parrott, Leigh, Bourne appear over and over. The puzzle is why Josiah, the greatest of them all, isn't buried here in his birthplace!

Josiah Wedgwood was born some fifty paces south of the church tower of St John's, the thirteenth and frailest of Thomas and his wife Mary's children, all of whom except one nevertheless in such a large family survived into adulthood. It does seem that Mary had been in confinement all her life for her eldest, Margaret was twenty-three when the baby Josiah was born. Thomas and Mary appear also to have run out of family given names for here, the name Josiah, the name they gave to their youngest, had never before appeared among the males of their extremely fertile and large family relations who, in 1730, occupied and owned nearly all the land in the town. The story of the arrival of the Wedgwood's is one of simple dimensions, and not unique. It is impressed with all the intrigues of Georgian family trading, couplings of very near incestuous coil.

It is impossible today, looking out from Josiah Wedgwood's birthplace, to imagine the rural scene of the early settlers for the contours of the land have been changed dramatically by excavation and mining. But the first claimant of all of this land without any doubt stamped his entitlements upon field, meadow, wood and brook by using the very name of that district - Barcardeslim, or Burwardeslym and Burslem.

In 1416, during those troublesome and cruel two war years, when Henry V fought, routed and reclaimed Normandy and became heir to the whole of France which his son inherited; Thomas Burwardeslym paid suit to the Tunstall court. This meant that he was established as a juror indicating a position of some importance, possibly because of his ownership of land and property. It is reasonable to assume that this man was a certain Thomas of Burslem having acquired his situation either in consanguine connection with the Audley's or in a purchase from that family when the line was breaking up. Whatever the reasons, three other suitors of the Burslem family were recorded by the Tunstall Court's Rolls during the following hundred years giving some substance to the name and the family's position of authority. In presumed descent, a Gentleman named John BURSLEM was born in the early sixteenth century, and, in his maturity he was said to have been an esquire owning a large house, DALE HALL, situated on the western slopes of Burslem's town centre. The site has been identified as being on the approximate land west of St Paul's Church nearest to Newcastle Street, and demolished prior to the church's erection in 1828. This John Burslem was foreman of the Tunstall Court Jury in 1563 and again in 1569. The other important families at this time, who were his neighbours and numbered as jurymen in the court rolls, were the Biddulph's, the Adams's, the Colclough's, the Crocket's and the Daniel's.

John Burslem owned 650 acres of land, that is twice the amount the monks owned at Rushton Grange which was then - at the time of John Burslem - in the ownership of the Biddulph family. John Burslem's land comprised and included the whole district occupied by the town today to which he let to farming tenants. And yet he was not a rich man, being inept in commercial enterprise and unwise in his friendships. By the time of his death in 1596 his personal possessions were mere household chattels and his land had been divided into property at Oldcott in Goldenhill and Brownhills. The Burslem's though managed to hold on to Dale

Hall and the tenanted farmland thereabouts from which they continued to collect rents. But in spite of a few further local auditory aberrations, John Burslem's descendants nevertheless moved on into solid money-making circles, particularly in mining, while others moved as clergymen and yet others became landowners in their own right. A granddaughter even became the Countess of Huntingdon part of the line which today includes the present earl. But more important to Burslem's history is the presence of John Burslem's grandson, another Thomas, who married Mary Ford of the Moss in Cheshire from which partnership came the issue of Margaret, their eldest daughter.

As Margaret was growing up, the son of a large farming family in nearby Harracles near Leek, Staffordshire, Gilbert Wedgwood, had made a decision to come to Burslem where some of his relations were practising potmaking. It was, in a way, an outreach from the protection of his Leek relations whose over-intensification of the farming lands slowed-down his personal and naturalistic commercial interest and opportunities. Gilbert married Margaret in 1612; they were cousins from the marriage of her mother's sister to John Wedgwood of the Harracles branch. Margaret Burslem was the eldest of two children - in a family without male issue - and she brought to the marriage a dowry of modest wealth in land and connection. Her sister, Catherine, married William Colclough of another famous family traceable to the court of Edward III and existing today in the Bagot family and the Swinnerton's.

Throughout the next hundred years the Wedgwood family in a line from Gilbert grew and spread across the land of Burslem using the minerals further found by excavation and taking advantage of the techniques brought into the region by other master potters the likes of the Dutch born Elers brothers of Bradwell, the Adams' family of Greenfields, the Daniel's and the Astbury's, none of whom had started as true natives of the district. By the end of the 17th century the area had become identified for its ceramic produce and the Wedgwoods were the most notable, due to their possessions for as much as their skills. The recurrence of the family name in the baptism register conveys the depths of the family: now they were true Burslem folk.

But it is not only the matter of the Wedgwood's joining a growing band of so called 'master potters' or even leading them. Certainly Gilbert practised the arts and manufacture of ware for sale, but Gilbert's important role, a role that distinguished him from his peers, was to found in his entrepreneurial skills, in the way he leased out land encouraging his relations to buy and work here, and in the education of his children to his own commercial ways, preparing the way and making a base for future generations of his family. These marketing and trading skills are found to be distinguished in many of his descendants, principally in his great grandson Josiah who employed Gilbert's business managerial talents and harnessed them to his own potting skills. Josiah like Gilbert benefited from special capabilities in spotting the right partner in marriage and in business. Both men were much sought out by their peers and made many famous friendships. And it all began with the roots from the seeds set by Gilbert.

A 17th century puzzle jug, said to be the first piece of Staffordshire ware ever to be signed reads, 'John Wedgwood 1691'. Of course, there are many earlier pieces of great value and of more artistic preference, but this single piece indicates how far the industry had developed some forty years before Josiah Wedgwood's birth. Yet it was during the next 20 years that Burslem mushroomed as the small potting village became overwhelmed with some 147 occupant traders - the majority by far being potters - settling around the top of the hill where the present town centre is today. In the 1720 map we find family names listed repeated over and over: Wedgwood, Lovatt, Allen, Beech, Daniel, Marsh, Wood, Cartlich, Read, Malkin, Steel, Leigh, Adams, Taylor and many more familiar names that have progressed through the generations. All without exception were famous potters of their time.

As all these developments were shaping up, Thomas Wedgwood and his wife and children steadily worked the Churchyard Works. Their cousins John and Thomas of the Big House were potters on the east side of Shoe Lane (Wedgwood Street) which stretched onto land known as the Jenkins Fields where they placed a windmill built by James Brindley. Their cousin Richard, husband of Catherine, owned the Over House and cousin Ralph Wedgwood worked the Ivy House opposite the Big House. Young Josiah grew up on the edge of this frontiers town around St John's where it had all began with the Benedictine monks.

As a child of twelve Josiah Wedgwood's life was blighted by a serious attack of smallpox which later recurred in adulthood to cause an amputation to his right leg. The adversities of illness and having to survive as youngest in a large family, distinctly directed his life and his future career. He was educated at home until he was nine, probably by his mother and sisters who taught him to read and write and do simple sums. Illness provided Josiah Wedgwood with the time to allow his mind to become aware of other non-manufacturing matters that were going on around him. He took notice of the history of his trade and learned by watching his relations practice the arts of throwing and moulding. It is not difficult even today to imagine the location and environment that Josiah Wedgwood lived in.

The Churchyard works and house lay in the oldest part of the town between the ancient church and an old alehouse then called the CROWN, or, the CROWN AND MITRE, today simply the MITRE. The house and potbank sat where part of St John's infant's school was later built and on land now owned by the firm of Heath's Sneyd Colour Work. Although it was the oldest part of town, at the time of the young Wedgwood, it was the least inhabited - the earlier settlers joining the newcomers in transporting themselves to the top of the hill in pursuit of clay and coal. To the north of the Churchyard an old lane, formerly known as Church Lane and later named Bourne's Bank after the family of Catherine Egerton's second husband, fell away into a huge pit which had been excavated, at first by the clay-getters, and then in 1719 when the Lord Macclesfield mined 150 acres of coal adjacent to the water courses north of the church. This massive pit can be seen still in the steep contours at the foot of Bourne's Bank beside the company ACME MARLS.

The view up the hill to its summit must have been like looking up at the mouth of a bellowing volcano. It was a hill on fire belching smoke and flames high into the sky! And yet, even amid this industrial turmoil, the young Josiah's house sat at the edge of the long alder wood as it undulated through Rushton toward Sneyd Green - side-lined, as if itself preferred to keep its own company away from its dirty neighbours. Black hovels and green fields heaving side by side.

When Josiah was fourteen he was apprenticed to his elder brother Thomas under whose tuition he learned the basic trades, being the custom of the times. The sibling relationship was however far from brotherly, Thomas inclined to laziness and to let the business slide. Upon completion of his training in 1752, Josiah commenced a small potting business some three miles south from Burslem at Cliffe Vale in partnership with an older man, John Harrison. It was a brief partnership which did not inspire Wedgwood except into the initiation of the general business side of potting as well as allowing him to train in the sciences of the trades. Josiah proved to be the strength of the business and it was dissolved two years later when he entered into partnership with the master potter Thomas Whieldon of Fenton, himself a ceramic scientist, who encouraged him to further experiment in the mysteries of the ancient trade. When he was twenty-nine Josiah Wedgwood was ready to return to his home town, still the centre of the Potteries, to prove to his many relations the uniqueness of his products. This time he set up at the very centre of the town renting the Ivy House from his uncle Ralph. This was the cauldron at the top of the hill! That everlasting fire at which he had gazed when he was a child.

Wedgwood outgrew Burslem. Within ten years he had helped to develop the industry into a fine art and taken it into the world's market places as well as into the dining rooms of royal palaces. He then occupied two potbanks, the IVY HOUSE and the BRICK HOUSE, known as the BELL WORKS on account of the calling of his workers in at the start of the day and to announce the firing and emptying of the kilns. The ringing of a bell became a standard practice adopted by all who followed him and was carried on well into the middle of the 20th century by the use of steam buzzers and electric sirens: marking the time it was in fact copied thereafter by the owners of all industrial premises throughout the world. Wedgwood was as full of innovation as he was progressive in the skills and science of his trade. He employed the finest and most eminent artists and crafts-men and firmly believed and practised in-house training for all his workers as well as caring for their welfare. He pioneered the use of turnpikes in order to get his ware to the western ports in good time for sailings and with the minimum of damage and breakage. But some say his finest contribution was his stimulation and part-financing of the Grand Trunk Canal, cut to be named the Trent to the Mersey Canal which was the first major permanent route across Britain since the Roman legions laid-out their straight roads well over a thousand years earlier.

This canal, inspired by Francis EGERTON 3rd Duke of Bridgewater, related through marriage to Josiah Wedgwood, is 93 miles in length. It was engineered by James Brindley. It's highest elevation is at Harecastle Hill from where it descends across Cheshire to meet the River Weaver at Preston on the Hill. In the east, it winds through the Potteries to meet the River Trent at Wilden Ferry (now a bridge) near Burton. The canal's elevations are controlled by a total; of 75 locks. The common width is 25-30 feet with a depth of four and a half feet. In the west the canal is carried by aqueduct over the River Dove built upon twenty-three arches - *a floating bridge in the sky, a mile and a half long!* In the east the water is carried over the Trent by an aqueduct of six arches and over the River Dane by three arches. But by far the most olympian of the canal's features is the tunnel that was cut through the Harecastle Hill, three miles north west of Burslem. The tunnel is 2,897 yards long and 8.5 feet wide; the arched ceiling is entirely lined with brick quarried and made from local clays on site. The struc-ture is designed for legging, which means that the horses were un-harnessed and led over the hill to the other side while 'leggers' or 'legging-boys' were employed to lie on their back on the barges and kick along the roof in order to propel the water vehicle through the length of the dark tunnel.

The digging of the tunnel was begun more or less at the same time the first clod of earth was ceremoniously dug by Josiah Wedgwood and James Brindley on 26th July 1766, while work also commenced at either end of the canal terminals. The entire project took eleven years to complete, during which time Brindley died and Wedgwood had moved all his works out of Burslem town centre and over its southern ridge near to Shelton.

Incredibly the Grand Trunk Canal opened up Burslem directly to the world. It increased vastly the loads that could be carried; it cut the time of transportation by many days; it literally eliminated breakage, and, it made Burslem a household name throughout the land - the town was, after all this had been done, placed in a commanding position at a central point of the kingdom, standing on what was then the principal transport route to be used for many years to come.

The now hugely successful and famous Josiah Wedgwood was living in his new home overlooking his potworks on the south-facing meadows beyond Rushton and Cobridge, a distance of only some two miles from Burslem. But the great man took with him his treasured employees, those special men and women he had personally trained. And he built houses for them close to his new factory which stood at the side of his canal. To this idyllic location he gave the whole area the name ETRURIA after the Italian region which produced the pottery he so admired and emulated and which re-introduced to the world. Etruria Hall stands today as part of the Staffordshire Moat House hotel and conference centre. It has been greatly renovated and added to. The district however is still named Etruria.

Two hundred and forty years ago, Wedgwood paid a Mrs Ashenhurst three-thousand pounds for the Ridge House estate comprising 350 acres. (This Mrs Ashenhurst was heiress to the local wealth of Colonel Ashenhurst, a Roundhead commander who led his troops at the attack on Biddulph Hall in 1647 which saw the Royalist seat pounded by a huge cannon known as 'Roaring Meg' see below.) Etruria Hall was finally built in 1769 when Wedgwood removed there with his wife Sarah and the first three of his children. The architecture was, by the standards of those times, quite modest and reflected the Georgian style which was dominant in the new-built mansions of the emerging capitalist middle-class of industrial Britain - the new county set. Modest it may have been but it boasted thirty-four rooms with an ample wine cellar and an ornamental garden laid-out by CAPABILITY BROWN. On the gentle west facing slopes, the views were utterly representative of the best of English shire and country life. Here Wedgwood entertained James Watt, Erasmus Darwin, James Brindley, Joseph Priestley. Willam Boulton and many other famous captains of the Industrial Revolution. Together these men met and compared experiments, talked of progress and innovation - their conversations and astronomical surveys were identified by the name of their group; the LUNAR SOCIETY.

It was here, in this growing industrial district which had by no means yet thrown-off its rural aspects, that Josiah Wedgwood died in 1795. His eldest son and heir had previously moved to Surrey but returned to live briefly on the Etruria estate after his father's death whilst waiting the completion of his own mansion in the Staffordshire village of Maer (a house sometime later occupied by the Burslem brewer, Henry Parker.) Meanwhile Josiah's former partner and nephew, Thomas Byerley, took over Etruria Hall as well as the running of the pottery factory. Later the hall became a ladies school operating there from 1824 to 1844. Lord Granville purchased the estate in 1858 and his iron-works' manager Colonel WS Roden came to occupy the hall after whose death the building was used as office premises for the Shelton Steelworks.

St John's churchyard holds no resting place for the Biddulph's though; that once grand family that brought the richness of aristocracy to the district and yet, at the same time, carried the black shrouds of sudden death and pestilence, disastrously saddling the family name with hate and fear as the ermine livery of their gold and purple carriages and horses turned black on the scourge of rats.

When Henry VIII dissolved the monasteries and the monks withdrew from power, many spiritual men were persecuted to their death, others fled the country; the bulk of the Catholic Church's wealth was seized, or by other unreasonable means passed into the ownership of wealthy families. Once again evidence emerges of deals done for family connections aligned to those of Norman descent quietly living in their shire hundreds. Many ditched their Papal faith and deferred to Henry, the protector and defender of the Church of England, while as many remained and hid their faith from public show, practising their traditions in detached groups in cells in sympathetic communities. One such family were the Biddulphs.

At the time of Domesday, a Richard de Forester is mentioned as one of the lords of Staffordshire. His second and third grandsons, viz Edward de Bidulfe and Sir Thomas de Bidulfe took the family through the lines of Biddulph, Gresley and Audley into the 18th century when the host name merged with the wandering Goring family of the Barony of Camoys down to Thomas STONOR whose own great grandson, Thomas, successfully claimed the title of Baron Camoys in 1837.

In 1539 Henry VIII gave the dissolved Hulton Abbey's Rushton Grange, its cottages and its farms, to a court favourite, James Leveson. A later family member, George LEVESON-GOWER (1815-91) became second Earl Granville with massive iron works throughout the country, notably the Shelton site as previously mentioned; land he acquired from the Wedgwood Ridge House estate. Earl Granville's second eldest son, CROMARTIE, (1851-1913) assumed the title 4th Duke of Sutherland and married MILLICENT, (1867-1955) daughter of the Earl of Rosslyn. Among the richest families in Great Britain, one of the Duke of Sutherland's homes was Trentham Hall.

James Leveson was a rich man in 1539 and not at all in need of any more Staffordshire property; he therefore promptly sold the Grange estate to his friend Richard Biddulph. His son Francis built Biddulph Hall in 1558, a magnificent Tudor mansion and farm which was the family's home until 1643 when, after the Civil War battle of Hopton Heath where the then head of the family, John Biddulph, was slain in the field, Biddulph Hall was bombarded and virtually demolished by Cromwell's army when all his land and properties were confiscated by Parliament. While his father lay dying at Hopton Heath, eldest son, also Francis, prepared to defend the ancestral home at Biddulph. There he held up with a number of strong Royalist friends and relations against an army led by Lambert Cromwell and was largely successful in repulsing the Parliamentarians until a huge cannon, known as 'Roaring Meg', was brought up to bombard and destroy the hall. Francis Biddulph surrendered after a battle lasting a week. The death of John Biddulph at Hopton now saw his son Francis as head of the family. But at the end of battle at Biddulph Hall, Francis was arrested and imprisoned for the next two years at Eccleshall. This was a disastrous time for the Biddulph family but even so, upon the commencement of the Commonwealth, and certainly by the Restoration of the monarchy, their possessions were handed back to them for such as they were as most of their residences had been reduced to rubble. James Leveson's gift of Rushton Grange at Burslem was the exception.

It is now 1647, a year which saw a virulent strain of the Plague pass through the countryside. Francis Biddulph, his wife Margaret and their children had just taken residence at the Grange estate upon his release from prison, having no mansion left to occupy at the destroyed Biddulph Hall. The Catholic landowning family of the Bagnalls had been tenants of the Grange by the subsequent marriage of Thomas Bagnall, town clerk of Newcastle under Lyme, to Jane Hammersley of the Ridge House estate, (the estate that Wedgwood had later bought). The caretaker tenant of the Grange at the time was Sampson Bagnall who quit the property immediately upon the Biddulph's return. The Grange House was quite rustic and Spartan compared to the lavish homes the family had been used to. The house itself was half-timbered and thatched with two annexes attached to the sides and one to the rear. Even so, it was identified as being the best house in Rushton and second to Dalehall where the Burslem family then lived.

The Biddulphs continued to maintain the old faith in secret and had a personal Catholic priest in attendance together with a newly employed governess, an Italian catholic woman named Catherine who had recently joined them. How the Plague was brought to Burslem will never be known. It will also never emerge just how many people were affected for the parish register was deliberately left unreported throughout the period by the clergy's refusal to allow interment in St John's churchyard. What is certain is that the epidemic began in the Rushton Grange district and spread to the lower reaches of Hot Lane where most of the victims lived and where sanitation was particularly bad. Here the entire community almost disappeared. So serious was the epidemic that many left the district never to return: the bodies of the dead were just as soon plunged into a deep pit on the Grange indicating the suddenness and widespread severity of the wretched disease. Had it not been for financial intervention by a number of master potters, which brought about the taxing of twelve surrounding parishes to account for substantial relief aid, Burslem, it is said, would have been entirely ruined by this fatal calamity.

Myth prevails that the Biddulph's governess Catherine, introduced rat-fleas through a bundle of clothes she had brought from London. She was said to have had a fine singing voice and locally known because of it as 'Singing Kate'. Because of the rumour of the rat-fleas in her clothes, Catherine and the Biddulph family were accused by Burslem people and blamed outright for the pestilence. The mass burials were sited on the condemned Biddulph's land and the plot was cursed with the awful name - 'Singing Kate's Hole' - she being one of the first to die. Nor did the Biddulph family escape for most of their children died also of the plague. Heartbroken and devastated at the loss of his family Francis Biddulph rode off into the night and was heard of no more.

After the departure of the Biddulphs, the Bagnall family returned and tenanted the Grange House to a number of Catholic tenants until 1688, the year which saw the abdication and flight from the country of the last catholic king, James II. Burslem was singularly protestant at this time and the catholic tenants of the Grange, fearing for their lives, fled from their home. Their fear was not without substance for, in the excitement of the routing of James, many Catholics throughout the land were persecuted and their property stolen or destroyed. The Grange in Burslem was not to be the exception as a mob from the town as well as from Shelton, climbed the hill into Rushton and ransacked the Grange House. The oldest and largest part of the house was reduced to rubble, but the smaller attachment towards the north end gable, used by the Catholic familes as a chapel, survived and was left standing together with a number of farm buildings. When events had quietened down, these few buildings were once again employed as a place of worship, albeit on the basis of secrecy as for some years to come a number of Catholic purges broke out, in particular the Gordon Riots in London of 1780 when once again the catholic community of Cobridge lived in fear of religious persecution.

By 1800, the old part of Grange House was still substantially standing and owned by the Warburton family, potters in descent from Ann Daniel and John Warburton. This family had been united with the Bagnalls by the marriage of Anne Bagnall to William Warburton, a member of the Cheshire family branch. Their grandson Jacob, the potter, friend and confident of Josiah Wedgwood, lived at the Grange until 1814 before moving to reside at Ford Green Hall where he died in 1826. But the farm was still maintained by tenants even when, in 1839 Lord Granville took up his options on the ownership of the adjacent land, Ridge House, and erected a number of blast furnaces for smelting iron on the Grange. All of the land beside the canal and neighbouring beside Wedgwood's pottery works, was occupied and became known as Shelton Iron Works. Puddling troughs, blast furnaces and steel rolling mills were added introducing to the growing site, its own coal mines, iron mines and stone quarries as well. At the time of Granville's death in 1891, Shelton Works was among the largest in the midlands and the most self-sufficient with minerals. The iron works together with its collieries had become the single largest employer in the district.

Shelton Coal Iron and Steel works were nationalised in 1946 and became known as Shelton Bar. In the fiercely fought economically competitive years of the 1980s, the company was severely trimmed and its workforce cut-back as it was returned to private ownership. In 1986 The whole area of the former Granville works was designated as the site of the United Kingdom's third National Garden Festival which turned out to be hugely successful. Following the festival's closure the land was sold and a giant business park and retail centre was built incorporating Wedgwood's Etruria Hall in the hotel complex of the Moat House.

Grange House and farms survived into the early 1900s but by 1930 the house had fallen into total decay. Today its site is unmarked but council houses in the south west corner of the Grange council estate more or less occupy the land on which the grand house stood. It is possible however to view a copse containing some overgrown trees which once formed a corner of the Biddulph's extensive garden and grounds. But probably not for much longer as new housing projects continue to encroach upon the locality. And still the parish church of St John's lies active in the northern vale unobservant of the Biddulph's entitlements, offering no comments on theirs lives; blind to their deeds, silent to their fate. Somewhere on the Grange among the cinders of industry, lie the broken pieces of unknown hundreds of plague victims. Lost people of Burslem.

The first pages of the parish registers of Burslem of 1538 show aged parchment hardly readable. A Thomas Heath is recorded as the first incumbent rector in 1532, prior to this it appears that ecclesiastic administration came from Stoke's parent church, St Peter's. There may have been earlier sheets of register but a fire at St John's in 1717 destroyed them along with the old wooden chapel nave. Rates records of dues paid to the lordship were commenced in 1563 when some thirty-two inhabitants were levied land tax. Records of 1601, during the closure of the reign of Elizabeth I, show that there were but 13 baptisms, 3 marriages and 10 burials. And, in 1616 still only 41 persons were liable to taxation. But, in the year 1676 an ecclesiastical census recorded that there were 444 baptised Protestants living in Burslem over the age of fifteen.

That same year the noted Doctor Robert PLOTT, historian, geographer and naturalist, passed through Burslem. The town was by that time considered important enough to attract such an academic traveller on his way to Lichfield. Plott found the place to be '*the seat of the greatest pottery carried on in the country.*' He found a '*sizable*' community making pots using four different sorts of clay and coal, '*all being dug out within a distance of half a mile*'. The famous historian reported that he had found a '*fair number*' of thatched cottages inside small hedged and fenced enclosures. At the rear and side of each enclosure, he found ovens - a '*hovel, no more than six feet in height,*' shaped wider at the base and cowled with a bottle-shaped furnace shell and trenched. Nearby were the traditional arrangements of sheds, coops and sties; for, there is no doubt, that the regular crofter was by now supplementing his income in pot-making having found a market for clay pipes and earthenware containers such as butter-pots. From this point on, Burslem's history becomes properly recorded and its subsequent fame handed on to following generations. But before further departure into that history and before leaving St John's churchyard, a small mystery remains to be considered.

In a later chapter we shall find that between 1835 and 1845, the Potteries had begun to come to terms with the struggles for workers rights amid the creation of early trades unions, and Burslem in particular was the scene of a number of serious consequential incidents of unrest. Several demonstrations took place over poor working conditions and pay, and two serious situations of riotous assembly broke out culminating in eventful disorder in Burslem and Hanley, both instigated by agitation from the Chartists. The first of these gatherings culminated from the strikes and lock-outs of 1836-7 and occurred on 10th November 1838 at a Chartist meeting in open fields in Hanley. And the second, by far the most serious and notorious, was fought throughout the Potteries ending in a violent climax in Burslem town centre in the middle of August 1842. A sad fact of the Burslem 1842 riot is that a young man from Leek was shot dead near to the Red Lion Inn. His body was taken by constables and laid out in the town hall from where it was returned to Leek and to his parents. Some historians have identified the boy as one, Josiah HEAPY; others refer to him as a local man, Nathanial JOHNSON. Legend and the mists of myth now enter the story.

Most agree there is a body in St John's churchyard of a young man who was supposed to have been shot in one of two violations. And, there is indeed a gravestone herein bearing the following inscription as a tribute to Nathanial Johnson:

**'Under this stone the body lies
Of a good and faithful child.
His father's hope and his mother's pride,
His life was Hasked but God denyed.
I went up town a sight to see,**

**And met with a shot which did kill me.
No mourn for me, I beg you make,
But love my sister for my sake.'**

While this epigram bears the sentiments of those troubled and uncompassionate times, the presence here of Nathaniel Johnson of Middleport puzzles, who, his gravestone memorial states, died on 12th July 1837 from a gun's shot. This leaves the question - which tumult was he involved with? The disorders throughout 1837 took place in Hanley, but there was certainly no reports of anyone being shot as a consequence. The infamous Potteries Riots in which the man from Leek was shot dead was a full two years off after Johnson's death. So, who was this man who shrugged-off self sentiment to beseech sundry mourners and beg a lasting love for his sister? What awful thing was he a party to that deserved such a dramatic end? And, where lies the man shot dead before the Big House on 16th August 1842? What of he?

More will be heard of the pottery strikes and lock-outs in later chapters. Perhaps by the end of the book the questions of Nathaniel Johnson will be answered. Meanwhile it's time to leave the potter's field and look at other records.

**This place of drama;
This field of peace.
What are we here?
We hold horizons in our hands
To offer to a waiting guest.
What would you choose to taste,
A hawthorne's sting, or bramble's wands?
A Lake, a field, a rippling brook
To sooth?**

**That you and I stood in this hour
And shared those things. Remember?
We were there.
Go now, and think.**

Chapter Two

METHODY AND REASON

'...The houses of the towns or villages were mean and poor, scattered up and down and Mostly covered with thatch. The manners of the inhabitants were not superior to their habitations; and their pleasures and amusements at their wakes and holidays were gross and brutal......'

(Ward, pg. 31)

'OI! YOU! What are you staring at? YOU! You - starer-bob! YOU!' A traveller would be wise to pass by hurriedly. Escape! Take care to move away swiftly for the HOT LANE gutter-snipes are about with their street cries which once echoed threateningly through the covered alleys hereabouts as gangs chased gangs: *"Rally-o, rally-o, one, two three; we are coming after THEE: one two THREE!"* A gentle and harmless - humourous in fact - sounding cry, but one filled with veiled accusation; drawing up and protecting boundaries. The battle is on. And, at the end of it, *each* time, the war would be resolved in a gentle kiss, or amnestied in exchange for a bloody nose! Rally-O was a chase-game played in back-to-back street communities until the real threat of community diaspora arrived bringing with it the ugliness of fear and jealousy, those two malignant frailties that set neighbour against neighbour. Then the children were hastened indoors from the cold out of the harms way of natures unsecured predicaments and perversity into the stifling comfort of predictability. Thus featherbedded, man rejected the tremulous passion of the young and how he himself was once young.

Derived from a Medieval field game locally called 'Prison Bars' - a game which set one half of a community against the other in raids, skirmishes, assaults and defence, locked together amid general pushing and shoving that might last up to a week - Rally-O disappeared in 1961. It stopped, almost overnight, when the last of the gas-lit street lamps were turned off, trickling away from the stagnant, stinking drains of slum terraces, shrouded by the damp fogs left leaden in the place of departed communities. It soon became a forgotten pastime as it sidestepped and bypassed the estates of new semi-detached council-countryside before it became lost forever in a maze of bucolic street names; houses with gardens at the front as well as the back; smokeless chimneys stacked with antennae and satellite-tracking dishes. The plans and plots of street-games are no longer remembered. Life changed for everybody in 1961 as the traveller stood impatiently at the portals of a new age of indulgence - consumerism. It was the year when Society came to be called Socialism.

> **And so, at the top of Time,**
> **where filaments hang in electric skeins**
> **touching the face of Gods**
> **in winds of webs and rains**
> **of brittle frailty; in carbon rods**
> **that stir the syrups of the Universe**
> **where nova-rich elements scout**
> **fluidly together to disperse**
> **in one last great illumination**
> **before the lamps go out.**
> **"We shall not see them lit again in our time."**

In 1961 the world paid homage to a young handsome man from the western hemisphere. His name is remembered best by his initials only - he had arrived to rule the world. And in that same year a lone handsome pilot from the east became the first man to fly in space and see the stars as they see themselves, unhindered. The stunning achievements of these flaming birds of passage - so much alike in all they dreamed of - were celebrated by the building of a tribal dividing wall straight through the middle of one of the world's major capital cities in order to keep their mutual aspirations apart. A world version of Prison Bars and Rally-O!

Into the 1961 industrial districts of Britain a migration of working men continued to flood into the old towns of the old Empire's centre where they were cautiously welcomed or rejected as whim and taste prevailed. They brought with them new cultures which swept into the cobblestone back alleys from which the English tribes had begun to escape. A nationwide road network was being hewn out of the countryside giving access to places which had previously been undertaken in a two day journey. And in Burslem, it was noted that the last gas-lit street lamp had been removed to the city works department at Longport; that most new pottery kilns were being built on a flat base and brought indoors to be fired by naked electricity embalmed in the vapours of mercury and platinum. Amid all these inspirational exchanges only the British poor in 1961 mourned the passing of the umbilical symbol of the past - 1961 was the year that the farthing was made obsolete! The great leap to the future was taken.

The traveller is safe now. The grubby street urchins have packed-up their games and their threats, and have left. And gone too have all those people who once lived and died in Burslem's Hot Lane. Dead, after living a somnambulant life groping through a few short crammed years of school and factory floor. Readin' ritin' and 'rithmatic on chalk-daubed slates, just around the corner from their homes; near to the potbank where they and their parents worked, a dozen yards from bed - and back. And the chapel in the next street - R.I. and Sunday school. The use of 'practical crafts' that needed not wit but sweat in the art of seeking comfort and solace in the hundred adjacent public houses, sited for convenience - 'The Old House at Home'. Life sagged away in those back street beerhouses, in other men's parlours, where drink was to be had in exchange for jam-jar pennies, where a surly landlord met all men's pressing needs with a critical look. **'Eh! What are you staring at, starer-bob!'** All gone now.

Touching Hot Lane, here is Nile Street. The traveller may stand today on the corner of what has always been the major crossroads in Burslem; where, straight as an arrow, Waterloo Road darts southwards, hurrying all things that will be hurried to the city centre shops, to the plastic-smelling offices draped with corporate swish. To places where eyeless computers wait in passive aggression.

At the west of the junction lies Burslem's once main shopping street - Queen Street. It sits on a sloping ledge cradling its over-sized public buildings in its apron, like a child-bearing pot-woman nursing her motherly breasts. And Swan Bank - foremost of the town's principal squares - straddling the A50, the former primary road that once carried all travellers from Goldenhill - the village at the Head 'o 'th Lane that overlooks the wide plains of Cheshire - to the south, to the Lane End and the Meir where the land drops to the pull of the West Midland's central magnetic conurbations. Meanwhile, on the crossroads of Swan Bank, the George Hotel sits quietly and contemplative within its well-approved geographic antecedents; rightly reserved and justly content in its prominence at the head of Nile Street.

Nile Street was named after the success of the battle of Aboukir Bay on the River Nile when Horatio Nelson defeated the French Toulon fleet on August 1st 1798, thus ending the sea phase of the Napoleonic wars with France. Within two years another great name would emerge, that of Arthur Wellesley, who, within fifteen years, would ride the fields of Belgium to destroy French power and expansionism forever as his new century un-rolled. And the names Wellington and Waterloo would afterwards be proudly carved on the name-plate of every first house at the start of a million new streets all over the Empire, as if each one was individually special in its personal dedication to the great general and his deeds.

The end of the 18th century began the time of Regency; the last two years of the old Hanoverian George III, the monarch who let the western colonies go. It was also a time of the consolidation of the 'gentleman' class who pressed the ceiling of the wealth of the peerage as well as imitating the lifestyles of the dukes and earls, the viscounts and the barons. These gentlemen, born out of manufacture, industrial invention and daring, built huge mansions out of English oaks laid out in the country estates of the shires around the fast-growing new cities of Halifax, Newcastle, Liverpool, Manchester and Birmingham as they out-matched the old industrial towns of Norwich and Lincoln. William Pitt was prime minister. Great Britain was the richest country in the world and most people felt content with their lot - even the working classes!

It was a time of naming streets after heroes and events rather than in the identification of locations and directions. The new industrial towns took hold of this and ran with the breathless patriotism of affiliation as well as competition. Today in the back streets of the run-down and reclaimed suburbs of these cities and towns - urban villas that shot up all across the north west and the midlands - there still can be found cardinals of Waterloo Roads, and processions of Nile Streets along with regiments of Wellington Streets, galleries of Pitt Streets and George Streets; Charlotte Streets, Gladstone Streets and many other long dead notables who stretched down from the Regency into the age of Victoria when it then became a formality to name each new terrace, an avenue, a court or a square after the Queen or another person of government. And if ever a local person's name was used in a home town, then, it was the height of recognition; it was something to be aimed for, a reward for a lifetime of doing good and practising good deeds - in giving back some wealth from whence it came.

Until the year 1700 the sparseness of the communities in Burslem reflected the system of Enclosure, ownership of land in the names of personal locations such as Malkin's Moor, Daniel's Croft and Robin's Croft; or in descent from the former common land as in The Hill, the Furlongs and the Hadderidge. The only roads were unmade lanes such as Packhorse Lane, Beeches Row and Hot Lane. Bourne's Bank, Burslem's oldest road, was at that time un-named - occasionally called Church Street as it led directly from St John's - and was an un-made path. And, while the pottery industry grew and more people came to live and work in the centre of the township, names were used to identify the sites of their 'potbanks'. Thus we find, by 1715, names being used to locate the potters and their hovels some of which were still in colloquial use up to the mid-twentieth century: Churchyard, Flash, Holehouse, Hamel, Knole, Ruffleys, Stocks, the Pump, West End, Rotten Row, Maypole, Shoe Lane, the Jenkins, and Greenhead.

All of these names are self-explanatory in describing their locations - Hamil, Holehouse and Greenhead have certainly climbed into the 21st century, their names remain the same and are still used.

As the population rose people began to inhabit the fields which lay between the old lanes and there came to be a need for more particular descriptions of residence. In these times, 1720-50, the land was given a more descriptive terminology: Hill Top, Bowling Green, the Windmill and the Stew Pool. Later came Ball Bank, Daniel's Row, Cockshut Hayes, Pudding Bag, and Furlong Passage. Meanwhile the manufacturers began to move away from the grime into the peripheries of the 'town that belched smoke', with houses reflecting their high position: Cobridge Hall, Bleak House, Longport Hall, Portland House and Bank Hall. Interestingly, by the late 1770s, these small townships started to grow faster than the main town centre becoming districts in their own rights but without self-governing autonomy. Longport, Middleport, Newport, Cobridge and the Sytch all turned inwards, looking at independence in their home lives as well as at their trades.

Hot Lane had its own special community who's roots were established along with those of old Burslem-by-St John's, Rushton, and Sneyd Green. These were potting districts long before the hill top began to fire where today the town centre stands. Brownhills was a growth area before Burslem, and in 1790 there were more workers living in Longport because of the expanding potbanks and their support industries brought about by the opening of the Trent and Mersey canal; much more in fact than in the parent town. Note the chronological constituents:

Date:	Description:	Source:
1086	1 tenant and 4 cottagers	(Domesday)
1563	32 cottages	(Church records)
1647	Population growth halted because of the Plague	(Ward - Bagnall records)
1666	41 hearth taxes collected - important houses only	(County records)
1680	70 houses	(Vide Plott - pub. 1686)
1702	27 baptisms	(Parish register)
1740	40 baptisms	(Parish register)
1750	Big House erected	(NS Field Club vl.LXXVIII)
1760	'...a hill inhabited almost entirely by potters.. a multitude of whom assembled...' etc	(Wesley diaries)
1761	First town hall, market, school, constable's rooms built	(Ward pg 235-236)
1780	159 baptisms (Parish register)	
1781	'...the whole face of this country [has] changed in about twenty years! ...inhabitants have continually flowed in from every side.'	(Wesley)
1810	256 baptisms	(Parish register)
1815	Waterloo Road built to link Hanley	(County archives)
1817	Union Buildings houses built by Wm Davenport	(Titles, deeds)
1819	Mount Pleasant and Stubbs Street Dalehall built	(City archives)
1824	Fountain buildings erected by E Wood for workers	(City archives)
1828-31	Newport Street and area built around St Paul's Church	(Davenport collection)
1830	308 baptisms	(Parish register)
1832	360 registered electors	(Poll returns)

Date:	Description:	Source:
1835	New market built on site of Ivy House potworks	(Burslem Health Board)
1837	394 registered electors	(Poll returns)
1841	Population 16,090 inc. Sneyd & Cobridge	(Census returns)
1851	A total of 4,000 brick and tile houses standing	(Burslem Health Board)
1857	Town hall demolished - new hall built on site	(Burslem Health Board)
1871	Population 22,971 - highest recorded of former Borough boundary	(Census returns)
1921	Population 42,444 - highest recorded of new borough which included Smallthorne and Chell.	(Census returns)
1991	Population 22,604	(Electoral returns)

There was a time when there were 14 schools in Burslem. A main line railway station linking the town to London. There were 21 places of regular worship, a principal hospital, an American consulate. A town hall with its own independent council; five substantial coalmines, a police station with a complement of forty constables. Hundreds and hundreds of potbanks and, one hundred and forty-seven public houses! Burslem's situation in the City of Stoke on Trent was as unique as the City of Stoke on Trent was in the County of Stafford - as its districts were to the town of Burslem - uniquely independent - fiercely so.

> *'The Five Towns seem to cling together for safety. Yet the idea of clinging together for safety would make them laugh... From the north of the county right down to the south, they alone stand for civilisation, applied science, organised manufacture... you cannot drink tea out of a teacup without the aid of the Five Towns; because you cannot eat a meal with decency without the aid of the Five Towns. For this the architecture of the Five Towns is an architecture of ovens and chimneys; for this its atmosphere is as black as its mud; for this it burns and smokes all night... for this it is unlearned in the ways of agriculture, never having seen corn except in packing straw... for this, on the other hand, it comprehends the mysterious habits of fire and pure sterile earth; for this it lives crammed together in slippery streets where the housewife must change window curtains at least once a fortnight if she wishes to remain respectable; for this it gets up in the mass at six a,m., winter and summer, and goes to bed when the public houses close; for this it exists - that you may drink tea out of a teacup and toy with a chop on a plate... [AND] ... Bursley has the honours of antiquity in the Five Towns. No industrial development can ever rob it of its superiority in age, which makes it absolutely sure in its conceit. And the time will never come when the other towns - let them swell and bluster as they may - will not pronounce the name of Bursley as one pronounces the name of one's mother... There you have it, embedded in the district, and the district embedded in the county, and the county lost and dreaming in the heart of England!'*

(OWT pg 5)

Hot Lane was first referred to at the end of the 17th century during the visit of the traveller Doctor Plott, although it was identified as a village community quite some time before this. In Hot Lane it is likely that its people came down from the High Lane ridge from Smallthorne rather than they climbed up out of Burslem. A current local street guide will show that it travels uphill eastwards and lies between Nile Street and Sandbach Road, a distance of some 300 metres; a short stubby street of no apparent good use. It has no houses, and is edged on its north side by a high bank of grassed earth used as a visual barrier to hide a sprawling industrial park behind. On the south side are a few other business premises opening directly on to the roadway. But there remain two buildings at the west end of the lane by Nile Street that provide extremely important links with Burslem's past. An obsolete wayside inn and a chapel!

It's difficult to conceive that this small location was once at a centre of Burslem's development as a pottery manufacturing town. Once more the imagination of the traveller would be strained to live again in the first centuries of the second millennium. Those years that led up to and came to rest in the 16th century would have seen the few farms and cottages clustered about St John's Church, and the small communities of Rushton, Sneyd and Hot Lane within a short walk away giving little sustenance to the few who lived there. But what they did benefit from was lifted straight from the earth - outcrops of coal and clay were abundant. The older villages of Sneyd and Hot Lane also were advantaged by the alder wood which provided more than their needs for domestic and marketing uses - a forest which provided a natural partition between the hamlets of Sneyd and Burslem/St John's. But it was Hot Lane that first provided the seemingly never ending coals for the district's pottery hovels, a site later developed as the Sneyd Colliery, a mass employer of colliers through the ages.

As the communities of Hot Lane and St John's grew, both sides took advantage of these readily availably minerals as they advanced towards the hill top of Burslem. As the St John's potters reached the upper shelf which was to become Queen Street, they turned aside, no doubt for fear of penalty for the encroachment of the lands of the Burslem family resident at Dalehall. Meanwhile, the Hot Lane community pushed towards the hill top along the lane that was to become Nile Street. With the natural geographic boundaries, it is likely that the Hot Lane and St John's community came together at the clay pit of Swan Square. These lanes, thus joined, provide both access and egress routes to the southern slopes of the hill top. A few years on saw push giving way to shove when, driven along by the organising pottery developers, the richer families began to employ the former crofters in groups to perform manufacturing tasks in their work and pay them a wage in annual hirings. The space was quickly filled - there was no where else to go. Thus the hill was conquered and the Burslem of today was born. But the traveller should not forget that Hot Lane and St John's were already substantial communities and indeed continued to thrive independently with their own chapels and schools.

Between 1690 and 1790 the Hot Lane residents lived with no particular outside influence in their small one or two roomed thatched cottages with walls made of broken saggars and sealed with saggar-marl and clay - 'Potting Peasant' is probably an appropriate name for them. The folk of these independent neighbourhoods kept themselves to themselves entering the town's small market only to bring in clay, coal and supple wood for packing. Most of their requirements were prudential to the cultivation of crops, animals and poultry; and the raw labourer even provided his own alehouses a number of which merely grew from lowly sheds or as simple ale-benches set at the entrance to hay-barns into which the imbiber collapsed after a long course of drinking.

It has been said that the Sneyd family hunted deer in these parts. It is a likely conception for the descendants of the Conqueror's army would have found a number of forests in the district ranging from Hanley along both sides of the ridge as far as Chell. But that must be left to conjecture for time has drawn its curtains across the windows of the local pastimes of the lordly; the memories of peasant life provide the only chinks of light in the shrouds of the past, found deep in the holes they dug which they back-filled with the waste they cast aside. Thus the first inhabitants lived according to the means of the land and in the ways the land and soil had directed them. But it was to Hot Lane that other methods came to guide their spiritual ways as well as their industries.

Methodism is the evangelical movement founded by brothers John and Charles Wesley in 1739. Governed by Presbyterianism, Wesley and his followers swept aside many of the faith's ecclesiastic traditions of the times in the rejection of apostolic succession and the ordination of the elders - presbyters. John Wesley set up an evangelical church after he was prohibited from the pulpit. This led him to preach in the open air at market places and wherever the poor and the poor workers gathered, for these simple people - often debarred and hardly ever encouraged to attend orthodox services - were his converts and followers. As an evangelist John Wesley travelled over 250,000 miles and preached some 40,000 sermons during his life. Advance notice of his arrival in a town would promote an excited congregation gathering hours before his arrival where some five or six-thousand people included many who would leave their workplaces just to hear him preach and sing along to his brother Charles' popular hymns. John Wesley's travelling preachers first came to Burslem in 1757 where they ministered from a horse block in front of the Legs of Man Inn. They found a town separated by two distinct classes: the manufacturing potters, who lived in the high houses at the top of the town, and the labouring potters who lived in the overcrowded poverty of the cottages that lay along Hot Lane and Bourne's Bank.

As with any newly developing frontiers' town, Burslem had both a static and transit population which took its only pleasures from the profusion of alehouses and the primitive delights found inside them. At this time the only two places of worship were the high Church of England at St John's and Sneyd, and the un-promoted Catholic church away at Cobridge. The rich and prominent of Burslem took their wives and children to the Church of England from which the poor people were positively deterred from attending.

The evangelical and open-air style in which Wesley's preachers conducted their sermons, sought its converts in among the shambles of slum dwellings, although the primitive style was at first scorned by the poor people who gathered to poke fun at the public ranting. The pulpits of the evangelists were the doorsteps in the lanes, standing upon the haystooks in barns, upon horse-stages and on boxes at the factory gate. Here the preachers were regularly abused and made fun of, encouraged by a gentry who wished to preserve their sanctity of traditional, safe and 'un-harmful' worship. But Wesley managed to attract a fair quarter of the town's leaders who infected not only their workforce but a number of their peers as well. It may be claimed that, if the master potter became a Methodist, his workers would follow suit by aping culture or compulsion. Soon a nucleus of local Methodist followers was established and within two years of John Wesley's heralds, the preacher himself came to Burslem. This was in the same year that the 30 year old Josiah Wedgwood consolidated his business at the Ivy House pot works after returning in the previous year to begin the triumphal conquest of his home town.

Wesley preached at the gates of Wedgwood's Ivy House and works on a rainy Saturday and Sunday in March 1760. Did the two great men - religious reformer and industrial reformer - meet? Records don't say, but it is highly unlikely, even though they would surely have found much in common with each other as history later records in the telling of their individual lives. The most powerful promoter of industrial science and the most compelling religious preacher, here in the Mother Town, sharing the same breath of air of that single moment. Imagine that, if you will!

Wesley found encouragement and a large following in Burslem and, duly inspired, he visited the town no less than 12 times over the next 30 years. But even before he arrived Methodism had already taken root and had been stirring in that most under-privileged part of the district - Hot Lane.

In the year 1759 a licence was granted to hold religious services at the home of William Lockett, a potter who lived in Cross Hill near to St John's church. This unceremonious event provided Burslem with its third denominational religion which itself took some tentative steps towards the opening of a religious house in the town's open market place before the erection there of the market building a year later. After the local Methodist cessation from the Macclesfield circuit - under the impulse of the Ridgway brothers, Job Meigh, William Smith and John Mort - Burslem together with Hanley, later to be joined by other Potteries towns, formed its own circuit. A small house in Hot lane was found in which to meet. This quickly became overcrowded and so Job Ridgway, an important master-potter from Chell, purchased a plot of land from Thomas Sherwin, a Burslem landowner, who was selling away his field known as KILN CROFT. On this parcel of land measuring **'nineteen yards by twelve yards'**, the old ZOAR chapel was built, immediately dubbed, 'the Salt Box'.

Potteries' Methodism thrived and nowhere faster and stronger than in Burslem where the first Sunday School was established near to Zoar in Hot Lane. And even Zoar became too small for its congregation which moved to a newly built chapel on the new rapidly growing Waterloo Road - BETHEL - in 1824. As Methodism splintered into factionalism so more chapels were built until, by the last half of the 19th century, Methodism in a variety of forms had become Burslem's most prominent and popular faith. Once a year it took to the streets in pageantry; in May when Sunday School Anniversaries allowed long processions of children to parade around the squares, the parks and the lanes: little girls in white flouncy finery; boys smart in velvet suits. Edwin Clayanger accompanied Hilda Lessways to a gathering in St Luke's Square to watch a sight well known to Arnold Bennett. The two young sweethearts stood on beer barrels and saw that:

> *'The whole Square was now suddenly revealed as a swarming mass of heads, out of which rose banners and pennons that were cruder in tint even than the frocks and hats of the little girls and the dresses and bonnets of their teachers; the men, too, by their neckties, scarves and rosettes, added colour to colour. All the windows were chromatic with the hues of bright costumes, and from many windows and from every roof that had a flagstaff flags waved heavily against the gorgeous sky. At the bottom of the Square the lorries with infants had been arranged, and each looked like a bank of variegated flowers. The principal bands....were collected around the red baize platform at the top of the*

> Square, and the vast sun-reflecting euphoniums, trumpets and cornets made a glittering circle about the officials and ministers and their wives and women....
>
> And almost in the middle of the Square an immense purple banner bellied in the dusty breeze, saying in large gold letters, "The Blood of the Lamb", together with the name of some Sunday School...,
>
> Then a hoary white-tied notability on the platform raised his right arm very high, and a bugle called, and a voice that had filled the fields in exciting times of religious revival floated in thunder across the enclosed Square, easily dominating it - "Let us sing."'

In 1798, a Hanley victualler, Thomas Cooke, bought a small part of the estate of Ellen Wedgwood. The NEW INN, in Fountain Place was already established as an alehouse and a well-respected visiting place for it possessed two clean water wells at the rear of the premises. Thomas Cooke was a professional in his trade who, in his lifetime, tenanted some four or five public houses. The offspring of such men are as a rule incorporated or drawn into their parent's business and preoccupations, or else they are completely turned away from it deterred by the scenes, sights and sounds their growing minds are forced to accommodate.

While living at the Burslem New Inn, Thomas's eldest son William was born in July 1806. This weak in body but strong in mind son was to rise to fame as a Doctor of Divinity who helped to pioneer religious and academic education in Ireland and in the North East of England.

The traveller will note that the New Inn faces St John's Square. Here a pause at the entrance of the inn to look along the square may still evoke the scenes of poverty, drunkenness and debauchery that the young William Cooke grew up with until he was fifteen years old. In this quarter of the town, he would daily have seen fights, prostitution, assaults and theft; and, when the 'wakes' were about, all the horrors of bull-baiting, cock-throwing, dog-fighting and other inhuman sights to appal even one with such determined parental protection. William Cooke was never to forget this backdrop to his young life.

The Cooke family were practising Wesleyan Methodists and William was educated in the faith from an early age turning to it eventually for his profession. At the age of five he was taught to read and write at the Wesleyan Chapel at Swan Bank and received his religious education at the Zoar Sunday School in Hot Lane. By the time he was thirteen the boy had become a respected secular and religious student with the Bethesda Church in Hanley and was one of a talented group of up and coming religious researchers. It was soon after his entrance to Bethesda that Cooke became completely converted, being spiritually called during an illness from which he was not expected to recover. His 'miracle' of recovery, according to his father, came through continuous prayer by which he was delivered from his sick-bed to become a devoted Christian educator and teacher.

In 1811 the Cooke family moved away from the dreadful tableau of St John's Square to keep a notable wayside inn, the Black Boy at Cobridge, and later, in 1819 to the Rising Sun in Shelton. But William Cooke had moved spiritually further on. He was so well respected for his energy in initiating night schools for children that he was offered the position as a principal preacher in Ireland organising Methodist colleges among Catholic communities. Later he moved to

Newcastle on Tyne where he spent most of his career teaching and writing a number of powerful theses and books on numerous religious subjects. It was in Newcastle on Tyne that he wrote CHRISTIAN THEOLOGY, a work which was for its time the seminal document on ecclesiastical response. Much respected by his colleagues, Cooke went on to become the President of the Methodist Conference and the editor of his faith's principal newspaper, the CONNEXIONAL MAGAZINE.

Cooke however continued to visit his 'home' church, the Bethel in Waterloo Road and in his later age in 1878 the great minister initiated and opened the DOCTOR COOKE MEMORIAL SCHOOL adjacent to the Bethel Chapel in Zion Street. The modest edifice may still be seen today, part of Broadhurst's Pottery.

Through William Cooke and others like him, the spirit of Temperance invaded the streets of Burslem becoming the vehicle of conversion for many in the Sunday Schools, temperance halls, alcohol-free hotels and cafes. Cooke remembered well his childhood overlooking the Square and doubtless he made sure that he and his colleagues would at least provide alternative ways for the lost sheep of Burslem.

It was these early Methodists of Hot lane who provided the balance to the scales of life that saw them tipped against the potters in the years between 1790 and 1850, as children as young as five were forced into a cruel industry beset with the poisons of dangerous substances and long bone-breaking toil amid lung-infecting swirling dust and smoke and breath-blocking heat. Such men allied themselves with the early trades unions and the Chartists, pitting their influences for the betterment of their peers.

The name of Bennett is not rare in Burslem. Even at the time of writing there are some 300 listed in the local directory. Many names of the famous will be found in the most obscure corners and backwaters, known and praised only by their contemporaries. So it would indeed be unusual if Burslem had only Arnold Bennett to laud with that inauspicious surname. There was his grandfather John for instance, unremembered other than as a progenitor of his famous grandson.

John Bennett was a shopkeeper who owned a number of houses near to his general stores in Pitt Street, then a gruesome place jutting from Nile Street and bounded on one side by a huge potbank while the even more massive Pinder and Bourne manufactory was just forty metres up the road. John Bennett's wife came from the Vernon family who were one of a number of small-time property owners that provided cheap lodgings in the middle of the town. Together they had five children, the surviving three all grew up to make something of their lives. The eldest John, was a pottery artist who went to London and found employment at the Lambeth pottery of Henry Doulton. He later returned to Burslem at the encouragement of his former boss who had become a partner at Pinder's, but after a short while he went to America where he subsequently lived out an unnoted life. The second eldest son, Enoch, trained as a potter and a teacher before becoming a pawnbroker after which he went on to realise his true profession as a lawyer. The daughter, Sarah, married a musically minded plumber before she took over her brother Enoch's pawnbrokers business in Hanley. Sarah herself was an accomplished pianist.

Pater, John Bennett, was passionate about his religion and had received his education at Swan Bank Wesleyan Chapel which had been established in 1796 just a few years after John Wesley had died. The high Gothic chapel was completed in 1836, a year which was as crucial to John Bennett as it was to be for the local faith.

There was no shortage of places of worship then. The Waterloo Road Bethel was thriving to a congregation of some 1,500, an Independent chapel was built in Queen Street in 1837, the year that Victoria came to the throne after whom the commercially developing street was named. In Nile Street the tall and spired Holy Trinity church, founded in 1798 and opened in 1851, pointed skywards, unharmoniously trapped between the ovens of industry. It's frontage seemed to disappear inside the factory itself as it stood side by side jostling for prominence with the factory gates of Pinder and Bourne's, whose co-founder, William Bourne, traded in the American market but failed. William Bourne was a personal friend of John Wesley who always lodged with him when he visited Burslem. Bourne later returned from the New World to die, after being ignominiously bankrupted, leaving a poor widow and seven children to be looked after by his brothers.

It was in the un-paid occupation of a Sunday School teacher that John Bennett and some of his colleagues made their mark on Burslem's historical rolls. John taught poor children to read and write from books and pamphlets as well as from the Bible and the Scriptures. Trouble loomed after a ruling at a Methodist Conference decreed that the teaching of reading and writing should not be given by the lay teachers. It appeared that some leading delegates petulantly considered that secular instead of spiritual education had become the practice of chapel instruction. These objections were strongly sounded stating that there were other places, not least at the home and hearth, where children should be taught basic reading and writing, and that it was not a job for the church to educate in any other way than by those methods that were to be found in the directions of the scriptures. It may be fairly considered that the underlying intent of the delegates, most of whom were civic leaders and employers, was that poor workers should not be allowed to rise above their allotted station in life. These were also times of Chartists' belief in worker's rights and employers had much to fear in the growth of political activity which relied a lot on the broadcast of news and of reported meetings by way of pamphlets and newspapers - workers must not be taught to read!.

John Bennett was very much a Socialist as were the growing bulk of the young Methodist preachers in the new towns - Chartism and Methodism embraced each other naturally in their policies for the poor.

The superintendents of the newly opened Swan Bank Wesleyan chapel accepted the conference's edict on education per se, and instructed its teaching ministers to use no published vehicle, other than the Bible, as a source of reading and writing. John Bennett and his colleagues refused to obey the superintendents who therefore promptly locked them out of the chapel and schoolrooms. This is what historian John Ward wrote about it in 1842:

> **'The managers and teachers of Burslem Sunday School could not be brought to yield to obedience to a power they had not recognised for many years, a separation became unavoidable...at last in the month of May 1836** (during a large eclipse of the sun!) **The trustees of the school took the very decisive step of locking the doors and leaving the shepherds to seek out fresh pastures and for such of their flock who chose to follow them ...Nearly the whole body of the scholars adhered to their teachers, and their parents and friends entered warmly on their behalf, into the strife.'**
>
> (Ward - pg. 242)

The trustees of Swan Bank Sunday School failed to predict these strong reactions and pompously ignored the emergence of a new chapel and school which was being erected at Hill Top above the Sytch. As John Bennett was walking away from Swan Bank he was met by the master potter, Enoch Wood, the principal benefactor of the Hill Top School, who invited him to become not only a teacher at the new premises but to sign up as a trustee and superintendent. John suddenly found himself among more the liberal-minded of Burslem's notables and it is clear that, from then on, he moved in better established social circles. The new congress of school and chapel at Hill Top thrived because of the rift over the teaching procedures at Swan Bank and a report in 1838 gave the numbers of attendances as 1,354 scholars supervised by 202 teachers with a considerable congregation of worshippers at the chapel. Against this opposition Swan Bank Wesleyans were forced to concede in its fight with its teachers in the face of a diminishing congregation. And so it re-introduced secular teaching. John Bennett and a number of his friends returned.

Hill Top was a magnificent building erected with fluted Corinthian pillars supporting Italianate balustrades with a Romanesque-fashioned open staircase on each side of the frontage climbing to an heroic portal and a concealed reception balcony. The main part of the building including the chapel, school and an attached house used as a hostel - formerly the public house the Falcon and Castle - were demolished in the late 1970s. A rump of its front pediment has been kept as an historically preserved relic.

John had married Mary Vernon in 1834. Within two years, at the age of 25, John had converted the front room of his terraced house into a shop out of which he sold many useful household items to his neighbours. Number 46 Pitt Street lay on the southern perimeter of the small district of Hole House some 200 metres from the town's market place. Originally this district had been a retreat from the smoky town in a pleasant pasture known as Hole Croft Meadow.

A fine house was built on the eastern slopes (where the Royal Doulton car park stands today) which overlooked the Out Lane as it wound away in front of it passing on to the moorland markets. The house, built around 1770, was owned by Samuel Malkin who was a great benefactor of the poor and brought his family up likewise - (the family owned many properties in Burslem which they provided generously for the needy and poor - 'SYDNEY MALKIN'S HOMES' counted among them Arnold Bennett's former house, 205 Waterloo Road until recently). An even larger house was built inside the nearby potbank belonging to James Cormie who began the line of notable tableware manufacture on the site which he passed on to his nephew Thomas Pinder and which ultimately resulted in the presence of Royal Doulton in Burslem.

Samuel Malkin's house in Out Lane fell into disuse before being demolished in 1800. This was prior to the Sneyd Holy Trinity church being later built on the same site. By this time, the part of Out Lane that ran between the George Hotel and the edge of the alder wood (now the northern end of ELDER ROAD) had been given the name, Nile Street in tribute to the famous battle. This new street was still rural with fields edged with hawthorn, while the Out Lane continued with its crude industries from the alder wood to Smallthorne under the name which had become commonly used - Hot Lane. But in John Bennett's time the whole district had earned itself a deserved solemn reputation as being a place which 'good and decent people' would never visit.

This early Victorian Out Lane/Hot Lane had by then become a claustrophobic district containing a shamble of tightly packed self-constructed cottages interspersed with coal pits, pottery hovels and marl-pits. There was no sanitation - there never had been, for this is where the plague took hold and claimed most of its victims in 1647. Hot Lane?

John Bennett's family grew up in the shadows of mighty bottle ovens towering above their tiny cottages among bestial filth as the ovens disgorged great gouts of black smoke from their burning turrets into the streets below. The very air they breathed was swollen with pollution and there was never any respite for the poor inhabitants who, troll-like, scuttled about their warrens in the agony of interminable work and restless sleep in overcrowded bedrooms; dreamless in bug and flea-ridden 'hot-beds'.

On the north side of Pitt Street was the sky-obliterating factory wall of the Royal Works which somewhat hid the horrors of the ghetto beyond it. Un-officially dubbed 'HELL-HOLE' by the townsfolk, one of its temporary inmates was Methodist minister and writer Christopher Shaw, who in his book 'When I Was A Child' - written under the pseudonym of 'An Old Potter' - vividly depicts a hell on earth. Within this abused patch of English soil, prematurely aged humans, physically and mentally emaciated, dwelled. They shared their brief time in the world with the vermin of open sewers, enveloped as one item in community filth. In this pit they were imprisoned, attended by all the symbols of poverty - pawnshops, animal-fat processing huts; leather-tanners and tripe-dressers, all sharing the inns and prostitutes with potter's labourers and colliers.

In the 'Hell Hole' was a gas works and the pall of death hung over the whole in a deep hollow out of sight of the Christian pedestrians and the temperance pleaders who hurried by to the sanctuary of the Sneyd Church, a blackened token of hope which parodied succour, living side by side with the charnel ovens of Pinder and Bourne where dispensable souls were incinerated on the furnace floor for the sake of the beautiful artifacts that emerged out of the other side.

Despite the recommendations of Royal Commissioners, children of 6, 9, and 10 were still employed as mould runners and dippers assistants; little mites whose only use was in their smallness enabling them to work in conditions too cramped for their giant masters; a smallness for the gain of a few shillings earned to make a contribution towards the keep of their large families; dependent on the idle ways and whims of the plate and vessel makers who chose the beer-shops to pay out wages given in the 'lump', while tearful mothers waited in the mean streets for any leavings. In the well of the mother's tears dropped aching illustrations of the differences between fat and lean.

If they did not die in infancy, children became adults the moment they stepped into the potbank. Here they found misery, physical abuse, privation and the orgiastic use and abuse of women and alcohol. Here were found contagions of social illness in all its pitiful starkness: death and scarlet fever; death and the use of lead and arsenic; death and silicosis, and that frightful disease known with naive cynicism as 'Potter's Rot' - pneumoconiosis. Death stalked these kilns; and death came like a blessed thief to provide for man's only release.

These were times of infant mortality of epidemic proportions. John and Mary Bennett's first two children, both girls, died at birth, one from whooping cough and the other taken by a common illness known as tubercular wasting - phthisis. John Bennett was determined that his family should escape from this Satanic world and through the strengths of his religion and self-education, his surviving children were spurred on to better themselves. Second son Enoch grew to match the determination of his father and reached to the middle-class heights of Victorian Cobridge. And it was Enoch's eldest son who made the Potteries famous with his stories of the Five Towns, becoming as a consequence perhaps the greatest realist novelist of his age.

The year the great Hill Top Chapel and School was opened, 1837, and Methodism was attracting more people to worship on a Sunday than all the pubs put together in Burslem could, Victoria became Queen. The world looked safe and secure to the rich English gentlemen, and yet at the same time the outlook was so bleak for the poor. By the benchmark of the post Age of Reason - never in history had the distance between the upper classes and the lower classes been so wide.

In Yorkshire, a singular unimportant event occurred as a working girl and wife of a young Yorkshire preacher named Joseph Kipling, gave birth to her first child while travelling around the dales and moors of Yorkshire and across the flat lands of Lincolnshire in the fervent caravan behind her husband's pursuit of life as a Methodist minister. The boy was given the first names of John Lockwood and received his primary education at a Methodist school in a mill town near Leeds. Here the young boy was desperately unhappy having been blessed with an unencouraged mind for artistic design which lay dormant under a curriculum of religion, arithmetic, reading and writing and French language. John Lockwood had the mind of a free man and happily the strength to break free. But his heaviest burden of youth was, as eldest son, to carry out his father's own aspersions planned for him to become a minister of the faith.

In 1851, when he was 14, an uncle accompanied him to the Great Exhibition where he was stunned by the novelty of art and the innovations of new crafts and craftsmanship. The Exhibition's self-contented proud Englishness at the dawn of modern times gave the young boy the necessary boldness to persuade his father to allow him to follow his enthusiasm for creative art and by the time John Lockwood was twenty he became a student under the famous architectural designer Sir Philip Cunliffe-Owen, master of South Kensington School of Art.

At twenty-two John Lockwood Kipling had completed his studies and was highly acclaimed as an outstanding student. He then sought around for suitable employment undertaking a number of freelance tasks in London, one of which was assisting in the design of the interior moulding for the Victoria and Albert Museum.

In 1860, John Lockwood Kipling came to Burslem to work as a pottery designer for Pinder and Bourne in Nile Street. During his sojourn here, he was encouraged by his employer Thomas Pinder, with whom he had an almost family relationship, to enter a competition for the design of the facade of the proposed new Wedgwood Institute. This he did in collaboration with a local artist Robert Edgar. Together they won the prize.

John Lockwood made friends easily one of them being the nationally famed artist William Muckley at the time teaching in Burslem as its unofficial art master and under whose tuition he improved his figurative design skills. He also began to influence the work of not only his colleagues at Pinder and Bourne, but many aspiring potters who desired to develop their own careers by attending the

Muckley and Kipling's art classes which were held in rooms over public houses in the sad absence of a formal school of art. It is still revealing to recall that, at this period, the Potteries had more natural artists in so small an area than in any other town in the whole country, and all their artistic skills were learned on the factory floor and at night school for there was no permanent teaching college in the town!

As the young teacher and designer settled among the potters he became particularly friendly with a Methodist minister, Frederick Wesley Macdonald, himself a newcomer who was some two years younger than Kipling but very much like him in background and outlook. Both men came from homes where religion and its domestic catechisms were actively promoted. Both had received a private education without having attended university, and both were welcomed strangers into a town countenanced with beauty as well as darkness. They were men with time for social romance while remaining alert to cynical irony.

Fred Macdonald was very much concerned with poverty and the terrible conditions of children working in the potbanks. Both he and John Kipling gave free lessons to poor children as a respite from their confined lives. Fred's life had percolated through a family of strict religious upbringing, his father being a Methodist minster in the Wolverhampton circuit.

The Pinder family were regular patrons of the Wesleyan chapel where Fred Macdonald preached. It is not surprising therefore that the interactivity of such a populist faith in such a small town should deign to bring together the social activities of the Pinder's, the Macdonald's and young John Lockwood Kipling. A picnic was arranged in the summer of 1863 at the popular man-made inland resort of Rudyard near Leek where the lovely countryside and placid lake attracted the young from the dark industrial towns of the four adjoining counties. Fred Macdonald took along his Yorkshire friend while the young Pinder sisters invited Fred's sisters who were visiting him at the time.

Alice Macdonald was the eldest child of the family and lived with her parents in Wolverhampton, thus it was perhaps accidental though fortuitous that she and John Kipling should meet. It is said that after the picnic meal had been eaten, the young folk strolled through the fields where another young picnicker and colleague of John's quoted from Browning's Childe Roland a line of poetry which prompted a reply from Alice who responded with the poem's following couplet applying it suggestively to the spirit of her brother's companion pointedly adding, 'He must be wicked to deserve such pain.' John Kipling found himself immediately attracted to the spirited young woman which led to further liaisons and a subsequent meeting with her family. These two independently charged characters grew together through their interest in art and in their self-concluded disenfranchisement from their families' religious traditions.

There were four Macdonald daughters in all; Georgina who married Ned Jones an artist who worked closely with William Morris and Dante Gabriel Rossetti and became a famous Victorian painter in his own right. Two other sisters, Agnes who also married an artist, Edward Poynter, knighted later when he was President of the Royal Academy; and Louisa who married a business man, Alfred Baldwin, and whose son Stanley rose in politics to become a British prime minister.

Like ships in the night the friends that came together at Rudyard Lake and passed by. Fred Macdonald moved away to Liverpool in 1865 and eventually followed in the footsteps of William Cooke by becoming President of the Methodist Conference. And John Lockwood Kipling married Alice and moved to Bombay where he took up an appointment as professor of architectural sculpture at the newly created School of Art. Their first child was born in Bombay in 1865 and he was duly named Joseph Rudyard, the second name given to note and bless the place where Alice and John had first met.

As for the potbank in Nile Street so instrumental to the story of Rudyard Kipling - Thomas Pinder died in 1867 after serving a life as a dedicated master potter, surviving his younger brother who was a partner to hand over the business to his great nephew, Shadwell Pinder. Looking to expand in the ever competitive world of ceramics and tableware, Shadwell took as his partner Henry Doulton of Lambeth in 1877. The firm was soon to become Doulton and Co. when in 1881 Henry Doulton acquired the company outright upon the retirement of Shadwell Pinder.

The family of William Bourne, Thomas Pinder's former partner, found supportive relatives and became scattered as many other potters did in the industrial shuffle of late Victorian pottery manufacture. The Bourne's had been an important influence in the development of the raw trade as it was emerging from the fields into organised industry. But it was to another family with the same name that religious notoriety came to visit.

At the great age of 88 John Wesley made his last visit to the Potteries perform the opening service of a new Wesleyan Chapel and school in Tunstall, the most northern of the six towns. This mighty edifice was opened on March 29th 1790 to accommodate a 1,400 congregation. The service booklet was delighted to report that the chapel was **'lighted with gas and warmed by heated air'**. Still ministering, Wesley however was being stalked by death even as he preached in Tunstall, and the weary reformer died but a few months later.

In the congregation that Sunday was an 18 years old carpenter named Hugh Bourne, born in 1872, from the nearby farming village of Bemmersley. Hugh Bourne was not a convert for his family had been practising Methodists at Fenton where they owned a smallholding from which they eked out a meagre living. Their arrival in Bemmersley when young Hugh was sixteen saw the transfer from their 'home' chapel into the Tunstall circuit.

As the Methodists were reorganising after the death of John Wesley, Hugh Bourne started to learn ancient religious languages in Methodist school groups. In 1799 he helped to organise a group of evangelists who preached at the pit-heads and on the slag-mounds of the numerous collieries around his home in the villages of Ridgeway and Bemmersley, setting up a chapel nearby in the village of Harriseahead. At the opening of the grand Wesleyan Chapel in Tunstall, Bourne saw in the scheme a departure from open-air preaching in a return to a hierarchical administration and away from, what he believed, were Wesley's intended beginnings. Bourne's ideals were based upon rude evangelism - liberal as to where one could preach and holding the right to self-communion in their own church. This differed critically to Wesley's own beliefs which, following his conversion in 1738, still kept him within the Anglican church often taking communion therein even though Methodists were forbidden to preach from its pulpits. Hugh Bourne longed for a time when Methodists did not have to take communion in the Church of England. This inevitably came about in 1795, four years after Wesley's death, but for Bourne the waiting had been too long. He was still only twenty-three and, some may have said, impetuous.

Meanwhile in Burslem, a young aimless man, William Clowes, had returned home having spent quite a lot of time in the teens his twenty years wandering on the east coast of England where he lived for some time in Hull. Clowes had been born in Ball Bank Burslem in 1780. His mother was Ann Wedgwood and was related to the Wedgwood's of the Churchyard Works. She was a distant cousin of Josiah.

Still unsettled, William Clowes attended a Methodist service at the Wesleyan Chapel in Swan Bank where he was dramatically converted and became an evangelist attached to the Tunstall society where he met Hugh Bourne whose group had grown to a membership of some forty young men and women. Although the two branches were not united their similar ideals of preaching drew the two men to each other and Clowes lost no opportunity in demonstrating what he and Bourne believed to be the basic attitudes and methods that the early Wesleyans had practised. Their boldness in their sermons earned them the name of 'ranters'; their simple dress and simplicity of language reflected their self-given name, 'primitives'. And they allowed women to preach from the pulpit - not that it mattered as the meetings were mainly held outdoors. For following his compulsions, Clowes was severely admonished by the Burslem Wesleyans.

Early in 1807 Hugh Bourne attended a meeting in Cheshire given by an American evangelist, Lorenzo Dow, who talked about open-camp meetings. This gave Bourne and his colleagues the idea of holding a festival-type of meeting in a large open place on similar lines as the 'revival' gatherings in America. As if by divine inspiration, the perfect location was found right on Bourne's door-step. Mow Cop!

Mow Cop is a hill situated at the highest point in the district. It is literally the southern tip of exposed rock of the Pennine Chain of mountains that form the spine of England, and it stands on the boundary of Staffordshire and Cheshire with magnificent views across the plains of Cheshire to the Irish Sea while, to the south-west, the tor overlooks the whole of North Staffordshire and the Potteries. Sometime in the 1740s a sandstone folly in the form of a ruined castle was built on the summit of Mow Cop by some long forgotten gentlemen community leaders of the district.

On May 31st 1807 a large crowd began to make its way up a variety of lanes leading to the summit of Mow Cop coming from all the surrounding villages, from the Potteries, and as far away as Manchester and the towns that lie along the Mersey. By all accounts it was a fine day and the majority had come in family groups dressed in summer clothes, children leaping about the exposed rocks - all in all one huge picnic.

Both Bourne and Clowes gave lengthy sermons and so successful was the meeting that other gatherings were arranged throughout that summer, eventually conferring upon the new connexion the status of its annual event where folk camped for several days duration on the slopes and fields that surrounded the hill. The Wesleyan governors were furious and made no exceptions when they expelled their wayward members en block. This immediately prompted Bourne to begin a new society, a break-away chapel based in the village of Stanley near Bemmersley. Meanwhile Clowes continued his own 'open' way of preaching even though he was forever being warned as to the consequences by the Burslem

Wesleyans. In 1810 the trustees at Swan Bank had by then had enough of Clowes's truancy following an open air meeting upon the heights of Ramshaw Rocks, a precipice on the range of hills called the Roaches on the Buxton road. The name Clowes was immediately written out of the congregation list of the Burslem Wesleyans!

Clowes and his followers were now unshackled and wasted no time in joining Hugh Bourne and his congregation. The name, Primitive Methodism, was formally adopted in 1812. And from this revolutionary break-away Primitive Methodism spread across the country much in the same way as early Wesleyanism had done through open-air preaching; across the east to Hull and particularly in the old London villages and in the south-west counties. William Clowes died in 1851 and Hugh Bourne a few months later in 1852. But it was not for another thirty years that the Primitives had their own permanent place of worship in the Mother Town of Burslem when the Clowes memorial Chapel was built in Church Street (now a much shortened William Clowes Street) followed a couple of years later by a chapel in Albion Street Middleport, (now Harper Street - also considerably altered after demolition).

These dissidents to their own faith emerged along with, and in the trail of John Wesley. Individually they attempted, through their religious beliefs, to improve the lot of the common people, those who were oppressed in their workplaces and those who were impoverished in their tenements. Two-hundred years were to pass from John Wesley's first ministration outside Josiah Wedgwood's Ivy House, where he created his famous Queen's Cream Ware, and the emergence of emancipated youth and the new social verite that came about in 1961. This social revolution did not so much filter back from across the Atlantic to where it was originally taken, but it leapt again from the industrial towns that Wedgwood and his ilk had helped to create. New cultures from the old Empire towns of Liverpool, Manchester and Newcastle upon Tyne. In Burslem throughout those two-hundred years many dissidents and reformers have walked across the squares and streets leaving behind great edifices of civic grace. Men who allied themselves to Methodism and social improvement. Men who sought change for it had become their time and not their father's

William Woodall, Thomas Hulme and John Wilcox Edge, politicians and civic architects; chartist such as Joseph Capper and trades unionist - William Owen and Samuel Clowes, temperance leaders the like of James Keates and the Ellis's. All of these men, and more, played their part in easing the route of their fellow travellers and in the improvement of life for the townsfolk of Burslem, and all of them were deeply reasoned, often doggedly Methodist and allied to its causes.

In 1961, Stoke on Trent City Council accelerated its policy of slum-clearance and regeneration. Bold in concept and well-meaning, sadly many great buildings were pulled down. Heritage that could not be replaced disappeared. And worse. Street upon streets of dwellings were bulldozed to make way for car parks that would never be used. It had taken two-hundred years to populate the Mother Town. It took the next twenty years from 1961 to 1981 to empty it.

The two modest buildings at the end of the rump of Hot Lane stand to remind the traveller of the erratic gait of the pace of time. Here still is the first Methodist chapel of Burslem inspired by John Wesley. It stands opposite the empty building of an old wayside inn, the Dog and Partridge. The chapel still has a good congregation, and the old pub was lately used as a meeting house for scouts -

Moorcroft Pottery now own it and it stands unused. The traveller should take note of the name plate of the inn which is preserved in its original form made entirely of coloured mosaic in the picture of a retrieving dog carrying its quarry. Empire emulating empire.

Cemented in the wall, at street level is a sandstone war memorial bearing the names of forty seven men from this one street who never returned in 1918 to pray with their families in the little Zoar chapel across the road. The houses have gone, the people have gone, just like England's old coin - a quarter of a penny, a far-thing, all gone in the changes of 1961.

Chapter Three

REFORM AND RIOT

> *'...and the workmen, suffering from these privations, became the convenient and ready instruments of the seditious demagogues, who had long been disseminating the deleterious doctrines of "The People's Charter", as the sovereign and sole remedy for poverty, and all political grievances...'*

(Ward pg. 585)

In the year 1825, a twenty-two year old serving woman, Martha Watts was handed down a sentence of death by the circuit judge at Stafford. Martha lived in a tenement in a claustrophobic square off High Street - now named Greenhead Street, Burslem. The proximity of a huge open warehouse which stored wet ball-clay dug and carried here by canal from Cornwall, influenced the naming of the square - Ball Bank. But, just forty-odd years earlier, the site of the slum tenement where Martha Watts lived, housed a substantial dwelling known as Over House, so named because it was, at the time, the highest and most important domestic property in Burslem. The house, and the attached potbank, and much of the land in Burslem, was owned by Madame Catherine Egerton - related by marriage to the family of the Dukes of Bridgewater and by descent from the Wedgwood and Burslem families. Such are the changes a couple of generations can make to the land.

During these four decades of super-fast growth - 1780 - 1820, (just part of one person's life span!) - the countryside discovered the consequences of redistribution of land, the progress of machinery and the evolution of the factories; the labour system and the movement of population to the towns. The High Street district of Burslem evolved from being surrounded by pleasant pastureland, through which wandering lanes wound from hamlet to hamlet, into becoming a filthy slum. It sounds like the consequence of a revolution - it was! To think, a rich landowner's estate, in the tumult of an overnight storm, becoming occupied by poor labourers in turn sharing their cottage life with an animal slaughterhouse and a maze of pottery hovels attended by stagnant ponds and shard mounds. It was here that Burslem's first poor asylum and workhouse was sited, a Bastille in which ordinary human beings stagnated in a refuge that housed a multitude of nameless and forgotten souls.

Linking Ball Bank with the Market Place and the rest of the town, a narrow doglegged, high unlit alley, still wanders between the hot walls of a potbank, unvisited by the light of day. Its name is known by the older generations of Burslemites as 'Jawnels' on account of the excavation of the jawbone of a whale in 1800; a relic of the early world, deposited here during the withdrawal of the last Ice Age six-thousand years ago. Even today, a walk along this empty passage, beneath dark walls of pottery ovens rising on each side blotting out the sky, will as much haunt the traveller with tactile pleasure as it will romance him with sensory caution. Evocative intuitions drop in the shape of tangible thoughts, captured simply by touching the encrusted rivulets of industrial grime-scale layered on crumbling factory bricks. The sounds of screaming animals, and sights of streaming of blood coursing along the gutters, may still be imagined by the receptive traveller. Martha Watts was born here, and here she lived out part of her tragic life, for what it was worth - a few shillings!

On 16th August 1842, an event occurred in Burslem that took both the working-classes, and the newly formed local administrations by surprise. Parliament did not fully understand its threat, nor did the people understand its gravitational power. Had it been planned, or even better organised, Britain might have been sloughed into a revolution that many workers had been promising since the French Revolution changed the face of Europe some fifty years earlier. As it transpired, the spark that lit the flame was snuffed out almost as soon as it took-hold, due, almost entirely, to the results of poor revolutionary management and ill advised co-ordination. The event, which may have changed the world, has slunk into Burslem's history, fabled only by wishful authors. Historians play the moment down; it is never referred to in the history-books of educational curricula, and yet it is one of those milestones that occur in a millennium - a missed opportunity, a change of mind - a hesitation on history's battlefield - best forgotten! On 16th August 1842, the history of the world could have been re-written here in Burslem.

The memories of that hot summer's day have long been confided to the archives of myth, to be looked back upon with the affection of vague nostalgia. Nobody, but *nobody*, at the time accounted for what was to occur during the day's events, or even remotely saw the opportunities that were presented. Nor did anyone consider the judgments and imprecations that would be left behind. It was an important day in the lives of Burslem residents, a day that could have inspired a definitive moment of history, an event that ought to have become enshrined in the chronology of the pilgrims of Britain's workers. And yet, that day has slipped by, as unremembered as are the people who fought here in the streets. Martha Watts was in another place in another time and knew nothing of it. But the fumbled key that opened and closed her troubled life also released the same shackles of pain suffered by her kindred townsfolk in 1842. The uncompromising doors of freedom are heavy indeed.

There was a time when some Burslem residents found it easier to walk to Hanley and Tunstall than to walk to Burslem. It wasn't until the 1820s that Burslem people had anything at all in common with the townsfolk of Longton. They hardly ever met and were as foreign to each other as if they were separated by an ocean. They even spoke a different dialect. Many still do!

Parliamentary boundary changes have been the cause of many re-arrangements of county and district areas and acreage. They happen today from time to time but with less upheaval to the communities than they did at the beginning of civic organisation. And it isn't just one enactment of impressive magnitude that moves mountains, but a number of tablets tumbling from the halls of Westminster over a long period of time, petitioned and pursued by the ordinary men and women in all walks of life. Many acts, in all their connected and varied ways, have produced dramatic consequences for the people, some have taken away common rights and some have forced restrictions upon them. And, through these diversely political administrations, the subtlest of changes have often brought the most far-reaching consequences in the day to day lives of the people through the ages. Man makes changes - man is changed.

The Member of Parliament for Wendover, shipowner and patriot John Hampden, was just such a man for change. A lover of his country, in his time he became a devout enemy of Charles I. Together with careerist politicians John Elliot and John Pym, denouncers of arbitrary taxation, Hampden refused to pay a ship tax levied by the king without the ratification of parliament. An ally of Cromwell, Hampden in 1642, was one of the gentlemen members who attempted the seizure of Charles which precipitated the Civil War. And, he was instrumental in the impeachment and the beheading of the king's principal adviser the Earl Strafford. Hampden was a rich but socially educated man who hated the power of the king and the court cronies. A Puritan who resented the court's Catholic leanings and worried about a return of the Roman Catholic faith. He saw revolution as an option, and planned for it.

Almost two-hundred years after the events that led to the Civil War, the name Hampden was resurrected when working men's political groups were formed in Manchester, Leeds and Sheffield. They called their meeting places, Hampden Clubs, after the man who had once challenged the absolute rule of the monarchy. In their own rules of conduct, these working class agitators pointedly adopted Hampden's ideology as well as his name. Their aims were straightforward - to give authority by law and in central regulation, the order to establish the fundamental rights of negotiation between master and servant in their efforts to formulate common and abiding rules of employment. These meetings conceived the humble beginnings of unionism for the non-trade general worker.

In 1827, a series national events began to unroll that were to bring about outstanding changes to the lives of Britain's citizens, and in particular for the new-town dwellers of the commencement of the post Industrial Revolution sprawl in Yorkshire, the North West, the North East, the Midlands and Scotland.

In June that year, the prime minister, Robert Banks Jenkinson, Earl of Liverpool died having resigned from office following a serious apoplectic fit. A liberal minded Tory, Liverpool had been in office for fifteen years, the second longest continuous term in the history of the office. He had presided over a shadowy and class-favoured system of government and managed to hold together his party which was being split over a variety of policy issues, the principal of which were the country's roll in foreign economy, free-trading and Corn law taxation. Liverpool's was the first administration - in a succession of Tory governments - which vocally proclaimed that its members were 'born to rule'. It was a time of individualism when, even though political affiliations were declared, many Tory members sat as independents; and many state ministers were culled from the hereditary peerage. The natural consequences of the Industrial Revolution began to emerge during his long administration, for it is during this period that Capitalist's assumed a novel power.

Since the start of productive industrialisation - the Factory System - towards the end of the 18th century, England had seen large and growing towns like Manchester, Sheffield, Leeds rise in ever widening 'conurbations', a new word; and towns, such as Stoke on Trent and the Black Country towns to the south, growing comparatively by trading relationships. None of these subtopias had independent representation in Parliament, for the English Parliamentary system at the time allowed for every county in England and Wales each to have two MPs irrespective of the numbers of people who lived there. Additionally, a number of county towns, considered over the years to have such importance connected to them and called 'County Boroughs', were also permitted to send two MPs to Parliament. However, in the geographic realignment of the population caused by industrialisation, the fortunes of the 'old' towns receded as they became eclipsed by the rapidly growing northern new centres of industry, which were led by innovations, invention and gadgetry supporting the textile trades. Borough ports on the east coast closed - the Suffolk borough of Dunwich, once an important eastern trading port, had in 1819, as a consequence of a diversion of its sea trade to the western ports, only forty-four houses. And yet, as a borough, Dunwich was still entitled to two Mps! The same applied to many of these early boroughs which became the subject of electoral abuse. In Cornwall it was rife, and in the ancient Wiltshire borough Old Sarum, seven resident electors continuously returned two Mps!

In such places parliamentary representation was handed down inside families, it was of particular benefit for those who could afford to send their youngest son to Westminster, for in those times MPs received no payments at all, but the influence gained of having and MP in parliament more than compensated these families. At worst these seats were purchased. Two of the consequences of this constitutional imbalance were, that the new industrial labouring classes were still being treated as they had been when they lived entirely as serfs sustained by tenant farming despite their acknowledged importance to manufacturing production - and, the emerging new middle-class, which had risen out of factory ownership - their members themselves becoming wealthy landowners - being constitutionally measured by the same yardstick as their own employees. These were the Capitalists who could now afford, out of their own pockets, to extend their powers and demand rightful representation for their domain.

Under Liverpool's administration, another kind of revolution was in the air, a social one, insinuated by the new rich and irritated by the population explosion of the poor as they converged upon the manufacturing centres. (In 1720 most people in Burslem lived in the countryside, sheltered in the surrounding farming hamlets - by 1801, ninety per-cent of the population lived within the confines of what is now established as the town centre limits, about 300 acres.) And yet this was manageable for the country, Britannia - as far as the new rich were concerned - couldn't be a better place in which to live; life for those at the top was awash in economic security, while strong international trading provided a lucrative remuneration for the daring manufacturer and entrepreneur. Opportunity was there for the daring. The only dark side had arisen after the wars with France in 1815 when returning soldiers found it difficult to find employment in a vacuum of European economic reconstruction. They were still classed as chattels to be used at the whim of the paymaster who paid their wages to be spent in shops and inns and on services which the factory owner himself directed, including the houses the workers lived in. Traditional 'accidental' revolution set to overthrow standing institutions, was easily negated by local master-led conciliation resulting in agreement by lip-service, promise and tactical adjustment. This was, as a rule, acceptable to the majority of workers who were as threatened by market forces as were the masters. As long as there was money to progress the week and food on the table life was tolerable.

In the post war years radical pamphleteers set-up a network of Hampden Clubs throughout the country of which there were some forty in the towns of Lancashire alone. During the period 1815 to 1827 riots were seen in the Spa Fields London, the Pentridge Rising, thwarted by the so-called 'Oliver' infiltration, and the fateful Peterloo meeting at Manchester. All of this agitation led to deep feelings of disestablishment through which all of this social unrest was brought to a head at the end of the second decade of the 19th century.

After Liverpool's death, the year 1827 saw his successor, George Canning, die in office, and the next prime minister, Viscount Goderich, resign after a few months attempting to patch-up a government which was in deep division over the growing number of problems in its economic policy. This brought to power the Duke of Wellington, hero of Waterloo. It was under this brief supervision, his first administration as Prime Minister, that England saw the return of Catholics to hold office, and in 1829, full Catholic Emancipation, which allowed members of the 'old faith' as well as other religious dissenters to become MPs and members of the House of Lords.

During Wellington's two years as Prime Minister (1828 - 30) radicalism began to push to the front of the political agenda. Unions of workers found initiatives to gather group strength as the disliked and irresponsible George IV died, his rule bringing to a close the long period of preferred laissez-faire under Hanoverian principles. A combination of civil events dominated by calls for political emancipation which heralded the inevitable constitutional change, levered the great general Duke into becoming a reluctant pivot in reform. Having experienced republicanism at first hand across the channel and, seeing a desperate need for government to preserve itself against growing urban unrest, he encouraged his Home Secretary, Robert Peel to organize the Metropolitan Police, while, in the chambers of power, he effectively split the old aristocratic Tory Party by his insistence on the retention of the old constitutional traditions. His doggedness caused the unhealed scars which eventually ushered in the new Conservatives, a unionist party which flowered to amazingly hold office for such long definitive periods that, even when the Labour Party had become the official opposition in the 20th century, it still easily held the administration with the will of the working classes.

The roots of the schisms command-driven by Wellington, even diverted the Whigs into an uneasy coalition with the Liberals and the Radicals, so that indirectly this first Wellington administration brought to the forefront the burning issues of parliamentary constitutional reform. But it was the bad harvests of 1829 -30, a year which saw a dramatic overseas trading slump which affected the whole nation, that accelerated unrest and a cry for parliamentary and social reform. In 1830, Prime Minister Wellington made a Parliamentary speech defending the established system of elections. The consequences of this impassioned speech turned many of his Tory members, seeking a lead on reform, against him and their vote was carried along with that of the Whigs. Wellington's administration was defeated.

Under Wellington's successor, Earl Grey, chancellor Lord John Russell brought the draft of his Reform Bill to the commons. The next two years saw parliamentary upheaval like such that had never previously been seen since the Civil War and comparable only with the divisions caused by Irish Home-Rule and the legacies caused by its civil war time dis-unities. In the late 20th century, only the European Union options and divisions can match it. Up to this point in history, 1830, aristocrats had ruled parliament - based entirely upon land ownership and rank. The new Act took into consideration the industrialists and new commercial middle-classes.

The Great Reform Act became law on June 7th 1832. In providing the vote to all males who held property with a rateable value of ten pounds per annum, the law gave a real circumstance and cogency to local administration which at once embraced, for the first time, most manufacturers and commercial traders. Electorally though, as its other base purpose had intended, it cut a swathe through all the so-called 'pocket boroughs' in an attempt to condemn the practice of buying seats to the parliamentary dustbin. It now meant that constituencies with less than 2000 voters had no independent parliamentary representation and those with a voting population of between 2000 and 4000 - traditional townships normally returning 2 MPs - were reduced to having only one. Twenty-two new constituencies were created in towns which were not previously represented. One of these was the new borough of Stoke upon Trent.

For the first ever time, the potters of Burslem and the other Potteries's towns went to the polls to elect a representative that viewed an interest directly concerning their industry and its trades instead of some absent landed aristocrat who lived in the centre of the shire, whom they rarely had opportunity to consult. On Monday 10th December 1832 the new borough returned its first two MPs, Mr Josiah Wedgwood II, who was sponsored from Hanley, and Mr John Davenport who, as a Burslem pottery employer, received his support from the town where he worked.

There were four constituent divisions to the new borough, Burslem, Hanley, Stoke and Lane End (Longton) - Tunstall returned with Burslem and Fenton with Stoke. The total number of people who voted was 1,175 which represented 97% of a ***possible*** electorate. At Burslem the votes counted that day numbered 672 for all candidates with the Longport pottery manufacturer, Davenport, beating the Etruria man, Wedgwood, by a hundred votes. Both men however were Tories who were sent to serve under a Whig administration. But, it must be remembered, that this was still very much an affair of men of substance, the middle-class wealthy pottery owners most of whom were able to cast at least two votes, one for their houses and other for their businesses.

Nor was the exercise a peaceable one with reports of hustings being disturbed, speeches interrupted by barracking and missile throwing, while at Stoke - where the count took place - a number of candidates and their supporters were jostled and injured. So fierce was the competitive response towards opposing parties that many had to take refuge inside the counting hall. In Longton, a related outburst saw the windows of the Crown and Anchor Inn smashed. Longton was the place where more trouble occurred among Burslem activists, who had travelled there and openly confronted Longton activists in the market place. But in Burslem it was said that tranquillity ruled overall, so much so that the election was hardly noticed by the ordinary townsfolk.

The names Wedgwood, Edensor-Heathcote, George Miles Mason, John Wood, Copeland and Spode were all pottery manufactures of great renown and wealth. As with the un-elected peerage that went before them, these men assumed their 'right to rule', and they made sure it was backed by legislation; for these men of 'new' money, grew in parliamentary power and persuasion. It was to be another seventy years before the first active working man - John Burns in 1906 - became a member of parliament and further eighteen years after that before the first working potter - Samuel Clowes in 1924 - took his seat.

Progress under new legislative powers meant developing a local organisation. Burslem's commercial traders began looking for support and parity among their fellows as early as 1813 when an attempt was made to organise a fellowship called the Chamber of Commerce. In the beginning their interests were presumed to have a better chance if the six towns fell in line with each other, federated together alongside other pottery manufacturers. But any thoughts of a corporative and long term alliance were quickly dispelled and each town warily progressed individually.

As early as January 1st 1814 however, a tariff was drawn up by the pottery manufacturers listing the standard prices of tableware regulating a ceiling and base-rate of selling costs. Meanwhile, general support and provision trades along with allied industries, went their own way and fixed prices of goods to benefit themselves. Both of these organisations meandered on without any formal structure until 1825 when the pottery manufacturers organised their own formal federation and the commercial traders followed suit. It is no coincidence that these events happened to match the time of the emergence of unions of workers who had been inspired by the belligerency of the Hampden Clubs for which a great deal of public support was now gathering. Thoughts of revolution were being secretly mooted among radical underground worker's groups.

One of the first, and the most notable, demonstrations of the collectiveness of the union of workers occurred in Tolpuddle, Dorset when a number of labourers refused to work, calling for better wages and improved working conditions. The local employers quickly quelled this action by invoking the law of the land and criminally indicted the workers for 'administering unlawful oaths', a law that was honed to suit the circumstances in order to provide the maximum punishment. The Tolpuddle Martyrs were transported to the colonies. This was in 1834. One year later, an unconnected Municipal Corporations Act, an appendage to the Reform Act, was introduced in order to strengthen the power of the town's new administrators by allowing common districts such as the Potteries (Stoke on Trent towns by this time were known universally as the Potteries) to amalgamate as municipal boroughs. The Potteries at first rejected this, particularly Burslem whose civic caretakers saw no benefits whatsoever in union with the likes of Longton. They, and, as it happened so did the Longton leaders, preferred to sit in isolation.

Also in 1834, the world's market and overseas trade, reflecting Britain's slump, was entering a very severe depressed state. Although the Burslem manufacturers were able to sustain the new slump in the national and international markets, they could only do so by engaging men under short-time working conditions and making ad hoc cuts to worker's wages. These privations were by comparison to their previous pay and job conditions, unsustainable and unacceptable to the workers. The parity of wages and the long-term market situation initiated a move a step closer to the consolidation of a local manufacturer's federation. Even so, the pottery manufacturers still resisted all out consolidation with the five other town's employers. Both Burslem and Longton manufacturers still saw themselves as leading an autonomous and selective industry. It was a time when they all were looking-out for themselves in order to survive against the universal depression. Unity bowed to self and covetousness. This inward-looking structure had been exhibited in a confidence born out of a unique single market, an individual produce made in individual potbanks; practices to be retained and cherished, inasmuch as their fathers and they had bequeathed them. It was a confidence they kept tidy in their own personal marketing abilities. Such was their dominion. Such was their greed. Such was their mis-understanding of the legislative trading reforms. Such was their failure to compromise with their workers as the government had compromised with them. Failure, as it were, to look to the future as an all-encompassing business with a respectful acknowledgement in the value of their workers.

It was over the simple issue of forming a law protection agency that Burslem held out against unitary federation. In 1813, the first recorded annual meeting of a newly installed association of manufacturers and commercial men, met under the title of Association For The Prosecution Of Felons. Thirty-seven 'respectable and notable' employers and men 'with interest' met at the town hall to form a body to protect their premises and property from theft against any person who carried out felony or insinuated felonious intent. They elected the potter William ADAMS Jnr as its first president and local solicitor, James PRESTON as its treasurer.

The Association employed the town crier to call a curfew and to report any of their workers who broke it. They also paid their own watchmen to gather information and pass-out rewards to everybody who responded to 'Hue and Cry' when called upon. The Association also paid further rewards when a felon was caught 'in the act' or upon oral deposition that led to an arrest. When a felon was brought before a magistrate, punishment was always meted-out in accordance with the law of the land. But the Association more often sought to dole out their own penalties which enabled them to create their own offences based on the 'byelaws' principle. Penalties often employed some deterring element of public humiliation such as being placed in the stocks. Even so, these early arbitrators were as uncompromising in punishment of the recidivist as they were as often merciful to the wayward. They were aggressive implementors of the 1824 Vagrancy Act which was intended to 'prevent wasters and sturdy beggers from wandering about and committing sundry questionable acts by which an easy livelihood could be gained'. These people included the 'idle and disorderly', common prostitutes who were found 'wandering in a public place and behaving in an indecent and riotous manner'. Pedlars and able-bodied persons refusing or neglecting work causing their families to become chargeable to the county. Men and women who falsely claimed poor relief and women (note the specified sex) who neglected to maintain their bastard children. The Act isolated and categorised people as rogues and vagabonds, and made offences of fortune-telling, begging, sleeping-out, gaming in public, neglecting the family and running-away and absconding. All of these felons the manufacturers prosecuted with full-blooded enthusiasm and often the innocent were caught up in wholesale purges brought to book and had-up in the symbolism which insisted that strong punishment made for good discipline.

The rewards practices, legislated by the Parliamentary Rewards Act, were very much of an inducement to provoke known criminals into committing crime, and an incentive to inform on friends for fictitious as well as actual crimes with the result that many real criminals went undetected and many 'innocent' people were wrongly punished. Additionally, receivers of stolen goods would offer the victim his own stolen property back 'undamaged and in good condition' for an anonymous compensation payment. Felons only had to pass from one town to another to escape detection and prosecution as one town's jurisdiction did not extend past its neighbour's boundary. Because many felons escaped justice in this way, the Burslem Association, under the presidency of Enoch Wood, therefore decided in 1824 to look at the feasibility of setting-up a general law agency throughout the whole of the Potteries. Negotiations at once broke down through Burslem's own insistence on securing the backing of an act of parliament in order to give its own Association greater prominence. An embryonic Potteries Police Committee was therefore disbanded in that year.

A typical case of crime and its punishment which the Burslem Association had to deal with was the prosecution of a coiner named Theodore MOORE who had a backstreet foundry in Hanley. Moore was a frequent visitor to the BLUEBELL, a new public house in Waterloo Road, where middle-class folk gathered to deal in business. His activity of cheating and passing-out forged coins was so prolific in Burslem that it was alleged that not one businessman had escaped being duped with Moore's worthless 'base half-crowns'. He was eventually cornered at the Bluebell but managed to escape over the Grange fields into his foundry near to the site where the Sentinel newspaper later set up its main office and printshops. The Hue and Cry following from Burslem failed to catch up with him that day, but in the end he was caught at home and pulled by manacles along Waterloo Road to the lock-up in Market Place. At his trial he demonstrated the confidence that defined his trade and went un-ashamed and un-bent to the gallows.

In 1829, Home Secretary Robert Peel introduced uniformed police to the streets of the capital and municipal legislation followed, extending the Metropolitan Police Act to the counties under the County Police Act. By 1837 Burslem employed a number of constables and part time specials who could be called upon in times of unrest. The job of chief constable had previously been an honorary position, indeed, in 1842 the holder of the office was Enoch Wood Jnr., then living in the Big House at the end of Moorland Road. But, in the wake of the serious rioting that same year, a full time post of 'Superintendent of Police and Fire' was created at Burslem, the first commander of the force being Thomas POVEY, who was given the potter John Shrigley's former house to live in and for use as duty accommodation for his constables. There was also a lock-up situated in his cellars.

These were times when the good order of communities were controlled by a handful of legislative instruments designed to protect the employer who was considered honest and above suspicion and accusation of gain by theft. Therefore the law dealt harshest with theft from the employer, misuse and damage to his goods and machinery. Cruelty to the employer's load-bearing animals was never tolerated - the mule was of value at a time when there was little interest in the neglect and abuse of children, particularly behind the enclosures of the home and the factory walls.

Workers unions in the Potteries had been growing in adolescence since 1825 when journeyman potters came together to set a standard price for standard produce - just as the manufacturers had proposed - each plying to control his own profit per factory, per trade. The difficulties for the workmen's representation, was underscored by the power in the wealth of the owner and very much depended on tact and diplomacy in the union's methods of negotiation, for the manufacturer was just as likely to sack his entire workforce and set-on a whole new rank of workers at a hint of dispute. During the ten years to 1835, the potter's unions grew in size and demands. And, just like the manufacturers, they failed to unify their political structures in a combination of all the six towns; thus their representations were primarily weakened.

In 1836, following in the wake of the great reforms of parliament and alongside the municipal changes taking place around them, the infant unions addressed the unfair system of paying-out wages by the 'truck' which enabled the manufacturer to pay less, pay in lump or, pay by tokens. This enabled some discriminated trades to unfairly get more, or less, than their colleagues, a cause of jealousy and anger. The truck issue very quickly became immersed in the national general agenda of improvement in wages, and so the potters allied themselves to pursue their own causes alongside those of the national agitators, even though overall there was no specific interest or concern by the national leaders in the pottery industry.

That year the Potter's Union was made up of 54 lodges each with its own rules. Although there appeared to be universal membership, paid affiliations were very much local to the town and the factory. This was to prove problematic in the industrial troubles which were about to descend upon the Potteries' workers.

Apart from wages and payments, the main bone of contention for the potter's unions was the employers' insistence on their rigid practice of 'Annual Hiring', a system which had prevailed from 1770 enabling the employer to reduce his workforce by numbers and for periods when work was slow. The practice of paying out 'Good From the Oven', which allowed the employer to pay his worker only for undamaged ware, was particularly resented because quality depended much on the skills of others. The unions therefore set about to rectify these unacceptable conditions of employment.

Lines were drawn as these unproven and untested societies faced each other across factory floors and in shops and market places. On the one hand were the new Federations of Pottery Manufacturers, and a loose Chamber of Commerce for supporting traders; and opposing them were the worker's unions representing the mass of workers.

In July 1836, union members from Burslem and Tunstall, who were employed by the same single manufacturer, withdrew their labour from 14 potbanks on the grounds of a cut in wages. The Federation of Manufacturers, supported by the loosely bound fickleness of the town's traders, at once resisted in the harshest retaliatory manner by closing all their 14 factories which involved the stoppage of 3,500 workers, the majority of whom did not belong to the union. The might of the district's Federation joined together and supported their 14 manufacturing colleagues, their strength lying in their shared financial contributions. They easily held out until September as Martinmas drew near - the traditional month of the annual fair hirings.

It was clear at this point that the employers had the upper hand when, encouraged by the new-tried Federation, 50 more factories locked their workers out. This meant that there were now some 20,000 potters unemployed caused by strikes and lock-outs throughout the entire Potteries district. The effects of the long-term lay-off were parlous for the employers and for their customers, though the worse of the consequences were off-set by the poor international market anyway. But the lay-offs and unemployment were catastrophic for the potters. So severe were the results of the restrictions in spending-money that the Chamber of Commerce now changed sides as the shopkeepers and market traders were compelled, in order to preserve their own businesses, to support the workers by credit sales.

The labour disputes were still unsettled by November and December when armed troops were moved from Stafford and assembled in Newcastle under Lyme in preparation of insurgence and open public disturbances. By January 1837 money was so low and the workers had become so divided that many simply wanted to return under the conditions which had prevailed before the actions. A large gathering of unionists met in fields by the Saracen's Head in Hanley. Many from Burslem that day suffered the ignominy of being chased-off by a small troop of fusiliers as it became clear that the strike was lost. Weakened and embarrassed, the unions conceded. The strikes were called-off on 27th January. The employer's total lock-outs had lasted just over five weeks from the Martinmas annual hirings, well into winter. But worse was to come.

The expectations of a return to a sound economy was too far off and a previously inexhaustible export market dribbled to a stop for all but a few major employers in the Potteries. Ahead lay severe industrial depression which was to last for two years with its effects being felt over the next full decade - 'the Hungry Forties' - during which time all elements of the pottery trades were devastated, a sad consequence which affected those first attempts at an organised trades union. Nevertheless, out of these early troubles a stronger manufacturers federation emerged, the beginnings of an independent political chamber of commerce was formed, and ultimately, though it was still a while off, more unified trades unions came forth.

One year after the Potteries' lock-outs had ended, Francis PLACE, a sixty-seven year old London tailor, a man who had in his radical beliefs and from street-corner meetings, agitated for the implementation of the 1832 Reform Act, drafted out a document which he called, the People's Charter. The draft contained six demands covering full and partial claims for full emancipation and voting rights of the working man. The completed document was published in 1838. Pamphlets were drawn from this which were printed by an eloquent Nottingham member of parliament, Feargus O'CONNOR, who ran a newspaper in Leeds. As Burslem and the other Potteries' towns were suffering terrible and awful times of starvation and poverty; their unions of workers in disarray, Chartism was born!

To dismiss the great Chartist Movement as a temporary aberration would be to refute the emergence and development of Great Britain's 1990s Labour Party, the same government that imparts legislation of populist authority to a socialist-minded country in the closing years of the 20th century. The Charter's demands were not new individually, but as a set of rules they were revolutionary for the times:

1. Universal male suffrage,

2. The abolition of owning property in order to become an MP,

3. The election of annual parliaments,

4. Equal size for all electoral districts,

5. Payment of salaries to MPs,

6. Elections to be held by secret ballot.

The realistic fact is that, except for the non-adoption of item 3, all these Chartist demands had been met by the time the first parliament was elected after WWI. Indeed, the original binding rules of the Labour party were based upon many Chartist principles, and the wording of the original Clause 4 of their rules literally echo the wording of Chartist rhetorical ideology regarding the distribution of accumulated wealth and the sharing of the benefits resulting from of their own labours.

On 10th November 1838, a large meeting took place, in fields above Bryan Street Hanley, at which upwards of 20,000 people gathered. Feargus O'Connor made a keynote speech calling upon support for the People's Charter. Some 10,000 signatures were there and then given. Was this then, the torch that lit the fire, much called-for and long awaited, to kindle belief in a complete union of workers?

The following year more meetings were held by local Chartist based in the Potteries which were unspecifically countered by greater solidarity between the employers who by now were looking for other methods of manufacturing ware and the use of machinery. They had learned the lessons of the strikes and lock-outs better than the workers had. Solidarity - be prepared - had become the employer's watchword long before it became the battle-cry of the unions.

The workers in Burslem by now had grown to become as militant as their counterparts in Longton and had started to move away from the co-operative socialism propounded by Robert OWEN upon whose agenda the trades union movement is largely based, and moved towards the radicalism of the Chartists. Among these converts to Chartism was a thirty year old Owenite, a potter named William ELLIS, a Burslem man who lived in lodgings near to St John's church, a short distance away from the Methodist teacher and shopkeeper, John Bennett, Arnold Bennett's grandfather.

Meanwhile, a new parliamentary election had been called in 1841 to support the administration of Tory Prime Minister, Robert Peel. William Davenport, who had represented the district for nine years had decided to retire and nominated Frederick Dudley Ryder, son of the Earl of Harrowby to be his successor, which seemed to many to be a hark-back to the ways-and-means of the rotten-borough system - cronyism - buying seats, though not for money. The election of Ryder was thought to be a 'walkover' but the emerging Liberal Party decided to field a radical candidate, John Lewis RICARDO.

Ricardo was not from the Potteries but his family was considerably rich from profitable dealings in a number of national business transactions. He was the nephew of the political economist and Jewish stockbroker, Jacob Ricardo MP, whose family seat was then Gatcombe Park in Gloucestershire.

Attempts were made to have Ricardo disqualified as not being resident or having a business interest here, but this was easily deflected by his appointment as a director to the newly formed North Staffordshire Railways.

The election was set for the 30th June 1841 and three candidates were nominated for the two seats: Liberal - Ricardo; Conservative - Ryder, and William Taylor Copeland - Conservative, who was an alderman of the City of London and whose local connections were by virtue of his purchase of Josiah Spode's pottery in Stoke.

The new electorate, authorised by amendments to the Reform Act, allowed for more worker's representatives to take part in voting and, naturally, the oppressed potters who had perceived to have seen themselves suffer at the hands of the employers and were still suffering much from the effects of the depressed market, turned to the Liberals to promote their causes at Westminster. The Chartists, fielding no candidates of their own, threw their whole support also behind the Liberal candidates across the country.

Copeland and Ryder had decided to canvass together as their manifestos were identical. Wherever they spoke to employers they were met with endorsement and campaign money, but when they attempted to meet the people they were booed and heckled to such a degree that it became pointless to address them. As a consequence of their disinterest in meeting the workers, the workers' activists and Chartists began to follow them around causing disturbances whenever they could.

On 23rd June, six Conservatives, including Copeland and Ryder were travelling by horse from Stoke to Longton when they were startled to be followed by a crowd of workers which gathered force as they went along. By the time they had reached Longton the crowd accompanying the candidates was up to some 500 people who were barracking them and preventing their horses from galloping off. Suddenly the demonstration began to get out of hand and missiles and stones were thrown causing injuries to the two Tories, in particular to Copeland who received some nasty cuts and bruises. The party made its way to the Longton town hall where it was given protection by the newly appointed office of Stipendiary Magistrate, Mr Bailey-Rose. But in the end, the bedraggled team were chased out of town. No further attempts were made after this to canvass or speak in Longton.

Disturbances were also reported in Hanley where Conservative banners were torn down and supporters were pelted with rubbish; and in Burslem, a number of beerhouses had to be cleared by the special constables after fighting had broken out. In Stoke, a mob threw stones breaking all the front windows of Copeland's pottery and then continued into the town where they lay siege to the Conservative meeting house. The result of the poll, according to the contemporary historian John Ward, was testament to the intimidatory methods of the Liberal's campaign - '...a practical illustration of the superiority of intimidation and violence, over the futile notion of independence in election tactics, and the great efficiency of ruffianism...'

Ricardo won four districts out the seven polled, but he easily won the populist endorsement, his election workers deterring as many as 278 Conservatives from casting a vote for fear of that very intimidation. It seemed, for the time being at any rate, that the workers had won the day. Ricardo himself, proved to be a very independent MP and continued to be elected until his death in 1862, supporting the railways and other transportation free-trade causes. He was of the coalition of Liberals, Whigs, Peelites and Radicals that came together in 1859 to form the New Liberal Party. At home, he was instrumental in bringing rail to Burslem with a main-line linking station at Longport. His popularity in Burslem, although he was absent from his constituency for most of the time, earned him the dubious honour of having the Railway Inn (Dalehall Inn), in Newcastle Street, dubbed, 'The Ricardo Arms'; and a new street in the St John's district was named after him!

The elections of 1841 showed the workers that they could, with organisation, democratically put favoured and like-minded sympathisers into parliament. It gave greater force to the Chartist movement and it brought a renewed energy back to the lapsed potter's unions. But neither the Manufacturers Federation, nor the owners of the private coal mines were ready to turn political power to any degree over to their workers. In late 1841, the coal mine owners in particular, began to turn the screw; cutting wages and creating longer hours. But by now the Chartists were holding public meetings almost on a weekly basis. Burslem was a stronghold of activity and their leader, William Ellis, was determined to make the election victory count. He led a group of Burslem Chartists to Stafford where they proceeded to disrupt a council meeting at the Shire Hall, their representatives calling for points of order on matters of social conscience. The meeting descended into chaos and the constables were called, but Ellis and his men escaped before any arrests could be made.

Between January and June 1842, the Lancashire mill owners began an organised scheme to balance their overseas credits which were considerably affected by the slump in the market. They implemented the simplest remedy and cut the workers wages. Coal mining was very much in crisis as a consequence of slow trade and a number of coal mine owners followed the lead of their Lancashire colleagues. The owner of the largest coal mines in North Staffordshire was the Earl Granville, the Duke of Sutherland's half brother. He was immensely rich and owned the Etruria estate and could easily have weathered out the economic depression without any recourse to disruption to his workforce. But Granville, in absence, did what the Lancashire mill owners had done and reduced much of his colliery wage bill by cutting pay. Another coal mine owner named Sparrow, did the same at Longton in July that year, but the colliers here refused to submit to his swaggering arrogance and walked out to a man.

In Leicester, a leading Chartist, Thomas COOPER, was alerted to the events in the Potteries and on 10th August he travelled with his group including another national leader, Arthur O'Neil, to Wednesbury in the West Midlands where he addressed a rally of steel workers and coal miners. It was clear that the two men were expecting something to happen for none of the subsequent meetings over the next few days had been pre-arranged. In the crowd that afternoon in Wednesbury were three Potteries Chartists, William Ellis from Burslem, Hanley Chartist and shoemaker, John Richards, and Joseph Capper, a Tunstall blacksmith and Methodist preacher. Accompanying them were a group of Burslem potters among whom were two brothers named Nixon from Middleport and their friends, Garratt, Dennison and Ball.

The Potteries had now become a focal point, a potential catalyst. And Chartists from Manchester, Yorkshire and the Midlands turned their eyes inwards to the anticipated collision with the employers that their Potteries members seemed bound for. Something very important was apparently going to happen in the Potteries. At the same time, the pottery manufacturers and coal mine and iron masters were hastily meeting to prepare contingencies for any possibility of attacks on their premises. Already miners had broken into pit-heads and destroyed carriages and machinery, dumping them into the canal and obstructing the passage of barges carrying valuable cargoes of coal and ware.

Under the chairmanship of Enoch Wood Jun., whose family were at the time in residence in the Big House, the Association For the Prosecution of Felons again met hastily at the town hall where they called upon the service troops stationed at Newcastle under Lyme to be prepared to assist at any disturbance at Burslem. They also swore in as many special constables as they could recruit and arranged for local Volunteer Regiments to be stood-to.

Feargus O'Connor was meeting with a large group of Chartist members at Bolton when they heard of an incident which had occurred the week before some forty miles down the road at Burslem. It was reported to them that, on Saturday 6th August, three miners who were collecting financial relief in Burslem's market place, had been arrested upon an allegation of begging and locked-up in the cells beneath the town hall. Notice of their incarceration was quickly passed around and a crowd of miners numbering 200 marched on the police station at midnight, their faces blackened to avoid identification. The crowd, including a Burslem labourer named Colclough - whose presence there, it was said was purely for causing trouble - easily broke into the poorly guarded lock-up and freed their workmates turning their attention to nearby shops and houses, breaking windows and looting as they fled. Among the numerous acts of vandalism was the smashing of the face of the town hall clock, an unforgivable sin in the eyes of the pottery manufacturers who had single-handedly put up the money for its erection! Troopers and dragoons were called from Newcastle but by the time they arrived the only people in Burslem were irate shopkeepers bemoaning the damage, and terrified residents hiding in their kitchens.

Thomas Cooper was now travelling north from the midlands with his growing band. He addressed meetings at every town on the way, and, on 13th August he arrived in Hanley where he spoke at a large meeting of the striking coalminers. The following day, Sunday, Cooper again spoke at Hanley and at Longton; on each occasion his audience grew in numbers. At the same time that this was going on, other principal groups of Chartists had begun to gather in Manchester in order to hold a giant peaceful demonstration to commemorate the 23rd anniversary of the Peterloo Massacre on August 16th.

In the morning of Monday 15th August, the largest crowd so far collected in Crown Bank Hanley once more to listen to Cooper; they had come from all over the Potteries; potters of Longton and Burslem mixing like brothers. Thomas Cooper's intended theme was to win by resistance to violence and disorder. But the radical leader impetuously introduced what some took to be a battle-cry - **"Do no more work until the People's Charter has become the law of the land"**. He inadvertently caught the riotous mood of the crowd during the hour long emotive and passionate speech as the crowd moved off in a mob to Shelton where they again took hammers to the machinery bringing work at the iron works to a halt. Another group attacked Hanley police station and scattered documents in the street and freed prisoners. At the same time the mob broke into a pawnbrokers and flung pledges into the crowd. The local tax office was next to be raided which the mob attempted to set on fire. Joining up with the Shelton crowd, the mob marched to Stoke where more damage was inflicted upon businesses. The police Superintendent Stonior was physically attacked and many of his officers received serious injuries.

Word of the march quickly spread and an even larger crowd began damaging property in Longton which then turned and marched to meet the Hanley crowd. The Longton rectory was burned down and acts of vandalism and arson were inflicted wherever the mob took itself. Meanwhile in Manchester the Chartists were being kept informed of events in the Potteries as they unfolded. The crucial question was being formed on everybody's lips - 'should we abandon the Peterloo demonstration and march to support our brother potters?'

Throughout the late day the whole of the Potteries from Hanley to the southern towns of Stoke, Fenton and Longton were at the mercy of the mob who had routed the police and other bodies of law protection. Houses of professional men and town officials had been demolished and set alight. Many properties were burned to the ground of a whim. Even minor damage involving the smashing of windows and complete disruption of official work affected the population as a whole. The Potteries was, for twelve hours, subjected to a regime of anarchy. The night sky was red with burning buildings. The streets echoed with drunken cries of violence and screams of wild jubilation. What would the morrow bring when it was Burslem's turn!

Meanwhile, Thomas Cooper and his friends, belatedly realising the implications of his statements, left the Potteries for Manchester with the assistance of Samuel Bevington, a Hanley master potter and Chartist. They were led along the High Lane ridge intending to get to Chell along a country lane which was normally deserted. However, the group became lost in the darkness and wandered off course directly into Burslem town centre. Here the fleeing incendiaries were arrested by watchmen who took them to the Big House where they found Enoch Wood entertaining Samuel Alcock, both famous manufacturers and both members of the Burslem Association for the Prosecution of Felons. The two employers took Cooper to the temporary house of a lawyer and magistrate, William Parker, whose Hanley home had been destroyed earlier in the day. Despite a lengthy interrogation, Cooper was surprisingly released and allowed to continue his journey to Manchester.

The day of Tuesday in Burslem began relatively quiet. The sun took to its climb over the eastern slopes of the Sneyd Green ridge spreading its bright yellow heat onto the shelf which supported the town's centre, its growing warmth shifting the sewer-mist out of the open gullies of Queen Street and into the marsh-valleys that lay along Bournes Bank. It was the day of the mass rally and demonstration in Manchester to commemorate the massacre at Peterloo.

Brothers, George and Samuel Nixon collected their lunch packs and left their mother's terraced house in Newport Lane and on the way called for their fellow Chartist and friend James Ball. The three met up with Burslem men William Garratt and Charles Dennison at the Bethel Chapel in Waterloo Road where they had arranged a rendezvous to walk together towards Hanley to join the procession they knew was heading for the Mother Town.

At the George and Dragon, the innkeeper, William Barlow, had already decided not to open that day until he was sure that the demonstration was going to be a peaceable one. His public house had already suffered from theft and disturbance the week before during the miner's attack on the lockup. Barlow was a worried man, for some of his more knowledgeable customers had alerted him that a gang of known trouble makers had been at the incidents of riotous behaviour in Hanley the night before and had every intention of joining in the days events at Burslem in order to target the stock of the alehouses and inns. What really concerned him was that the ringleaders lived just across the road in the Holehouse.

Watching the dawn from his south facing bed chamber, Enoch Wood Jnr. - tired after his interrupted night and the arrest of Cooper - looked out over the Swan Bank and Square. Already small pockets of men had gathered in groups weighing-up the days agenda, dressed in their overalls and aprons like clusters of mistletoe berries hanging from black branches at the junctions of every street. There they loitered about the lanes and alleyways, steadily growing; as does early autumn fruit overhanging hedgerows.

The President of the Felon's Association, Alcock, had instructed his servant to lock and bolt all the doors and to place wooden shutters across the windows of his house in the Sytch. Wood had himself retired to the back of the Big House with his wife and children. He would not be chased out of his town like many other potters been! In Hanley, the gathering crowd had moved from the now overcrowded Crown Bank into the more spacious Bryant Street fields, all the time making preparations for the march on the Mother Town.

Also heading for Burslem was Tunstall Chartist Joseph Capper. In the weeks before, Capper had been advocating that the Chartists should confront the authorities head-on for he saw no progress being made by negotiation; a strange directive for a Methodist minister. Two nights before, he had preached outside the Wesleyan Chapel near to his home at 29 Piccadilly, Tunstall, and on that occasion he had totally advocated that any such confrontation should be conducted with peaceable decorum on the part of the Chartists and that sheer strength of numbers would go a long way to show the employers that their ranks would not be broken. As he climbed the Scotia Bank, Capper stopped by at several houses where people had gathered in groups, and he prayed with them for peaceful success.

Thirty-two year old John Bennett was also at prayer. His wife, Mary, who was with child Enoch, - who was to become the father of Arnold Bennett - knelt with him and their eldest boy John in the parlour of their house at 46 Pitt Street. John was no Chartist but as a Methodist minister he knew where his allegiance lay.

Not far from Bennett's home, the district of Holehouse was a cauldron of activity with people milling about and gathering sticks and stones and other missiles in anticipation of the day's coming events. Among these was the poor labourer, John Colclough, a young man of great strength and resilience who had been with the rioters in Hanley the day before, and he had indeed been present at the release of the begging miners from Burslem's lock-up. Even now, in this hot morning, he was still intoxicated by the battles he had fought and with the ale he had consumed during raids on public houses the night before. His behaviour was inflammatory as he went about the lanes and alleys urging men and women to pick up what weapons they could and to join with the marchers coming from Hanley.

Eight o'clock saw the arrival into Burslem's confines a platoon of fusiliers and a troop of dragoons under the command of Major Trent who had been stationed at the barracks at Newcastle under Lyme. Their headquarters were to be the yards of the Legs of Man Inn in Market Place where a regiment of 200 special police constables were being sworn-in and fortified at the same time by glasses of hot port. Joining the Newcastle troopers was a Burslem volunteer regiment led by Captain Powys, a retired soldier who was a local lawyer and magistrate.

During the next hour, as the morning progressed and the summer sun became hotter, the crowds in the Burslem streets grew and grew. It seemed as though it was a Wakes day, for many wives and their children had turned out in their summer frocks and Sunday suits parading up and down singing and cheering around and around the town's central walks.

Thunderously vocal, the march from Hanley reached the crossroads of Waterloo Road at Cobridge. The parade stewards had heard that they would be met in Burslem by marchers from Macclesfield and Congleton who had spent the night bivouacked in Leek, but they weren't sure of a time of any rendevous as no co-ordinated programme had been set. By Warburton's potbank, the head of the march was met by the brother's George and Samuel Nixon and their friends who had made up their own group which had now grown into a strength of about forty or fifty Burslem men.

'The lions are here...the lions are here... we have come to deliver freedom...'

The crowd were singing, no - *shouting* at the top of their voices the words of a popular Chartist anthem...

'...the lion of freedom has been set loose from his den...
And we'll rally around him again and again...
Again and again... again and again... hurrah hoorah...
Again and again...'

There were no law enforcers to stop and disperse them on Waterloo Road, the thoroughfare that was now to emulate the actions of that great battle in Belgium against the French.

It was just after 9 o'clock when the might of the march reached the centre of the town. Together they numbered some six to eight thousand. From the rumble of continuous voices, high pitched, unheard commands were shouted detailing the action. The intention of the Chartists leaders was to hold a rally at a point in the Market Place where sermons would be heard and a notice would be handed-out to the person in charge acting as representative for the employers. None of this agenda had been proposed to the employers let alone passed out as information to the majority of marchers. It seemed that most people and factions were in the dark by omission rather than be design.

As the march entered the town, it became at once clear to the Chartist leaders that the employers had taken their own precautions, for many of them were genuinely surprised to see the large opposing numbers of troops and specials who had stretched a line across the top of Swan Bank in order to prevent access to the Market Place where the town hall and the lock-up were sited. The employers had learned lessons from the previous weeks events when the colliers had easily freed their comrades from the cells. **'Let no man pass!'** commanded Major Trent as he turned to Captain Powys whom he had placed in command over a platoon of horse cavalry should there be any necessity to charge into the Chartist's ranks. Now twenty past nine in the morning. In the town centre the march and the troops stood face to face. It was a stand-off.

What happened next was to play a crucial part in the outcome. The Chartist's demanded the right to pass into a public place of their choosing where they could hold their prayer meeting and to hand-out their demands. Major Trent told the leading Chartists that he would not allow them access to the market place and instructed them to disperse into the fields over by the Jenkins and into the Hamil. But he was ignored, more than likely because he wasn't heard. At the same time, some five-thousand marchers from Leek had reached Smallthorne and were progressing in a long line descending down the lane to the town centre. Joseph Capper and his followers were meanwhile holding a meeting of their own, separated on the other side of the town by the official cordon. And all the time the local people were wandering around jeering the troops and encouraging the Chartists into action. The riot was now just minutes away. In retrospect, it became clear that Trent's commands had either not been heard, or had been ignored; whichever, the information for dispersal had not been passed around. The fatal combination of lack of communication and poor leadership not only caused the inevitable conflict, but it decided its outcome. Had the crowds moved into the Hamil fields, it is highly likely that a peaceful demonstration would have gone ahead. As it was, the lions insisted on their demands.

There were now so many people crammed into such a small space that anyone so minded could commit crime at will. This situation was put into effect by the group of men from the Holehouse who, resident in the poorest part of town, seized their opportunity to go on a looting spree. The nearest premises to them was the George and Dragon Inn where they had no problem in breaking down the doors and gaining entrance to the bars where they plundered the ale taps and raided the wine cellars. Money was stolen from William Barlow who was punched to the ground while his staff were threatened with assault if they stood in the way of the mob. The leader of this group was the Holehouse labourer, Colclough, whose nickname was abbreviated to 'Cogsey'. They held the George and Dragon to a man until an appeal was made from Barlow for intervention. Captain Powys now had little alternative but to relieve the old inn.

A small platoon of dragoons quickly entered the inn at the rear and, using the flat blades of their swords, easily evicted the intruders who were by this time well drunk. That is, most of the intruders fled, probably all with the exception of Cogsey who had the drunken courage to resist, taunting the dragoons with a stick until, by overwhelming numbers, he was picked up and thrown into the street.

The crowd on Swan Bank by now had become very agitated. The front lines were being pushed against the horses flanks that were rising onto their hind legs determinedly controlled by their riders. Hymns were being sung out-chanted by Chartist's songs, overlaid by the shouts and screams of men, women and children. Cries of jubilation, of pain, of anguish, of joy and fear. Bugles were blown on both sides. Horses whinnying; jeers from the crowd echoing in the shouts of the constables. The options that Powys once commanded had now disappeared. He only had one choice left.

The Riot Act of 1714 was introduced to suppress the Jacobite reactionists when, in those former troublesome times, it had become almost impossible to quell outright civil disorder. Although the Riot Act was only repealed as late as 1967, a few of its most strict elements have been retained by the subsequent Public Order legislation, including the definitions that pertain to riot itself.

A state of riot occurs when twelve or more persons continue together in a violent and turbulent manner to the terror of the people whether or not the object of the meeting was lawful. There was no doubt in the mind of Captain Powys that day that a riot was in progress, and he had to act accordingly. Astride his horse, Powys unrolled the order of the law. A small document which had been prepared and signed by the magistrates, Alcock and Wood. The dragoon commander tried in vain to make the crowd listen but the pottery workers were having none of it. Most of his words went unheard except by those marchers at the front.

'Our Sovereign Lady and Queen chargeth and commandeth all persons being assembled immediately disperse themselves and peaceably depart to their habitations or to their lawful business, upon the pains contained in the Act made in the first year of King George, for preventing tumults and riotous assemblies. GOD SAVE THE QUEEN'.

It was the first and only occasion that these most powerful budget of words - an awesome declaration - had been used in the Potteries. It was a statement that commanded silence during its reading and it proclaimed that all persons so gathered must disperse within the following hour or else be proceeded against as felons and suffer the consequences of death and severe punishment. It was, in its most potent sense, a declaration of war against the civil population.

The troops had now ended their skirmishes and had regrouped behind the lines. News of the reading of the Riot Act filtered back into the crowd, losing its urgency and threat the further it retreated as the crowd grew more confident by the sheer numbers present. By the time Powys's words had reached the back of the crowd, his words had diminished into an ineffectual whisper. The Chartist leaders, under John Williams and the Nixon brothers and friends, continued to call for a meeting with the employers while Joseph Capper's group supported them from the top of the hill. The march from Leek was about to enter the town and were some two hundred yards from Swan Bank, while at the same time, Cogsey Colclough, or Cogzinelly as some shouted after him and his gang, broke out from the Red Lion where they had drunk the inn dry.

In an unfortunate piece of timing, the loudness of the chanting mass hid the declaration of Riot and it was consequently not heard by the crowds lately arriving who were prevented from going forward by the Hanley procession who were now milling around looking for action. This gridlock brought the Leek march to a halt outside the Red Lion Inn as they pushed and were pushed back trying to grasp hold of any scrap of information that might tell them what was happening. The full implications of the situation was not imparted to the new arrivals, nor did they know that the Riot Act had been read out. Such was the confusion that no one knew exactly what was happening and what was required of them to comply with the law under the terms of the announcement. Some twenty-thousand people innocently stood in an unmoveable block chanting their slogans, expecting information, instructions; anything that would convey the next move!

The riflemen prepared a redoubt formation backed by the horse cavalry with the hundreds of specials in support at the rear as the protagonists faced each other across Chapel Bank and Swan Bank. In the front line, swords had been drawn, bayonets fixed and muskets loaded as the minutes ticked away, the crowd having little sense of time, nevertheless were alert to the occasion. And still men were arriving into the Square from Moorland Road and Waterloo Road oblivious to what was happening at the front, enjoying the summer's day out and singing songs.

On the hour, Captain Powys rode to the front just behind the first line.

'Clear the Streets!', he called.

The great pressure of numbers gave the soldiers no option but to drive forwards swiping their swords and thrusting their bayonets in front of them. The men at the back heard the crack of distant gunfire while, those at the front, reeled, many on each side trying to flee as one. At the front, it was a scramble for safety but, at the rear the newcomers continued pushing forwards, blind to what was happening out of sight, deaf to the sound of the conflict and ignorant to the situation. No one at the rear knew what was happening until the smell of gunpowder of the kneeling front rank riflemen of the redoubt reached their nostrils.

One group of men who grasped the occasion and gloried in the excitement and the tumult was the drunken crowd that had been thrown from the George and Dragon and had invaded the Red Lion. Foremost again was Cogsey Colclough who led his men, urging them and encouraging them by his leaping up and down between two troopers and disarming them, mainly by surprise, before falling to the ground where he picked up a cudgel with which he began to strike the underbellies of the horses causing the animals to unsaddle their riders. In his single moment of fame, people seeing the soldiers tumble to the thrusts of Cogsey started to chant, **'Hooray, hoorah...hoorah for Cogzinelly'**, over and over. A rain of stones showered over the mob into the ranks of soldiers many of whom retreated. But even as they did, the dragoons had begun to regroup for another charge. Even then, the crowd at the rear, comprising totally of the moorland's marchers, continued to play their marching instruments and sing their marching songs.

By now the Hanley marchers were well into Swan Bank and were preparing to invade the Market Place while the Leek marchers, in front of the Red Lion, continued their push forwards. Powys, who had now found his armed redoubt was still holding the standing line, gave the command **'Fire!'** The cracking and the sounds and smells of gunpowder igniting and exploding were hidden by the terrible shrieks of people being hit by musket balls. Men fell to the ground. Many turned and trampled over their fellows in their fearful escape. The men at the back now knew full well what was happening at the front. The crowd scattered, leaderless. Some men carried away their wounded comrades as the special constables gave chase along the streets and lanes into the fields. Swan Bank and the Square was cleared by the soldiers and it was emptied more quickly than it had been filled. The core of the riot had faded away - the employers would now exact their revenge.

Though several of the rioters had been hit by musket fire, the list of casualties and the severity of their injuries has never been revealed for the majority of those struck took-off, escaped unidentified, their injuries treated in the anonymity of their homes by their families and friends. One man who didn't escape unharmed had arrive with the Leek marchers. After the first volley of fire, the young man, a shoemaker said to be named Josiah Heapy, lay dead in front of the Big House hit in the head by a musket ball. His body was carried by a constable into the town hall where it was later collected by his family and taken home. His final resting place even today is lost, though his memory still haunts Burslem lanes. As all this was happening in Burslem, an even greater crowd of some hundred thousand were demonstrating peaceably in the streets of Manchester as they marched with restrained dignity to the Free Trade Hall and market place.

Over the next few days, many of the accused ringleaders of, what had now been called the 'Burslem Riot', were arrested as preparations were made to try them at Stafford Assizes. O'Connor and other northern Chartists departed from Manchester wondering what would have been the outcome of the Potteries' Riots if they had decided to come in concentration to Burslem instead of holding their ineffectual demonstration in the north-west's capital. The Stoke MP, John Louis Ricardo, was overheard to remark in a Westminster committee room, that he had been so very sorry to hear of the consequences of his poor constituents' innocent demands for the Chartist's principles, but that he saw no future in worker's representations.

Some 274 persons were brought to trial of which 54 received the severest punishments of transportation for life, and imprisonment from between 21 years and 7 years. Of the main Chartists, William Cooper was sentenced to two years, John Richards - one year. Of the local Chartists, Joseph Capper received two years in Stafford Gaol, William Ellis was transported for 21 years and died in Australia. John Colclough (Cogzinelli) was accused of riot in Fenton and Burslem and for freeing the miners with the assault on the Burslem lock-up the week before, and for breaking the town hall clock! He was sentenced to transportation for life, although, after sixty years in Botany Bay, he returned to Burslem in 1903 where he died quietly, unremembered for his part in the riot.

The eldest of the two Nixon brothers, George, was sentenced to two years imprisonment while his sibling Samuel received 15 months. Their friends, James Ball - 15 months, William Garrett - two years, and Charles Dennison - one year. During the whole of the Potteries riots, hundreds of smaller sentences were handed out, particularly against women and children whose offences had been mere fringe involvement in a series of raids on shops and houses and of looting. These punishments did not reflect the severity of sentence in length or time, or in their participation during the riot, but were inflicted in response to the wrath of the employer. Sentences of between three months and one year were imposed involving long shifts at the prison's treadmill or picking oakum, a practice which skinned the individuals' fingers until they continuously bled openly - a legacy of imprisonment which they carried to their death.

For the moment, the Chartists were silenced. They drifted from town to town, meeting and talking to crowds, in a mixture of political conspiracy, religious revival and calls for emancipation and equal opportunities. But the riot in Burslem had shaken the hierarchy and the manufacturers heeded the warning.

In April 1848 a mass meeting of the Chartist movement was held on Kennington Common in London. It was to be the movement's last gathering of such proportion, and it signalled the end of the road for its leaders.

Two famous photographs made by the great early pioneer of press photography, W E Kilburn, are held in HM's Royal Photographic collection. The stark images depict a wide view of the Common with a crowd of workers gathered all about a central wooden stage on which are standing the chartist leaders. Their president, Feargus O'Connor, had called the meeting to present a mass petition calling for the immediate implementation of a programme of worker's rights. The government, remembering the Burslem Riot, thus considered the Kennington meeting as a prelude to a similar civil violation, this time in the capital, involving a much larger and disciplined crowd. The Prime Minister, Lord John Russell, advised the Queen and her family to move out of London to their home, Osbourne House on the Isle of Wight. Once more revolution stalked the streets of England.

In France the troubled King Louis-Philippe abdicated and fled to England. As a new republic was declared across the Channel Victoria remarked to her diary that, as a result of the worker's demands, there was a feeling of great uncertainty felt here throughout the land... **'I tremble at the thought of what might await us here'**, she wrote. Her consort, Prince Albert, however associated himself with the worker's claims for release from poverty, and he encouraged the Government to do all it could to help the workers and the unemployed. He exclaimed in a personal letter to the Prime Minister on the day of the Chartist meeting on Kennington Common, **'I would be exceedingly mortified if anything like a commotion was to take place.'**

Even though confidence betrayed them and fear stalked them, the government were assured of a win, for the Chartists were now but a shadow of their former selves; much of the zealotry had been steamed out of the engines of the movement. Too many had gone to prison for their cause; too little had been achieved.

The seriousness of the situation was not underestimated as the Duke of Wellington himself was put in overall command of 10,000 army troops while 120,000 armed special constables had been sworn in. The Chartist's had anticipated a gathering in excess of 200,000, instead some 20,000 turned up. And the 'great petition', said to contain some 5 million signatures only revealed some 2 million, many of which had been deliberately spoiled and duplicated. O'Connor, still an MP, was persuaded to meet the commissioner of the Metropolitan Police. During the discussion the waning leader accepted the position of the Government and its primary role as protector of the people. That the whole crowd would not be allowed to march upon Parliament in the time-honoured tradition as they had threatened, but that O'Connor himself and a few associates would be permitted to deliver it to the Speaker, was the best deal. O'Connor accepted the terms offered him by the commissioner of police. At this, the meeting on Kennington Common peacefully dispersed and it was left to O'Connor the next day to address Parliament with the pleas of the Chartists. It turned into a fiasco for him as members talked over him and read newspapers. Parliament and the monarchical constitution had come through intact as had the Metropolitan Police in their first great test of controlling civil disorder. But the administrative institutions had been roughly shaken as well. Among the Conservative's greatest theorist's, parliamentarian and writer, Edmund Burke, on his deathbed fifty years earlier had written, **'The King, and his faithful subjects, the Lords and the Commons of this realm, - one triple cord which no man can break'**. In his powerful opposition to the freedoms of democracy, Burke's final testament prophesied the fate of the Chartist movement.

The two daguerreotypes of the great Kennington Common meeting were purchased by Prince Albert for he wished not that Victoria's subjects should learn through the new art of photography, the power the masses could command. The pictures fully capture and evoke the memories of that day. Dark sky, a sullen crowd, motionless; just a few banners of protest and the ominous construction of a tall factory chimney in the background - unlit by fire, unmarked by the emission of smoke - a black, sad obelisk symbolising the frustrations of the day.

But, from the theatres of Kennington Common, Manchester and Burslem; by the presence of Chartism in history, the governments were made to realised how close the country had come to an accomplished worker's revolution. One of the consequences of Chartist insistence and its later progeny, the working commissions, a number of legislative changes were introduced, none more important than the launch of an enquiry into the conditions of child labour in factories and mines; hours of work and hourly rates of pay for the working man, both of which ultimately led to broader care and insurance for workers in the greatest industrial nation in the world.

From 1848 rafts of social legislation was floated into law in an attempt to outlaw the evils and consequences of bad practice in the workplace, in schools and on the domestic front. It was the Police Act of 1856 that introduced the maintenance of compulsory forces throughout England and Wales seen in London as a successful civil peace-keeping force when compared with the military. In 1862, the government made grants available to educate children up to twelve years old, and in 1870, the Elementary Education Act made local authorities duty-bound to accommodate education programmes. The urban working classes were given voting rights in 1867, and in 1872 the secret ballot was introduced. It was even time for monarchical intervention as Prince Albert - and no one more than he had understood how close the throne had come to being overturned - personally addressed a working-men's meeting shortly after the Kennington debacle which went a long way to reassert the monarch's 'one family' strength to the working classes. These years saw the relaxing of the Queen's detachment from her people by often bypassing the wedge of her government on public occasions, superintended by Albert until he died.

Locally, after the industrial unrest, in 1843 the pottery trades picked up for a while largely due to a full order book from the United States of America. In 1844 the Potteries Emigration Society was formed to raise funds to purchase land in Wisconsin America which was named Pottersville. The six years to 1850 saw many families travel across the ocean to settle in a community which exists today. But by the year of the Great Exhibition serious emigration had dwindled to nothing and many who went out to seek out a new life returned penniless. The numerous potter's unions trundled on, slowly amalgamating in wearisome progress throughout the rest of the 19th century, until, in 1906 it finally became recognised as a properly constituted national union under the title, 'The National Amalgamated Society of Male and Female Pottery Workers - NASMFPW.

Feargus O'Connor was a beaten man. Although he remained a member of parliament, some three years later, it was clear to his few remaining friends that he held unstable illusions and in 1852, the leader of the Chartists became completely mad. He died in an asylum in 1855.

Perhaps, in his deranged mind, he might have saved a thought for the summer's day in Burslem, when, as he was celebrating the Peterloo Massacre with his followers in Manchester, a last minute change in orders would have deployed a greater mass to the Potteries where the outcome of the Potteries Riots would undoubtably have been different!

By virtue of the Police Act 1856, the local Association for the Prosecution of Felons handed over law enforcement to its police force, and relaxed its authority to meet from that day to this only for an annual dinner, the longest continuously practising organisation, though today un- accountable, in the Potteries district. For the poor, crime then was an incentive to betterment. It was instinctive. Punishment was to chasten even beyond retribution; beyond confession and further, beyond remorse. Life in Burslem was considered so cheap that most were willing to take their chances viewing lawlessness as an evil road which, out of necessity, they were compelled to plod. The penalties were the severest the law could administer. Martha Watts was a Burslem woman who succumbed.

When Martha Watts appeared in the old dock of Stafford Assizes in 1825, she was charged with larceny - the theft of a small sum of money from a companion with whom she spent the evening drinking in Ye Olde Crown Inn, just around the corner from the dreadful Ball Bank.

Martha was a serving woman at Ye Olde Crown and, during a casual conversation, struck-up the acquaintance of a travelling salesman who had become a little worse for drink. The man, flush and flash with his money, repeatedly called for drinks to his table where he engaged Martha in conversation aimed at securing her later favours between the bed-sheets of his rooms. Martha sat with her gentleman whenever she came to serve him and, noticing his careless inebriation, she took but a few shillings from his jacket pocket while he wasn't looking. It was a foolish attempt at making a small profit but her honest instinct failed to respond and her weak resistance gave way. And she may have succeeded in her felony but for the jealous attentiveness of a 'friend', similarly employed as a serving woman at the nearby Duke William Inn, who sat morbidly watching the whole incident. Martha was betrayed to her drunken companion who complained to the innkeeper and she was taken straight away to a magistrate to be indicted. Later, from the dock, the tearful woman pleaded her remorse and asked the judge to consider the fate of her two young children who had no father and who would have to face the world alone. The judge would have none of it and she was sentenced to be transported for seven years. Her children were ordered to be placed into the care of the town's beadle until they could be reunited with their mother on her return.

Upon her arrival in Australia Martha would have been taken into farm slavery. If so, here the story of her life ends, for history does not record whether she returned home on completion of her sentence. As with so many who were transported she simply disappeared. If she was lucky, she would have been employed by a considerate employer and she might have been very fortunate to have married a goodly man. Whatever, it is likely that she died in Australia, maybe as a result of the bone-breaking activity of the workplace, or from one of the country's indigenous diseases. Nor does history report on the lives of Martha Watts' two children. Apart from a few lines in a contemporary newspaper reporting her crime and punishment, it is as if Martha Watts and her family had never existed.

The Great Reform Act and the subsequent Municipal legislation, together supported by enactments of improved poor law and better social security: the hard fought-for agreements of the early potter's unions emblazoned in the accounts of the Chartists deeds for the emancipation of workers, eventually drew the causes together as governments and employers learned the value of ordinary people. Among the tens of thousands of Burslem's unknowns, the name of Martha Watts would have no special meaning at all. But, unlike the overwhelming armies of Burslem folk who have passed anonymously through its streets and its lanes and fields, Martha Watts is remembered by history simply for slipping her hand into the pocket of a drunken gentleman and stealing a few shillings. All her contemporaries have been forgotten.

Physically, **Burslem** lies at the southern tip of the Penine Chain.
Looking down on the **Roaches** across to Burslem
only 10 miles as the crow flies.

Westport Lake
An eerie and lonely place when you are by yourself

The Jawnels
A name given to an evil place where the jaw of a whale was found. A relic from the last Ice Age

(Below)
The Sytch to Brownhills
The old Liverpool Road

The Sytch entering the town

The last remnant of the Back Sytch

The West End of the Road to Lancashire as it was known locally

(Below)
The entrance to the Road to the Sytch and Liverpool

The Wedgwood Big House
Moorland Road stretches to Smallthorne. The bottle oven of Moorland Pottery can be seen in the centre of the picture

(Below)
Lord Shaftesbury's Burslem Ragged School
where poor children learned the 3 'R's. In the 1960's it was a dance school

This is Waterloo Road and it was once full of such houses.
Arnold Bennett's family home at 205

(Below)
The Leopard - Bennett's 'Tiger'
Note the roof line of the old houses and the hotel stretching back at the rear

The Haywood Brother's Hospital in Moorland Road
Now being redeveloped by Burslem Community Development Trust

Malkin's Folly. Burslem Town Hall and Queen's Hall.
The Town Hall was opened in April 1911 and closed the same day

Entrance to Madame Reymond's House, Moorland Road
Re-mortgaged at least 4 times to pay for the upkeep of the North Staffs Symphony Orchestra

Madame Reymond's House
The top stone lintel over ground floor window carried the name "Beethoven House"

76

The modern Post Office
Closed 1993. Hamil Road winds up to High Lane in the centre back

(below)
The rear of the Wedgwood Institute with the empty Leopard Hotel on the right
In the background the Grange in front of the Hanley sklyline

The town entrance of Jawnells
The High building to the back of the picture was the Liberal Club

(Below)
Burslem's first commercial bank
Kept afloat through the efforts of Enoch Wood who underwrote its credit facility. To the left is Cock's Entry

Newcastle Street which replaced the old Packhorse Lane
In the background is Porthill Bank and Dimsdale

Once the White Hart Music Hall
Where Fred Horry spent his last night in Burslem before shooting his wife dead

The Packhorse Inn
at the top of Packhorse Lane
before demolition

(below)
Corny Eyes
and the former Railway Inn

The Town Gardens before Ceramica

Bycars Road
The old route to Tunstall which wound below Stanfields before turning into the Pinnock Fields

Middleport Canal looking towards Longport

Chapter Four

HUCKSTERS AND EREMITES

> '...the inhabitants, who met, in their different towns, as well as aggregately, induced the government to admit "THE BOROUGH OF STOKE ON TRENT" ... as it comprised the largest parochial division, and prevented the jealousies which would have arisen, if either Burslem or Hanley had been made head of the Borough...'

(Ward pg. 61)

There's something about triangles that attract us. For a start they don't suffer fools gladly, nor do they encourage opposites. We may look at a single line and know instinctively that it requires two poles so that its opposites can conform - each end is compatible to the other - when one turns, the other responds. Whereas a square, now a square *definitely* signifies compatibility - it has four corners aligned in equal fortification, each facing the other across a central space. This straight square has an epicentre that measures relatively from its opposite partner: the epicentre is a point that is often coveted by the challengers occupying the four corners for here stands control. And this position, this central point, is jealously protected when won. The balance of power in the square becomes more tenuous if the square is stretched to a rectangle - the field of play then becomes critically narrowed - the contest now runs up and down and it is each of the narrow ends that are to be won; the centre is irrelevant. Yes, it is the triangle that is the difficult battlefield - it has no proportionate centre, therefore the middle is disorienting to the contestants. Its shape is teasing, uninviting, unconventional. It's a bit-pattern of deterrence, something to be shared but not owned. And yet, whoever controls the triangle does so from an unassailable position of power, and may do so from any one of its three corners.

The city of Stoke on Trent is like a triangle. Sometime in the past its three corners strove for the ultimate control of the single unit. Two of the players failed utterly, for they just didn't understand the perverse difficulties of the triangular field of play. No more impact upon Burslem's decline is to be sounded than in the echoes of the resonance of the long struggle between independence and federation nearly a hundred years ago. Having its beginnings in the sublime confidence of the 1870's and 80's, Burslem marched arrogantly into the battlefields of twenty years of open warfare with its neighbours that lasted from 1890 to 1910 and which culminated in the last tired battle of that final year straying into the long and miserable retreat of the 1920's and the 1930's. The three sides of the triangle then framed the three elements of defeat: humility, tenuity and futility. Like dominoes, they fell onto each other as confidence fell with the decline of power and resulted in: the re-settlement of people out of Burslem town centre: the decline of Burslem's commercial trade: the universal acknowledgement of Hanley as the city centre and Stoke as the civic centre.

Trade in Burslem certainly isn't what it used to be. Don't take the word of a chronicler, ask the president of the Chamber of Commerce! The battle for city-centre commercial status has been fought and lost a long time ago. The fall-out from the conflict can be seen in the streets, the lanes and the squares. Victorian buildings, piles of civic pride, lie between the emptiness of long demolished properties like some snaggle-toothed gargoyles. The alleys leading to the backs of shops are unvisited, for behind the frontages dereliction is cautiously hidden away. The people who made the town, who gave it a heartbeat, have been evacuated, the architects and the builders have gone; each and all by way of their own preferences have escaped into the countryside. But there was a time ...Oh, and what a time it was...!

Burslem's Chamber of Trade was properly inaugurated in 1851, the year of the Great Exhibition. Then, there was nothing seemingly to fear for the old English shopkeeper. The employers were rich and the employed had a choice of jobs. A regular professional army was easily conquering resistance to imperialism overseas; trade abroad depended much upon Great Britain. Trade at home could not be bettered; everyone could afford to shop, most could afford to own a cheap one. Never had the term, 'Nation of Shopkeepers' been so appropriate. Slums and degradation there were, starvation there wasn't, even though there was a majority of undernourished workers there was always fish, fowl, offal and vegetables available; stew and broth was staple; bread and beer was compulsory. Although poverty was strident in the industrial towns and the countryside, it affected only the staple workforce. The poor didn't get poorer, it was just that their numbers kept rising, their masses continuing to increase the town's population, whereas those who managed to rise from the factory floor became richer as a consequence of a well-stocked labouring market. This bourgeoisie moved into the suburbs. Then came conflagration in Europe's summer fields of 1914, that Boys-Own adventure that promised the contestants on all sides that, as victors, they would be home by Christmas!

Of course the Great War changed most everything in Europe except in Great Britain, 'this sceptred isle' which remained an island. Great Britain was the only participating empire to emerge from the war with its monarchy intact; the 'Triple Cord' - the King, his subjects and the Lords and Commons - had held once again. And in many ways, even in a land made to become 'fit for heroes', the majority of people simply wished to return to many of the safe ideals of the Edwardians. All they wanted was the best of the old times and the best of the new. And, who could blame them! But their good times could not be retrieved, the juggernaut of Empire was wandering off-course.

In the Potteries from the middle of the 19th century, due entirely to its central location, the town of Hanley had emerged as the district's main commercial seat. It held nothing different than the other shops and markets of the other towns, for in fact each town offered its own specialist commodities distinct from those which its rivals were able to present. Hanley was simply the most central in communication, it was also the highest point and contained varying topographical levels of descent from a high hilltop linking its divisions with ease and luring one street into the next, unlike most towns which responded to the draw of a central market place. (Even JB Priestley later praised these 'swinging' elevations in a description of Hanley as one of his favourite shopping centres.) But by the middle of the 19th century Hanley had become the most populated of the Potteries towns.

The Six Towns of the potteries in fact progressed in relative isolation until their amalgamation as a unitary borough in 1910. But it was the reckoning of the past and future, a catalyst of time - that came to insist - what was to go forward with the people and what was to leave behind. This was a judgment that had to made in the 1930's - by then it could not be deferred any longer. To consider the subtle post-WWI changes in Burslem and the effect that slide to slump had upon its trade and commerce in that single decade, the 1930's, the traveller has first to assess the impact of the collision of fiscal culture that exploded in the Mother Town on Thursday 31st March 1910 and how its inhabitants came to terms with it. For some wary Burslem anti-Federationists at the time, the decision to enter into civic partnership with the other Potteries towns was tempered by the thoughts that at least the new council house would be based in the Mother Town; where else, since this is where the great industry began. And, as it seemed to those self-confident Edwardian gentlemen who carried on the traditions of their Victorian fathers, the Burslem folk were the better-placed and more experienced in civic matters than their potting relations in the south of the district.

Burslem had been a market town since an act of Parliament in 1825 which gave the town permission to regulate its own market, its lighting and watching and its guardianship of law and order. The Poor Law Reform Act 1834 allowed the appointment of a Board of Guardians. In 1848 the Burslem Board of Health was formed by Act of Parliament. The conditions of that Act stipulated a yardstick that bound the Board to legislation. The qualifying yardstick legislated that during a period of 7 consecutive years, the death rate of an applying town should be identified with a criteria - as having a mortality rate of 23 in every thousand. Burslem, because of its industrial illnesses, easily came within that measure! To be a Board member an individual had to have an estate worth at least one-thousand pounds, or was the occupier of a premises with a rateable value of thirty pounds. The Burslem Board of Health lasted until 1878 when the Burslem Borough became incorporated. The Board of Health had however released its management of the town's workhouse which was situated at Green Head - a site today occupied by a car wash business. In 1838 the workhouse accommodated some 152 paupers the majority of whom were the elderly and infant. The following year, a new workhouse at Chell was opened after Burslem's union with neighbouring Wolstanton which had jurisdiction over Tunstall as well. And so, the old 'bastille' at Burslem, as it was known, was taken into use as a barracks for the local volunteer regiment.

The structure of local government in Britain has its diagnostics in Norman Britain, but its machinery became activated as a sociological concept in Elizabethan times when responsibility for a town's poor was commanded by law with each town providing a rate relief for the assistance of its abject weak. In 1597 the first Poor Relief rate was introduced to cope with the numbers of poor people who were flooding into the large towns increasingly at an alarming speed. By the end of the 18th century, poor relief was administered in the main by the clergy. In the Potteries this responsibility was properly undertaken in 1825 when the district adopted the legislation of the Select Vestry Act 1819. The first civic officials were therefore made up of churchwardens and parish overseers and meetings took place in the vestry of St Peter's Church in Stoke. The Stoke Vestry Committee at first comprised of 2 wardens, 4 overseers and 20 elected members from which an equal proportion were selected from Burslem.

It was a most haphazard set-up and it seemed that it was established only to defend the individual's corner wherein business was discussed in an ad hoc manner enjoined by much shouting and occasional brawling! In its second year the committee never met and was disbanded due to non-attendance. While all these frustrated attempts at civic compromise were going on, a number of interested manufacturers and traders in the four main towns of Hanley, Burslem, Longton and Stoke, had begun to meet on a regular basis to discuss the towns' trade and economic auditing to their mutual benefit. Fatefully, these masters of industry chose Hanley as the regular venue for their meetings. The Reform Bill of 1832 changed the method of local administration for all time. It preceded the Local Government Act of 1835 which gave considerable powers to locally elected representatives.

In 1857 Hanley applied for and received its Charter of Incorporation as a Borough. In the twenty years since the Local Government legislation was introduced, its town civic leaders had been pushing ahead with vigour, providing the town with a host of municipal functions which included a higher grade school, electricity, gas confederate through the British Light Corporation, and they commissioned and built a large concert hall, the Victoria Hall, behind the former Victoria Hotel, which was at that time being used as Hanley's council house. The consequences and privileges, encompassed by the status of Borough became much sought after; Longton achieved the recognition next in 1865; Stoke and Burslem in 1874. Subsequently, because of its large population - over 50,000 residents - Hanley qualified to achieve the even higher status of County Borough in 1888.

A federated district had been advocated by many manufacturers over a long period of time but by the 1890's it reached the top of the populist agenda responding to a stronger and more persistent force which advocated full unity of the Six Towns under one council. In 1895 the Duke of Sutherland roundly commended Federation and offered to give his estate at Trentham as an inducement to progress - although it was obvious that he was gaining for himself a personal incentive wherein a unified administration would enable him to clean up the River Trent which passed through his land causing a constant nuisance by silting-up due to the factory waste deposits which were dumped in the river's tributaries. Though Sutherland's bait was never taken-up by the union of towns, the offer provided the breeze that whipped-up the spark which fanned a more insistent flame to Federation.

Over the next thirteen years the Potteries' towns were drawn into conflict, lined-up against each other on opposite sides, a triangle of contestants as it were, for and against amalgamation with the main protagonists lining the angles on each side of Hanley which stood haughtily at the apex. In Burslem the principal individuals and the ordinary people were so divided on the merits of Federation that the fight was taken into the streets. A poll was organized in 1903 the result of which revealed that 2,670 townsfolk were against joining with the other towns, **an overwhelming vote by six to one against those who were for Federation!** It was accepted by most Burslem people, and strongly affirmed by the anti-Federationists, that Burslem had the services that it required for the next 20 years; its own gas and water authorities; it was well ahead of its neighbours in elementary education as well as in its art and technical schooling in the ownership of the Wedgwood Institute. What's more, the town was about to embark upon the building of a principal school of art in the fashion of a college.

Although a number of powerful committee members tried to force the issue, the six towns of the Potteries continued independently for the next 4 years during which period a cross-boundary group was formed, the Potteries Association For the Promotion of Federation, chaired by the Duke of Sutherland himself with the support of Major Cecil Wedgwood of Barlaston, Thomas Twyford, a master pottery manufacturer of Hanley and, Leonard Grimwade, a distinguished Victorian potter and inventor of Stoke upon Trent. In 1905 this committee's membership boasted of a peer of the Realm, 3 serving mayors, 5 aldermen, 15 magistrates, the presidents of each of the six town's chamber of trade, a co-opted member from the leaders of the new Labour Committee and its parent organisation the Potter's Union, and the rector of Stoke, Henry Venn-Stuart, who advocated support unofficially on behalf of the whole clergy.

In a long first debate on the merits of Federation, Venn Stuart argued that no matter what it cost the rejection of unity would only postpone the inevitable in future years. During this speech, the Stoke rector issued an obscure reference to the district which many took personally; **'...in such landed towns, we must not huckster about a penny or twopence on the rates...'** - the implication being that even after a union each town should be able to contribute whether by loss or by gain. It was an issue that returned time and again as some of the towns continued to feel discrimination alongside the commercial popularity of Hanley. Inevitably the writing seemed to be on the wall that Federation was going ahead sooner or later. Still Burslem continued alone believing that it could enter later after first becoming a County Borough in its own right in a speculative attempt at merged with nearby Wolstanton, when it could taste the brew that its neighbour Hanley had enjoyed for the previous 17 years. In reality Burslem was extremely jealous of Hanley, **'that pushing Chicago'**, as Arnold Bennett's Old Wife, Constance Baines described it caustically; the town that had stolen Burslem's trade; that **'grasping and unscrupulous Hanbridge'**!

In 1907 the Burslem Federation Board again petitioned for a referendum of electors and this time the difference between for and against had considerably narrowed; 3,240 against the union, 2,074 in favour, representing a turn-out of 74% of those *eligible* to cast a vote - the population of Burslem that year was 38,766, *which meant that some 32,000 townsfolk were disenfranchised!*

The feasibility of a Federation was moved forward and became an election issue that year. From July onwards a succession of meetings were held by the Local Government Board who were recommending union based upon those, already adopted by the London Boroughs, employing a system of differential rating. However, these London proposals were largely rejected as being inappropriate for the Potteries. And in the slow wake of the Potteries endeavours a new proposal, suggested by Frederick Geen a Stoke businessman, was tentatively promoted. Geen's proposal also suggested a form of differential rating but allowed for an interim catching-up process which happened to be beneficial to the town of Stoke set against Hanley.

An enquiry was held at Stoke Town Hall in the week of the 8th January 1908 conducted by government officials. Burslem immediately sabotaged the procedure by withdrawing on account of the role of the official's chairman, John Burns, whom they accused of bias by vocal interference. A bill was nevertheless presented to the House of Commons committee supported by Hanley, Longton and Tunstall but emphatically opposed by Stoke, Fenton and Burslem. So negative was the Commons' primary presentation that the whole package was indifferently sent without comment to a Select Committee of the House of Lords. At the outset the Lords accepted the principles of Federation and, what's more, accepted the scheme deposited by Frederick Geen, on the elementary premise that it appeared to have the most public support.

It was at this point that any plans Burslem had to influence its own unitary status appeared sunk. The Lords had decided that by the majority of will, they the Lords would recommend the installation of a federated borough for Stoke on Trent whether it be voluntary and with cooperation, or by coercion and compulsion. In a weighted dictum the chairman, Lord Cromer, pointedly exclaimed, '**If local public opinion cannot decide about local government there is no value in public opinion at all**'. Faced with a domestic rout and complete defeat, the Burslem committee under the chairmanship of Sydney Malkin, put forward an amended aimless scheme based upon the total valuation of the rates with added costs applied to towns holding on to individual assets. It was cynically noted that elements of these principles were bound within the statement of Mr Frederick Geen and overall were not dissimilar to the Stoke proposal. Hanley didn't seem to care either way, its civic fathers had known all along that their town was going to be the main commercial centre whether it stayed as a county borough or merged to make a larger coalition. But the Mother Town was resentful as the tug 'o war with Stoke lumbered on.

The fervour of patriotism heightened into chauvinism in widespread public anger. Parochial zealotry was publicly demonstrated; an intolerance was now voiced, a bitterness which had existed since 1870 within the towns' traders' associations, which had helplessly watched-on as their more dedicated and financially rich customers now travelled to Hanley by the new trams to purchase specialised commodities. Arnold Bennett voiced his own concerns when he graphically placed the consequences on the modernisation of communications. He referred in private correspondence to his life in Burslem in the 1870s when:

> '*...there existed less than two miles of tramlines in the entire district and only two trams, drawn by horses and travelling between Hanley and Burslem, twice an hour.* (And in 1908) *Now electric cars run about everywhere, from Longton in the south to Tunstall in the north......And it was precisely the rapid cars which at last broke down the stubborn individualism in the separate towns and brought about their federation and the triumph of Hanley, the central and largest town...For a penny or twopence, in a quarter of an hour, the man or woman with money to spend could be in Hanley, and not all his love for his native town would keep that man or woman out of Hanley...*'

And of Federation in his fiction:

> '*It aroused fury in Bursley, which saw in the suggestion nothing but its extinction of its ancient glory to the aggrandizement of Hanbridge. Hanbridge had already, with the assistance of electric cars that whizzed to and fro every five minutes, robbed Bursley of two-thirds of its retail trade... and Bursley had no mind to swallow the insult and become a mere ward of Hanbridge. Bursley would die fighting.*'

To 'die fighting' was the rallying cry which whimpered soon into silence, for in December 1908 the Royal Assent was granted to the Potteries' Federation Bill. The fight for the commercial centre had been long decided, now the Mother Town entered into a new battle - which of the Six Towns would host the civic centre?

The three triangular contestants in this encounter were Stoke, Hanley and Burslem. Longton's communications were considered inadequate, and in any case Longton had no interest in the clash other than to support, along with Fenton, the nomination of Stoke as being of their kith and kin. Hanley supported its own claim, although its real interest was in commerce. But Burslem saw the civic centre issue as paramount to a return of the trade it had lost to Hanley. Enter Sydney Malkin, principal parochial pro-Federationist!

Malkin's amendment to the Federation Bill had been based upon each individual council's precautions against 'asset-stripping'. And his own personal scheme of retrospective asset valuation, coupled with a tri-lateral retention of individual profit in service revenue. Malkin was an alderman and had been twice Burslem's mayor in successive years. By virtue of these offices, and his council seniority, Malkin became Burslem's principal trouble-shooter. He seemed to be well placed to negotiate civic-centre status on behalf of his town. The question was, as a pro-Federationist, could Malkin settle with the Burslem 'antis', and could he deliver the prize of the new borough centre being stationed in Burslem?

It has to be noted that at this point in the process the amalgamation of the Potteries towns into a federated unit was a fait-accompli with the Lords looking to the ancient town of Stoke becoming the administrative centre. Malkin and his committee must have known this, so surely any civic expenditure from Burslem's coffers would have been better used to get the best possible deal out of the inevitable merger. Vanity and pride prevailed and the entire agenda was misread.

Sydney Malkin was born in 1865 and an absolute contemporary of Arnold Bennett being just two years older than the author. His father, James, purchased The Mount at Penkhull, a well-positioned modest mansion overlooking the south of the Potteries towards the county town of Stafford, built in 1803 by Josiah Spode II. James Malkin was a tile maker whose own fortunes rose when he married Annie, a daughter of Joseph Edge a prominent Burslem potter. James Malkin, his father in law Joseph Edge and Edge's friend, Benjamin Cork, collaborated on tasteful earthenware which they successfully directed to the cheapest end of the market. They opened a potworks in Queen Street on the site of today's former School of Art building . Sydney Malkin and John Wilcox-Edge, sons and heirs of the two principal partners, inherited the business's of their fathers while Mary, third daughter of Benjamin Cork married Frederick Macdonald, the Methodist minister whose sister Alice married John Lockwood Kipling. From these Burslem lines descended the poet Rudyard Kipling and British Prime Minister, Stanley Baldwin. Thus are dynasties created from humble beginnings.

By 1900, Sydney Malkin had acquired all interests in the business of Malkin, Edge and Cork and had opened large new premises in Newport Lane, Middleport. Malkin was mayor of Burslem in 1907 and had become very much involved in the amalgamation of the towns as a pro-Federationist, as indeed was his cousin, John Wilcox-Edge. As a founding member of the committee of the Federated County Borough, Malkin was brought into direct conflict with Frederick Geen with whom he clashed on a number of occasions. He resigned in petulance protesting that Geen was little more than a petty dictator who refused to make concessions on behalf of his town Stoke, and in particular Malkin resented the intended purchase and administration of the money-making independent Burslem Water Company.

Having quit the steering committee he turned towards the interests of Burslem's Independent Federation Committee, believing that here he could use his influence more potently. But Malkin resigned from that as well, tetchily complaining that Burslem's anti-Federation committee members, who by a long way were in the majority, were unreasonably and fiercely radical. He now became marginalised finding that his own unswerving views had pushed him into a lonely corner of the triangle of decision making.

Sydney Malkin was still however chairman of the Public Works Committee and, in his supervision of civic building and management, he obliquely saw an opportunity for Burslem to become the civic centre. His train of thought and his stance was huckstering - if only Burslem could possess the most up-to-date administrative facilities, so modern that the decision to locate the new administrative council house could not be conceived to be placed anywhere else in the Potteries other than in the Mother Town! Under Malkin's direction his committee brought forward a proposal to build a new town hall from scratch. So daring was the concept that Burslem's full council were beguiled into acceptance. So far as civic buildings were concerned the town had an abundance. Its existing town hall was only fifty years old; although its fine ball-room and concert facilities were inadequate for large audiences and comfort and its acoustics were poor, it was more than adequate for Burslem's own needs as an administrative centre. The Wedgwood Memorial Institute, opened in 1869, was a superior educational forum, while the new School of Art, built and opened only five years in advance of Federation, was considered as the leading artistic and technological conservatoire of its type in the Potteries. Nevertheless, it seems that Malkin's plan in agreeing to the amalgamation of the towns was to bring the process of centralised local government to Burslem. This he would not be moved from. But others, in the south of the district had similar thoughts, none more pedantic than the powerful lobbyist Frederick Geen.

Both Malkin and Geen knew that ultimate central administration would reside in the town which could provide the best facilities, even if those facilities were offered to be built retrospectively. Almost stealthily both Burslem and Stoke made plans to build new premises and to flamboyantly extend their existing appurtenances.

Stoke Town Hall had been commenced as long ago as 1834. Progress on its completion however was excruciatingly slow with the north wing only being completed in 1842. The south wing of the frontage was still being fabricated in 1850, although many of the committee rooms were at that time in place. What Fred Geen and his Stoke council did was to recruit the services of London architects, Wallis and Bowater, to re-shape the interior rooms and to build an attached concert hall at the rear. Already Stoke Town Hall was the largest in the six Potteries towns, built in stone block with four giant Ionic columns standing upon a central portico over the main entrance. A large council chamber stylishly based on a round inner arena inside a square hall with Grecian amphitheatrical dimensions, was fashioned in 1888. Other rooms were re-deployed and the huge concert hall was lavishly embellished with heraldic enamel and be-jewelled decorations interlaced upon scrolled plaster mouldings and carved imitation tapestry. So mighty was the edifice that the only name to adorn it was King's Hall, after Edwards VII, although it was only given it's new name - the same - at the convenient time of the coronation of George V. The whole was ready for use in 1911.

For many years Burslem boasted a number of theatres; what it didn't have was a concert hall of the proportions of the Victoria Hall in Hanley. Malkin sought to rectify this by building a brand new civic centre attached to which would be a grand hall. He persuaded Burslem council by the strength of both public and committee lobby to approve the construction of such a development. His personal appointment of Messrs Russell and Cooper of London as architects got the commission under way at the beginning of 1910. Just as the King's Hall was, the new Queen's Hall was completed in 1911 at a cost of a hundred thousand pounds, and named after Queen Mary, George V's wife.

The Queen's Hall and new civic centre was built on what was at the time a waste corner of a triangle of land in the centre of the town. From the very beginning the triangle had been used as a tip from which shard from adjacent clay pits had been piled. It had formerly been part of the Burslem estate managed by the Over House and had come to be Burslem's traditional meeting place when in the 17th century the maypole had been sited upon a flat shelf of its down slopes. The western corner of the triangle had been an ideal site to erect Burslem's first town hall as well as its second town hall over the same position - now named Ceramica, since 1911 it was always referred to as 'the old town hall'. The public market was also built here on the waste opposite the Wedgwood brother's Big House. But in 1900, the land where the Queen's hall was to be built by Malkin was still largely derelict occupied only by a Methodist Mission hall and a disused wooden Music Hall, formerly the Wedgwood Theatre. Known as the 'Blood Tub', it had been owned by a popular variety entrepreneur, Matthew Hall, who presented acts of a bloodthirsty theme, murder and mayhem. In the late 19th century Arnold Bennett knew it and called it Snagg's Theatre when it was being used as a meeting room for a worker's action of strike:

> *'...from its green, wooden walls came a sound of humanity in emotion. Before the mean and shabby portals stood a crowd of ragged urchins....*
>
> *"It's a meeting of the men", said Edwin.*
>
> *"They're losing aren't they?"*
>
> *He shrugged his shoulders. "I expect they are".*
>
> *She asked what the building was, and he explained.*
>
> *"They used to call it the Blood Tub," he said.*
>
> *She shivered, "The Blood Tub?""Yes. Melodrama and murder and gore - you know."*
>
> *"How horrible!" she exclaimed. "Why are people like - like that in the Five Towns"?*
>
> *"It's our form of poetry, I suppose," he muttered, smiling at the pavement which was surprisingly dry and clean in the feeble sunshine....*
>
> *...Snaggs', dimly lit by a few glazed apertures in the roof, was nearly crammed by men who sat on the low benches and leaned standing against the side walls. In the small and tawdry proscenium, behind a worn picture of the Bay of Naples, were silhouetted the figures of the*

> *men's leader and of several other officials... The smell of the place was nauseating, and yet the atmosphere was bitingly cold... rows and rows of discoloured backs and elbows, and caps, and stringy kerchiefs. They could almost feel the contraction of thousands of muscles in an involuntary effort to squeeze out the chill from all these bodies; not a score of overcoats could be discerned in the whole theatre, and many jackets were thin and ragged; but the officials had overcoats...*

Clayhanger. Book II chapter XX

There were then, in 1911, seven town halls operating in the Six Towns of the potteries! Each in its own right providing an integral concert hall. The King's Hall held, 3,250 people; the Victoria Hall, 2,580; Tunstall Hall, 1,100; Longton Hall, 950; Fenton, 550, and with Burslem's new Queen's Hall seating 1,600 with an upper room, the Princes Hall, accommodating 550 people, culture in the Potteries was clearly well taken care of even if it wasn't totally patronised. Additionally, Burslem's New Town Hall held the police and children's courts; a dozen committee rooms and a central open courtyard with a gallery which could be opened into a mezzanine area.

Thus there were three possible towns that were vying for civic centre status: Stoke, Hanley and Burslem. Which one would be victorious?

On March 31st 1910 the corporations of Stoke, Longton, Hanley and Burslem, and the town councils of Tunstall and Fenton were severally dissolved. The constituency of the new borough was named Stoke on Trent based upon its location under the provisions of the Select Vestry Act 1819, pre-proposed under that name to become a county borough under the provisions of the Local Government Act 1888. The Charter for the new borough was extended from the County Borough of Hanley in the name of the Mayor, Aldermen and Burgesses of the Borough of Stoke on Trent. On the same date all the provisions of Municipal Corporations as they related to the individual towns were at once cancelled.

It was deemed appropriate for the venue of the first meeting of the new council to be held on neutral ground and it was therefore convened at the North Stafford Hotel in Stoke with a division of committee meetings to be shared among the other town halls for the time being. The first mayor was Major Cecil Wedgwood who defeated Fred Geen. Geen's proposer for mayoralty was his adversary, Sydney Malkin - the irony was not lost upon the on-looking councillors from the other towns! And overnight Burslem, with a population of some 40,000, found herself with two majestic buildings - one, brand spanking new - with no specific use and with nothing to put in them! Two administrative council houses with nothing to administer! Little wonder that the people laughed at Burslem's second town hall in amusement at their ironic dubbing of the building as Malkin's Folly!

To be fair the Queen's Hall had its share of occasions. The City's annual Art's Ball was held there until the School of Art lost its autonomy and effectively closed in 1974. And it was the preferred choice for the diners of all sorts of associations from the Felons, the Chamber of Trade, the annual Police Ball and all the potbank dances and do's over many years. The weekend public dances were a regular feature from 1935 to 1970 as were hundreds of concerts, ballets, light opera and operetta's and stage shows. The Queen's Hall was a popular venue for all these until nightclubs and other entertainment venues began to appear by the 1960's. But by then, Burslem's waning star had dipped below the southern horizon as Hanley began to expand into its suburbs of Shelton and Etruria.

In the 1920's, trade and trading in Burslem was as strong as any of the other towns but the insidious choice of centralisation for shopping preference drew more and more shoppers into Hanley aided by approachable road networks and the lure of department stores. To go to Hanley was to have a day out. It was an excursion which often included the whole family as the day's shopping preceded a visit to the cinema or the theatre and a fish and chip supper before the last tram or bus took them home. A local phrase passed down from these times still prevails in many of the 'Six Towns' - "I'm off out for the day", as though there were no other place in the world, - **"I'm going up Hanley Duck!"**

For a short while after the Great War, the immediate British economy was strident during a period of economic adjustment, and people did expect a return to pre-war Edwardian standards. While for the serviceman, the social aspects of life had not seemed to have changed in the years between 1914-1918. However, the expectations of those - mainly women - who had been left to fill their places at home, had been widened by their wartime experiences. Many of Britain's anticipated leaders were dead, and those who were left, who had emerged from the carnage, were compelled to look urgently to the calls of the people for them to fulfil the social needs of the lower classes. The creditable social reforms begun by the Liberal government before the war had to be carried on more than ever. The backbone of the 20th century had already been fractured in its first twenty years. There was to be no going back - the war of empire had proved that. In a speech that stunned many of his audience, the under-rated 20th century social legislator, Lloyd George said, in an attack on property ownership and the traditions of inheritance:

'Who is responsible for the scheme of things when one man is engaged through life in grinding labour to win a bare precarious subsistence.... and another, who does not toil, receives every hour of the day, every hour of the night, whilst he slumbers, more than his poor neighbour receives in a whole year of toil?'

Even so, the 1920s saw Great Britain trailing in the industrial market as the new industrial nations, America and Japan, easily caught-up and began to overtake a Britannia which of necessity clung on to its dominions in the old empire. The 'Roaring Twenties' did not happen in Great Britain, not at least outside London, and most certainly not inside the Potteries. And yet it was during the 1920's that Burslem enjoyed its finest and most popular trading period. There were a number of reasons for this but one of the most important was the decline of the capitalist platform beginning in 1918, as distinct from other criteria among which none is more important than the simultaneous rise of political socialism and socialist legislation.

Between 1910 and 1920, the majority of the new council members and administrators in industrial Britain came from the manufacturing classes who were the substantial property owners born out of the years of Victorian and Edwardian enterprise and opportunity. They were men of means, men who had a traditional say in how the districts were run on a level which fitted in with county and borough stature. It was expected that their sons would have taken their place in hierarchical precedence - the so-called right to govern. But death in the entrenched mud of Flanders had ended their 'as-of-right' rostering to council and parliamentary entrance alike. Instead, room was made for the independent commercial class who had remained static with a strong local home-base. There were of course a number of established traders on the new Stoke on Trent council, Geen himself and Malkin were of old family status, and wherever these men stood they remained at the top of the power pyramid. From 1920 though, the district councils of the Midlands and the North West were more often than not made up of members who were either shopkeepers or their representatives or their affiliates. Stoke on Trent council during this period had a large majority of such self-made men while Staffordshire County Council absorbed the 'landed' among its 87 members comprising of:

23 manufacturers of importance; 13 farmers; 2 physicians, 2 clerks in Holy Orders; 4 peers of the realm, 1 baronet, 2 Members of Parliament; 7 members carrying the military rank of colonel and above, and at least a dozen knights and 'Gentlemen'. Indeed, the only members who could qualify to have come from the working classes were the members for Burntwood, who was the manager of a drapers shop, and the secretary of the Society for the Leek Silk Twist Manufacturers.

1918 also saw the final split of the National Liberal Party, many moving to support the Independent Labour Movement; and the true end to the traditions of laissez-faire. Two years later saw also the optimum emergence of the Labour Party financially supported by the unions of which there were some 4 million trades union members by the end of the war. More parity was granted in 1918 when all men over 21 and women of the age of 30 were given the vote. But Stoke on Trent now lay quite comfortably behind the front lines of political manipulation as political influence moved briefly from Liberal to Conservative. In a short while though the Stoke on Trent Labour Party began to organise itself earnestly moving with comparative ease to the forefront of local politics aided by a full membership of trades unions.

The Federated authority after 1910 worked in much the same way as the separate town councils had, with the members fighting for their own parochial causes. At first the full council was made up of a majority of Conservatives and Liberals and Liberals who had become Conservatives. These men championed their political parties behind the soubriquet of Independent, for the populist conception in local government was one of honesty in independence. It was important that the public was omitted from the political forum - to this end party divisions were never publicly expounded, thus restricting the general public's interest and participation in civic service. In other words, politics - which had taken the place of 'born to rule' or conservatism - still belonged in the safe hands of the ruling classes; so far as the public were concerned, it was enough that their interests were represented by their employers and providers, therefore their betters. And so to the general public these trading councillors were seen to be above politics - as politicians the shopkeepers could call themselves by any name - most used Independent.

But soon they controlled the council to suit their own lifestyle, holding their meetings in the daytime for only they could afford the time away from the workplace; their full monthly council meeting was held on a Thursday afternoon - a preference born out of the practice of arranging their half-day closing on a Thursday. This idiosyncrasy, whether by design or otherwise, was perpetuated to the end of the 20th century. By this mantra, until the Labour Government of the late 1990's began its policies of regional devolution and civic reform, many workers who were unable to get time off work during the day were prevented and deterred from becoming councillors.

The traders held power on the crucial planning committee and were influential in the decision- making affecting town centres, particularly judgements affecting their own commercial generation. They also held power in deciding the merits of new applicants for business, alteration and extension, being careful that their own trading wasn't affected by unwelcome speculators. Thus each lobby fought its own corner, each of the town's councillors responding to his or her own insular representations.

In the absence of political grouping, the Independent councillor therefore contrived to influence his committee's decision-making in his own patch by tying other strings to his bow - the Watch Committee sat to elect constable and to make promotions in the police and fire service - Education Committee chose headteachers, all of whose selections were open to nepotism and seduction and the play of favours which were expected to be returned. Other councillors selected the coroner, the chief medical officer. And it was the Licencing Committee that debarred publicans from committee membership. Fine, despite the obvious that the Licensing Committee was easily controlled by other members who had trading affiliations with publicans and who probated themselves to members of the powerful Association of Licenced Victuallers - **no conflict of interest here then!**

Paid officers of the council were ingratiated by councillors and vice versa, having a common interest in advantage in pecuniary matters as well in fraternity favouritism.

Additionally a third bowstring was added by which councillors owning membership in one of the powerful clubs or secret societies, used the pact of brotherhood to bring other influence. Indeed these men often changed allegiance as political strength waxed and waned or tribally prevailed - Outfalls, Catholics, Freemasons, Felons, Rechabites and Buffalos - even to holding cross-membership. The southern town councillors of Longton, Stoke and Fenton, were traditionally escorted into Freemasonry while the north town's offices were Catholicly persuaded. Oddfellows and Forresters lodges were abundant in grand order and wizardry. All through the Potteries the towns were each independently influenced by antediluvian prioritization and polarisation organised and administered by the traders and shopkeepers. No problems here just as long as the commercial geography and hierarchy remained in place - nothing out of their control should affect the balance of hierarchy in the high street!

In the Britain of the 1920's very little had been done since 1918 to relieve poverty and ease the daily conditions of the poor which incorporated the whole of the working classes. The domestic front's turning point arrived in 1926 with the modernisation of the Central Electricity Board which overhauled the production and distribution of power and lighting. This massive economic leap forward became administered under the powers of new local government reformations introduced in 1929. The so-called Chamberlain Act cleared away the local Boards of Guardians freeing-up the convoluted independent national health and unemployment insurance regulations introduced by Lloyd George as far back as 1911. The role of the Guardians was now handed to the county and county borough councils. From 1929 the issues of housing, so far as it affected the working population and the problems of homelessness and overcrowding, were tackled head-on. Local authorities were given the right to purchase and build council owned and maintained houses. The Mother Town, in common with its neighbouring sisters, began the task of slum clearance and the clearing of the warrens of tenements and shared-facility cottages. Nearly all of these blighted properties were located inside or in close proximity to the town centre. In squares and triangles and pieces of commonly available land.

At first slum clearance wasn't seen as a problem by the councillors and the programme was indeed embraced with open arms as heralding the birth of a new town, a new beginning, spearheaded by social housing provision which in turn would encourage a fresh distribution of new spending money. And much of the early clearances were targeted at the outlying communities such as Hot Lane and the Sytch which turned out to the trader's benefit, for these measures brought the residents from these distant areas closer to the town centre to reside in lodgings there. But as the decade turned into the 1930s, the Stoke on Trent Labour Party had grown in sufficient political stature that it was able now to influence the acceleration of the slum clearance programs. The council was compelled at this point to turn its attention to the heartlands of the shopkeepers, the old town centres, which had been greatly neglected as singular units of accommodation since Federation in 1910.

In 1930 the slums in Burslem had been largely unaddressed. Baker Street (Clayhanger Street) housed a potworks together with a forge and some twenty cottages. Nearby Massey Square, (Chapel Lane) was almost a little village by itself with upwards of 700 people living there in back-to-back narrow lanes, as was Ball Bank, High Street and New Street (Greenhead Street) with 120 cottages; Davenport Square, (Wycliffe Street) 600 people, and the dreaded Holehouse, (Holdcroft Street), 1000 residents. It was determined that all of these shanties, skids and ghettoes had to go, and the construction of new housing estates was commenced to accommodate the removing town dwellers; brand new streets of houses with little patchwork gardens, flung up on land formerly owned by mangers of exhausted collieries, providing tidy little houses built in the countryside of Stanfields and Sneyd Green - once the fields of the Audley and Sneyd family, in fields where deer was hunted on horseback. The people, formerly living in the overcrowded town centres, were given country residences leaving the vacated town centres much less populated. Almost overnight the effect was felt by Burslem's traders as they lost the custom of some 2000 residents to Tunstall of all places - that sister town which suddenly became the nearest shopping centre to the people who had moved to Stanfields - and another 2000 looked to Hanley - the nearest market for the people who had moved to Sneyd Green.

Another irony for the once powerful town centre traders came by virtue of the back street shops which were always attendant but always out of sight - exclusively serving the tenement dweller, remaining open long hours after-hours, tolerated but never encouraged to join the Chamber of Trade nor even cloistered by its membership list. These rag, tag and bob shops in unvisited thoroughfares, where the majority of goods could be purchased for less that a tanner, of course were also subject of the rehousing policies, for they were at the very heart of the slums. Although they had managed in the past to evade the prohibitions insisted by the council that houses were for housing and not for retail, their owners were informed that they were still houses as defined for the purpose of slum clearance. But in the houses on the new estates, commercial trading was strictly prohibited under penalty of forfeiture of tenancy. Many of these shopkeepers who succumbed to the regulations hung up their aprons and handed on their stock, but there were those - the more enterprising - who bought private houses in Middleport and on the sprawling estate on the east side of Burslem pleasure park.

The Park Estate had sprung up during the Edwardian housing boom when the lower middle classes seized the opportunity of emulating their 'betters' in Cobridge. These older estates in the 1930's were invaded by the cleared-out shopkeepers of the town centre. The slum clearances had caused the back street shopkeeper to move on, and so they collected their wares and simply opened up the front room of these houses, placed a counter across the middle of the room and worked it as a shop. Park Estate was full of them!

At this time there was no legislation to prevent or control this odd pursuit of retail trading and, because these itinerant shopkeepers were able to undercut the prices of similar commodities being sold in the town centres, they were able to provide cheaper goods at a reasonable return to the customer. Cheap-jacks, they were known as. In such places credit clubs, dividend savings and lending-club enterprises thrived. The established town centre traders were under threat again, having lost trade to Hanley, now they were having to cede much of their business to those very people they had sought to represent, people they had re-housed for the improvement of the town. What irony! And these cheap-jacks were intimidatory for though they weren't aware of it at the time, it was the start of a new peril that would affect future trading fashions and styles forever. It was an unforeseen affront to the men who had controlled every aspect of council business and town management since 1910, a slap in the face to those who had themselves created the social policies that they were now forced to accede to and promulgate. By the instigating of their programme of slum clearance, they had endorsed their own commercial death warrant.

The minutes of Burslem Chamber of Trade meeting of October 1934 say much in the absence of detail, but speaks volumes in the vitriol of its reporting. Witnesses to it have certified that a long debate took place in which loud anger, jealousy expressed and personal resentment was exchanged over the single topic on its agenda. Rarely had a trader's meeting been so well attended that its business ran well over the allotted time preventing the customary pint and pie supper in the room of the inn set aside for refreshments.

For some time, ever since the slum clearances had begun to take effect on trading, the town shopkeepers had watched helplessly as their custom sifted away into other districts. This was bad. But what stirred them into action now was the private-house businesses which were deliberately encroaching upon their staple commodities such as clothing, ironmongery and many other lines which were considered to have been the exclusive items for sales in the town centres. The popular name the estate shopkeepers called their businesses was 'general stores', but the derogatory term for these estate outlets was, 'parlour shops'; it was a name that was to find itself enshrined in parliamentary legislation. These 'commercial houses' were places where locals and residents could acquire anything they would reasonably want without travelling the journey into the town. The goods were cheaper - so what if they were only imitative and lacked the quality of the real objects! - the supply satisfied the demand and the parlour shops thrived.

The Staffordshire Sentinel reported upon Burslem trader's meeting as speaker after speaker complained of the rackets of the parlour shop traders as the air in the near airless room in the Leopard Hotel filled with accusation.

"It places the trader in an unfair position", commented W.E. Cropper, the president. *"It follows that, if an individual can sell without having overhead expenses, he is capable of unfairly cutting prices."*

The Sentinel's correspondent reported that, at *'a number of houses on the Burslem Park Estate it was possible to buy anything from a pair of socks to a hat at any time of the day or night. Even on Sundays.'*

What was happening in Burslem had suddenly become a situation that affected most of the industrial towns in the Midlands and the North West as their Chambers of Commerce grouped together to fight the problems of 'unfair trading' as they saw it and termed it. The Burslem Chamber of Trade overnight found itself in the forefront of the leading national lobbying committee organised to challenge the rackets of the side street shopkeeper, and it introduced its own local plans to combat it. The Burslem chamber set up a disciplinary register of admittance of traders from which it promulgated extremely stringent rules. The first three rules were utterly and aggressively terse:

1. **Trading from private houses shall be illegal.**
2. **A licensing clause shall be introduced and implemented by the Licensing Committee.**
3. **No new parlour shop shall be allowed unless a need is proved to the Licensing Authority, and only then if those traders are suffering hardship due to their clearance schemes.**

These plans and complaints were gathered from across the country and Parliament was petitioned resulting in a formal legislative control of rates and taxes administered under the Sale of Goods Act to be effected by the local authorities. But the damage had already been done with the exodus of the people from the town centres. Burslem Chamber of Trade was extremely anxious and did what it could to contain its traditional custom. It organised events such as 'shopping weeks' where prices were slashed and concessions were given on the purchase of goods from neighbouring shops. Sales weeks abounded throughout the year with the introduction of special seasonal sales to encourage the customers back. The Chamber made formal applications to the bus companies to bring shoppers in from the council estates once or twice a week and urged the council to improve road communication. No longer could the town centre traders sit back and enjoy the custom of a captured clientele on its doorstep; those shoppers had to be recaptured and preserved for the sake of the trader's own self-preservation. Burslem Chamber of Trade even sent a delegation to several of the consolidating departmental stores such as Marks and Spencer and the Hanley companies of Bratt and Dykes and Messrs Huntbach, but were only successful in bringing in a branch of Woolworth which they succeeded in doing by the gratuity of the Bellingham family who donated a piece of land on which stood two of their old shops in St John's Square to be held by Woolworth rent free for ninety-nine years. Coinciding with all this commercial ferment, the Burslem Wholesale Co-operative Society opened its new emporium at the portals of Burslem's main shopping centre. The Chamber of Trade didn't know which way to turn as the giant store cast a huge shadow along Queen Street.

The Co-operative Trading Association was formed in Brighton in 1827 by Dr William King, a local reformer for working-men's rights, which advocated the principles of self-help, the realisation of common capital and the protection of mutual insurance. It designated the subscription of a small amount of a man's weekly wage in order to raise sufficient funds to open a general store in which manufactured and garden-grown goods would be offered for sale in order to fund its contributors at a cheap rate. In these times of worker's reliance on commodities owned by the employers, and shops and stores that were in the main stocked and doled-out by the factory owner, worker's co-operation began to thrive. By 1831 there were some 300 co-operative societies in the land, the greatest number of which were established in the textile towns surrounding Manchester where the North West of England United Cooperative Company was founded, an organisation based largely on the persuasions and leadership of Robert Owen who advocated a mutual exchange of goods and jobs in work exchange bazaars.

In 1844, a group of textile workers in Rochdale, Lancashire, set up a business in a warehouse in Toad Lane where they manufactured and sold provisions and clothing. Its immediate success was judged by the customer who was given an accumulating dividend on each item bought. This was achieved by the seller depositing the difference between the retail and wholesale price back into the business to be used as shared profits, part of which was paid out as customer dividend. By 1882, the Rochdale Pioneers, as they were known, had achieved a share capital of eighty-thousand pounds sterling and listed over 5,000 members. In 1872, the newly named Cooperative Wholesale Society had almost half a million members and had diversified into dealing in a variety of goods which started out from Crumpsall near Manchester where a biscuit factory was opened. A dairy was opened in Ireland in 1889; a bacon depot in Denmark in 1900, and a even a tea plantation was established in Ceylon.

Because of its association with the working classes, the CWS started its own political party in 1917 under the title of the Cooperative Party. But its aims were so closely allied to the principles and rules of the Labour Party that it very quickly became an affiliated consort deciding to remain in retail where it would continue producing, **'a better class of goods - of our own brand - with an acknowledged sign of superiority.'** Nevertheless, the Coop Party retains its singularity to this day.

James Colclough of Burslem was an early pioneer of trading cooperation. He was a potter at the Soho Pottery in Waterloo Road when, in 1895, he encouraged a group of his fellow workers to put a small portion of their wages aside in order to share out the collected results in needy times for the purchase of provisions in bulk. Buying commodities wholesale soon resulted in a surplus of cash which was shared-out as a mutual dividend. Realising the potential, Colclough made an approach to the Manchester CWS who sent their representative, E L Griffiths, to Burslem to organise a committee of men to administer a cooperative. In 1901, a suitable premises was found at the top of Newcastle Street where the Burslem Industrial Co-operative Society opened its registered office, below which was its first shop, selling bread! A year later the society boasted a membership of 390 with a sales turnover of £3,791.00 returning to the society members a dividend of tenpence halfpenny in the pound. The most important Co-op contributor during these early years was Fred Haywood who saw his own opportunities arising after the resignation of James Colclough who felt that he had the right to become automatic president.

Frederick Haywood was born in Burslem in 1876. Having received an elementary education he entered the pottery industry where he remained as a labourer until he was twenty-two when his interest in the cooperative movement brought him into contact with the Colclough brothers and the original society members, in particular James Stanway, a pottery manager with Doulton and Co. Haywood firstly became the society's part-time secretary in 1902 receiving a small gratuity for his services, and in 1904 he took the job full time for a pittance of 35/- a week, half what he could earn as a potter. But Haywood, unlike others, could see that success of the coop was self-evident by virtue of its North-West prototype - the promise of richer prizes off-set the hardship of a poor salary for the time being. A year later, Stanway and Haywood supervised the enlargement of the premises in Newcastle Street so that it became a wholesale shop as well as the central offices. Meanwhile branches were beginning to open throughout the Potteries and Wolstanton under the name of Burslem and District Co-operative Wholesale Society. There wasn't a commercial outlet or undertaking that the coop didn't venture into including a penny bank, dairies, music salons, shoe makers, clothiers, funeral directors; until 1910 when the largest bakery in the district was opened in Newport Lane to facilitate a regional distribution. The direction the society had progressed under Haywood and Stanway was pursued with a bold and ruthless development policy until, in just a few years there wasn't a commercial range or commodity the coop wasn't involved in, pushing their limits even further by becoming so much a part of people's day-to-day lives with door-to-door deliveries of coal, milk, bread, meat and confectionary in exchange for tokens. And even in the commission of a brass band and choral society for their employees' participation: the Society turned on mystical success. To be employed by the coop from school was to be given a job for life!

By 1914 membership in Burslem District stood at 9,181 with sales of £182,000. Sales in 1918, by the time WWI had ended, had leapt to half a million and with a membership of 17,000, it schemes indicated just how much Burslem folk had come to rely upon the coop during those troubled war years. In the two years after the war ended, in June 1920, sales figures had doubled to one million pounds with a membership reaching 25,000. And so it continued in its success. The highest of the society's membership reached 74,310 in 1958; the highest sales peaked at nearly five million pounds in 1968, and between 1953 and 1960 sales never fell below 4 million pounds per annum.

And so in 1932, the Burslem and District CWS opened the magnificent new emporium in Queen Street fitted with the most modern features such as an electrically operated lift between floors and a mechanical device which elevated furniture onto various levels and directed furniture into its main window display. 1934, as the depression eased slightly, a new Coop Federal Dairy opened at Sneyd Green alongside Holden Bridge with other depots throughout the city following. In the 1950's, during a period of low commercial enterprise, Burslem CWS ventured into building American-styled large multi-commodity stores, One of the first was Krazy Kuts in Hanley which undercut every supermarket then in business in the district. This brought in profit which required a tighter rein of financial security as the private companies fought to challenge their leadership; and it led, in May 1968, to Burslem's incorporation with the Leek and Moorlands Co-operative Society which was made contributory to a further series of amalgamations in 1970 when the whole became the North Midlands Co-operative Society Ltd as it competed head-to-head with other American inspired private superstores. In 1972 NORMID ONE opened its huge doors to customers at the out of town store in Hamil Road. The coop had survived at the expense of the private shopkeepers who, by the late 1970's, had almost given up the chase. But from then on, the coop's competitors became as fiercely ruthless as the Co-op had been to the small town centre private single-commodity private shops.

Fred Haywood, a good friend of Sydney Malkin and strong supporter of Federation, was made the city's second Lord Mayor in 1926 and was knighted for his services to the Co-operative Movement in 1931. He retired in 1935 and was sixty-eight when he died.

One troublesome matter for Burslem Chamber of Trade was the demolition of the old police station, the former house of the potter John Shrigley, which stood at the rear of the 'shambles' as the rear of the market hall was known. The council knocked down both buildings in 1936 leaving only the enclosed meat market and Norris's Brewery bottling plant standing. The new police station was built on another triangle of land at the bottom of Hamil Road which had for many years been owned by Pat Collins, a fairground proprietor, who travelled the district with a popular fun-fair. Here today stands the present police station opened in 1937, much extended and modernised in recent times.

On the land vacated by Shrigley's house, the Chamber of Trade saw an opportunity to reintroduce residential housing into the town, and it begged the council's housing committee to build houses on the triangular site in Market Place. The Chamber's plans included building a block of rising flats of the style which were being erected in Birmingham on the vacated site to accommodate some sixty apartments, but the planning committee - now no longer the stronghold of shopkeeper conservatism - could not agree on the principle, and so they rejected the application on grounds that the site had never been designed for housing purposes, it being traditionally the town's civic amenities centre. Once more the irony of a civic centre without civic amenities was resurrected - two vacant town halls - no mind that the triangle had once been occupied by a line of terraced cottages accompanied by the popular Bluebell Inn and the Turk's Head tavern, a domestic centre ever before it was designed as a civic centre.

The whole issue of the decline of town centre trading had become a matter serious enough to unite the city, as the separate chambers of trade came together to formulate a campaign to replace old houses with new, and for the practice of building houses back onto slum clearance sites. A united and strong deputation was organised. And the Lord Mayor, Alderman John Arthur Dale, and the Town Clerk, Mr E.B. Sharpley, carried the trader's petition to parliament where they presented it to the three local MPs. None of this of course had any effect in Burslem's specific case, for the council, weighing the interest of local housing needs against the preservation of town shopping, were compelled by the law they had themselves encouraged and now had to impose, to continue with its slum clearance and rehousing policies. New estates were initiated at Ball Green and Mill Hill, then Norton and Smallthorne, and later Chell and the Burslem Grange. Although sited in pleasant pastures, these new developments were built on cheap land beneath which were warrens of coal mining tunnels.

The Second World War, 1939-1945, effectively ended the civil war of commerce as everyone buckled down under food, fuel and clothing rationing which continued in the main until 1948, coinciding with the council's second major tranche of slum clearance which saw the demolition of old property in Longport, Middleport and Brownhills. Immediately after the war, through the continuing restrictions of goods caused by rationing, the town centre shops had re-established control and were continued to be aided by legislation: by the levying of disciplined rates, by intrinsic specialisation, and by health and safety restrictions which were now becoming more stringently applied to the retailer. In Burslem there were a selection of good quality shops and a diversification that temporarily retained the local shopper who then had little money to spend and was particular on what to spend it in a catchment that lured people from Tunstall and Smallthorne.

In the 1950s extensions to the George Hotel placed it, along with the Leopard Hotel, in a town which was among the top five visited market towns in Staffordshire. James Norris (Burslem) Ltd was an extremely versatile and high quality wine and spirit merchants, while Alcock's and Bew's in 1955 advertised the sale of television receivers, record-player and records along with furniture, wirelesses and cycles to an increasingly diversified public whose newly implemented employment legislation - the 1946 Factories Act - ensured a proper wage for a 44-48 hour week.

Looking back once again to the time of the Federation of the Potteries towns in 1910, Burslem Chamber of Trade reformed itself that year and adopted the title, Burslem Traders' Association. Its membership then numbered 78. It reached its all-time high of 140 members in 1939 and by the time of the Coronation of Queen Elizabeth II, the total membership was a reasonable 106 serving a population of some 40,000. But, as the 1960s drew near, membership began to recede as commercial trading patterns turned towards youth fashion capturing a distinctly new and specialised source of spending power.

Better communications and the popularity and availability of the motor car improved and encouraged access into the town centres and to the doorstep of the large multi-range stores. By 1964 Hanley had become the magnet for the new conception of chain stores and High Street departments as they were called. Stoke, Longton and Burslem attempted to keep up with the draw but the market place had now become an arena of competition the like of which had never before been seen outside the USA. And the traditional grocery shops of food excellence and variety, gave way to dividend shops and stamp and catalogue buying. Pioneering super-markets such as local stores Swettenhams, Victor Value, Cee'N'Cee, and Taylors, in direct competition with the Co-ops, took over the vacuums left by the parlour shops which were gradually returned to housing. And once again the single commodity town centre shops were adversely affected. Now the council played its joker card on Burslem's hand. Councillors decided, with naive witlessness and shortsightedness, that as the demise of the six town centres continued, it presumed that a lineal collection of towns such as Stoke on Trent geographically was, the entire district would be better served by one central shopping centre.

It was in 1964 that the third and final tranche of housing slum clearance was commenced, and it affected the Mother Town's commercial position seriously. During the next five years until 1970, more than 10,000 people were uprooted from the St John's and Middleport districts in a rush of land reclamation and environmental improvements the likes of which had never before been seen. The entire community of St John's was cleared and laid-out for car parking for visiting vehicles that never came. A row of shops was demolished in Queen Street, a location which saw also the bulldozing of four public houses with the loss of rows of miniature Georgian architecturally valuable buildings. Elsewhere in the town, the Elizabethan styled Red Lion Inn was not only pulled down but excavated from the earth in favour of a bleak brick box. The grand facade of the meat market and town centre Victorian brewery had already crashed in rubble. And, during the same period, hundreds of distinctive pottery bottle ovens were ploughed into the ground. In the place of these irreplaceable monuments, plain-box architecture was erected, alternatively the land, too much land, was left as a consequence bare and derelict. One hundred public houses were demolished in Burslem during the 1960s and what was once a two mile long main thoroughfare, Waterloo Road, filled from end to end with houses, factories, shops, schools and places of entertainment, was left like a gaping mouth of broken and missing teeth. A railway station, public baths, three cinemas, two theatres, six chapels, removed in the dust of black magic - like the people - all gone. Gone!

In the new Millennium the Mother Town of the Potteries strives to compete for a place on the country's heritage trail. It still has exceptional examples of Georgian buildings and Victorian architecture and is managing to hold its own with the other towns as it comes to terms with the fact that its history remains its only selling point. But commercial trading has disappeared. Membership of the Burslem Traders' Association, the Chamber of Trade, stands at 12. It has no Freemasons' lodge nor does it have associations supporting other antediluvian or Catholic confederation. No Oddfellows, no Buffs. No guilds of retired classes of industry, no athletic clubs, no swimming groups, no choirs, no council. It holds none of the elements that raised it from the fabric of the civic structure which those Victorian proprietors handed over to the town's traders - all those local entrepreneurs who put their party politics aside to serve local government, believing that party politics had no place in the town halls - they needed not the rhetoric of party while the steam of individual enterprise blew out and prevailed - what they did for themselves they did for others and honestly believed that it was good for the citizens! Those Liberals and Tories had no reason to campaign under the banner of a political party; their's was their right to rule as employers and providers. That is until the Labour Party began to influence local elections by their committed adaptation of, and adherence to, the total unrepresentative system of forming an administration - he who passes the winning post first, controls all.

Between the two World Wars the Conservatives dominated national politics, even though throughout this period they consistently returned the least number of votes. The best example of this slanted voting system is demonstrated by the outcome of the 1922 election when the Conservatives were able to form a government with a substantial majority of seats and yet only polled 37% of all votes cast. In simple terms this meant that 63% of those who voted including a percentage of the population who were disqualified by reason of law, were entirely deprived of their preferred direct representation - a minority of elected Conservative members disproportionately held full control over the lives of its citizens. The labour party subsequently learned these lessons well, and from this morbid perception, Labour activists and politicians began to apply it to local government elections in a long term strategy to become the national government.

On travelling back to 1910, it is to be seen that the controlling party in the new Stoke on Trent Borough was made up of those Independents whose affiliations led them to act quietly in the interests of unseen, unpublicised political agendas. In the beginning the Independents were able to retain control by virtue of a voting system that allowed them two votes, one each for their residence and their business. By such gratuitous means the same men were able to influence politics in a number of towns. In 1910, in a country of 45 million, only 8 million had voting rights, and no women at all could vote. It wasn't until 1918 that voting rights were given to all men of the age of 21 and women of 30. Thus, from the end of WWI, proportion numbers of working class members began to increase; men who were made up of the artisan groups and unified commercial retailers such as the Cooperative Society - who were barred from membership of the official trader's associations - the ceramic unions, the miners, the railway workers and power groups. In the national elections of 1910, Labour had won 42 seats in parliament even though the Party had only been formed ten years previously. By 1918 it had secured 22% of the country's votes with 63 seats in the Commons. Four years later it would become the official opposition party.

A man for his times was Enoch Edwards who came to live in Burslem in 1875 when, at the age of twenty-three, he was appointed secretary of North Staffordshire Miners' Association. Born at nearby Talke, Edwards had worked in the pits since he was nine but his capabilities for manual work ended after an accident in 1873. He held executive positions in the Midland's region and in the National Miners' Federation. He was drawn to local interests and benevolence and was elected to the Burslem Council, prior to Federation, where he later became an alderman and town mayor. By political inclination Edwards was a Liberal and had earlier stood unsuccessfully as a Liberal candidate for Hanley. But, as his trade union the NMF was drawn into the Labour fold, Edwards stood as a Lib-Lab for Hanley and was elected MP in 1905. In 1910 he won again, this time as a Labour candidate, again for Hanley. But his home love was at Burslem where Edwards helped to organise the local Labour party which then had its core support in Tunstall. Here it rose hand in hand with the Methodists and the Coop Movement. He supervised the erection of the Miner's Hall at the junction of Moorland Road and Park Road in which he lived.

It was during the ill-fated miner's strike of 1912 that Edwards' health gave way. The memorial on his gravestone in Burslem cemetery records that he died, **"shortly after the calamitous miners' strike of 1912 which accelerated his death"**. It is tempting to consider that the many public commitments of this dedicated man hastened his death rather than the ill-advised fractured withdrawal of labour which he had personally advocated. Those early trades unionists and working-class politicians, granted one iota of power, often sought to indulge themselves - perhaps in self-preservation - perhaps because they were thrust forward by others less ambitious or too lazy to play their part in many affiliations that were on offer. At the time of his death, Enoch Edwards held three union presidencies, he was a Member of Parliament, a borough councillor, an alderman and secretary to at least two antediluvian associations and member of others. This was an excess that many other Stoke on Trent men and women of politics emulated until the slow process of Labour's Electoral College system effectively ended plurality in 1992.

Edwards encouraged others to pursue high position in the interest of the working classes, in particular he nurtured his union colleague Samuel Finney who came from the same village and had worked in the same pit as Edwards. Finney succeeded his mentor as President of North Staffs Miners' Association in 1888, and in the position of Secretary of the Midlands Miners' Federation in 1912. Closely following in Edwards footsteps, Finney stood for his vacated seat as a Labour candidate for Hanley in 1912. He lost but gained a seat for Labour in the North West Division of Staffordshire which, in 1916, was centred on Burslem and included Tunstall.

The 1918 boundary adjustments caused new elections to be held and Finney became the first Labour MP for the new constituency of Burslem Division, which again included Tunstall. In the general election of 1922, Sam Finney stood down at the age of 65 and moved to retire from public life to Wales where he died in 1935. Finney was succeeded by a thirty year old Scotsman, Andrew Maclaren who won the seat by the small margin of 205, although, a year later in 1923, he lost the seat to the Liberal candidate, William Edward Robinson, by an even smaller majority of 63. Robinson's tenure was short-lived and he resigned his seat after only 12 months because of ill-health enabling Maclaren to return to parliament in a 1924 by-election with an improved majority of 606 against the Liberal candidate.

Maclaren was a member of the International Labour Party and represented Burslem until 1931 when the General Election was contested after the sterling and revenue crisis brought about by the on-going rippling effects of the Wall Street crash and subsequent international trade depression, which came to a head in August that year. Prime Minister, Ramsey MacDonald, dissolved the first Labour government and formed the National Government in which he was to continue as Prime Minister heading an administration mainly comprised of Conservative ministers. MacDonald was expelled from the Labour Party, and in the October election of 1931 Labour returned only 52 members - none were from the constituencies of Stoke on Trent. The Potteries, like many of the northern working class districts, had turned their back on Labour, albeit temporarily. Maclaren lost his seat to the local Liberal candidate, William Allen. In 1935 Maclaren was back again and retained the seat for Burslem throughout the years of WWII, even though he resigned in 1943 to become an Independent member in a demonstrated show of resentment over Labour's welfare programme. Maclaren was very likely, and probably always had been, a Liberal at heart, though he was undoubtedly a hard-working constituency MP and was well liked. He left the district in 1945 and died in 1975 at the good age of eighty-two. As an MP he had also held the position of City councillor.

In the heady days of the landslide Labour Government after WWII, the Stoke on Trent Labour Party became thoroughly organised in the re-arrangement of the three constituencies, now called Stoke North, Central and South. Labour's active workers came from three main sources: the socialist intelligentsia based in and around Hanley: the ideological trade unionists: and by far in the greatest number by ordinary workers and their families who made up the rank and file of party activism.

With Maclaren now an Independent, Burslem and Tunstall Labour branches selected trade unionist A E Davies as its new parliamentary candidate who was duly elected and served until 1953. In that year, Burslem's Labour Party selected a woman from the North Staffordshire village of Milton; a long serving trades unionist and party member, Harriet Slater had trained to be a teacher. This choice reflected Labour's new preference for local people who had given ordinary time and extraordinary dedication to the party system and its rules. What's more, at branch level the Party was able to maintain local ideological control directing its MP to its own agendas. Married to a pottery worker and City councillor, Fred Slater, Harriet was the daughter of a pottery kiln fireman. She also sat as a City councillor and represented the Co-operative Party as its national organiser. Her obedience to the party line won her the privilege of becoming the Parliamentary Labour Party's first woman whip. She was duly honoured with a CBE for her services in public life.

By the 1960s, Stoke on Trent District Labour Party was dominated by groups of selective right wing clique members who orchestrated the principles of open recruitment to Labour Party membership by restricting it to personal selection and by invitation only; and, more often than not, only to friends and family members. Thus from this period it is easy to identify dynastical sequence in the chambers of local government in Stoke on Trent. John Forrester, a teacher at a local secondary education school, and a local councillor, was selected by Stoke North constituency party as its parliamentary candidate in 1966. Like Edwards and Finney before him, he simultaneously held the positions of Member of Parliament, councillor in the City Authority, secretary of the Constituency Labour Party, as well as trhe chairmanship of a number of representative committees - echoes of entrenchment - they say that 'none shall pass!'.

Forrester held the seat until he himself was rejected by a national change in party mood. Labour's embarrassing defeat in the General Election of 1983 under the leadership of prominent left wing theorist, Michael Foot, led to factionalism and a further lurch to the Left in many districts of high unemployment. It was at about this time that the Labour Party's Burslem Branch adopted a Marxist interpretation to the party's rules in a lateral alliance with extreme parties much like those in Lambeth and Liverpool. Burslem party nominated hard Left candidates to the council in order to oust what it saw as conservative-minded, non-assertive rightist councillors. Led by Burslem, during a period of left-wing radicalism, 1983 - 1992, the extreme left of Stoke North Constituency Labour Party, topped-up by additional factions of similar activists from Kidsgrove and Tunstall Labour parties, contrived to deselect John Forrester and replace him with the constituency's second women MP, Joan Walley.

This new faction were indifferent to which part of the country they recruited from, though it seemed fortuitous, though irrelevant, that Ms Walley had been born locally. Introduced during the catastrophic miner's strike of 1984/5, Joan Walley responded and fitted well into the Left's requirements - herself arriving as a left wing surcharged councillor from Lambeth. But, the failure of the miners to prevent pit closures; the ensuing anti-trades union laws; and locally the divorce of the hard Left Kidsgrove Labour branches from Stoke North to become part of a boundary reorganisation taking them into Staffordshire Moorlands, saw off any further inroads that the left could make. The council slunk back to its previous position of soft right, and Burslem electorate was again marginalised.

National local government elections since 1918 mirrored the growth from weakness to strength of the Labour Party in Stoke on Trent. The results of the 1919 borough elections in the Potteries show that no officially organised party member secured a seat in Burslem. All elected candidates were returned as Independent and those who declared themselves openly political referred in their description to their affiliations as well as their occupation or union: ie. Labour/NUR, Labour/Potter, Labour/Co-op. Labour council members only became distinctive by party association in 1931 after the Judas betrayal of national leader, Ramsay MacDonald. Conservative and Liberal Independents were always difficult to dislodge, and pointedly it wasn't until 1925 - fifteen years after Federation - that the councillors allowed Labour's first Mayor to be elected, Burslem councillor Sir Fred Haywood, who served to the fealty of Labour/Co-op. The demise of the Liberal Party had a great effect on those council members who were formerly able to describe themselves as Liberal: they had no name and they had to look elsewhere for affiliation; some hid in the Tory ranks; the majority became Labour party members.

By the middle of the 1930's, the increase of Labour council members was so rapid that it could be seen that control was very quickly going to pass into the hands of men and women who had traditionally been the servants to the masters. Now the masters had to consider their long-term position as councillors, lodged as they were in a city where candidates had become reliant upon shopfloor votes. It is from these times that the council started to be run by political preference. Although members now came from the ovens of the potbanks, the footplates of steam locomotives and the dark pits of the collieries, other councillors, standing under the banner of Labour, held positions of supervision and ownership in their occupations; schoolteachers, businessmen, and particularly publicans and shopkeepers: men needing to retain their community positions. Many traditional conservatively pared men and women simply joined the growing local Labour Party, and by these diversions and deviations the heart of the council remained a middle-class engine just as it was designed to be, driven by those who could afford the time to attend meetings during the day and those unqualified people who sought unearned recognition among their peers.

There is evidence at the end of the 20th century that in the near future local government administration will radically change by the devolution of responsibility and regionalisation. But whether it will become more open and accessible for the average British citizen who is currently learning to adjust in a multi-racial and ethnic society, time only will tell. And politics will continue to respond to the pull and sway of men and women who practice to monitor opportunity, for already it can be seen that the traders and their associations have staked their claim in any forthcoming regime by the devices of city-centre group management and commercial partnerships with the local authorities.

In all of this grand scheme it must be remembered that local government was designated in 1888 when powers were given to County Councils to manage their own roads, health asylums and local police. From this point in time travelling forwards, such a wealth of social and social security legislation has been implemented by elected representatives to whom the trust of the people has been delegated. So much so that Britain has become the most governed country in the world by a variety of statutory instruments that were devised to suit the times, even without the benefit of a single comprehensive penal code. And in massive quantity these enactments owe their roots to local needs tuned by, their adjustment and their amendment. As much money, if not more, is collected from the trader and business manager than all that emanating from ordinary household tax, enabling business to still have the deciding say on how the collections are spent in an arena where local planning legislation, as of right, favours the applicant.

Towns as traditional trading centres have severely declined throughout the country because of better road communications, the common availability of personal transport, the placement of multi-commodity centralised shopping, all of which has led to exclusive shopkeeper to shopper personal one-to-one shopping centres. It is impossible to see alternatives such as those the parlour shops created in the 1920's and 30's. And yet it was within the triangle of trading - manufacturer, retailer, purchaser - that the citizen's parlour shops were the first to begin the erosion of traditional town centre shopping. The ground of the commercial triangle is today still being held tenuously by the three local participants - the council, the trader and developer, and the citizen. And each relies on the others to maintain a wobbly balance.

But it is already obvious that, unlike the other two, the traders on their side of the triangle are prepared to move the playing fields to stay in control. As before, they will not be easily dislodged from their power bases.

Chapter Five

MURDER AND MARTYRDOM

> *'The churchyard contains about two acres... Among the numerous tombs and monuments in the churchyard, none has claim to especial notice, either for style, legend, or the names recorded...'*

(Ward pg 223)

All about the Mother Town lie un-marked graves of families and individuals, supine and in dumb testimony to the town's growth. Forgotten paupers lie restless beneath the clay at Chell and at Greenhead, nothing now is left of them but discarded piles of earth and dust and chalky bone: nor even their poverty is remembered.

The landscaped Grange hides fossils of unknown Plague victims mouldering in ancient fecula. In overgrown gardens, long over-earthed and claimed by piles of other musty things, lie dead families, generation upon generation. Behind a wall at the top of the Sytch are the fallen headstones of the Alcock family; Samuel Alcock who built and owned the mighty Hill Top Works, is hidden among the wiry grasses and the dock and the poison ragwort fighting for possession with more poisonous litters of man in sleepless incumbency. Chapels that have become workplaces still have names of donors and benefactors chipped into cornerstones. Grey slate plaques fastened on the end of a row of terraced houses tell, in fading lists, of young warriors who died in twentieth century wars; young men who failed to return home. Ceramic street-names cracked; dried-up terra-cotta water fountains; dedication plates bearing fragments of words in praise of dead aldermen, councillors and committee members, proud that they merely lived longer than others in their times when death was more commonplace than birth. Death is everywhere. Those who could, those who would be, those who deserve it and those who didn't are all buried in the shadow of the church Christians and sinners dealt with alike. Here, in St John's two acres of resting soil, the everlasting bits - finger joints, fragments of cranium and teeth of famous potters, manufacturers, schoolteachers, labourers, doctors, shopkeepers, publicans, pimps and prostitutes; and all their wives and all their husbands, and all their children lie together in the community of the dead mingling with the pottery shards of their trades.

Most graves in St John's Cemetery are pitifully Spartan; simple and mere factual in their message - green slabs of lichen unadorned by religious trappings. That is, except for the one tasteful marble obelisk near the north entrance by the car park. This is the memorial to a murderer said to have been 'more sinned against than sinning'.

Down by the dustbin
I met a dog called Sid.
He said he didn't know me,
But I'm pretty sure he did.

(Nursery rhyme by Michael Rosen.)

William Marwood was born in Lincolnshire in 1820. On 1st April 1872 his name, without attracting the public's attention, entered the pages of Burslem's worst chronicles. And yet his notorious deed is no longer remembered by anyone. He never visited Burslem, thank God, but he killed a Burslem man and that event caused the greatest stir in Burslem's criminal history. A riddley-rhyme will suffice as a clue for the time being.

"If Pa killed Ma, who'd kill Pa?
Why, Marwood"

Friday 12th January 1872.

- The front west facing door of the town hall was secured by the un-hurried janitor inserting his heavy keys to employ a series of double-barrelled locks which enabled two polished brass knobs to swivel freely, marked to bar and impede the burglar from any felonious intent and to prevent the vandal from his wicked wrecking whim. Beneath the stone-faced canopy, three men stood away from the teeming rain, heads together, bowed in conspiratorial conversation. It mattered little to them that they were keeping their hansoms waiting, while horses kicked at cobblestones impatiently, as bowler-hatted cabbies sat above their traces, heads bent, with muffled shoulders hiding their faces darkly; still as shining stone like gargoyles poised to swoop from the roof escutcheons of night-clad churches.

"I bid ye goodnight then gentlemen. And, I hope the evening went well for ye." The three who stood together each nodded their assent simultaneously as the tallest, the speaker, continued before the others could vocally respond, moving sideways to greet the approaching key-keeper.

"Ver' good, ver' good Nathe. Couldn't have been better for a full house. Well done lad. See ye next week."

"Right! Goodnight then gen'lemen."

"Goodnight Nathe." the others replied.

The caretaker moved away, hunched against the driving rain, pulling his overcoat tighter into his neck. Holding on stiffly to his bowler hat, the old man slowly swerved in and out of traffic on the still busy road, deftly avoiding the straining heads of two horses pulling a people-filled trolley clanging along the street.

"Well done lad, *lad indeed!*" he muttered to himself, irritated by the tall man's reference to Nathan Faulkner's social rank and without mind for the respect of the age of this septuagenarian public servant. He hobbled passed a group of rain-soaked revellers as he pushed into the passage of the Leopard; there he was greeted by his friend, octogenarian Albert Goose, who at once handed him a freshly pulled pint of porter. Here they conversed at once, as though resuming a conversation began by apprentice and master many years past: Albert, coughing phlegmy curses through his pipe about his silicosis, and Nathe cursing the impotence of his game left leg, ruined all those years ago by a fall of coal in the Sneyd Pit. It was 10pm on the dot and both men were creatures of habit.

Meanwhile, back across the road:

"Well, how d'yer think it went?" enquired the taller of the three sheltering under the portico of the huge civic building.

"Alright." replied a smaller and rotund man with rimless spectacles. But the third, a younger man, came back with more enthusiasm: a thin, also bespectacled, clerky-type: "Very well indeed. I do believe at last we are getting somewhere".

"It wasn't a large audience, but it was a new programme after all and everyone seemed to be able to grasp the noted symbols, which made a change", returned the first man, whose name was Josiah Wolstancroft Powell, "Very refreshing, very refreshing indeed", he continued, maintaining the lead in the continuity of the conversation.

"I thought Nichols did very well" commented the rotund man, "He's coming along smartly, him and his mate from Milton, that collier Jim Cope."

The rotund man steeped praise,

"We've got a good choir here Joss, thanks to you."

"No-oo", insisted Josiah Wolstancroft Powell with genuine modesty, "It's thanks to all of us and our perseverence with the new system. Now all the Potteries can sing to the heavens. Gives 'em something to do other than lining up at saloon bars morning noon and night."

J W Powell and his two friends in music and in civic administration, pottery owner George Howson, whom he had known all his life, and lawyer Arthur Ellis, son of the Reverend Philip Brabazon Ellis of St Paul's, were talking about the debut of their newest musical undertaking, the Staffordshire Potteries Choir and the continuing development of the Burslem tonic-sol-fa project which Powell had introduced here some twelve years past.

"I know we have won competitions; the last big one, the national at the Chrystal Palace, and that's ten years ago. Eh though, I think this choir's ready to take us forward as long as the orchestra's can get their act together and stop dominating the choirs. Bloody bands!"

"Aye", agreed Howson, "as long as the conductors can keep up with the choir masters and forget their daft insistence of music craft. Anyone would think we'd come to hear *them* instead of the singing".

"We'll get there gentlemen", said Powell, "Sight-reading is here to stay. Why, every school in the district is teaching it now. There lies the future of singing, and performance, mark my words. The future of Burslem music is bright"

The young Ellis turned his head away from the others and gazed along the Square as best he could through the rain, and fixed his sight at the top of Fountain Square where it sat directly across from St John's Square. There he saw three open pieces of land, cobblestoned open spaces surrounded by new buildings in architectural tribute to his times, bequeathed from the necessity of ancient toil. His youthful eye saw a changing Burslem, moving from out of the eclipse of its sister-town Hanley, into a golden pond born from the eddies of an isolated backwater. He saw, through his own eyes, what his two aging companions couldn't see; these men who, with his own father, had pioneered the Victorian decades in the consolidation of labour, a world of business and the fabrication of corporation. He compared *their* Burslem with the vision of his own new town, a place of leaders and leadership. *They* could remember a time without music and entertainment, and times when an unsettled tidal society existed without arbitrary communication between classes. A prominent demarcation line where on one side poverty stood in sad isolation, while the rich, on the other side, lived in greater, happier and healthier insularity. His two companions in their times had known riots in the streets, bloodshed and blood-letting. Now the children of those same townsfolk lived together under the conciliatory subjugation of the industry which directed all their lives. The young Ellis walked a few steps into the un-abating rain. And, nodding, he endorsed the comments on music of his two associates.

This self-congratulatory conversation continued for a further few minutes under the stone umbrella attached to the building in which the concert had been held during the earlier hours. The magnificent Italian carved slabs of Hopton stone that climbed in sheerness upwards to greet the skies, were supported in their endurance by Corinthian columns of diverse Ionic and Doric fashions gathering to its assembly at the summit of its tower, shaped like a vase, an appropriate structure which, in its turn, supported eight carved stone sea gods holding on their backs a four-faced Roman numbered clock. And at the very top of all of this architectural coordination, stood the life-size gilded winged angel of victory, of civic pride and endeavour, holding aloft a halo of laurel leaves - the greatest tribute to its Burslem benefactors.

Inside the dark building the concert room lay quietly, hugging its silent echoes to its cubed bosom. It had been designed as a ballroom with a sprung floor and with bouffant glass festoons cascading in the shimmering glow of the latest ceramic gaslight. Alabaster angels were suspended from the walls overlooking the luxurious arena where faery myths dance among the plaques of the Burslem coat of arms. Here enamelled shields adorned the mouldings of the ceiling and high arched railing spaces. At the east end of the room a stage had been erected on which many concert performers had come to deliver their programmes and share their talents. Behind the wooden stage tiering was a giant heraldic painting looking down upon proceedings. The whole of this effectual grandeur and its rich embellishments were deceptively and modestly concealed from outside prying and impertinent eyes by the doors that only admitted giants - doors three inches thick secured with solid brass plates and locks; for this was a citadel to the rich, to be viewed only by the notable and the important of the town's inhabitants; its administrators and aldermen. To the majority the ballroom was a forbidden place, a town within a town wherein the poor were never welcomed: no idiot would tune his danse-macabre here, no cripple would limp upon its polished floor, for this island was moated by forty-eight winding stone stairs that only the able-bodied could possibly negotiate. Only the fit and straight were permitted its use.

And at the top of this formidable and prohibitive staircase, that which climbed serpentinely from the lobby, weighed with cast-iron balustrades and mahogany hand grips, was the mayor's balcony on to which, dignity stepped from the grande ballroom to command everyone and everything below it. And below all of this grandeur of majesty, in a different space and time, lay the workings of offices and the trappings of storerooms, committee rooms and council chambers;

where clerks worked from eight 'til six each day. And these civic workings were themselves styled above the engine rooms through which roamed colon-like tunnels of prison cells and damp and dank passages, around coal boilers and bunkers, weaving, unseen from all righteous eyes, to and fro along tunnels to connect the police superintendent's house nearby. The whole was a pod, a civic cocoon, an organised anthill fixed by compartments through which all walks of life in the town could pass, just as long as it kept to its allocated areas.

Powell was the master of all this; he was the town-clerk as well as clerk to the governors of the Haywood Hospital Charity Trust; secretary to the Star Mutual Building Society, administrative respondent to the Staffordshire Advertiser and many other civic associated responsibilities. But his principal interest lay in the development of choral music in Burslem and the Potteries. That is where his heart sang most in tune and its loudest. Young Ellis was concordant with these passions. This was his rightful inheritance.

Powell shouted for his hansom, and with a snicker, the patient horse shook the rain from its velvet flanks at the touch of its driver whip and elegantly drew up alongside the stone canopy.

"Now then gentlemen", he reminded them, hinting by the expression in his voice of the consequences, "do *not* forget. Next week we will perform our final revisions, and, from the commencement of the following Monday, we will ride the Walkurie into the tumult and among the storms of the greatest test, the ultimate examination. We *shall* have success."

The two associates agreed heartily as the music master disappeared into the black cabinet, and with a loud snort of disrespectful approval, the shining horse clattered away towards Newcastle Street heading for the dip and the climb up to the tree-lined avenues of Porthill leaving the others in a thin cloud of its body-steam awaiting their own transport.

As the cab passed the top of St John's Square and Fountain Square, its incumbent was suddenly thrown forward as the gallant mare reared and bucked, steadied and brought to a standstill by the technical craft of an angry driver.

"Gerrite-ov-it yer silly bugger! D'yer want ter get y'erself killt! Yer silly sod. Bugger yersen off yer drunken sod!"

And, as the cabbie's whip brought the event under control he leaned back to calmly address his eminent passenger.

"I'm very sorry your worship. Some daft youth is trying ter gerr 'imsen killt. 'E walked straight in front of the 'oss 'e did. Its th' trouble wi town these days. Drunks ever where, ever where there's drunks".

The horse settled. Powell looked towards the Fountain Square and saw the inebriant culprit half running, half stumbling into Liverpool Road, apparently aiming his contrarious body to the illuminated doorway of the White Hart Music Hall. Powell at first thought the man derelict but saw that he couldn't be if one could afford a bright suit of a good cut, carrying a cane stick and a top hat which sat awry on the crown of his head. He had, according to the cabbie's repetitive journey report to the tired Powell, fled across the road as though the very Devil was in pursuit, causing him to look neither left nor right, straight into the path of the accelerating horse.

"The silly sod! The silly bugger! This is what Burslem's become - a place for drunks and thieves! What a terrible place!" The cabbie railed throughout the cab's traverse through Longport and up Porthill Bank.

The picture of the lurching man disappearing inside the public house was redrawn in J W Powell's mind's eye by the driver's mutterings as he attempted to allow his own thoughts to race ahead to a crackling fire and a bowl of Mrs Powell's hot soup before his bed...

...MINUTES LATER...

...The back room was dark. On a wall that backed into the yard of Wood's potbank, at the far end of the room, a wide stage had been set two or three feet above the floor. The bar was sited at a spittoon's level beside the stage causing the audience to look up at the performers and down upon the activities of the bar staff. Tobacco smoke hung densely in a heavy and wide pall, hanging above the puddles of fancy-dressed hall-fanatics that swilled around tables in mis-matched couplings. There were no windows visible, just black cloths that hung in odd wall spaces hinting as covers to hide some dusty jalousie, thereby preventing the interference and invasion of street light, the moon and other curious and prying eyes. What artificial light that struggled to take hold came across the room from the pallid stage footlights and wall lanterns lit by flickering batwing gas-pipes from behind the bar; and in the unlit empty spaces, the gloam was punctuated by the drawing upon of smoking pipes, cigars and paper-wrapped whiffs. For the inhabitants of this claustrophobic confusion, two young men drew drinks and three pretty girls passed them around the tables in trays of tankards and glasses. There was a combined smell of turpentine, tobacco and sweet face powder, all of which minglings from time to time was overwhelmed by wafts of body sweat and the putrid aroma of wet dirty clothing drying from a heat generated by unwashed bodies.

On the stage stood a man in a purple jacket, his grease-painted face leered over a flounce shirt and a huge polka-dot bow tie. He wore baggy trousers spun in the MacDonald tartan the bottoms of which trailed over two odd shoes, one black and one brown. In his arms the clown held a forlorn bundle of clothes which were surmounted by a fire-clay head which was painted with mobile lecherous eyes attached to sockets in its brow over a hinged jaw that flapped mechanically when the clown spoke for it. A sidelong leer was fixed in the eyes of the dummy and its mouth drooled in deadly lust. To this baggage, Norman (The Prince of Pals) Copnall, was crooning a duet with his stuffed protégé; a London Music Hall song:

> *He's a dear old pal of mine,*
> *He helped me when I was down,*
> *Lent me his aid willingly*
> *With a smile, not a frown.*
> *And if the day should come,*
> *And my lucky star should shine,*
> *I shall always be most happy to say,*
> *He's a dear old pal of mine.*

Most of the audience were totally unmoved except for a small group of the 'Prince of Pal's' followers who, with chorused uniformity, shouted enthusiastic applause as they joined in the second verse. With two swift bows the clown walked sullenly out of sight, dragging his now forlorn pal behind him. Two minutes later, 'The

Prince' was at his mates' table effing and blinding along with his companions, mouthing fake thanks to a dummied audience who were offering, in their turn, no praise whatsoever in expressions of blank appreciation. Amid crude hilarity, the 'Prince' was once again among friends - his pals. On the stage his place had been taken by Arthur Durber, the emcee, the innkeeper.

"Ladies and gen'lemen. Before our next artist - or should I say artistes - for these are the little gals you have all been waiting for," to which salivating nod and wink a number of men in the dark pit interrupted him and chanted -

"Bring 'em on, wheel 'em in Arthur", as their female consorts grunted with insipid coyness while others squealed with uninspired encouragement -

"Now then, now then, if you don't mind. Decorum please, (Oooooh, 'ark at 'im, 'E's swallered a dickshernry!) let's have the best of attention if you don't mind, ('we don't mind Arthur') for the finest and prettiest ladies in town tonight - and that includes those lazy tarts and farts across at Hall's Theatre - (much laughter) Yes, we have for your honourable dissertation the famous French Tableau d'amour. Gen'lemen, you won't be going home cack-handed tonight, that I'll warrant and wager." (More laughter).

"Before our tremulous tableau takes to the stage, I would like to remind you that next week we shall be bringing to Burslem that most famous contortionist act, Madame Ferenola and her troop of inside-out girls. See the fire-eater and witness with awe the extinguishment of the eternal flame. Where it goes is a mystery which will be revealed to you next Saturday in the only receptacle capable of accommodating this fantastic event".

With a flourish of his arm, sleeved with green banker's cuffs, Arthur Durber bowed deeply to his house-guests and departed the stage. The gas was turned down leaving the room with even less light, while the mournful tinking of an off-stage piano resonated parlour music.

Amid the dark the groups nearest the stage sitting on the front forms moved closer to each other. Furtive meanderings began, real or imagined, an imperceptive sway, things were happening, but just out of sight. Furniture was being arranged in unobtrusive preference; improved adjustments, while, at the back, drunken men lazed on the side-pumps dreaming drunken dreams and flinching in sleepless nightmares. Among these was a heavy man of angular proportions and an aggressive demeanour. His body was emerging from an all-day session on strong gin, his eyes glazed and bloodshot and startled as though he had just wakened for the very first time; and, finding himself in a music hall, he was shocked that he ha that this was his fate. Here was William Jones. Two years earlier he had been a manager of Ravensdale Iron Works, a good job from which he had been dismissed on account of his habitual drunkenness. Why Jones, a man of previous good character had turned to drink, no one knew, what's more, in these parts no one cared. It had been said that he had been briefly married but his wife had left him for another man, but there is no proof of this for Billy kept his private life to himself, and the woman had either left the district or had, er - well - disappeared! A brief spell as the licencee of a back street pub in Shelton saw him reach into the fearsome depths of alcoholism. He had lost his job as a publican and skulked into the criminal underworld and beerhouses of Burslem. The Mother Town had accepted him wholeheartedly into the pits of crime within her bosom. Here, in Burslem's backstreet underworld he was among pals, of a sort.

Bill's head rolled in a stupefied self-interested world of drink. He had to remain awake, aware now of his surroundings; to be in control in the event of a revolt of those he had tamed to his rule. In recent months he had fought the best and, in the town of the wicked, he had become the most wicked and therefore he was the strongest. At his arm a woman lolled uncomfortably in an undignified semi-coma. It was difficult to judge her age for she had the delicate look of a discarded angel, but her brown hair was matted with unspecified greasy ingredients and spread untidily about a wan, heart-shaped, rouged face. Her head drooped forward into her neck and a glisten of spittle dropped from the smear of a badly painted mouth. Her clothes were shabby and dark, and on the pump beside her lay a discarded straw bonnet and a shawl. She was as old as the life she led, clinging on to the times she knew best and to the men, any man, who would have her. Her two children, separated from her at birth, had known no grandmother for she had died under the wheels of a shraff cart, crushed into the flinty cobbles of a back-lane; herself a waif, not knowing her own mother who had been dispatched long ago to the Australian prisons for stealing a few coins from a gentleman client. Three generations of maidens with maiden callings, to whom no man would betroth their name in lawful bonding - these women who captured, in succession, their mothers' illegitimacy - the atrocious dowry of the ill-reared progeny. The vulnerability of Elsie Watts had attracted William Jones, she lived under the caprice of his brutal whim, and therefore, his protection.

The door that serviced the toilet and the street outside suddenly flew open. Cold rain splashed in over the wooden step as inmates cursed the interloper. The piano-player stumbled through the notes of 'The Old House At Home' as the top-hatted figure of Fred Horry stumbled into the room. This young man of twenty-eight years adjusted his eyes to pick out a figure, a friend, an enemy; a place to sit. His light silk suit was soaked and his leathern shoes squelched as he made his way to the side pump where he fell-in at the side of Jones. Flinging his cane and hat on to the seat beside Elsie, he mumbled some imperceptible greeting, steam rising from his wet body. His face was mauled with anguish, creased by years of alcohol abuse and with sleeplessness.

"I said champagne! Girl! Girl! Bring my friend and me champagne. We will drink a toast he and I - no - two or three, and we'll drink it to the grand illusion of life. Life! And to the bitter-sweet flower of the vine whose fruit fulfills endeavour, perseverence and honesty. And thrift and all things decent and good. By God, this night shall be remembered forever. I have it writ, my good friend William, I have it etched upon the tributes of my own sweet memories and those of my father. Nor can it be ever erased, for tonight, my dear friend, tonight shall be blessed in Heaven and Hell together."

Horry's cultured accent and Shakespearian affectations boomed around the room but burdened nobody. William Jones stirred, but he only moved at the call for champagne. Now he observed the newcomer sullenly as the waiting-on girl ran to the business of serving the best of the bad drinks in the house.

"Fred? Freddy boy, you look wet - inside and outside. What's your business? What outing are you on tonight? A drink, a song and a whore no doubt. I know you Freddy my lad. So, what's it to be? What merriment or mischief are you about to call upon the Devil as well as your God?"

Elsie opened her red tired eyes to observe the squatter who was causing the undue raucous. Seeing that it was Fred Horry, she fell back to her terrible reverie, uninterested by the state of the newcomer. Fred Horry laid his head closer to Jones.

"Tonight my friend", he whispered, "tonight murder is to be done. I have searched the town from the George to the Mason's Arms; from the Leopard to the Swan, and back to the Queen's Head again. I have given them all fair warning that the angel of death is about. Tonight, many now living will die. They will die in the shower of silver bullets that rest in my pistol, waiting. In the rain of retribution and in the storm of anger, they will die". He paused and as he stared, he scrutinised the inscrutable face of William Jones. "My friend", he hissed, I hope you will not be one of those who dies tonight."

Jones drew away in order to focus his own eyes upon Horry's face. A stare of mutual fear and loathing filled the inter-communicating space.

"Show me your gun!", Jones demanded, and poor Fred Horry, reduced by the stare and the intimidating command, submitted and produced a shining single-shot pistol from his jacket. Jones took it and handled it with the finesse of knowledge and custom.

"A pistol eh! And what would you be wanting this for my young mate. This is no good, owd lad. No good unless you wanted it to kill someone and only kill 'em once. What's it to be, a dog or a man?"

"A man, William, a man. Or, maybe men".

"Oh", countered Jones mockingly, "More than one dog eh? Might be a team of men - a company of curs, eh?".

"Might be, William. Tomorrow you will know for sure when you will count them lying in the red purged gutters of Hell, that are the streets of Burslem!"

The rumour had reached Jones earlier in the day. Horry had just returned, that day, from a protracted tarry in the Hanley brothels, and had since been searching the town in a drunken state, wildly threatening all his friends and sundry persons that he had returned to settle the state of play with the miserable dogs who had been lying with his wife. Those so-called friends who, even while he was abroad entertaining them and squandering his father's finances on them in drink and impulsive hospitality, were, in their turn, repaying him by entertaining his fair and sweet wife in his absences - or so he thought. Behind his back he had heard their whispers, hints and innuendo - or so he thought he'd heard them. Had taken in all their insults, the secret and scarlet truths, tales, distortions and allegations that he alone and been debarred from knowing. His anguished mind informed him that he'd been cuckolded so many times, that she lied through her denials to his accusations. Tears and anger he had shed in pain. And he had apologised in remorse when he confronted his rarely sober mind, even though, at the same time, ever more gathering menace erupted in violence at his home. So much so, judged by the public reports of so many shocking confrontations, that the young wife could take no more, and in the end had fled with her three children to the home and succour of her father-in- law in Lincolnshire where she had been given protection from the man they both had once deeply loved. Here at last she found shelter from the deviations and destruction of Fred Horry's version of love.

"D'yer know how to use this pistol Freddy my friend?"

"Oh yes, indeed I do sir - I do indeed. I have purchased this gun from a specialist in Nottingham. And I have practised with it across the Grange fields. Twice this day I have struck a tree at ten paces, and, should it have been a man, then he would have lain dead these four hours past."

"And have you found your enemies, these 'four hours past'. In your searches about this foul town? Who now lies dead? Who remains still under the threat of Freddy's silver gun?"

Fred Horry retrieved the pistol from Jones' grasp and waved it wildly in the smoky air of the room.

"They know I am here", he cried, "Their time is nigh. The Devil himself is about tonight".

Not a soul present stirred, not an ear took notice of the drunken masher. Except Elsie who moved irritably, glanced morbidly at the wavering pistol and went to sleep again. The gas-light was turned down once again as the master of ceremonies climbed back onto the stage where the far corners were rendered even darker in the stygian gallery. A lace curtain had been lowered in front of the backdrop hiding a troupe of assembled lady performers.

"Gen'lemen. For your indulgence; for your innermost delight and discerning discretion;" - those who had come for the show grew instantly quiet in sensual anticipation - "you are about to witness the most delightful digression in town tonight. These ladies have travelled all the way from Paris - for these performances are banned from practice throughout the Empire - in Paris, where they have enacted their tableaux in every high house of acclaimed and established repute. This is no cheap show" he spat in distaste, "where men hide behind the doors of censorship. This show gen'lemen is all about purity that even the constabulary were fain to bar in this town of Christian reverence. Sirs, your perusal has been endorsed by the highest office in Burslem, that of the honourable town clerk. And so without further ado, I give you the most famous and splendiferous, Tableau d'amour la Francais!"

The piano struck up a rolling theme reminiscent of verdant vales and meadows in spring. Babbling brooks chattered quietly from the keys as the curtains rose to a tense hall of unified breathing. There was a short burst of clapping from the table where the Prince was entertaining his guests, but the rest in the room stayed quiet.

The stage lights had been dimmed and it was just possible for the audience to make out a group of wispy, pale figures at the rear of the stage. The people on the back pumps couldn't see much clearly, hence the earlier movement and adjustments of seating positions. Now, the ghost-like figures moved slowly among the flowing of silk drapes creating a feigned mist which was followed and emphasised by the bass notes that rumbled from the piano. There were a number of these transparent curtains which served only to diffuse, even more, what light there was so as to present an inert view of the tableau. This was the view restricted to the audience by the manipulative, collective thickness of the drapes; but, as each thin sheet was raised in its turn, the detail enacted upon the stage became clearer. Slowly, and seductively, the female figures were assembled to assume a pyramid position, and as each curtain was lifted the breathing of the audience became more audible; noisy inhalations followed by urgent shushes.

The stage itself was a cramped affair, but each movement of the bodies thereon prompted gasps from the men from whose numbers were heard the odd sacramental cry - or an introspective oath - a plea - oh God! Oh my Heavens! Six scantily dressed women could be made out, swaying vaguely through the gauze; feet shakily fixed on a cushion of white cloth. Above them, three others stood upon their shoulders, and two more above them, their legs apart in careless posit. At the very top a small white figure stood palely alone; SHE, the celebration at the apex of the polyhedron, becoming clearer as the curtains continued to lift singly. And then, as the last piece of flimsy lace dropped to the floor, the tableau was uncovered - Oh Glory! Oh consummation! In utter disorientation, the black house-curtain fell and it was all over in an instance. Men gasped aloud, for in that brief pinpoint of time they had glimpsed a revelation that supported all of their fantasies. Six women, their breasts hanging away from weightless robes; three others with white alabaster bellies in the firmness of stroke; and two with dark triangles, in a tangle of dewy and luxuriant shade; and at the apex, the virgin child, with breasts moulded to the smallness of a fairy: a virgin angel, a child-woman, a sister, a daughter that brought forth pride, urgent arousal, erotic hope, social endangerment. In this room all man's forbidden passion had been aroused, and for a few, sated. This is what they saw in the blink of an eye, oh dear Lord; *'I wot nought how the world is went'*.

Behind the black stage curtain there was a flurry of movement, jolly squeals, a curse or two from a feminine voice. The triumphant French pyramid had collapsed through the most basic of Anglo-Saxon fissures, while cheeky girls tumbled off the stage. The rumbling piano was stilled. The emcee was quick, like a hare, to jump back onto the stage where he immediately began to introduce the next turn, as if to smash the cup, before it spilt, and disperse the insistent mood of the men in the crowd.

"The Harmonious Dukes. Three young men from Fenton who will delight you in their rendition of songs from the London shows," Arthur Durber babbled, as he dashed breathlessly after the retreating models.

Amid this milieu, Elsie's snoring responded to a kick from Jones, as she caught her breath in a throttled cough and cursed him for waking her. Horry was fidgety. His body was rocking backwards and forwards like an imbecilic doll.

"I shall do with them all before the day is up. All those who took advantage of my dear wife, her vulnerability, her generosity and, AND - my friendship! Tonight will see my revenge upon the dogs. Those hounds that lay about my bedroom while my children slept, not dreaming of their mother's betrayal". Horry rambled on, muttering threats and curses.

"It takes two yer know," Jones interrupted his friend's meanderings, "There's no smoke wi'out the fire; that's my experience", he said bitterly. "And I shall never forget...for one day... that one day...". Jones's mind entered its own private thoughts, blackly reflecting in his clouding face. "That was betrayal! Only women know how to perpetrate it. That cowardly incision. Women", he derided, "are the curse of man. Mother, wife or sister. WIFE! Oh wicked wife!"

So frightening had Jones's demeanour become, like a sudden storm about to explode, that Horry broke-off his own frothy rambling to watch his companion's spiteful strain with some fear. The image behind Jones's eyes was far-off, not in this room, not in this town - a beast crouched, a cat watching a cat, watching an invisible prey.

The tragic Shakespearean litany took hold of Horry once again.

"You say my wife, my dear Jane has given herself? You say it is she I should dispatch and not those vile robbers who countenanced and lured her? To her I should cast my anger, that my knife should cut out the innards of hell from her used body? That blessed haven in meadows of virtue that once was all mine, that I so miss, shall be no one's again? I should - kill her?"

Jones re-entered the world

"Who have you killed tonight my friend? It's eleven o clock and time is passing. The drink and the courage is deserting you. In two more hours you will be as sober as the judge that comes to pass his sentence. And when you are sober again you will not know your enemies for they will be your friends once more, your bosom pals. And your wife? - She will be there looking over your shoulder with the eyes of Delilah; insolent lips telling you mischief, canting on your allies. Time is running out."

"But Jane, my Jane. I love her so, I do so dearly. I want her home, I want my children. And things will change. I should kill the dogs that lusted her and shamed me."

"No my boy. Those friends you speak of are still your friends. All women are betrayers. Go see your wife and ask her to her face. And look behind her eyes as she shields the truth, as she turns away and vents you with her tears. And hear her say that it is you and you alone she loves, while even then she aches for the other who is absent from her bedroom, in that bed where your babies were conceived. Then think of your friends, how they companioned you and solaced you when you cried. And then, if you still cannot believe; then, and only then, return and dispatch them one by one."

Tears of folly and mawkish irritation welled in Fred Horry's eyes, and he began to weep freely into the noisome smell of Jones's jacket as he buried his face into his unshaven neck, crying, crying as Jones lays his arm around the gentleman dandy of the George Hotel; a rich man's son who had thrown away wealth in drunken kinship and false friends. Together they rocked forwards and backwards; a terrible cradle, a frightening lullaby, an evil commination of threat.

> **'Old Pal, Old Gal,**
> **The nights are long and wear,**
> **Old Pal, Old Gal,**
> **Each day seems like a year.**
> **Shadows they come stealing**
> **Through the weary night;**
> **Always find me kneeling**
> **In the candle-light.**

**The long night through, I think of you,
Old Pal, why don't you answer me.
My heart's embrace, an empty space,
These arms that held you tenderly.**

If you can here my prayer

Away out there,

Old Pal, why don't you answer me?'

The turns on the stage had been changing.

"...Truth? 'ere, this is the truth this is! Gospel truth! I woz an 'igh wire man once. That's right, yes. D'yer know what they calls 'em? Fun- am - bul - IST - Eh? I can tells you lady, there's no bloody fun in that game! 'Ere, I woz up there once - UP - you know - Eh? - and I woz about half way across this wire when this woman - eh, with a tight fitting frock on - eh - tight! I'll tell yer, she had to have a dose 'o Parker's purge ter get into that frock - tight! What a figure! Just like an 'our-glass I can tell yer lady. Lady? She woz no lady. I could see a Palfeyman's pawnticket pinned ter the back of her collar - one and a penny farthing to redeem it - I know, I can tell yer alright - Truth! Anyway, this woman, shall we call her a woman? - go on then - she woz walking the line towards me. Coming towards me - all front she woz like a bleedin' frigate - I didn't know where to put meself. Eh, what would you governor - hey - no - cheeky - I'm telling the jokes - there's only one comedian 'ere. That is, except for the emcee. 'Ave you seen his suit? Suit! - Loud? - if it woz dumb and still on the dummy it would deafen the Household Cavalry - And there she woz - this woman - what a duchess - in 'er tight-fittin' frock - I could see 'er bloomers right through it - tight? And there she woz comin' for me - forty foot up off the ground. Well, I'd got me pole in me hand - Aye-aye - 'old on lady - me balancing pole - What d'yer say madam 'What a big one' - you wait till after the show, I'll show yer! Truth! Any way, give order, 'ere was this trapeze woman 'eading straight for me, well - I didn't know whether to turn round and toss meself off or stay there and block 'er passage.....'Ere, what would you do sir? Truth do yer want? I'LL TELL YER THE TRUTH!"

THIS IS THE TRUTH ABOUT FRED HORRY.

Frederick William Horry arrived in Burslem the same year that Enoch Bennett took over a pawn-shop at 90 Hope Street Hanley. Although, at this time, Hanley was the largest of the Potteries towns, it was a mere blot, a simple stockade compared to the sprawl of other industrial conurbations in the Midlands and the North West. Hanley, even then, was parochially identified, within the coherence of the district, as the place to conduct business and the place to shop. A year after these un-noteworthy arrivals, Arnold Bennett was born in a backroom of his father's meagre little shop and Fred Horry married Jane Wright. The year, under-lined in the calendar of all Bennett fans, was 1867.

Horry bought the George Hotel in Burslem where Jane was a barmaid, and he settled down to a domestic future set in the traditions of innkeeper - a position, situated within a town's trading structures, of social eminence. Five years on from this date saw the Bennett family returning to its roots in the Mother Town where Arnold began to absorb the experiences of the town's comings and goings from the basement of his grandfather Longson's shop at the bottom end of St

John's Square. From these busy little rooms below stairs, the boy viewed scenes and occurrences that would eventually return to him to excerpt and summarise as he began to write down his realistic tales of the Five Towns.

The year 1872, which saw Arnold Bennett already committing to his memory sights and feelings from the draper's basement - his inspiration for the setting of The Old Wives' Tale - began propitiously for the five year old boy, and it was the year he began his education at the Wesleyan infants school which stood on the east side of Swan Bank at the rear of the architecturally Italian chapel adjacent to the north side of the George Hotel. From the first moment he sat on his wooden stool with his chalk and slate, the boy began to hear, smell and taste everything that was Burslem: the constant rumble of industry, the lung-clogging smoke and the sour aromas bourne in the dust-filled air. He was never to forget these sensations nor the detailed town activity that he observed daily and which he potently committed to his mind. Subsequently, the world came to know Burslem as well as Arnold, its streets, its contours, its layout, its architecture, its industrial legacies; but more especial, its people.

For many Burslem folk 1872 heralded other diversions; fancies and anticipations, hopes, pleasures, riches as well as poverty; mediocrity and danger - much like any other year. But, for the innkeeper of the George Hotel, the year was met in the company of the shrouded reaper, who had followed him from the moment he had departed from his place of birth, waiting his turn across the seasons of five years to claim his evil harvest. The season was now come - the reaper and the merchant met, in Burslem. Boy Arnold was oblivious to this conjuration and its outcome, for even as he sat at his school bench, yards from the marital bed of Fred and Jane Horry, his two fellow villagers lay painfully dead in some anonymous flatland many miles away on the other side of the country.

Arnold Bennett never knew Fred Horry. As close as they had been geographically, their stars had past but briefly and had never collided. Indeed, the Bennett family and the Horry's were completely unmindful of each other's lives; in stellar terms, their planetary trajectories were oblique. And yet, for a while, in the fleetest of connections, Arnold Bennett and Fred Horry shared the same orbit. In that iota of time, the author's neural structure recorded the event that had drawn their stars together in the vastness of the Cosmos. One day in the future the novelist would be compelled dig out the detail in order to write the story of the young tragic man in bittersweet prose about easy streets and blind alleys which they both knew well enough though never shared.

Looking back on the years that the gregarious innkeeper came to dwell among the potters, it is appropriate that most contemporary observers come to view Fred Horry as a manic, happy and sad, popular pal, for these were awful times in which the ordinary townsfolk took their pleasures where they could, and such people are drawn to the flamboyancy of happy spendthrifts just to catch the smallest glimmer that the lightning bolt emits. The tales of Fred Horry's thrill-packed roller coaster life on the rides of the beer house pleasure-grounds of 1860/70's Burslem, were once legion and legendary. Today those follies have been forgotten, packed away into the dusty packing cases of the past. And yet, so completely encircled was Horry by his adopted friends that, upon his death, they dedicated to him the marble memorial in St John's churchyard. Despite his many misdemeanours and his subsequent felony, that famous phrase - 'He was more sinned against than sinned' - is the motto remembered most about the life of a 'good old pal'. The stories we know of Fred Horry were perpetrated by his sidekicks and perpetuated by myth, distortions which even Arnold Bennett, with fictional complicity, added to.

Bennett's account of the crime and hanging of Daniel Povey, the domestically enslaved husband of a murdered drunken wife, - the event in The Old Wives' Tale which was inspired by Horry's own trial and execution - is employed by the author's reversal of the sequence of the roles of victim and perpetrator. Through the craft of the writer, Horry can be seen as a thumbnail sketch of Povey, and the deeds of Povey have falsely become interpreted as the deeds of Horry; indeed Povey **was** 'more sinned against than sinning'. Horry and Povey both remain in the mind as sad victims, confused in the deeds of their individual acts of murder, a case of fact becoming fiction with fiction prevailing, as it were, in authenticity in both cases. The crime of Horry has been trivialised by historians to such an extent that the memory of his sad wife Jane has been betrayed. Today we say, 'poor Fred Horry' with a little sadness, for his life is a myth and it is safer to ignore the truth with a smile and a snigger than to face truth with hurtful honesty. Yet there, behind the tattered shrouds of deception, the uncomfortable truth forever lurks waiting to be turned over. We often see it written in the ambiguity of a gravestone's verse, or in the rhymed confusion of some wicked bar-room monologue.

> *Would you like me to tell you a story, sir,*
> *Of the 'orribleness of war?*
> *Well its half past six in the mornin' sir,*
> *When the clock struck five to four.*
> *There was something went wrong with the works sir,*
> *And the enemy wanted a fight.*
> *So they lay with our right on their left sir,*
> *And we lay with our left on their right.*
> *And I wanted a Turkish Bath sir,*
> *But the colonel said, 'There's no 'ope,*
> *For the drummer-boy's drunk all the water*
> *And the bugler's swallowed the soap.'*
> *I lay down and cried in my anguish*
> *But the colonel said, 'Lad, never mind,*
> *But you haven't got on any trousers',*
> *So I went and I pulled down the blind.*
> *Then the bugler tooted his tooter,*
> *And I knew that the foeman was nigh,*
> *So I rushed out to buy some tobacco*
> *And a cannonball flopped in my eye.*
> *I could scarcely see for a moment,*
> *Which I thought was very unkind.*
> *Then the colonel's wife dropped in to see me*
> *And said, "Ere, shall we pull down the blind?'*
> *Then the enemy clustered around us,*
> *And the colonel went clean off his chump.*
> *And the horses got up and stampeded,*
> *And the camel's had all got the 'ump.*
> *Well, I was drinking my whisky and soda,*
> *When a shot struck me somewhere behind.*
> *As I couldn't pull it out in the street sir,*

I went in and pulled down the blind.
And the bombs lay around me in thousands,
And still they continued to drop.
So I paid for the dozen I'd eaten
And walked out of the oyster shop.
And the bullets were buzzing around me,
And one nearly blew off my head.
There were cannons to the right and cannons to the left.
But I just went in off the red.

The Huntsman public house in Westport Road is a modern looking inn. It has no special interest and formerly had two previous names, the White Hart, sometime known as a 'music hall', and the Victoria Hotel. However, in 1720 it stood on the site of a number of dwellings occupied by important potters around the summit of a locality known as, and eventually named, The Hill. In this important setting, at the head of the Packhorse lane, were the potworks of Thomas Cartlich of the 'olding' branch. Nearby was the house of Burslem's principal medical practitioner Doctor Mawson, who was also a dentist, barber and apothecary. Then there were John Lovatt and Samuel Horden, two counting clerks and important people in the town's administration.

By the end of the 18th century The Hill was in the process of being occupied by the developing Wood family, and by 1830 the whole area was lodged within the enclosure of the massive Fountain Works which presented its impressive frontage to occupy the north side of Newcastle Street in a sprawl of bottle ovens, warehouses, selecting bays and packing barns. The perimeter wall stretched in protective crenellated brick like a huge fortress with its wide arched entrance looking for the world like a crusader's high castle. Only the main entrance remains today, a reminder of the powerful status of the mighty industrialists of capitalism. The rest is a heap of wasted archaeology buried beneath houses and streets.

Nearby stood the towering Hill Top School and chapel which owed its existence to Enoch Wood in benevolence and patronage. Built in 1836, the school that year received John Bennett, Arnold Bennett's paternal grandfather, as its superintendent after his expulsion from Swan Bank Wesleyan. Opposite stood the great expanse of Samuel Alcock's visually unique potworks, like some Helenic palace rising virtuously from Trojan ruins, a building claimed by Arnold Bennett as the 'finest in all Burslem'. And close by was the Royal Hotel, an alehouse of luxury with a long bar, a room for dancing and, at the rear, a famous bowling alley. Further towards the town was an old cottage tavern, Ye Olde Crown, much in the same condition it is today as it was in the 1830s. And in the direction of the Sytch, the Liverpool Arms and the Royal Oak added old fashioned flavours to nine public houses extending themselves overall in this small district to a total of twenty-three, taking in those found along the numerous adjacent side streets.

The Sytch was a remarkable town within a town, a separate entity on the northern edges of Burslem. Down here was a tabernacle, a water mill and a street named Lancashire which turned on itself to troop back to the top of the Hill where the Lord Shaftesbury's ragged school still stands, built in 1840, making it one of the oldest building standing that retains its original shape and design. In more modern times it became the Shaftesbury School of Dance where many Burslem ballroom students practised the arts of waltz, the foxtrot and rhumba.

And the graves in the small plot hidden behind a high old wall are still there; the last resting place of the great potter Samuel Alcock of the 'Sytch Works'. This is where his house was and his garden, now protected inside the confines of the Wades' Manchester Works.

The Sytch! A cluster of back-to-back cottages, unadopted by the council, unlit for many years while its sister neighbourhoods wallowed in yellow shimmering gaslight. Unmade streets and alleys among which were small potworks, and blacksmiths; a mill and millrace; rural poverty at the edge of a substantial mansion, Brownhills Hall. Here the Oxley Brook mingled with the Burnhayes Brook diverted by culvert under the Liverpool Road rolling down to Longport and Etruria to meet the River Trent at Stoke. It was in the small long demolished tabernacle of the Sytch that Josiah Wolstancroft Powell first introduced his tonic-sol-fa system of music reading - the Sytch men became the first potters to sing in majestic unison - 'O Holy unity!' Once the district was pleasant country land. The first potters lived here. Out of these acres, Tunstall grew as well. And yet, in such a short time, the savage poacher of terrestrial wealth had taken his poke and moved on, relentless in his conversion of all things simple into the mystery of manufactured riches.

Along with the potworks came the workers own hovels and overcrowded tenements and cellars. Hidden from the town was Ball Bank, a squalid backyard of a pottery. In 1815 it stood as part of the town's militia barracks and attracted the miserable camp-followers of vagrants and prostitutes. And it was here that in 1845 the barracks was transformed into the Mother Town's first workhouse following the introduction of the revised Elizabethan Poor Laws. Ball Bank was a cauldron in which brick ovens towered over ant-like people sucking them into the furnace flames in an endless procession that trailed beyond the factory gates and never to be seen again. Ball Bank provided the entrance to a long narrow passage that ran between two roaring potbanks, slicing through uneven factory floors, emerging at the other end nudging at the mighty doorway of the town hall. No resident with a modicum of self-preservation or moral decency would pass through this rude alley. Arched between the solicitors practise of Arthur Ellis and the post office, it's warning shadows seemed to convey to all that eternal, fearful and curious message of abandoned hope. Nightly came cries and squeals of animals in their death throes, for at the top of that queer alley was the town's abattoir, sitting cheek by jowl with foreboding houses lying in permanent darkness amid wretched sounds of agony and death. And yet Ball Bank was where many residents preferred to live for here was the warmth of the hated ovens as well as the obtainability of fresh flesh food, so different to the bleakness of the 'Hellhole' behind the George Hotel in Nile Street, which had nothing to offer for the town's jettisoned humanity.

Public houses were everywhere, in each dark nook they crouched. In shadowy crannies they sat like fat rats waiting to pounce on those with a penny to spend and a memory to forget. Here among these drinking dens was the White Hart Music Hall, providing the crudest entertainment in its dark back rooms. Bawdy and salacious, it was a magnet to criminals of the lowest calibre and an attraction to those who tempted fate in the pursuit of an excitement never available and not normally optional to decent Victorian Christians. It was to this debauched house that fate lured Fred Horry, a young buck burning his father's money from the lining of his pockets.

In 1866, Henry Parker began to acquire a number of beer houses in Burslem which he supplied with pale mild and heavy bitter beer from brewhouses in Regent Street. In a short time, Parker's brewery was established and a good percentage of Burslem's public houses were bought and supplied by the former soldier. One of the houses that Henry Parker eyed-up covetously was the old George and Dragon coaching house which was owned by George Blake, an innkeeper of high standards who, not having relations himself willing to take over the inn, was looking for a purchaser so that he could move into retirement. A year after Parker had opened his brewery, he employed Fred Horry of Boston, Lincolnshire, the son of a well-to-do Lincoln beer brewer who he looked to as a financial partner.

Shortly after he arrived William Frederick Horry took a room at the George and Dragon from where he communicated to his father that the old inn was up for sale. His brief managerial position with Parker was soon terminated when Fred Horry came up against his boss over the sale of the George. At the age of Twenty-three, Horry paid out his father's money to secure the ownership and to steal a march on his former employer, a deal which his father seemed most pleased that his son had achieved. The business endeavours of his only son, so far off in fields afresh, conveyed to the Lincoln brewer that Fred had at last become a man of the world. A wayward youth, Fred had brought with him to Burslem a reputation for high living, heavy drinking and a penchant for the services of professional women; but what else could have been expected from him having lived all his life in a public house and a brewery? For such gregarious individuals, men with an abundance of ready money to spend on the pleasures of life, friendships are never far away. And it is perhaps reasonable to say that an important attraction to the purchase of the George was the proximity of a pretty woman. Fred found friends galore in the Mother Town, all waiting in the barrooms of what was then Burslem's principal pub, while he held out his right arm to the dainty hand of George Blake's comely twenty year old barmaid, Jane Wright, the chaste and speckless daughter of a local potter.

Now, the cynic who believes not in honourable love at first sight may bend a knowing nod to the fleeting passions of the taproom; and many will acknowledge, that in such haunts, graciousness is rarely a redeeming feature among the ire of drunken lust: and yet, this loving couple loved at once in purity, were married within the year and had been graced with the birth of their firstborn. In quick succession Jane was confined twice again bearing healthy infants; thus tied, for the rest of her short life she was enclosed in the cloying domesticity of mother-hood.

Fred Horry had become a Burslem man, locked in the traditions of the Mother Town's renowned capacity for adopting outsiders. He had friends, a pretty wife and healthy children, a home and an imperial position in the hierarchy of the town as an innkeeper. But his life was as incomplete as it was destined to be from its very beginning. Fred was born to die young. In a life cosseted in well-off family style, he had observed the conviviality of the astonishing world that surrounded his father's occupation. Each day he saw the magic of the drinker's vortex, the spangled universe of the inn, an arena that only children of innkeepers and publicans of a lifetime in the trade can know. It is a world seen through a changeling's eye, an awesome view into the chaotic theatre of Bedlam, to be understood and made sense of only by the crafty appliance of a cosmic kaleido-scope. Children born into such places are either devoured in the maw, succumbing to the pleasures and pain of intoxication, or they break-out, often to move happily and successfully in and out and about other human worlds. Fred Horry was of the former ilk. He was consumed by the indecorous passions of the world of alcohol and its temporary and shallow high-times. As with all alcoholics he was unable to comprehend his tragic situation, nor could he ever come to terms with his predicament. And Fred was cursed with dual bad luck by continually being unable to reach the goals he set himself while at the same time having an abundance of cash to fuel and sate his addictions. Horry's - or it should be said, his father's - money, provided for the necessary demands of a young wife and three children. It also supplied a golden pond into which his friends often dipped to turn the lucrative fins of a daring and errant trout. Daily their pocket money was scooped and doled to them in exchange for nothing more than a few hours of companionship as they all travelled round and round the merry-go-round town picking up the jettisoned dregs of society; an entourage for Fred, an accompaniment of mock servility and patronage that played their tunes for him in exchange for shillings.

Among Horry's friends was the Reverend Alfred Watton, an educated polymath, a scholar who had chosen the church, not for the gentle embrace of its Godliness, but as an easier option to access academic status and position. Watton had come to Burslem from Shrewsbury following curacies in a number of Midland's towns, the longest stay of which was in Nottingham, the lace town whose underworld he grew to know well enough and which knew him as one of theirs. An immigrant in Burslem he settled down well and married the daughter of a rich insurance patron, Dr John Morris, succeeding the Reverend J F Armstrong as the rector of St John's Church in 1869.

The bonding of the good rector's relationship with the innkeeper Horry lay in the mutual comforts of the church's Sacramental cup and the spirit measure of the public bar. Watton, in the Mother Town, was instantly drawn to the charismatic landlord who was, by 1872, an inescapable drunk, unable to reform from his well known habits which now included the regular beating of his wife. Unable to reform, even though he repeatedly suffered bouts of agonising delirium manifesting in horrific seizures and fits at home and in public places, Horry was happiest in drink. Watton showed similar traits examples of which were demonstrated in the pulpit where he was often seen swaying precariously, and from where he delivered a good number of unusual and obscure sermons which served only to disaffect him from his confused parishioners.

It was during these years that a large and fraternal group of men had formed itself into a club in the George and Dragon's bar. It was an association of heavy drinkers which included the loquacious Ravensdale steel manger, William Jones, who would be often observed drinking for longer hours each day in his pilgrimage to rehabilitate his tormented mind. Into this room crept the vices of greed and sloth, shying away from honesty and industry. In this company of errant gentlemen, Horry was unable to resist abusing the status of his eminent situation. The whisky bottle was as much at hand in his private domestic quarters as it was in the smoking rooms. His daily tours around other men's hostelries were devouring his health while his attitude to his wife and children had a particularly deleterious outcome. He was morose, aggressive and violent and he became convinced that Jane's defensive withdrawal into herself and for the protection of her children, was a cover for imagined infidelity. He became convinced she was having affairs with other men in his absences - these beleaguered insinuations he was unable to erase from the alcohol induced turmoil of his imagination. And the whole image was thunderously amplified by the canting of his friends who not once hesitated to pay lip-service to Horry's begged questions, as they resorted to lying about the amorous activities of their fellow courtiers with Jane.

But how could poor Jane find time for such matters clandestine? Here she was with three babies, a house and a public house to supervise - time for an affair of the heart? By God, if she had found a moment in that Hellish maelstrom, who could have blamed her for taking a minute of respite! But Fred did love Jane, more than either of them could possibly know; it was a love born crippled out of a selfish and disproportionate relationship - an intimacy of possession, which was the only material thing that Horry could relate to. Jane belonged to *him*, and he betrayed the drunkard's symptoms of battery when in doubt. Meanwhile Fred continued to ride his boozy carousel around the town amid a gang of acquaintances, weak-willed, more and more convinced that he was being cuckolded, a shame he was unable to confront.

It all came to a head early in march 1871. Jane's children - for they could never be called Fred's by virtue of his neglect and abandonment - were then age three, two and one. Throughout each day Horry was permanently drunk on spirits. Though his friends adored him, Jane now hated him and locked him from their bedroom. Accepting his domestic fate and not much caring about it, the Burslem innkeeper moved into disreputable accommodation in Hanley. His fits became more frequent as his friends slowly departed from his company seeing his endowed wealth sloughing away in another town. His lack of funds arrived sooner than later for, as a consequence of being informed of his son's mindless disregard for his family, the Boston brewer cut Fred's allowance and Fred was forced to sell the George and Dragon to his former employer Henry Parker.

Reduced to becoming homeless, Jane took her children off to their grandfather's fine home in Lincolnshire where she was provided with warm, comfortable and permanent quarters. In the ensuing twelve months away from Burslem, Jane found the comfort and respite she and her children needed away from her flawed marriage. Fred kept only in touch by the odd letter while he regardlessly carried on with his life of debauchery, aided and abetted in his fateful mission by the godless Alfred Watton, service friend to his wayward would-be prodigal who, in moments of sanity, still yearned after Jane and his children. It was Watton who introduced Fred to his 'private' Nottingham friends where, in a year of frequent visits, Horry frittered away what money he had left. He was, it seemed, bent on pleasurable suicide: drinks and jinks with any and most casual tavern women.

Known in Nottingham as the 'Lavender Kid' on account of his bright suits and gay attire, of which his pink calf-skin gloves were a prominent feature, he paraded himself along the riverside as a 'gaily dressed inamorata' as the prurient trial press reporters later dubbed him. But while the 'Kid' mashered arrogantly down Nottingham's byways, beneath his ne'er-care-less exterior there brooded a mangled heart and a disturbed mind which carried fragments of all the deadly sins gathering to respond to the evilness of self-hate. In unsubdued anger, Horry now sued his wife for divorce, citing a number of Burslem men as co-respondents associated severally and individually in adulterous acts with Jane. Of course none of these allegations had any substance, everyone knew this except Fred Horry whose aching recall was animated by his now only friend, Alfred Watton who continued to urge Fred to seek conciliation with his wife in order to properly identify Jane's indiscretions. But the matters were never tested beyond the imagination and in any case, by January 1872 the former innkeeper of the George and Dragon was in desperate straights.

Returning from Nottingham Fred immersed himself in a week of total and uninhibited promiscuous behaviour living in a Hanley brothel near to the former home of the Bennett family in that inappropriately named 'Hope Street'. In the daytime and the evenings he roamed the streets and lanes of Burslem not missing visiting one single pub as he searched for and challenged all men to account for even their briefest contacts with his wife. Sometimes he walked into the deepest hours of the night always ending up in the music room of the White Hart sitting with sundry drunks and with the drunken woman-beater William Jones. And there they drank champagne until the early hours singing along with the rude local artists until the two depraved companions lapsed into uneasy unconsciousness.

One morning Horry caught his train to Nottingham where he bought more ammunition for the revolver he had swung threateningly around Burslem. Over that weekend the raving man lay in his crumbling apartment turning over his life and the diminishing choices he had left. The horrid ghosts queued along the landings of his mind to feature in the dissipation of his young life, the assumed treachery of Jane, the tell-tale cim-camming of his posturing friends, the plausible lies of his pastor and the arrogance of Victorian Burslem; all bore down on his flagging shoulders in heavy thrall. Fate had already made its decision when it accompanied him in the first moments that he stepped into the streets of the Mother Town five years earlier, and now Fate declared its intentions for Fred Horry.

On Monday 15th January, while still drunk and angry and in great despair, Fred Horry arrived on the doorstep of his father's house in Boston where he begged for an interview with Jane; but the parlour maid had been instructed to turn him away. Fred persisted and forced his way into the lobby to be confronted by his father who was intent on dismissing him forcibly. At this point Jane appeared and, quickly assessing correctly her husband's erratic behaviour, took a conciliatory course and agreed to accompany him to the door where he began to make his final plea for salvation and, if necessary, to make his final farewell to her.

Alone now with Jane, Fred explained his case, the reasons for his jealousies, feebly expressing his true love and promising full retribution if a reconciliation could be formalised. A tearful Jane had lived her short life to the whim and abuse of drunks and declared she would have no more to do with her sobbing husband. She told him to leave. She sent him away. Outside the porch Fred Horry appeared to draw himself up resignedly, as though he had accepted the inevitability of his plight. And then, in a strange and far-away manner, he asked his wife's assistance in lighting a cigar, saying that he would leave peaceably afterwards and vowing that he would make no attempt to molest her or see her again. Jane turned to fetch a taper and Fred retrieved from his coat the Nottingham revolver. And, pointing it at the back of her head he shot her with a single bullet. She died instantly. The murderer made no attempt to run away, he stood over the fallen body weeping inconsolably. Nor did he deny his guilt to the constable who came to arrest him shortly afterwards.

At his trial at Lincoln Assizes in March, Horry pleaded guilty; his final words to the jury were to affirm his love and devotion for Jane claiming that it was provocation and jealousy that had led him to commit this single act of madness; an unsolicited aberration, the insanity of revenge. Fred Horry was hanged at Lincoln on April 1st 1872; all fool's day.

'He had followed her to Lincolnshire, and he was maddened by her defiant refusal to reconciliation. Upon her refusal, he killed her.' quoted the crime reporter of a local newspaper transcribing the prosecutor's allegations.

Back in Burslem a petition had been instigated begging clemency for Horry's life. Thousands signed it, but it was rejected by both court and the Home Secretary. On the day of the hanging curtains were drawn in houses over many parts of Burslem. A special service was given by Reverend Watton at St John's Church. And friends clubbed together to erect a memorial in order to place it at the front of the Norman tower. Nor was Jane forgotten in the memorial tribute. He was twenty-eight, it said, and she twenty-six.

At the wake friends sat on the long benches, at the narrow tables and all along the side room of the White Hart music hall. The musty room, dark enclaves, leather pumps yellow with tobacco and stained with body-sweat, sweet sticky, sweet smell of death. In the White Hart peopled mourned for a murderer who had once belonged to a respectable family; but it was for sure that the patrons of the White Hart were now his preferred family. And he was one of their own.

'The name of Horry has so long been connected in the borough with everything that was manly, humane and honourable, that the tragic event came upon our fellow-townsmen like a clap of thunder.' (The Potteries Examiner - 22.1.1872, reporting the murder of Jane Horry) Media rhetoric such as this abounded throughout the potteries, but particularly so in the Mother Town. In spite of this, and the many public petitions appealing for clemency, justice moved inexorably forwards; and:

'After a careful consideration of all the circumstances'... (the judge) **was unable to discover any sufficient grounds to justify him in advising Her Majesty to interfere with the due course of the law.'** (Court report of appeal Lincoln Assizes 1872)

On the Sunday following Horry's judicial hanging, Alfred Watton ordered the solemn ringing of St John's bells, whilst he made personal his conducted service for Burslem worshippers to 'accompany poor Horry's friends.' A funeral card was sent abroad giving notice of this service on which were printed references to Horry's qualities without noting his aberrations or his wrongdoings. These, of course, were Watton's personal sympathies: **'He died as a man, a Christian and a Martyr. He was more sinned against than sinning. Peace be to his manes!'**, he preached. And the memorial obelisk prominent in the churchyard carried a similar sentiment for two people so misled in life:

> 'Sacred to the memory of
> **William Frederick Horry**
> **Born 17th Dec 1843**
> **Died 1st April 1872**
> **Also Jane, his wife.**
> **Born 17th Feb 1846**
> **Died 15th Jan 1872'**

> 'This monolith was erected in affectionate remembrance
> Of the above said W.F. Horry
> by his Staffordshire Friends.'

A man may be looked upon in life in many ways. His deeds, may be saluted in his lifetime and yet be forgotten after his death: or in death, his memory beloved while his influence in life overlooked. Horry was a friend to his living public - a martyr to community benevolence perhaps; but what he did, he did only for himself. While he surrendered to the false pride of being popular among his peers - he became, that which he desired - the desire of the impetuous young - a champion in his adopted town. And yet, was this man no more than a wife-beater, a womaniser, a drunk and a common murderer? The truth speaks somewhere strong through simple truth - that he lived in Burslem for six years: a rich, irresponsible young drunkard, who wooed and married a young local barmaid, ill-equipped in her inexperienced life to compromise her flattered luck to marry one so rich - an educated foreigner in a backward town: they had three children in three years. And even his thoughts on his deathbed were not for his flesh and blood but for his Burslem friends and those imagined enemies:

'I thank my dear friends of the Potteries for their sympathy and pecuniary assistance. I feel that I have been deeply sinned against and wronged, but pardon those who have done so'; his last letter to Watton, written in grandiose self-pity.

To the end Horry continued to insist that Jane had been unfaithful to him - it was his only defence - maintaining that it was the seductress and her seducers who had brought him all his troubles to bear. In all the pages of his numerous final letters, he expressed no thoughts for Jane; indeed, his three children were not even afforded the most meagre of words or of one note in but one sentence.

Meanwhile Watton was damned profoundly for the tone of his memorial service, and his insensitive epigram about sin was openly criticised by many civic notables, expressed even more so in Lincoln than in the cynical Potteries. It was easy to see, through Watton's disguised comments about Jane in his sermon, that his sentiments for her were cold-blooded and amounted to nothing less than reportage of petty tittle-tattle, a prevarication to protect the character of his drunken friend. His sermon was much too blatant for the creed and the church to sustain, so that he was condemned and was never forgiven for it. In a rare sober moment shortly afterwards, Watton seemed at long last to perceive just how far he had taken his protection of Horry's name, and he inanely, and insultingly claimed that he spoke his sermon to promote his personal opposition to capital punishment. In exampling the death sentence handed down to Horry, he was merely, he said, expounding his own principles of Biblical penalties in their use as punishment for the ultimate crime of murder.

Watton's own life at this time was punctuated by landmarks of drunken irresponsibility. On the death of his father in law, Dr Morris, Watton succeeded to the wealth of his business which he proceeded to squander; and, as trustee of St Paul's Church in Dalehall and St Peter's in Cobridge as well as St John's, he almost caused their bankruptcies by mis-management of their finances. Watton considered life to be an ailment, his erratic views allowed him to suggest that the practise of bull baiting and cock fighting should be restored after they had been banned by law since 1835. Manically depressed, Alfred Watton blew out his heart with a shotgun in his Middleport rectory (today the site of Middleport park) on 20th January 1886. His tombstone in St John's says little for his life and nothing of his death.

In the intervening period between the hanging of Horry and the suicide of Watton, fate caught up with the third of the three fallen friends.

By the late 1870's, William Jones, a large-framed heavy man, had become a famous Burslem bully. Totally committed to drink, he was obese and bore the stigmata of alcohol in his physical being, as well as in the degeneration of his character and his attitude towards his fellow human beings. He was frequently violent as his criminal record lengthened. In 1878, the former iron manager had become a social outcast even among his criminal peers. At his lowest ebb Jones resided in Ball Bank alongside the abattoir with a young prostitute, Harriet Green, with whom he had been having a casual relationship. A wayward but apparently sensitive young woman, who loved Jones for nothing more than that she was in love with him, she kept his house and prepared his meals.

On the evening Jones murdered Harriet, he calmly walked into the White Hart Music Hall, his hands dripping with blood, and, when questioned as to his demeanour, he boldly announced that he had helped in the abattoir with the knock down of a bullock. He was afforded permission by the innkeeper to wash his hands in his private wash basin and to remain in the public house, which he did, drinking until he was drunk, before two constables came to arrest him. The police had been alerted by an awful row accompanied by a woman's screams coming from the house in Ball Bank, and on entering had found the body of Harriet Green, dead and blood-soaked.

At his trial at Stafford Assizes, Jones calmly faced the death penalty. But, with a display of grand impudence, he put forward a defence under his own counsel of accidental death, denying murder. The woman, he claimed, had come to remonstrate with him over a small domestic misdemeanour while he was at his supper of bread and cheese. During the row, Jones alleged that Harriet attacked him physically at which he fought her off by waving his hands about in defensive gesticulation. It was purely accidental, he argued, that the woman had got in the way of the knife which he was using to cut his cheese, the consequence of which she sustained several wounds to her neck and head, of which a number were assessed by the pathologist as having the severity of carrying potential fatal injuries. This pathetic excuse framed Jones's defence to intentional killing, so cynically feeble, but it saved his life! An abject jury apparently seemed able to identify themselves to Jones's circumstances and found him guilty only of manslaughter, whereupon the judge, not disposed to similar tolerance, sentenced him to penal servitude for the rest of his life, stating in a flat obiter dictum that he **'had indeed been fortunate in acquiring the services of a lenient jury'**, or else he would surely have hanged.

Companions three who had shared the same style of life, ceremonials which reflected not the shamed and averted face of the Mother Town and its society. Three accursed comrades chained together by life's temporary pleasures, pursuing a mode of self-gratification to the exclusion of all dignity and decency. And yet, in spite of their common abominations, it is the case of Fred Horry that is remembered lastingly.

Following the announcement of his hanging, there bore into the Mother Town a tidal wave of contagious adulation, a carnival treasure ship awash with the interest of the doings of Fred Horry; an extravaganza of morbid curiosity which caught the full imagination of the salacious majority. In addition to the memorial obelisk placed in St John's churchyard, there followed a stout and pathological business in Fred Horry memorabilia. Ryles' the printers of Waterloo Road - those cartographers who produced the famed 1720 map of Burslem - published a facsimile of Fred Horry's last letter which went on sale throughout the town for sixpence. Further, a rewarding trade was achieved in the sale of the murderer's portrait and, to top all of this, a perniciously devised memorial card which sold throughout the whole city in public houses at twopence each, a levy which raised a handsome profit for the Burslem publisher!

Over a few weeks, in equal numbers in its late editions, the Staffordshire Sentinel ran many letters both for and against the glorification of the career of Horry. It was noted that by far the greater bulk of correspondence laid complements to the man as a popular personality, sympathetic in tone as to his final circumstances, and regretful of his fate following his judicial punishment. A more ambivalent correspondence was reluctantly entertained by the editor who let the subject run its course, and there were the occasional contributions of serious criticism; but these letters were largely ignored by the provocative town watchers who out and out seemed to want to worship a hero. However, a certain section saw through it all. One irate parishioner wrote:

'It appears that this Christian Martyr for whom Burslem cherishes the highest respect was nothing more than a drunken publican who drank himself into delirium and killed her in a fit of jealousy'. And another: *'....a horrible and grotesque instance of popular canonisation than the glorification of this drunken innkeeper for murdering his wife could not be imagined.'*

Such pragmatists contributed but few observations to the avalanche of hero-worship, and their comments passed without response. The phrase, 'judicial murder' was on the lips of most people and could be heard shouted aloud in the taprooms of the town. Although it could not be said that Fred Horry was a man for his times, for all times throw up accounts of excess living, debauchery and the waste of high-life, Horry was treated to the kind of reverence accorded to the demise of a leader or trend-setter. In such episodes can be found intemperance hidden behind closed doors away from the public gaze; such parody allows only the most celebrated practitioners entry into public legend.

Jones's brutal and savage murder of Harriet Green was but one step further than that which many men doled out to their women each day. An ugly and bloody crime meriting a brief report in the court's archives. And, ought not the insidious manipulations of Alfred Watton deserve even greater condemnation? Did he not encourage Horry and Jones, members of his flock, by affording them the support of their pastor who faced them with a side of the clergy that was far distant from the blessed creed; black sheep who warranted better guidance and deliverance; a priest taking the same sacraments as liars, cheats and women-beaters? And was it not, by the consequences of his bizarre ministrations and the damaging effects of his wayward preaching, that his congregation turned away from the church, away from this depressed and pathological preacher who was so attracted to suicide and death. Who then will remember the names of Jones and Watton as time steps precariously and selectively along the plank of wayward deeds? Horry had infamy coming to him anyway. If he had he not abused and killed Jane he surely would have died a notable drunkard's death, famed for the coins he spent in the same sad sheds he shared with the preacher and the iron manager. And really, weren't all three lives as featureless as each other, sharing in their own way their empty days and nights while passing out their anecdotes of ill-advice to the rest of the forgettable drifting dregs, unmemorable the decades pile up, on and on?

Poor Fred Horry does not deserve the sympathies of our times for his reputation lies in the arbitrary cruelties of his own. And yet comparisons may be drawn today in timeless envy, greed, covetousness and revenge. He was a rich and privileged man who played-out the games of the poor with the poor in their own arena. In the country of the blind, it is said, the one-eyed man is king - but it's a dangerous land in which to live and enact another's life.

In 1908 Arnold Bennett's The Old Wives' Tale was published and the story of Fred Horry was once again told through the deeds of Daniel Povey. Bennett's description of the brief appearance of this anti-hero in the dock of Stafford's Assize court, the cousin of main character Samuel Povey, told how a local councillor was brought to justice for the murder of his alcoholic and abusive wife. Daniel was a well respected trader, neither drunkard nor debaucher. Finding his wife intoxicated one day and incapable of performing the most simple of household chores, an ensuing argument resulted in the accidental death of this unwholesome harridan and the total remorse of the pathetic spouse who had been cuckholded for so long by no fouler seducer than the gin bottle.

Upon Povey's conviction he was sentenced to hang despite a petition got-up by the townsfolk begging the leniency of the court. Daniel duly met his fate at Stafford Gaol and a memorial service was held in Bursley where a procession made its way to the church led by the Prize Silver Band. Black-edged cards were produced for distribution:

> **'Sacred to the memory of**
> **Daniel Povey**
> **A Town Councillor of this town**
> **Judicially murdered at 8 o'clock in the morning**
> **8th February 1888**
> **"He was More Sinned Against Than Sinning"**

Bennett had his narrator say:

'Loafers, women and children had collected on the drying pavements...In the great bar of the Vaults a barman was craning over the pitchpine screen that secured privacy for drinkers... The rector spoke too long... the immense multitude began to disperse by the eight streets that radiated from the Square. At the same time one' o'clock struck, and the public houses opened with their customary admirable promptitude... Such was the massive protest of Bursley against what Bursley regarded as a callous injustice... in a town of over thirty-thousand souls there are sufficient dregs to fill all the public houses on occasions of ceremonial excitement. Constance saw the bar of the Vaults crammed with individuals whose sense of decent fitness was imperfect. The barman and the landlord and the principal members of the landlord's family were hard put to it to quench that funeral thirst... At five minutes to three the Vaults spewed forth a squirt of roysterers who walked on the pavement as on a tightrope; among them a bandsman... his silver instrument only half enveloped in its bag of green serge. He established an equilibrium in the gutter.'

The novelist could not resist fitting the story of Fred Horry and the stir of the wake that day into his master work. The funeral celebrations in the town's public houses were well known to Bennett having spent his infant school years living in his grandfather's shop at the bottom of St John's Square. Although we know they never met, for a brief period of time Horry and Bennett trod the same cobbled lanes and daily passed each other by the George Hotel heedless to their own and each other's ensuant reputations.

**"If Pa killed Ma, Who'd kill Pa?
Mar-wood."**

At 6.am, All Fool's Day 1872, Frederick William Horry was led to his place of execution at the prison in Lincoln Castle. Having drunk a large tumbler of brandy the murderer was in chirpy mood as he allowed the executioner to bind his wrists and blindfold him. Within minutes Horry was dead, it had all gone smoothly even though this was the hangman's first execution.

Having read many reports of the frequent occasions of long drawn out death, decapitation and of the sights of condemned men and women struggling for hours at the end of a rope waiting to die, William Marwood, a Lincoln cobbler, had been experimenting with the length of a rope and the design of the drop so that it would be effective in order to cause instantaneous death.

He approached the governor of Lincoln Prison with his results and offered to give a demonstration. Marwood pleased the governor who employed him on the spot and immediately handed to him the execution of Horry as a probation.

Marwood went on to become the most prolific hangman of his times because of his technique, hanging some 175 condemned murderers. Of the twenty-two public executioners employed since 1593, William Marwood became the most respected and the methods he first used on Fred Horry were continued by every executioner until the last person was hanged by Albert Pierpoint in 1956.

WEDNESDAY 17th JANUARY 1872

The three men stood at the north entrance of the town hall. They laughed and slapped each other's shoulder in praise of their evening's work.

"Well, Mr Powell, I think you can be duly proud of your accomplishment tonight. This indeed was a night to remember. What a choir!"

"And what an audience," enjoined young Ellis concurring with his mentor Howson in congratulating Josiah Wolstantoncroft Powell on the concert of English choral work.

"Well, Gen'lemen, we can all be satisfied with the way it went. Burslem, nay, the Mother Town's folk, can rest abed tonight with the echoing sounds of Gloriana ringing through their dreams. This is a great town; folk have never been so well off - there are no dives or dens, and if there are we shall drive 'em all out, for this town is set to be the Vienna of the North. Long live Burslem!"

"And all of its good folk!"

"Aye - all of 'em."

Nathan Faulkner sidled up to the three.

"I've done and all locked-up now Mr Powell," coughed the key-keeper churning the mucus inside his livid lungs, heavy with pneumoconiosis, "I'll be off if you please sir."

"Aye, off you go Nathe, I shall see you in the morning prompt. Oh, by the way', he called him back, I don't know that beggar who killed his wife in the east counties do I? Sentinel said something about him keeping the George, blessed if I've heard of him. Horry, I think the reporter has him. Never come across him have we Nathe?"

"No sir. Not you sir, although I 'ave made 'iz acquaintance once or twice. A good bloke they say he was. Always ready to put his hand in 'iz pocket. Them's the sort for me every time."

"Ah well" countered the town clerk, "what we don't know can't hurt us can it?. Hey, cabbie!" he shouted to the driver, "Porthill and home".

Old Nathe stumbled across the Market Place to claim his waiting pint and the company of his good friend Albert Goose.

Chapter Six

MUSIC AND MYSTERY

'*...every nation of the civilized world numbers some eminent individuals whom it is proud to place in its historical annals, as the founders of its greatness... so the cities or places which ushered them into life or notice feel a natural and parental regard towards the objects which reflect upon them so bright a lustre.*'

(Ward, pg 427)

Opposite Burslem park, facing a seldom visited rural walk-way cut out of reclaimed industrial land, stands a one hundred year old house. In Moorland Road, these days an easily bypassed and unnoted carriageway, striking only for its un-featured shapelessness, the late Victorian three storey house stands unassertive and unpretentious. A window sign modestly announces that this is the office of Arthur Edwards, an accountant. It sits in a terrace - a villa - a set-back row with low, fronted walls guarding tiny blue-bricked entrance yards. Alongside the house is a covered cobblestone alley which leads to a passage connecting with Reginald Street, before it turns back to join the main street again. The whole length of this back alley services the shared lodgings of the regimental walls of a potbank, the Moorland Pottery - the Chelsea Works - as well as the backyards of Arthur Edwards' accountancy and a number of poky anonymous chambers. Over the high wall, the visitor may behold one of a handful of bottle shaped pottery kilns still left standing in the Mother Town. Its sensuous lines say all there is to be said about the potter's art; an evocation of smooth hands on wet clay, a solitary sentinel of industry; the last icon of a terrible beauty.

At one time, the whole row of Moorland Road frontages claimed the tenure of lordship, not only of factories and offices, but the recreational proprietary of the district's swimming baths, where teams once competed in that most popular sport of the potter, water polo. A slipper baths was housed inside; washing facilities for men and women to avail themselves, carrying underarm their bar of green soap wrapped in their tatty towel with which to perform the weekly ablution of an all-over wash, a pleasure denied them in the toilet-less deserts of back-to-back industrial houses. **'Cleanliness is indeed, next to Godliness'**; commanded their religious mentor, John Wesley, warning them to note his ordinance: **'Slovenliness is no part of religion.'** The grease-slicked water of the public baths, with its syrupy smells of soiled flesh spiked with DDT and chlorine, was as precious to the health of the potter as was the freshest of moorland streams to the thirst of the shepherd.

In this row the Potteries' District's stipendiary offices was once situated, as was the bureau of the American trades consulate for the area. A tax collecting office. The central post office was nearby, and, the Moorland Cinema! On the other side, the present steps of the rural walk-way once shook to the steel shock of steam trains as engines rocked through the station and under the smoke-filled tunnel below the road. Once upon a time, through many hours of the day, Loop-Line trains collected travellers from Burslem Railway Station, or, set them down alongside shunted wooden carriages of coals and iron and white dry pottery dishes and wet grey clay, while families queued on west-bound platforms for annual holiday 'specials' to Rhyl and Llandudno, via Kidsgrove and Crewe. Port Vale football club lay within a bladder's kick at the foot of where the Victorian pleasure park is now, a horticultural flash, flung like a balm wrapped in a soft chamois blanket across the cruelly scarred back of former coal mines and sunken pits.

All previous activity is long past. The house remains - 76 Moorland Road - in Alexandra Buildings. Its flat isolation still holds the power to lure the camera's lens to a view that forever sits in another time. Through its doors are carefully folded-away memories, set, to be examined only inside the dusty albums of the mind. And, from its stiff transoms - behind those creaking doors, locked away in former bedrooms - windows that once watched the views of the bustling park across the way. Now those scenes have faded like the faces of the room's former occupants. Featureless memorials: the broken bandstand bereft of brassy Sunday music; stilled one rainy afternoon when the band did not turn up to play. And the park's duck-pond, hoarily iced in winter, reflecting bare, brittle trees' branches, fretted black in a pallid pool of sky.

In indifferent watchfulness, the house dozes. But, in an odd unguarded moment, the house seduces the eye of the indifferent watcher as they pass by - a turn - a glance of sunlight, luring the gaze - the lungs of brick, beneath the parched skin of stuccoed pollution, sigh again with the loneliness of life and the pain of love.

11.00am, Christmas Day 1926.

As was their custom, the quaint pair took the short cut up the hill to the town's centre, climbing slowly out of the smart location of Charles Street, Hanley. The stroll had been planned to encourage an appetite before luncheon, for they had chosen roast beef and had instructed their daily housekeeper, Mrs Maddocks, to prepare a Yorkshire Pudding which they wished to eat with a baked potato and thin gravy. They paused briefly beside a stone-built Romanesque forum, the Tontines, a structure that housed the meat-market, the interior of which was marked with a slab-stone floor supporting a sprawl of trestles and boards from which traders sold farm foods out of crates; butchered meat and home-prepared groceries. And above the commercial arena was a cockloft, from which hung as many squealing children as chickens, all in crying fun, a game of greed, little mouths gobbling for attention.

Outside the front door, where Ionic columns and pointed pediments protected folk and fare, choristers had been organised in a wide circle and were singing Finnish carols beside a tall Scandinavian pine tree lit by electric bulbs in variously coloured hues. The tree had been raised here, in the very centre of town less than half a mile from the couple's home: a gift from the Danish royal family, a diorama from far-off days when grisled men wearing horns ruled the land from longboats out of fiords. And, as Norse consanguinity still freshened the palace of King George V, a singular-minded king who ruled in a bloody continent over a bloody empire, it might have been reflected, by those squealing children of the Potteries, that the king's mother was a Dane and his deceased father was a German, and he was monarch of the English in the departing days olde England.

The walk was routine. It had been undertaken often over the two years since their return from his committed regional travels. Over those years, they had been commonly observed by the town's habitues as they strolled ponderously, linked by arm and conversation; a private communication set apart in moated unity. Now and then they chatted with fellow passengers, but only when it suited them. As a rule they kept themselves apart, and in the main the townsfolk left them thus.

In the two years since they had been living in Hanley, the perambulation had taken place on a daily basis; sometimes even when the rain fell. After a while it was noted that the occasions were reduced to a weekly trek that was no longer apparently constitutional. An ordeal, it seemed, adherent to discipline. To the hordes who were about that morning, these quaint yoked figures passed without public attention or preoccupation.

Christmas day was bright, the grey sky carried its clouds well even though a stiff breeze bore an icy chill down from the north through the loping streets and alleys. The brighter clouds tussled with their darker siblings in a quarrel that threatened snow. In Upper Market Square and all along Lamb Street, through Miles Bank and into Piccadilly, crowds of festive merry-makers, all wrapped and muffled in overcoats and cloaks and long-flying scarves and woollen helmets, thronged over the polished cobblestones. More people clung to each other in pairs, and families wandered aimlessly, articulating babbling sentences into complements of the season. Friend's and stranger's hopes for good wishes were exchanged - the weather was criticised:

"Ooooh, isn't it cold!"

"Brrrrr, it's cold enough to snow"

"Brooh, is it going to snow?"

"Nnooh, it's too cold to snow."

The quaint pair passed by.

The woman was tiny and she wore black causing her to look tinier against the other darkly attired folk. About her small frame hung a hooded silk-lined full-length cape. The silk lining shone deep-red, and now and then the breeze blew the curtails wide giving out a splash of colour as if beguiled by dropping blood. Her companion, who may have appeared to any un-informed onlooker to be her son, was also dressed protectively in a black overcoat with the upturned collar hidden by a swinging dark blue scarf which, in motherly regulation, she might have made him wear in deference to her maternal concern. They stood to one side of the Market Place deciding whether to take morning tea at the nearby Angel Hotel where jolly patrons arrived and left in waves, passing from the cafe into the adjacent Grapes public house where the intoxication of music-hall and drink beckoned. They paused a little longer than necessary in their moment of indecision.

Hanley is the capital of the Potteries, and that day, as capital towns do in times of celebration, the streets and shops were garlanded with festive decoration. People, for the moment, enjoyed a brief assuagement from poverty and unemployment, even though it was seasonal for their trades to do well. And for the most of them, those revellers had worked in the potbanks up to that very morning. These brief holiday periods managed to catch a brightness in northern towns as the factories shut-down allowing the sky to become clear from smoke, where the air could be briefly taken in great gulps of rare purity. In such times, the worst of the bad times were forgotten, though only just for a moment.

This day a choir of twenty or so were singing by the Christmas tree as lustily as any were ever previously heard. The show was led with over-gestured animation by Mr J Weston Nichols; the choir reacting to their conductor as puppets do to a puppeteer, smiling and bobbing as he was. The fusion of singers was ending a stout rendition of Adeste Fideles and sopranos, Misses M J Bennett and Moulds, together with Miss Grant, contralto, Mr Hall tenor and Messrs Haughton and Malkin, basses, made preparations to sing the lively, 'Twas On A Winter's Eve'. Mr Nichols noticed the quaint couple's approach from the busy Parliament Row. He smiled at them in fond recognition to which alert signal the little woman raised to him a black gloved hand in a gesture of trembling response. Here the two waited in the bitter cold while the sextet concluded, after which the strains of a folk song, unknown to the majority of bystanders, were struck by a brass ensemble at a given cue from the conductor. The choir, taking in their turn the conductor's second prompt, began to hum the melody. Their voices were almost inaudible in sub-tonic contrast above the descant air.

"Madame, it's so good to see you out and about". Nichols had moved away from the choir and greeted the quaint pair. "And John! So good to see you too." He addressed the woman full on with concern. "I do hope it's not too chilly for you Madame. These east winds across the Square from the Green are so capricious. You must take care, keep warm; you are much too precious for us to be parted from you. And what would the hall's masters think if we got you laid-up?"

The choir master bowed deeply. A small man with a fine nose and a narrow face topped with ginger hair now greying through the shine of a high forehead. Here were piercing, though friendly, blue eyes that long ago had been startled out of the breathlessness of urgent youth into the complacency of a slowed-down, yet still active, middle-age. He sported a smartly cut moustache giving him the cheeky look of a clerk caught in truancy, for though he was not, that is what he liked to be. And about his neck, this clerk wore the office trappings of a woollen wrap; and woollen fingerless gloves were drawn from about his hands as he offered them in an extension of his soul in an amplified performance of greeting. He thus held dearly the covered hands of the woman's escort, rubbing them and lifting them vigorously, as if to steal some of the companion's hidden power.

"Choseph", the little woman chided, "you fuss too much. Von day, mark my verds, von day you vill learn dat people haff to make zere own vay in zere own lifes, no matter vot pressures may come from ozzer vell meaning persons". She glanced curiously at her own companion and issued a hardly audible criminating grunt intended to be heard only by him. Both men smiled, amused for different reasons.

The woman's voice betrayed the high-pitched weakness of age, yet still retained a modulated force that had long ago been perfected to chasten the listener. The accent was soft however, and, without giving way to the impurities of English, it was instantly identifiable as foreign, though pleasant - once attractive - once sensuous: Germanic. Despite the length of time she had lived among the potters she had not lost, nor wished to lose, her native origins. But she loved it here, and she loved the English. And she saw the potters as men of earth, water and fire, just as she saw their produce, the things they made with their hands; raw beauty.

"G'morning Joe". The tall man enjoined the courtesies. "Choir in fine fettle. Nice, neat programme. Who's up at Burslem?" A greeting, two statements, one question.

"George Wade is taking a group before moving on to the Sneyd. Young Caddick-Adams is up at Wolstanton. Oh, did you hear that the Middleport Union folded last week?" "Yes", replied the tall man, "It's a great pity. It is indeed. They've put so much work into their repertoire, and were really just about ready to take-off. Such a shame, and more the shame for Ed Leigh."

The voice of the tall man was taller even than his physique. Sonorous. His words were delivered, rather than spoken, with the inspiration of tutored elocution. His comments to his friend had been composed from polite triviality and yet were measured and meted out in sacred sentences. He was briefing, he was observing; watching; consulting and instructing all at the same time. Here was a man for whom words meant little; the brevity of their content was therefore impossible to misinterpret or misconstrue.

"Zat iss ze trouble viss ze Potteries, Vonce you haff soms-sing decent, vonce you haff soms-sing precious, alvays soms-sing comes along to spoil it. If it isn't zer conductors it iss zer producers. If it isn't zer chvoir, it is zer orchestra. Zer Potteries is full of music, good music; and what's more, good musicians. Look at mine own maestro; look how he has been treated!"

"Now-now", cautioned the tall man, "All that is in the past, and Madame, you shouldn't be bothering yourself about the whys and wherefores of Potteries music. Now its time to relax for both of us. To break away from the hurly-burly of music production. You have earned your rest." "I know, I know", interrupted the quaint woman excitedly, "but it is just not fair ven ze whole of zer district vonce had zer finest orchestra in zer whole country. Oh my, vat ve haff missed!"

The woman's voice trailed away as her face appeared to withdraw further into her hood. And yet the face did not withdraw from the coldness of the icy day, but it was for other reasons that the woman retreated. The hood was merely a hiding place.

Across the Square a line of children had formed a chain by taking each other's hands. Each child drawing the next along, skipping around the Christmas tree, a dancing snake, singing their wordless carol of perpetual annoyance...

'...Ding dong merrily of high, Hosanna in the Highest... Glor, or, or or, or, or or, or, or or , or, or or, or, or, or, ...(and on and on) in Excelsus......' until their guardians and protectors were compelled at length to parade their charges away in exchange for headaches and raw throats. Christmas lunch approached in a whorl of dance, a whirl of squealing.

The tall companion sensed the woman's retreat and placed his long arm about her frail shoulders.

"Come, Madame; I feel we have been out far too long." he asserted with deep firmness.

He ushered her towards the open space where the fountain stood dry, and, although she resisted for a moment, she walked with him yieldingly. With a shrug of reluctant relief, she permitted her frailty to endure his gentle physical persuasion, though not before she paid her respect to each and every member of the choir. And, to the brass players, she offered a collective thanks with a gracious movement of her hand for the rendition of her favourite hymn. It was a wave of regal sparkle received as it was given by an appreciative group of musicians. It was an occasion when their queen had been in attendance.

"We shall see you Madame in the new year. Soon, I hope. And you, John, you sir, must please come to our rehearsals in Burslem's Queen's Hall. Don't forget, the fourteenth of January. We miss you both so much, we all do." The choir mumbled a solemn agreement behind. "And I, I miss you immensely." He finished. Joseph Weston-Nichols gazed deeply into Madame's hood, and he saw a pale response of acknowledgment in a face he did not well know for the ratchets of age and pain had turned across the pale face since they had last met. A weather-tear coldly stood on the lower lid of his eye and he blinked it away. It seemed to his choir that he was weeping. He wasn't, but he may have been. "We miss you so much, dear Madame. Come back to us soon." The scene grew dark as the clouds dipped lower. In what had been a brief urban intermission, his choir had sung to its patron. In the hood he saw the lips smile. It was a smile that said much to Joseph Nichols.

The two men shook hands once more. It was to be the last time the three musical companions would be together again. Madame's cloak swept the cobblestones delicately, her protégée

in slow step beside her escorting the almost divine figure back home. Nichol's watched their return into Tontine Street, his friend towering steeply above the en-cloaked invisibleness, a firm arm directing the route. It was a fascinating image of a son guiding the retreating steps of his devoted ma-ma.

Midnight...

A photograph stood in a silver frame atop an oak bureau. It portrayed the image of an extraordinarily beautiful woman in middle-age. In the picture, the woman's lace-sleeved arm stretched to rest a hand upon the shelf of an alabaster plinth. Finger-tips, hardly touching, gently laid against a vase of English roses. A delicate hand, an extension of femininity from a satin-clad hour-glass body. But, it was in the face that all the beauty was held. All the beauty.

> *"Sea-Kings' daughter from over the sea,*
> *Alexandra!*
> *Saxon and Norman and Dane are we,*
> *but all of us Danes in our welcome of Thee.*
> *Alexandra!"*

In the evening, Madame had taken a little broth, the tiniest amount carried within a teaspoon from bowl to glottal mouth, drooling; offered with the gentlest of care by the dark man who stooped beside her. Lunch and dinner plates lay with assembled food, untouched.

They had talked a little while about music. They had talked, pausing frequently for the woman, the quaint woman, to take in raw-red breath. They talked of

Burslem's Arts Ball which they had both attended earlier in the month: a scene of artists and civic patrons parading themselves in the ballroom of the Queen's Hall in the annual celebration to show pride in their art. There, in the Mother Town, famed for its ceramic art and design; famous for its artist sons and daughters. A school of art of which Madame was herself proud to have been made an honorary patron.

The house in Charles Street where the two resided, was full of the memory of sound. A record - some orchestral piece - Scandinavian - had been playing. And it was thus as it ever was that they had found the house shortly after midday when they had returned from their stroll; full of music, memories of loved remembered songs. But now the only sound was the slow tick of a grandfather clock counting out the long minutes into hours as the second half of the day moved to close over midnight. Emptying echoes drawn into the static accumulators of lonely hours of ages. Christmas Day was nearly done. There had been no callers. No one knew the seriousness of the situation.

A round mahogany table sat in the centre of the square living room covered by a chintz cloth decorated with classic embroidery. A huge bowl of fruit rested in the Jasper cradle of a Wedgwood centrepiece. And close to it stood a pile of music manuscript, a sheet of which lay open revealing its straight lines, its little dots, its flags and its tails, crisp in yellowing code.

This was an old house. The walls of the room were high and the angles of the walls in the corners were rounded. A modest glass chandelier lit only those objects which lay directly beneath it in a dimness that hung without spectacle from a moulded ceiling rose. On the street-wall, velvet curtains dropped in looping drapes to the floor, each with tapestry tie-backs hanging loosely, half concealed by the fronted leaves of a potted aspidistra. The curtains provided a shroud, drawn together to keep the cold out whilst preserving the vaporous warmth of the sick room, smelling of embrocation and pink ointment. Liniment, oils and syrups. Aromas of the dying.

Samplers of stitching were everywhere. Some pieces had been framed and were galleried along the walls amid numerous credentials and certificates of proven achievement. A green velvet chaise longue tucked itself into an inglenook on another wall while three leather armchairs comfortably accompanied it. There was a leaded-glass bookcase in another corner which exhibited the seasons greetings cards on its flat top. And a small grand Bechstein piano held a prominent position, standing upon a thick Persian carpet which seemed to cover the whole of the floor with patterns of oriental curls and swirls. The room was like the inside of a music box, a container of paraphernalia; domestic bits and bobs covered by a mother-of-pearl lid, not so much half open but half closed, permitting only the briefest of glimpses into a world lost in the past.

"Play for me, my John. Just for a little while, until I fall asleep." Madame lay full length on her side upon the other of the pair of chaises longue. She lay tucked up, swaddled in a cream knitted shawl. Her face was thin, her features drawn; and her white hair, still as thick as a maidens, splayed over a plumped-up cushion. Each of her physical movements engaged the mental mechanics which enabled her to cope with breath-drawing pain. Her smallness resembled a tiny trapped barn mouse; quivering features hidden timidly from an expected fate.

The maestro gazed in honest love at the old woman. He was amazed by the gossamer translucency of her skin, so unblemished, so delicate, lying stilly waiting for some insect-like wondrous metamorphosis. He yearned for the tips of his fingers to grasp in thrall those useless twisted digits of her own hands: those talented fingers, those jointed companions of brilliance that once brought forth so much grace and feeling to music. Now they could perform no longer. Now they endured naught but the fiery rack of rheumatic anger. Although her face was but a sunken skull, her thin lips smiled giving shine to her once pretty face. He saw her beauty still even though her eyes were cowled by cumbersome tiredness. Oh how he remembered her stern beauty! That blonde, blonde hair. The fragility and sensitivity that had deceived many into thoughts of love un-spurned. That brave composure; those ice-blue eyes; that blonde, blonde hair!

His hands lay across the ivory keys oddly still, teeth of mammoths that had so often released his own passions and desires. Those keys he now touched with love, the same keys she had once stroked herself in loving sensuality. This was her piano; this though was his instrument, and the greater sound of his soft playing extinguished the remorseless clock.

Sombre notes began to roll across the room: SONATA QUASI UNA FANTASIA, the way in which she had once played in such languorous interpretation. To the moonlight, adagio sostenuto and allegretto. Time wandered, bourne on waves of music, passively across the manuscripts of ages - Beethoven through to Bruch:

'Drearly sings the autumn wind,
Through the pine woods stealing;
We must depart beloved land,
Though vesper bells be peeling.

In shadows deep thy streams are hid,
Cold mists envelop our dwelling;
O forest green, too soon the axe
Thy fairest glades be felling.

As stricken hosts our oars we ply,
Our heartfelt griefs concealing;
O island set in the Northern sea,
Arise, thy heights revealing.

Arise, and our exiled race receive,
For frail are the crafts we are guiding.
Yet still of Viking blood are we
In the ancient song confiding.

Where the storm-waves lash the rock-bound shores,
And the mount of fire be gleaming.
Ah! There we will pass the winter's night,
Of our future glory dreaming.

The silence ached. The voice of the ticking clock recaptured the tune-filled space. Hands on the piano were stilled by the song's ending. The noise of a motor car rattled in the street outside. Some revellers larked in the coldness of Old Hall Street playing a drunken game of chase outside the unlit fire station. And laughter chirruped from the town; from the Trumpet Inn, from Burton's Store, and loudly from the ancient houses of the Woodman, the Just-in-Time. And far beyond in Parliament Row, and over into the Market Place, the tall tree stood, aglow with excited fingers of electricity. Hanley had not yet settled.

Madame dozed fitfully. Her lips twisted in a pained grimace.

4.00am...

She stirred. Her head involuntarily moved to rise. ***"John!"***

The weak voice startled him. Faint nightlight strayed through a thin gap at the meeting of the curtains. He got up from his chair and knelt stiffly beside the settee.

"I'm still here, Madame - I'm still here. Shhhhhhhhh." He stroked her moist forehead and gently adjusted her cushion. "I'm still here. I shall not go away. Do not worry that I shall leave. I shall stay with you. And the doctor will call shortly, and we shall see that you will be up again. We shall see. I will never leave you, my dearest love." His quiet voice softened even more to nurse her pain. Perhaps she had not heard him, heard nothing at all?

Slowly and faltering he hummed a Grieg song into her hair: Silber, Sylvia, Solveig's Song: whispering into her silver hair. Her breath was shallow and she had no strength left to resist; no inclination to open her eyes. Into her tired mind, he helped her to put away her dreams, one by one; and with each stroke of his hand he counted them individually.

He tried to give her water but her lips would not respond, her mouth declining the drops in resigned refusal. That once, just once - a murmur - the moment when she had woken him from his own exhausted sleep. He had heard her last word; a goodbye raised with urgent power. Her last, and yet it was like a baby uttering its first. With all the final effort of her dying frame. A word, for him alone. A memorial to their life together. **"JOHN!"**

December 28th 1926.

> *'The procession moved off from St mark's parish church in Shelton led by the Reverend Prebendary, Mr F Kay, accompanied by the Reverend R M Thompson, the vicar of Leek, a family friend. The principal mourner was her adopted pupil who sat in the first of two coaches following the hearse. The tall man, in his late forties, was seen to be weeping, his head bent forward and his face hidden by a black handkerchief.'*

(Extract from the Sentinel)

An affecting moment for John during the grave-side rites, came when the old Danish hymn tune, arranged by C E F Weyse, was performed by a muted brass ensemble. The strains of the song were simple and the beautiful hymn could be heard in the distance across the winter's brittle grass, humming through the leafless trees. It was the same hymn that the ensemble had performed in the Market Square just a few days earlier. It was a song which had been a favourite of Madame's father, who also lay here, her mother also - it had been played at her father's funeral in another century. Now she would rest. But she would rest yet not in total peace, for to achieve abiding sleep, her spirit would have to wait another thirty-four years.

Later that day, it began to snow.

June 1959.

> *'We are pleased to report today the eightieth birthday of Stoke on Trent organist John Cope. Mr Cope has been the City organist since 1945 and, although he does not conduct, or have any practical responsibilities these days, he still kept in touch with colleagues and friends in the music world, but rarely attends concerts. As well as the organ, Mr Cope also plays the violin and is accomplished on a number of other instruments. Asked about his musical influences, Mr Cope referred to a liking for Wagner and Elgar. Of his early influences he said that, "I ..generously acknowledge the debt I owe to my mentor, Madame Reymond, and for the opportunities she gave me."'*

(Extract from the Sentinel)

Thursday 6th April 1962

The Evening Sentinel reported the death of John Cope, Stoke on Trent's organist, at his home at 47 Charles Street Hanley. A black-lined photograph, taken in profile of the musician's handsome face at the age of eighty, was printed on the front page.

Wednesday 12th April 1962

Today was the funeral of Mr John Cope, the organist of Stoke on Trent and former conductor of the North Staffordshire Symphony Orchestra. The principal mourners were his son-in-law and daughter, Mr and Mrs Forrester-Warden. Among others paying their tributes were, the president of the North Staffordshire Symphony Orchestra, Gilbert Sherwin and officials, Mr C Caddick-Adams and J Caddick-Adams. The present conductor, Mr P L Rodgers, also attended. The service was conducted by the prebend of St George's Church, Newcastle under Lyme, Revd. H H Wellings assisted by the Revd. A Edwards of St John's Church, Hanley. Following the service, a small group of family mourners left for Hanley Cemetery, where the body was laid to rest.

March 1999
(Journal of Fred Hughes)

This day I visited Hanley cemetery. It was a typical English spring day, the wind was high and it still forcefully held the winter's ice. It was raining, of course, and the combination of strained elements conspired to whip away words from the microphone of the portable recorder. Constructed sentences were impossible to articulate. The grave was central in the beautifully laid-out cemetery, alone on a gentle rise overlooking Hanley's Victorian pleasure park. The simplest of tributes made of granite; a stone cross on two rising pedestals on which were carved the memorials...

Idon Holst Familie Gravsted.
Fredrik Idon Holst. d,1899
Julia Holst. d. 1893
Karen Marie Elisabeth Reymond. d. 1926
John Cope. d. 1962.

Was this it then? Surely there was a story?

The Santa Claus Lady.

This is a story of Victorian drawing rooms. The swish of long black frocks; the turn of crowned hats. Gaslight and whisperings out of cupped hands; guarded glances from behind cowled fans. The story of Madame Reymond and her protege John Cope is about social partisanship, jealousy and cant. It tells a tale that embraces the mystery of Scandinavian fairytale, myth and legend. It touches upon fame and fulfillment and yet exposes frustration and failure. It alleges fraternal influence but hints at factional control. Someone - an archivist? a relative? a friend? left but a few clues to their lives.

A Potteries music critic, Frank BUTLER, in an obituary in the Staffordshire Advertiser in 1926, said of his subject:

> *'I never knew anyone with a more enquiring type of mind. No phase of artistic or intellectual life was passed-by unless she had made some enquiry into it. And I never knew anyone more kind to children and animals."*

Butler referred widely to the life of a young Danish music teacher who, for a good part of her life, chose to sojourn among the dark, smoke-depressed and clay-laden potbanks of Burslem, the Mother Town of the Staffordshire Potteries. Certainly she was a traveller, we know from whence she came, and we know that she arrived, but not the exact day. Why she came and where she was bound we shall never know. What message called her here? What brought her to make this detour? Perhaps she was a little errant in her wanderlust? Perhaps there was some divine input? Whatever it was, the potter of those times will only confirm that she appeared among them one winter's day, as Christmas approached, in a fall of snow - pure white, in the land of the black furnace-flame and the oven's roar.

As far as is known, Butler's obituary was one of only two local tributes made at the time of her death. The Staffordshire Sentinel however printed a warm appreciation, (We regret to announce the death of...etc, etc.) but certainly there were no national contributions. Another, a later writer and local music critic, Reginald NETTEL, claimed in his book published in 1944 analysing 'Music in The Five Towns', that:

> *'...above all she loved the orchestra. She saw that the musical developments going on around her in the Potteries could not attain fruition if orchestral playing remained in such lamentable case. She prayed for a conductor...There came to her a young pianoforte pupil. A boy of remarkable musical ability; a boy with all the makings of a great conductor.'*

Nettel called music in the Potteries, 'Cinderella Music', mildly accusing those responsible for its impoverished state, and the City of Stoke on Trent for its lack of interest and support when other districts, Liverpool, Manchester, Leeds and Huddersfield, had by 1905 raised strong societies patronised by powerful and dedicated manufacturers who anchored the arts and the training and retention of good teachers to the sideshow of their wealth.

In his ornate journalistic style, Nettel attested that Potteries' music had suddenly found a 'fairy godmother', one who used her own funds liberally, and her classical talents unselfishly, to help create an oasis in a musical desert. To quote his lofty appraisal:

> *'No princess in a Hans Anderson tale ever had the fairies' gifts in greater abundance than this Danish lady who so unexpectedly came to brighten the dark face of Burslem.'*

This eloquence is matched by Butler's languorous tribute where this mysterious observation is made:

> *'I know a little tot who, upon seeing Madame for the first time at Christmas a year or two ago, immediately called her the Santa Claus Lady.'* (Of course Madame, as we now know, was noted for her black red-lined earth-sweeping cloaks fastened at the neck with the enamelled head of a lion, her own face half concealed by the hooded bonnet.)

Both good men, finding no appropriate definition to catalogue her musical importance, stopped short of the term, 'principal doyen of the arts' - a description so close to being pressed by their pens - and fell to sentimental commentary as they wrote in praise of their subject. Indeed, Butler had seen her as a mentor, a teacher who had encouraged him to read more widely and to become a musical journalist. Both critics were admirers of her talents and of her personality but, at the time of her death, they both well knew - as Nettel significantly declared, that *'...she was without many friends... Her enemies never left her alone, but a few staunch friends she had to the last.'* Maybe it was true then that none knew her better than children and animals.

So, who was the 'Santa Claus lady', the 'fairy godmother', who appeared to have been so loved by some, singers and musicians, and hated by others, patrons of the arts, who came to condemn her with petty and snide malevolence? If we turn to written records we find little information. A woman who was at first taken to the hearts of the potter, embraced by his celebrated welcoming parochialness, in fair exchange for the novelty of a strange talented outsider; and yet in the end, it was the same famed Potteries' insular bonds, woven so strongly in ties of tradition and fellowship, that slipped loosely away, shamefully undone when they had used her up, when her resources were finished with.

A small package of papers and cuttings lodged in the Potteries Reference Library, present the only substantial record of her life here. Little is recorded of her private life. All those who knew her at the height of her importance have long since passed on, all personal memories forgotten or lost. A rummage through the archivist's small parcel of information whispers of fame, shouts of personality, and hints of romance, but says nothing of fact. An assembly of notes tied together with a letter or two and a few odd photographs. Apart from this there is a short entry in a dictionary of local biography, and two brief chapters in Reginald Nettel's assessment of Potteries music. No written or recorded music remains; no sounds, catalogues, portfolios by which to assess her quality and merit her achievement. And yet, in the years that strode across the two decades of Victorian and Edwardian England, it was just possible to measure the Potteries' weight against the high marks of Britain's greatest period of orchestral and choral music. A flickering candle lit to fire a beacon in the cover of a long night. And the music teacher played her part in its illumination. That is all. So, is there a story to tell?

In the last quarter of the 19th century, the Burslem suburb of Cobridge became the very model of a red-brick terracotta village, a place where the town's new commercial middle-classes had come to reside away from the smoke and grime. During that time, Cobridge became an important social link lying in a sprawl across the great 1815 Waterloo Road, half way between Burslem and Hanley. It was here, in 1881, that Enoch Bennett built his six bedroom modest mansion, number 205, where his eldest son, Arnold, spent his last years in the Potteries before hastening to London, called to a world of letters and to his destiny. As one door shuts, so another opens.

In 1887, the Holst family of Denmark came to occupy a house directly opposite the Bennett's at number 218 Waterloo Road. Strangely, and inexplicably, their 34 year old daughter, apparently a spinster, arrived ahead of them, alone and unaccompanied. Born in 1853 and christened Karen Marie Elisabeth Holst, she appears to have been the only child of Frederik Idon Holst, a master cooper of Copenhagen. A rumour circulating shortly after her arrival, implied that she had emerged from mourning her husband whose name had been Reymond. However, this is without substance and researches have failed to discover the origin of the name Reymond - not indigenous to Denmark nor found familiar in the eastern European Romantic countries, nor even during the Parisian years of contemporary impressionism. Papa Holst came to Burslem some weeks later with his Danish wife Julia. The family in exile was complete.

Karen Marie Elisabeth - although, as far as is known, none of these given names was ever used either by her or any of her acquaintances - always Madame - had studied music in Denmark under several noted teachers including the celebrated conductor and composer, NIELS GADE, which qualified her admirably for her occupation as a music teacher. But why the family had come to Burslem in the first place, under whose persuasion, at which member's instigation, remains a continuing mystery. It is unlikely that in his profession as a cooper, the father would have been attracted all the way from Copenhagen by the limited trades in pottery crating, or even to the manufacture of oak barrels at Parker's brewery - (would he not have preferred employment with the larger manufacturers in nearby Burton on Trent?) It may not be presumed therefore that Fredrik Holst, as head of the family, had come to pursue his career in Burslem. There are no references to relations living in the district nor has any inditement been made to any other branch of the family being resident in any other part of the United Kingdom. Wife Julia had no profession and her life here seemed to be one of concealed and private domestic activity. The reasons why they came must lie unresolved locked within the recesses of Madame Reymond's previous and subsequent musical career, itself a conundrum of fame and failure.

The Holst family was not without financial strength for they were enabled at once to acquire two houses in Waterloo Road Cobridge - in that 'classier' part of Burslem - a domestic property at 218 and a music salon in the same road leading to Hanley from directly out of Burslem's town centre. Trades directories between 1890 and 1896 list Reymond has having a salon at 176 Waterloo Road, a regular entry which states that she was **'Madame Marie Reymond - music teacher'**. In this same period the directories do not refer at all to the name and trade of her father. She apparently was the householder, her parents were presumed to reside with her, perhaps in retirement. Were the family so wealthy as to be able to live without substantial income?

From the beginning Madame Reymond began to establish her credentials and within weeks the register of her music classes was reasonably filled. The town held a relaxed and healthy competitiveness among a growing number of music establishments which included the Morfey brothers who had premises at the head of Waterloo Road and in Market Place. It was a firm which spawned more than a generation of music teachers and musicians to whom they sold and provided instruments. At one time the Morfey's employed H K Hales, said to be the principal character of Arnold Bennett's 'The Card', as a piano salesman before he departed, firstly in competition with the brothers in a shop just next door, and then turning to the sale of bicycles and classic motor cars, from other premises in Market Place and Newcastle Street. Another music entrepreneur was Thomas Nicklin - yet another Arnold Bennett ingenue - who made pianos at Liverpool Road, and John Bruckner who tuned organs from 37 Waterloo Road. In addition to these noted practitioners there were a host of other names in the directories of Burslem who advertised to teach music from their own parlours to the new middle classes.

Madame Reymond competed modestly, and yet it was she, or perhaps her name, that brought an intriguing light to the district. She was doubtless an excellent teacher, but it was that name that offered a peculiar undomesticated relationship; it symbolized professionalism, Victorian pride - 'salon-taught', it promised. Her name was not so much a name than a title. And, she had *'that'* accent! <u>Mad-ame</u>, with a long emphasis on the second syllable reflecting French art, *rich* patronage; it was this *en-touche* respect to the arts that the middle class housemanager of Burslem, wife of the dour pottery manufacturer, found compulsive. They lived in Cobridge among the wealthy merchants, and Arnold Bennett and his family lived across the road.

The great three novels - the CLAYHANGER trilogy - follows the dynastic course of a Burslem printing family through a twisting pattern of love, deceit and death. Much of the location is set in Cobridge and in the real house of Bennett's father - the Clayhanger home in the books. The novels are hugely autobiographical and,. In 'THESE TWAIN', the third book, Bennett describes a musical evening at the home of Edwin Clayhanger and his wife Hilda. These musical gatherings, 'at homes' or soirees, were very popular in Victorian middle class England, and it was through this social channel that Edwin and Hilda chose to enhance their growing community status. Hilda, the prime mover, chose her guests by 'invitation only' as her cards attested to, although all those invited knew that the musical evening was to mark Tom Swettnam's betrothal to a Scandanavian beauty, Manna Host.

> *'Miss Manna Host of Copenhagen. Manna Host was twenty-three, tall and athletically slim, and more blonde than any girl ever before seen in the Five Towns. She had golden hair and she wore white... She spoke English excellently with a quaint, endearing accent, but with correctness. Sometimes she would use an idiom... exquisitely unaware that it was not quite suited to the lips of a young woman in a strange drawing room; her innocence, however, purified it... what impressed the company even more than Miss Host's accomplishments was the candid fervour of her comprehensive interest in life, which was absolutely without self-consciousness and fear... somehow beneath all such freedoms and frankness she did not cease to be a maiden with reserves of mystery... All gazed at her piquant blonde face, scarcely pretty, with its ardent*

restless eyes, and felt the startling compliment of her quick, searching sympathy. And she, tinglingly aware of her success proved equal to the ordeal of it.'

This description fits Madame Reymond as well as any photograph. Of all the women in the Clayhanger trilogy, this brief snapshot of a real person says much for the author's sensuous attraction to the mature foreigner in the way that a young lusty Arnold Bennett must have perceived his neighbour. He obviously knew of her expeditionary attitudes towards Potteries music for it is later recorded that he 'greatly admired her work and the causes she supported.' But they probably would not have met intimately while he was residing in his family home for the young twenty-one year old was leaving for London at the same time the Holst's were arriving in Burslem. Any subsequent meeting is not recorded by the author and in any case, at the time of the publication of his first novel in 1898, the Holst's had moved out of Cobridge. And yet Arnold Bennett, writing These Twain in 1916, conveyed in this book a more felicitous chronology, writing as though he felt through the sensuality of his character Edwin Clayhanger, that he did indeed know Manna Host intimately. In real life, at the time of These Twain, Madame Reymond was sixty and Bennett forty-nine. Bennett's female characters were always aesthetically stronger than the male. Something about the presence of Madame Reymond attracted him deeply; something that stayed with him, a sensation which he had to tell his readers about.

An appraisal of the library's photographs of Madame Reymond show a fragile sensuality, a pacific aura which she seemed to have retained throughout her life. Indeed, judging by the later photographs, it could be said that age enhanced her fair looks. The archive pictures are of a child's flashing smile in wide and eager proportions in the confidence of an expected destiny. Then there are those of a young woman bearing the poise of adolescent sexuality; and then, in a third phase in which can be seen strong lines vividly depicting a condition of maturity and confidence. Lastly there are pictures of old age and calm refinement. In all stages of this person's development, the pictures show a lady possessed of distinctive Scandinavian translucence - not beauty, but expressed wistfulness, the kind of folky naturalness which is served best by the accompaniment of Norse wordless songs of nature. All this in the cokey crucible of the Potteries.

There is evidence that from the start of her residence in Burslem, Madame Reymond had a remarkable friendship with her sister emigre and countrywoman, Alexandra the Princess of Wales, with whom she held a written correspondence in later life. Father, Frederik Idon Holst, added his personal homage to this association when, in 1897 during a royal visit to Stoke on Trent, he was **formally** invited to present Princess Alexandra with a pair of maple-wood milk pails which he had personally hand-made for the Copenhagen Great Exhibition of 1872. Originally intended to be presented to Alexandra's father, King Christian IX, on the occasion of his silver wedding. Something, some matter which has never been identified, caused that presentation not to happen - the silver wedding celebration took place but Holst never got to make his presentation. How close was the relationship between the Holst family and the royal family of Denmark is also a mystery - royal protocol forbids hypothesis.

At the time of this civic presentation to Alexandra in Stoke, Mr Holst was accompanied by his daughter, who was then age forty-four. And she in turn was attended by her most accomplished pupil John Cope, who was eighteen.

John Cope was born in Milton, an eastern suburb of Burslem. On the lanes leading to Leek, the small Staffordshire moorlands village grew out of the footrails of the once mighty Bellerton Colliery. John was himself the son of a miner, and at an early age the parents discovered that he had exceptional musical talents, learning on the family piano and on the local church organ in a vale of ardent Primitive Methodism. His talent brought him to the attention of Madame Reymond who travelled frequently to the Cope home to supervise the twelve year old's tuition; and it was at the age of twelve that Madame undertook the full-time musical education of John Cope.

The Staffordshire Sentinel's obituary of Madame Reymond contains the information that she had adopted the boy. This knowledge had become a public talking point during the years of fame; it was this title-tattle that promoted the later protracted criticisms jealously levelled against her, that John Cope's parents had scandalously 'sold' one of their children to the teacher who had possessed him in a Faustian fashion. The truth seems to be that the teacher, quickly appreciating the pupil's potential, advised the parents to allow him to reside at her home, much in the same way that a potter's apprentice would have lived with his master's family. It is not unreasonable to suspect that Madame Reymond's passionate insistence in the boy's musical talent, and that the boy's musical life would be wasted without proper tuition, seriously impressed the parents. Here was the leading music teacher in Burslem offering her patronage to their talented son. What a great honour for the Cope family of Milton.

Upon acceptance of this form of contract John Cope's life was changed forever; he was to be a musician not a coal miner. And it says much for Madame Reymond's musical reputation, and her international status, that she at once enabled her young pupil to be sent to Munich for exemplary tuition under the great Bavarian master organist, conductor and composer Josef RHEINBERGER (1839-1901). It says more however for the strength of her finances, for she alone provided the money to facilitate Cope's studies in England and Bavaria. It can only be imagined how that boy from a poor Potteries' family felt - privileged? Chosen?

In 1897, Madame Reymond and her father moved to 76 Moorland Road where a row of terraced superior houses had just been completed. The new house faced the recently opened recreation park and was particularly convenient for the town's busy railway station. Developed some forty years previous, Moorland Road had become the prime location for prospective business/residential sites. The house was chosen with sufficient dimensions to accommodate the family's domestic and business arrangements. It cannot be said that Holst's or Madame Reymond influenced or commissioned the building of the terrace but the deeds show her to be the first owner. Above the arch of the adjacent service entry was a stone tablet bearing the name, ALEXANDRA BUILDINGS 1897 - named after the Princess of Wales!

The frontage, as it was when it was erected, is ornamented with local stone with the windows of each of the main front rooms supported with modest flat-faced Ionic pillars. In a central position above the front entrance of number 76 is a stone carving of a Grecian lyre, and the letters of the name, BEETHOVEN HOUSE, originally carved in New Roman type-face into the stone lintel, may still be seen having been blotted-out with cement some years ago.

Mrs Holst, Julia, had died in 1893, and was buried from the house in Waterloo Road and interred in a modest plot on the western slopes of Hanley Cemetery. Reporting on the funeral, Frederik Idon Holst was described by the Sentinel as, 'a white haired dapper old gentleman'. He himself lived only a few months after the move to Moorland Road, Madame Reymond and John Cope being the sole occupants thereafter. At the time of her father's death, Cope was still studying in Munich while Madame Reymond undertook the tasks of furnishing a home and a music salon. It was as though she was preparing a home for her protegee; she even had installed at 76 Moorland Road, a stylised and personalised tuition organ built to the specification and the construction of J Kendrick-Pyne, the great music master of Manchester Cathedral. John Cope returned from his Bavarian studies in 1902 and at once took up the baton and conducted many of the country's famous orchestras. He was twenty-three years old.

From 1898, Madame Reymond founded the BURSLEM CHORAL UNION paying for its upkeep with her own money. This extraordinary orchestral union was the first of its kind that incorporated instrumentalists playing alongside singers in rehearsal sessions, each division using the same annotated manuscripts, unlike other choirs which were trained to be independent of the orchestra reading from different sheets and with their own choral director. The Burslem Choral Union instantly became the most successful ensemble in the classical style of tuition and performance.

In 1904, John Cope, at madame Reymond's insistence, founded the NORTH STAFFORDSHIRE SYMPHONY ORCHESTRA which held the first of its famous annual concerts at the Victoria Hall, Hanley, in company with the Burslem Choral Union, the NORTH STAFFS DISTRICT CHORAL SOCIETY and the HANLEY GLEE AND MADRIGAL SOCIETY. All of these groups were variously patronised by the Potteries' foremost citizens and philanthropists, principal of whom were the Duchess of Sutherland and J Kendrick-Pyne and a number of gentlemen of the district including the mayor, the town's councillors and other civic leaders. These were times when it was expected that such benefactors should provide culture for their citizens, and many successfully did so.

Madame Reymond was the orchestra's financial secretary which allowed her to carry much weight in the selection of programmes which frequently included music by Beethoven, Bruch, Behrend and the works of Niels Gade. Many European composer's works were performed in those early years of the twentieth century, and yet, Potteries' repertoires rarely included the works of contemporary English composers which most northern orchestras had permanently added to their programmes, often performed by the composers themselves. This was a basic error of management and production later to be laid solely and unfairly at the feet of Madame Reymond when attendance at Potteries classical performances began to decline under the age-old dilemma of regional preference; the facilities of the dedicated halls of Manchester, Birmingham and Liverpool, each one close enough to reach out and capture the committed audiences of the Potteries, and each one jealously guarding the patronage of one or more of the great English Victorian and Edwardian composers and conductors.

Among the promoters of English music was the Potteries born composer HAVERGAL BRIAN, who was himself encouraged by Edward Elgar to perform English programmes. The 'Cinderella Music' that Reginald Nettel parabled in his book was not far short of the truth. Havergal Brian, in an article written for the

Staffordshire Sentinel in 1909, dissertated on what he saw as **'an orchestral crisis in England'**.

The prolific Brian, who was also a journalist and music critic, had for a long time been making angry waves against the directors of regional orchestras whom he alleged had deliberately been ignoring the works of the front-line English composers in preference to the, so called, 'high standards' of continental countries, the Germans, Austrians, the Russians, Hungarians and the Scandinavians. Using his home town as an example, Brian pointed out that in Weimar, the 'home' of Lizst, Wagner and Berlioz, there resided a smaller number of inhabitants than in Stoke on Trent, and yet the concert audiences in Weimar were large enough to sustain season after season of locally produced work which attracted the attendance of the rest of Europe to its famed music festivals.

Of course choral music was at its zenith in the northen industrial towns during these same years due entirely, for a generation or so, to the practice and participation of the tonic sol-fa system invented in 1855 by a Hull Sunday school teacher, John Curwen. It was from this point in English choral music, that working class people were given a voice, learning to sing by sight and sound following the local leadership of Burslem's town clerk, Josiah Wolstancroft POWELL and a Hanley pottery manufacturer, George HOWSON. Successive Potteries' choirs were at the cutting edge of tonic-sol-fa tuition and Powell's STAFFORDSHIRE POTTERIES CHOIR won many national choral competitions, based as they were at Burslem Town Hall. There was certainly no shortage of choirs in the Potteries district.

As the drum roll of choral music and performance gathered pace into a thunderous tumble, good local orchestras were hurrying to keep up. Was it to be sight and sound for everyone or, time-honoured annotated music for a few! A dangerous rift had been forged between the two factions which many saw was underscored by the seductions of class distinction. This openly affected the recruitment of good technical instrument players to the Potteries orchestras. The problems were exacerbated by the difference in interpretation and emphasis. By virtue of two musical systems running side by side, many orchestral conductors couldn't be bothered to spend the time arranging concerts for instrument players to read from annotated sheets while simultaneously a choral conductor was leading his choir from coded phonetics as though on the same platform. Rehearsals merely resulted in a poor show of bad communication. The conflict between orchestral musicians and choirs was well noted and criticised; and the Potteries received its most damning public criticism following the first performance of Coleridge-Taylor's The Death Of Minnehaha at Hanley's Victoria Hall:

> *'The chorus sang the words... as if they loved it... Excepting for a few minor blemishes, their performance was most excellent. Not so that of the orchestra! And here we must raise a protest at the treatment the work received at rehearsal... The accompaniments were inefficiently played, many of Mr Taylor's best effects "missed fire" completely, and occasionally certain instruments took long rests that were not in the score'.*

(Part of a quote from the Musical Times)

As Nettel observes:

> *'If this were a unique example of failure to recognise the importance of orchestral rehearsal it would be bad enough, but similar behaviour occurred time after time.'*

These problems highlighted the lack of good conductors and musical directors and, as a consequence, many good and competent musicians left to join orchestras in Manchester, Leeds and London, leading only to a strengthening of the position of the choir master in the Potteries at a time when musical vogue was for large oratorios. They said, quiet wrongly, that the purpose of the orchestra was to support the voice. Unison had turn to discord.

Although these problems also existed in a large number of northern towns, the situation in the Potteries had reached a critical point, that is, until John Cope founded his North Staffordshire Symphony Orchestra. For a brief period, - 1904 - 1914, and even, to a lesser extent, throughout the personnel depleted war years, the Potteries orchestra was among the finest in the country. Many things of course changed after WWI, including the sponsorship of regional orchestras. A residue of talent was absorbed from the provinces into the orchestras of London, Birmingham and Manchester, a fate which had been predicted by Havergal Brian, not wholly because of the war, but because of public disinterest and disinclined patronage. And yet, throughout his own substantial literary output, Brian, the defeatist, was often supportive of his local colleagues and eloquent in his praise of their individual enterprises. But, at the same time, while agitating for an 'Englishness', he did little in a practical terms to deter his colleagues from employing the devices of self-destruction. He was content to remain distanced, using his newspaper column as a barrier, as he continued his warnings against self-indulgence, foreign over-intensification and non-committed attitude to nationalist programmes. Brian however was as provincial as the next, and so his remarks and warnings were lost in a general inclination and movement towards regionalisation.

The oddest absence in Brian's critiques were praise for the North Staffordshire Symphony Orchestra. He never once commented on the innovations and prefecture of the work of orchestras energised by Reymond and Cope, even though he was of Cope's age. Good, bad or indifferent, it seemed that Brian simply ignored their contributions; and yet, how successful the alternative might have been; how exciting if composer, conductor and producer had been able to perform together! Perhaps Brian took exception of Cope's refusal to conduct Brian's composition, 'First English Suite'. But Cope at this time had fallen foul of Potteries patronage and much that he did locally was ignored; Cope refused - not because of the value of the work - but because he was unsure of its reception.

While Brian, 'The Awkward Cuss' - to give him a name made famous by North Staffordshire's the New Victoria Theatre - was busy criticising musicians and patrons and company directors without mercy, Madame Reymond was writing over-familiar letters of encouragement to English composer Gustav HOLST (no relation to her family), and receiving correspondence from SIBELIUS who accepted her invitation to become a patron of the NORTH STAFFORDSHIRE ORCHESTRAL SOCIETY, an association which she attempted to provide an umbrella for the whole of the Potteries orchestral music. And even at this time, she was continuing a long-term correspondence with the now Queen Alexandra, while Cope was getting on with the practical business of training and conducting the

Burslem Union, rehearsing them in a nearby timber merchant's sheds and the crate yards of the Moorland Road Pottery, a place used in the 1950s by the famous potter, Susie Cooper.

In the meantime other Potteries music directors were fighting their own corners, none more impressively than the 250 strong TALK 'O' TH' HILL CHORAL SOCIETY, a choir which had won many national competitions under its conductor and musical director James WHEWALL, a local coal miner, from the same colliery and village as the two Potteries trades unionists and MPs, Samuel Finney and Enoch Edwards. Whewall was another man who found fame out of adversity, invalided out of the pit - the same one that Finney left following his own accident - with a serious injury. Another who turned to the succour of music.

At the same time that Madame Reymond was enjoying written social intercourse with the Danish Queen of England, James Whewall and his company, were giving a command performance before King Edward and Queen Alexandra at the Royal Albert Hall. At his greatest moment of triumph over his competitors, music critics were asking him to comment on his future aims and targets for his fine choir: Whewall replied, with typical working class sang-froid when initiating the truth, **'Nothing! And we cannot exist as a choral society, for the Potteries already has too many'**. At a time when it seemed that the whole district was singing, the musicians were muted, except that is for the wonderful orchestra of John Cope, playing to enraptured fans in Manchester and Birmingham, yet so detested at home.

With his huge scope as a musician and conductor, his wide talents as a teacher, Cope continued to improve his orchestra and honed the skills of his players to the international respect he himself had earned. Relying upon the practical arrangements of separate sectional rehearsal, he brought together individual elements to form a collective, an immaculate regiment which responded together to the demands set-out by the master - his musicians played to support the choir and the singers were integral to the whole: Cope's singers needed not a separate choirmaster, for the conductor's holistic approach enabled them all to see the bigger picture and therefore the end result. But, neither Cope nor his mentor, Madame Reymond, had any public money coming in to aid their own depleted resources. As a consequence, Madame Reymond instigated a compulsory contribution scheme to which Cope's musicians made small payments for the prestige of performing under the Burslem maestro. It was to be another cause of accusation levelled against Reymond by the town's elders when the day of reckoning came.

In late 1905, the Burslem Union was considered by Cope to be good enough to enter a competition. Although he personally disliked competitive performance, 'crude and unethical to his trade', Madame Reymond saw it as a way of improving the financial situation which would be bolstered by the prize money. She also considered that success would bring the necessary publicity to encourage local public interest and provide wider a patronage which was able to give pecuniary support.

The competition, at Morecambe, Lancashire, allowed for a number of professional players to be included in the orchestra. Cope took only his amateurs and they lost by just one point to the winners who had employed four professionals to play a tricky violin section. Instead of Burslem turning out to greet the national runners-up with positive commiseration, Cope and his orchestra were met with indifference and scoff. It was now that the town brought the full force of its petty anger and jealousy against the woman who had dared to teach them art: teach art to those who understood more about art and artists than she would ever know! This **foreign woman** who had presumed to lead **them** out of a cultural desert. Were they not the inheritors and legatees of the skills and art of Josiah Wedgwood? They needed not the likes of this female intruder to teach them music, for, were their singers not already rated among the country's finest choirs? They cared about her 'arrogant ways' as much as they cared about the 'vainglorious' Arnold Bennett who had deserted his home town to make an awful lot of money by 'caricaturing' its people and its language! Reymond! Bennett! Cope! Brian! Artists? Pah!

For her part, Madame Reymond quietly saw the potters as, 'feeling people', who lived in a place where great beauty was refined from the dirty earth. Here, in this industrial cage, she felt that they needed a refuge. Was there not a time when they asked her to deliver them from their ovens? Happy to receive all her experience and all the money - her own money - money that she was prepared to invest in them? And, when money was scarce and failure was writ, they backhanded her explanations, pooh-poohed her high-minded attempts, made fists at her financial loss, pulled faces at her fine countenance and, carped spitefully at her achievements. With the consummation of huge irony, the potters discovered that they could never forgive Madame Reymond for her talents, her undaunted demeanour and her valiant strength. They would never excuse her for her commitment to the music she wished to share with them. Even when she brought the LEEDS PHILHARMONIC CHOIR to Hanley, to show people what they could achieve themselves, the potters saw it as haughtiness intended to wound them. And, worst of all, they were loathe to ever pardon her for introducing them to the talents of one of their own. A man, who, but for her tuition and encouragement, would have been but a chapel organist, a musically-minded coalminer. They could never forgive this foreigner for bringing to them the finest symphonic conductor the Potteries had ever known! Envy and Pride, the two worst social sins, conspiring together to defeat kindliness and selflessness!

Turning once again to THESE TWAIN and Arnold Bennett's descriptive skills: when he produced the final book of the Clayhanger trilogy, he was a long way away from Madame Reymond's execration. And yet he knew the anguish she must have been suffering - for had he not endured himself the potter's censure for omitting Fenton from his phonetically preferred 'Five Towns'? He knew first hand how cutting the potter could be, how they would turn against her:

> *'...The other women were a little saddened by the thought of all the disillusions that inevitably lay before her...*
>
> *Manna Host simply replied with the innocent characters of a fairy tale:*
>
> *"I adore the Five Towns. You do not know how English you are here... I Love You..."*

And Bennett concluded:

> *'...but disillusions were inevitable...'*

But, in spite of her disillusions, Madame Reymond stayed committed, inescapably bound by the chains of Destiny that the fates had planned for her.

Looking back from a distance of nearly a century, it seems today that her single most important success was to give the Potteries an extraordinarily competent musician who founded an orchestra and choir which influenced local classical music like no other before or since. And, at its best, this union gave force at the time to the belief that a national college of music excellence could be founded here among the raw blackness of industry. And maybe it also promoted the myth in some quarters that Madame Reymond from Copenhagen had met her Destiny here in Burslem, the Mother Town; but that the stars had let her down by failing to shine upon this prescribed rendevous.

It has been asserted that her piano craft had a dimension and scope not often encountered in a provincial town, that she had a musical fluidity which revealed astonishing accomplishment; that she had such choice of musical rendition that she could instantly select the mode for anything she might have been called upon to play. And, she displayed more than her musical talent by demonstrating a total understanding of all the fine and classical arts associated with social response and high commitment. Thus, she claimed, that she read all Bennett's Five Towns novels, 'more than once', because she said, she was 'a part of them'. Who then could better empathise with her real life character than the author Bennett, and she with the content of his books - an integrated absent partnership - a deep unspoken relationship between the writer and this 'pretty lady' of the Mother Town?

Realistically, without Madame Reymond, John Cope would indeed been a good pianoforte performer; a competent organist. But, because of her guidance, he received incontestable and unassailable references. Such was his musical progression, and such was the pride she felt in him after Munich and Rheinberger, that she needed to prove to the people of the Potteries that they had among them an artist of international class, and to show them they she had discovered him for them. Indeed, she went so far as to engage the HALLE ORCHESTRA to play at the Victoria Hall, Hanley so that her protégé could conduct it, no matter that it was at her own expense. She wished only to illustrate to the Potteries music lover what she could achieve for them and what she was prepared to do to accomplish it. But the petty-minded lateral Burslem burgesses viewed it all as self-glorification - sensitive and vexed that a 'Northern Seas invader' had presumed to tell them what was good for them. And yet, to Burslem, Madame Reymond gave all she could give without consideration of her own losses, or contemplation of her own gains. People of the Mother Town, in their parochial ways, just didn't comprehend her unselfish generosity. By the principles of their own insular lives, making-do in poverty and self-achievement by social climbing, were the only ways they knew.

John Cope meanwhile, kept his own counsel. A pointed stick in his hand said for him all he wished to say, as he gave light to the spirit of orchestral accomplishment. Through his talents, and perhaps for the first time in their lives, potters could experience live performances of the works of Mendelssohn, Mozart, Beethoven and Schubert under the rooves of their own concert halls. But Madame Reymond had been terminally wounded by the people of Burslem. She vowed to leave the Mother Town.

In 1919, the music teacher was financially broke. It was the year that John Cope bought a house in Hanley and departed Stoke on Trent to tour with the CARL ROSA OPERA COMPANY as its principal conductor taking with him his mentor as his constant companion.

In sublime contrivance the Burslem elders blamed the two for 'desertion', and she alone for the crime of 'abduction'. And then, Madame Reymond's Burslem Choral Union was broken up and dispersed.

Cope went on to conduct many of the country's best orchestras in most of the finest concert venues in Great Britain. But in 1924, Madame Reymond's constitution for touring weakened and they returned to their home in Charles Street Hanley. At long last Cope's talent was being recognised in his native Potteries and he resumed his position as conductor of the ailing North Staffordshire Symphony Orchestra. Under his direction once again, and the orchestra came to thrive under the batons of Sir John Barborolli and Harold Gray. Cope's credentials were now unquestioned and he, but not Madame Reymond, was instantly forgiven. However, in a rare conciliatory mood, the Potteries musical administrators were forced to acknowledge Madame Reymond's services and promoted the performance of a concert at Hanley's Victoria Hall on April 6th 1925 performed by Cope's orchestra which accompanied Reymond's friend, the great Belgian pianist, de Graef. One of the items preformed was the OSSIAN overture by Niels Gade and fittingly, both the British and Danish national anthems were rendered.

Madame Reymond continued to enjoy a well earned respite in the pleasant gardens of the house in Charles Street until her death a year after this famous concert, appropriately at Christmas, the mid season of winter in which she arrived here. She was buried alongside her father and mother in the unpretentious grave in Hanley cemetery. It's a plot that is marked with nought but a simple stone cross and carved words written in the Danish language. When she died, Madame Reymond was seventy-three; John Cope was forty-seven.

It was soon seen by all how much the death of his special friend and inspirational mentor had greatly affected him, and he quit the orchestra to take-up the complimentary post as organist for the Stoke on Trent Corporation, as well as sharing his ceremonial tasks as music master of both Newcastle under Lyme High School and Orme Boys School. In his later years, he enjoyed some success with the Stoke on Trent Operatic Society, but he never ever really captured the international status or the fame that Madame Reymond had envisaged and planned for him.

Beethoven House in Moorland Road was sold and became offices, and Burslem returned to its dark and musically deprived backwaters. Even so there have been some notable success stories, the Royal Doulton Choir was extremely popular and nationally acclaimed before it was terminated, as was the Royal Doulton Prize Brass Band. In recent years, Burslem's Queen's Hall has been blessed with highly professional performances of the North Staffs Amateur Operatic Society; but the golden years of the town's music died when John Cope left with his beloved counsellor. He eventually married and had a daughter. John Cope was eighty-three when he died in 1962. And, like his mentor, he bore handsome looks to his death. Both had been countenanced with natural reflective and pacific physical and spiritual attractions.

On her seventieth birthday, Madame Reymond received a gift of a beautiful gold and pearl brooch in which her initials, KMER were inscribed. The brooch was surmounted with the British Royal Imperial Crown. She was also given two large farmed photographs, one of the late King Edward VII and the other, a portrait of the then Queen Mother when she was Queen Alexandra. Both photographs were signed and accompanied by a handwritten note from Alexandra commending

Madame Reymond on her:

> '...*splendid work for music in North Staffordshire during 34 years. We must all be most grateful to you for your wonderful work and its benefit to the Country*'.

A brief postscript was added:

> '...**Wishing you a happy future in our beloved Denmark.**
>
> **Your friend. Alexandra**'.

Alexandra died in 1925, just a few months before death caught up with Karen Marie Elisabeth Reymond. Neither woman returned to the place of their birth, but they both made huge social contributions to their adopted country.

The relationship between John Cope and Madame Reymond was undoubtedly made in the heavens. Their lives mean so much to the romantic and yet so little to the historian. Their influence to Potteries music was short lived, and yet, how great it could all have been.

When Cope died, his body was interred in the Holst family grave in that modest Hanley potter's field. Teacher and pupil, friends sharing the deepest of love, together again. Once upon a time in the Potteries, the light of two stars from far-off parts of the Universe crossed. And, having come together, they passed as one into Paradise.

It is said that a story has no end until its theme is resolved. But life, we know, is not like that. Most people are born and pass without note, only a few leave their names and their deeds to posterity. Hundreds of millions have been and gone, and hundreds of millions are yet to travel on this planet. Billions of people whose lives are not recorded in the books of fame; billions of lives whose story have no end, no themes resolved.

Postscript.

> *Mortgage and Conveyance*
> *dated 12th October 1897*
> *from Mr William Mellor (vendor)*
> *to Mrs K.M.E. Reymond, widow.*
> *For the sum of;*
> *one thousand eight hundred and ninety-seven pounds.*

The above is the heading of a title of a deed in relation to the new house, 76 Moorland Road. This deed mentions the name, BEETHOVEN HOUSE, and in each transaction the signature of the mortgagee is appended by the title - **WIDOW**. Over the next ten years, Madame Reymond re-mortgaged or borrowed to a total of one thousand and twenty-five pounds against the property. Among the lenders were the Rev Charles WERNICK, the rector of Abberton, Colchester; John BOURNE, a Smallthorne earthenware manufacturer; and money from the personal estate of the wife of Charles Edwin Henry GOODWIN, the noted Hanley jeweller. There is little doubt that all of this borrowing went to the up-keep of her orchestra and choir. As with most lives, mysteries remain. The life's journey of Madame Reymond is no exception.

A corner of the Fountain Works
Still standing in 1999

(below)
The Old Packhorse Lane
The main road to Newcastle until it was taken over by the giant Fountain Works of Enoch Dodd

Once the front of the American Hotel facing the old Main Road to Hanley

(below)
The Melly Arms, Lower Street
The only domestic building standing in the huge St John's estate which once often housed some 10,000 people

The skylight window of the New Inn
Said to have been made to admit light to the painting school of John Lockwood Kipling - Rudyard Kipling's father

Arthur Berry's favourite pub
The old inn can be seen to the left of the hotel rebuilt in 1885 - on the right is the entrance to Bourne's Bank. The old road to Hanley.

High Street - now Greenhead Street
Looking towards Ball Bank. There were once worker's cottages all along the left side. The Dolphin stood where the car is.

The Fountain
Replaced in 1992

The Washington Stores
Where William Moorcroft developed his unique artistic creations. A tunnel connected the Studio with the main Macintyre Pottery on the other side of Waterloo Road

(below)
The fine architecture of the Hill Top Chapel
Admired by Arnold Bennett. Demolished in 1979

The American
Officially opened by Enoch Wood in 1834.
The right bays were added after extension in 1890

Colin Melbourne's sculpture of Henry Doulton in Market Place

"Show me yours and I'll show you mine"
Men and women's toilets on the pottery of Burgess & Leigh

(below)
Outside the offices of Burgess, Darling and Leigh

How well the presence of the ghosts of long dead potters can be felt in these cobblestone alleys
Burgess, Darling & Leigh, Middleport

(below)
Where the Battle of Burslem Raged
The George and Dragon that sat at the site occupied today by the ground floor left side windows

A courtyard at Burgess, Darling & Leigh
"Make do - make fit!"

(below)
Lancashire
Overgrown

The favourite pub of workers at Dunn Bennett Pottery
Now demolished to become part of Steelite

(below)
The courtyard of Moorland Pottery in Moorland Road
Once occupied by Susie Cooper

The only sculpture of Josiah Wedgwood that depicts the great potter as an amputee with a wooden leg

(below)
The south perimeter of the Wedgwood estate of 'Over House'.
Nearby was an ornamental lake.

The Dog and Partridge
The last house in Hot Lane, once home to a community of 5,000. Now there are none!

The great art of the potter

Once the cultural centre of Burslem, Bournes Bank
The Palace Cinema on the left, the Coliseum on the right

(below)
1970s Burslem
left is Alcock's Warehouse. In a period of 5 years it became a classic car showroom, and a nightclub called 'Strikes'. The Salvation Army Citadel has also been demolished.

Things that lie underground
Preparing for Ceramica and discovering the Victorian toilets. Such a waste!
They were reinterred

The Royal Express, Bournes Bank
Well known as the "Jig Post".
Note the worn step!

Market Place
Familiar scene of the centre of Burslem in the 1950's

Celebrations after the Battle of Waterloo
(Curtesy of the Adams collection)

The memorial on the tomb of Nathanial Johnson
Wrongly named as the man shot in 1842
who we know to be Josiah Heapy of Leek

Chapter Seven

ARTS AND ARTISTS

'...*Socrates, the greatest of the Grecian Philosophers, in all his conferences and discourses, sought to lead his scholars to an acquaintance with themselves. We wish the managers of our schools would, in this respect, imitate the example of a heathen teacher; for we infer, from the visible fruits of the instruction imparted, that it too frequently tends to make the learners, when out of their pupilage (sic), forget themselves; and to regard their slender acquirements somewhat too highly - that it produces a degree of self-confiding independence, quite at variance with that Divine and most apposite lesson, "As the clay is in the potter's hand, so are ye in mine hand..."*'

(Ward, pg 38)

Art, it is said, can be fashioned in the oddest, the most obscure and unlikely places, and by using the strangest of devices. A ball of clay in the hands of a potter is base earth until the wet printless fingers mould and make. A sable, a quill of hogs hair, a pen or an iron nail - for what is art if it is not craft, if it pleases oneself and gives joy to others? Pick up and sharpen a wooden clothes-peg, wash out a piece of sacking and turn out a bagful of torn-up old clothes. Make sure there is plenty of time to spare: rough hands become a handcrafted makeshift Jenny which, in the old days, has produced the most beautiful and the most useful tapestries to grace the cold tiled floor of a workman's meagre kitchen.

>   **In the wide front of a chimney's breast,**
>   **Sat a bent and ancient iron chest;**
>   **Black-leaded - O you know how -**
>   **With doors on either side of its bow,**
>   **And hooks suspended over the blazing coal**
>
>   **Supporting an encrusted cast-iron kettle,**
>   **To hover above the cinders red and full,**
>   **Held steady, grabbed with another hook,**
>   **With clinkers of black in a blacker nook;**
>   **Blacker than sin, blacker than black to look.**
>
>   **A padded sofa standing against the wall**
>   **With shadows cast out of a shivery hall.**
>   **A cheap chaise-lounge, against the wall it stood,**
>   **With knitted covers on the ends of wood,**
>   **And padded too, sitting atop of an old pegged-rug.**
>
>   **All hours I've watched my mother sit**
>   **Grasping at a sharpened stick a peggin-out;**
>   **All night long, till my father, an old man,**
>   **Spit blood across the fire bars' painful pan.**
>   **- Pegged-rug, in colours made from things thrown.**

Billy's coat, and Arthur's worsted trousers,
Shirley's skirt and Hilda's compromisers -
Ruptured and all torn-up and sorted into piles,
Then put back in patterns for test and trials
On smelly sacks, stuck in for miles and miles.

The whole laid out across the floor
In pride of place for warmth and layer,
For shine and new, and comfy on the legs
As though the life was grateful for the pegs
That made it - even for the whitlows and the segs.

The dog would lie on't. And bugs would grow inside
To breed bigger bugs to roam for far and wide.
And then mother'd take some more old rag
And tear it up to mix it in the bag,
For better they who louder brag.

A blessing. A comfort for all to take.
A place to warm an aching back.
A covering to stand for years 'til rug's demise,
Among the soil of a pauper's house
With the bugs and the weevils and the lice.

Another sack, another coat
Another pair of pants to cut.
Another cardigan and skirt,
Another pegged-rug o'er the dirt.
A piece of beauty - a poor man's art.

In 1914, when public houses in England and Wales opened daily at 5.30 am and closed at half past midnight, the length of permitted hours was discretionary to the brewer and publican; most, in the industrial towns, used their best time to catch the shift workers going to and from the factory and, as a consequence, a clutch of beer-houses grew around the factory gates. In the country, where the farm labourer came and went and was hired on a day to day basis, the public house was more flexible and seemed to be open at all hours. And, if the doors were shut to allow a rest period for the publican, they would just as soon be re-opened if the customer's knock demanded it. The sounds of un-tuned pianos barreling trivially from the parlour amid clouds of fag smoke and smells of old beer and old clothes, were manifestations of pointless lives. Memories which remain only for a few of the most ancient. The pub was the old house at home; everybody had at least one on their doorstep.

It is from these times that memories of the comfort of a central stove-pot fire with the publican's mongrel lying lazily in front of it are evoked. That cur of nondescript lineage had pride of place, lying in the multi-coloured patterns of a pegged-rug done-up out of rags by the artistic imagery of the women of the house. A sharpened stick to poke the holes through a sugar sack and a shove of a swatch of granddad's grey or dark blue jacket to make a contrast alongside a swathe of bright green or a floral print of a sister's frock, long since rendered down out of useless thrall having served two elder siblings previously; out-grown and handed down.

In the Potteries no one knew those public houses better than the artist Arthur Berry. In 1979 Arthur Berry recited his award winning story, **'A Lament For The Lost Pubs Of Burslem'** in a broadcast on the local radio station, BBC Radio Stoke. It was a soliloquy, a contemplation of his own collected memories of the public houses which he frequented. Premises which he enjoyed as much for their patched-up and improvised architectural contours as for the patched-up folk who sat in them in long, leisurely intervals in the shadowy taprooms in timeless afternoons. Berry, first and foremost a painter, loaded up his pallette with the crude and raw colours of life in order to present his startling descriptions of dark interiors that made homes for crooked-bodied and bent-minded men and women as they played-out their lives with a deck of cards, a box of dominoes, a pint of stout, a glass of mild: gnarled hands of whist loaded with jokers.

He identified and exposed the torture of his fellow men such as 'bookies', out-of-work window cleaners, and the butchers of the meat market who killed animals in the streets and carried their carcasses into their stalls, after which humorous slaughter, they went for a pint or two at the nearby, 'Hole in The Wall' or the New Vaults, next door. These butchers were....

> **'Bucolic, red-faced men given to quick repartee and with a liking for drink. One, I remember was a short, breathless fat man with a polyp nose and a straw beamer. His unfortunate nose looked very vulnerable as one saw the wicked curve of his well-worn bone-hafted knife being sharpened. It was said that he ate raw meat and that he had worms that tickled the back of his throat and caused him to cough all the time.'**

Nor did Berry omit and excuse women from his cholic humour in his descriptions of the 'weaker sex - the distaff side' as drinking women who, 'sat in snugs squat as frog.... with knees the size of hams'.

> **'Such a woman was Mrs Potts, God rest her soul. She never stopped eating pork sandwiches all the days of her life, and her great chops must have chommeled** (coll) **herds of pigs down. I do not think her stomach had been empty for half a century or more. And she would sit there, night after night, filling her face with pork and Guinness.'**

The Mother Town in Berry's time was full of pubs with hidden rooms guarded by broken doors boarded-up with hardboard panels for unexplained reasons; doors fastened with brass latches that rattled identifiably; penny weighing machines that never worked and stood unused in corners. And the pubs were full of 'Popes of the Taverns' and hierarchies of high placed and respected 'drinking Mafiosos' who never worked and never suffered illness. 'Shilling women and wing-collared councillors', where pot-women performed impromptu fertility dances on table-tops. Like the pegged-rugs in the potter's hearths, this was beauty; cruel, harmonious realism.

Berry, like Arnold Bennett, counted journalism as a feature of his work, though he was never employed by a newspaper nor did he submit serious articles to them. Although his rough narrative style could not be further from the polish of Bennett's realistic compositions, Berry nonetheless possessed a portfolio of realism just as dramatic and as richly subtle. Berry's writing was - like his painting - a strong collection of portraits in which can be seen representations of hard-bitten people drawn in pitiless caricatures. In his art forms, his people were not so often physically different from Bennett's own characterisations, but, whereas Bennett sifted through the mind, Berry thrust his images straight into your face, beating the mind and the mind's eye with remorseless shame. Both men were artists, analysts, good reporters. Both men knew public houses, but only one was comfortable inside them.

> 'How terrible has been the loss of the stove-pot. These magnificent, dark stoves that were once the heart of every taproom. Elegant, black shapes that stood there with such dignity, like totems. To sit against these on a winter's night, and feel the rich heat, and see the amber beer was a benediction. Men would come at early-doors to get a wooden seat against it.
>
> To watch a publican's dog lying asleep in front of one of these stoves was to watch luxury. The loss of these stoves was a great blow. Men have watched fire for millions of years. To give a form, like a stove, to hold the fire was a perfect blending between nature and art. And to watch a publican lift the top and put a shovel-full of coal on was to watch a High Priest attend to a Ritual of Life.
>
> To go into the Sea Lion in Waterloo Road, and to get in early when the place was fresh-mopped, and the new beer mats were laid out on the tables; the ashtrays were clean and the stove was crackling with fresh coke, and the red quarries were gleaming, and the bar-pumps were shining, and the dominoes and cards were waiting, and the publican had got a clean collar and tie on, and all the world was shipshape. This was happiness, or as near to it as I've ever come.
>
> And, what could be nicer, fresher than a newly whitewashed Gentleman's? I have patronised public houses because the Gentlemen's smelled so fresh. But then, I have patronised pubs for very strange reasons.'

Arthur Berry was born in Smallthorne, a village on the eastern outskirts of Burslem, on February 7th 1925. Smallthorne still holds a dwindling colony which once belonged to a moorland hamlet that grew on the far side of the High Lane ridge, itself an outcrop in the rippling shallows of the Peak District and the Pennine Chain. In early times, the farming community extended from the valley lands that forded a fast flowing tributary of the River Trent. Here was Ford Green lying below Smallthorne, a smaller hamlet which stood across the brook at its most convenient section separating lower North Staffordshire from its higher lands as the county's northern boundary approached Leek, the Queen of the Moorlands. The oldest house in Stoke on Trent stands in Ford Green today as it did in 1580 when the Ford family extended their modest dwelling during a time that witnessed the growth of their farming lands, lusher under the bleak ridges of Norton le Moors and Brown Edge.

The Fords were an old family whose undefined roots probably lie amid the scattered remnants of Norman Conquest. They were Lancastrian in their support for Lord de Audley who was killed at the battle of Blore Heath during the Wars of the Roses. And in the Civil War, their flag was raised for Charles, although they remained quiet throughout that turbulent time, afraid to reveal themselves to the skirmishing Roundheads for fear of attack and destruction. Happily, they were left unmolested. And later, the Young Pretender's Highlanders, in their travels south, also visited Ford Green Hall in 1745, but once again left the occupants unharmed as they passed by along with the Stuarts into oblivion. When other times insisted, the Ford family embraced the Quaker faith during periods of religious austerity.

In 1590, Mary Ford, of the Moss, was married to Thomas Burslem of Dale Hall. The eldest daughter of that union, Margaret, married Gilbert Wedgwood, the founder of the great Burslem potting dynasty.

On the eve of the first Great War of the twentieth century, Smallthorne was home to some ten-thousand inhabitants; mostly they were the families of colliers, chain makers and fustian cutters. They knew nothing of Cavaliers and Roundheads, and cared even less for the Fords who had departed more than a hundred years before.

At the time of Berry's birth, Arthur Berry's father was age twenty and employed as a colliery bricklayer at the nearby Bellerton Lane mine. There had been a regular history of mining and miners on Berry's paternal side going as far back as three generations. Suffering the restrictions of coming from a poor working class background and being part of a large extended family and the privations it brought, it had always been his father's intention to improve his own lot in life and therefore, by doing so, to improve his immediate family's welfare. To this end the father took on an extra occupation as a barman, working in many of the numerous public houses in the back to back village setting. Eventually he was granted a liquor licence of his own and moved his wife and young son into the cramped fixtures of the Albion Inn in Croft Street Smallthorne. It was in this small back street pub that the family lived when Arthur was 12 months old. The smoky environs of the public house were his first recollections, memories he carried with him throughout his life.

There were a number of close associations with the licenced profession on both sides of the family, and in the midst of these tough industrious flinty folk, Arthur Berry grew up very much aware of his working class antecedents. His maternal grandfather, a patriarch affectionately known as 'Owd Turp', had been a long-serving publican who had retired from the Forrester's Arms, at the 'top of the bank', to a large house in Garlick Street on the Burslem side of the High Lane ridge. We have it on Berry's own authority that the aged, cantankerous, straight-talking moorland labourer in his story, **'A Visit To Cornelius'**, was drawn from his experiences of visiting his grandfather who lived alone attended only by the occasional servitude of his dutiful daughters and his small but vicious black mongrel dog. In this dark tale, hierarchical working class patterns of disjointed family duties and respect are explored with raw accuracy. It's impossible to leave the story without being affected by its aching view of the awful expectancy of sameness; to see the future as a crouching griffin monitoring the inevitable happenings that would arrive the next day as they had the day before.

The Smallthorne of Berry's childhood contained all that he could expect from life. In these narrow backs his future stretched out before him; cobbled alleys, long-lanes of cheap-jack manufacture in a make-up and make-do existence; church schools and Primitive Methodism; a society enslaved by the lines of paternal precedence, old men bound by the chains and ties of staple industries.

> *'As a little lad, I was always playing down the backs, and, somewhere inside me, I've been playing down the backs ever since. Backs are the backs of streets. Only terraced houses or tunnel-backs*

have them; and all the backs have little water closets and coal-holes. And all the way down to the end of the streets these little coal-holes and lavatories are seen disappearing into the distance. Some of these alleys are cobbled and some have been covered in asphalt; but many are just flattened and uneven earth. But outside most folk's back gate you'll find that they've either put a bit of concrete down or tarmac, or built a surface out of the ages of ashes, spread day after day for years and years...

I've watched old folk going in and out of these lavatories. Watched how a cat sits on top of a gate. Watched how it watched me back, and watched how it would jump on top of the back-kitchen roof and walk across the ridge of tiles. I have seen dogs snarl with their noses and bare their teeth under the bottom of the gates, and watch passing dogs bite at them and snarl back, and understood that there's nothing more that dogs like than having a fight with a dog that can't bite back.

These backs always had a smell of dog-muck and smoke about them. There was always dogs leaving a pile and somebody having a fire and somebody pulling their face "'E wants' reporting, that owd bugger does - 'E always has a fire on washing day"...'

The houses in these streets are all the same size with the same size roofs, the same size doors, the same number of bricks. Everything on each house is in the same place, repeated again and again... But the diversity of human life has civilised their uniformity... All this came out of poverty... out of lives that were often filled with the drudgery of work and more work, most of it boring and monotonous or dangerous. Or worse still, no work and no money for the mothers of poverty to raise big families out of.'

There was a great distance between the two communities of Burslem and Smallthorne, far greater than its actual few-thousand downhill steps betrayed; a huge awesomely imagined distance that separated the town's boundaries by eons, for the residents of the different communities stuck together, distanced from each other by tribal isolation. The mile and a half long journey - downhill all the way to Burslem - was rarely travelled by the ordinary person having no purpose to visit. It could just have been a hundred leagues distant judged by the culture and fellowship that stood between the two townships' constituents. In Burslem there were potters, white-faced with dusty chalk: in Smallthorne, colliers lived, burrowing and burying themselves deep into the earth, black-faced with fine coaldust. Through the lives of these alcohol-ambushed and work-weary kinsfolk, viewed with the mesmerism of surprise, of awe and anxiety across the public bars and through the cracked parlour doors and crazed windows of the taproom of the Albion, Berry saw his own tomorrow. Amid the reckless anticipations of the growing and impatient child, the boy witnessed his own future's bleakness, its emptiness, a silent scream dressed upon the grim, drunken faces of the colliers. These were the faces that came to be representative of his artistic style: wide-eyed children behind low desks in darkened schoolrooms; half-faced men caught in profile and bent to machinery in factory sheds; white-faced ancients, unsmiling amid rows of blackened vegetation in broken down allotments where black-eyed miners took their Sunday respite. This was the crop of the publican's son, a harvest that one day the artist would garner.

When Berry reached the age of ten his mother initiated a move from the pits and pubs of Smallthorne to the rural district of Biddulph. The 'flit' came upon the family suddenly, though well-considered by the mother who worked long and arduously behind the scenes in order to improve the family's environment. The move would also enable Berry's father to continue his work in the collieries in the new area. However, the father was very much set in his own ways and he did all he could to resist the evacuation from his beloved public houses and his 'rounds' with his mates. But Mrs Berry was to have her own way, not only securing the tenancy of a small farm cottage, but negotiating her husband's new job with the manager of the Victoria Colliery. And so, Biddulph it was to be.

Here was freshness. Long open meadows away from the pit, a rugged land with craggy outcrops of rock at the rolling tail of the Pennines; a house in down-land, braved inside the harsh contours of millstone grit as it settled to the flatness of Cheshire. It was in this moorland village that Berry resumed and completed his education and from where he began his journey into art and painting.

In 1938, when the young pupil was fourteen, Berry passed an examination for entrance to Burslem's School of Art. In the meadows accessible to the family home, Arthur had developed an interest in making sketches of the natural views. This line drawing was encouraged by his mother having had his skills brought to her awareness by an observant and liberal minded headmaster who favoured the pottery industry for his pupils rather than the pits. Berry's father however, had long since cast his labouring lot in with the coal mines of Biddulph. Here he found hard earned security out of which he manufactured simple expressions to remind his son that there was nothing to be had from life without working for it with manual endeavour and physical exertion. When time approached for Arthur to leave school, he advised him to go out and 'get a proper job. There's 'nowt to be 'ad from painting and art.' He cautioned his son that if he became an artist he would be without a wage and would always be poor. 'Theyt always be a three and seven-pence ha'penny man', threatened his father; and yet, when Arthur's academic achievements had been fulfilled his father would always greet him pleasantly and with some degree of hidden pride; 'Howdo Rembrandt!,' he would salute his son. Arthur, his mother and his headmaster won the day for the young man's future, and Arthur's life was pledged to painting.

To the young student from the open fields of Biddulph, Burslem was a revelation. A town rich in the ore of artistic freedom and flush with contestants engorging themselves on larger than life architecture; to Arthur everything was huge, it felt as though he had been transported to another part of the planet, a haven which was a capital, a country of art and artists.

At the time, the Mother Town housed the most renowned school of art and design in the county of Staffordshire. Its superintendent was the most radical of educators, an established artist named Gordon Forsyth, mentor to nearly all of the great Staffordshire pottery artists of those times. Here Arthur Berry became a disenchanted pupil, impartial to his studies but eager to tread his own path. Other interests drew him and no greater lure had Burslem for him than its public houses of which there were an abundance. In 1943, when he was eighteen, Arthur legitimately entered their taprooms and parlours where he met his fellow students and their teachers and held long beery conversations about everything, even sometimes including dissertations and the judgement of modern art and art's modern practices. But, outside there was war, and with WWII upon them, these conversations were more geared to the interests of the ways of social discourse rather than in art study.

In these establishments of profligacy Berry found his inspirations among the careworn powdery-white faces of the slip-house man, the dipper, the mould-runner, the fettler and the stouker. Idlers and 'out of work window cleaners'; bookies' runners, boom-breasted prostitutes, pigeon fanciers, gamblers, tinkers and vagabonds. Here he discovered affiliations with industrial and social self-abuse, discordant standoffs in family neglect and careless welfare, men and women who had become out of touch with the values of hearth and home. In this comradely cauldron he discovered the specialty of idleness for he was compelled to observe men and women who had been cast of the shores of contemptible ablution, starved of love and ignored by salvation, awash in the tears of depression caused by the lack of work. The shout of self pity and the silent whimper of old age and loneliness were the street-cries he heard.

The young man from the backs of Smallthorne bucked at methodical teaching and, even though his principal was a teacher who allowed the freedom of independent design, the relationship between Berry and Forsyth was forgettable. From Burslem, Berry went to London, somehow having buckled down to pass his examinations for admission to the Royal Academy of Art where for the next three years he spent his time in South Kensington leading the life of a Bohemian. Despite his leaning to the aversion of work and spells of downright laziness, in all truth his qualifications for admittance to the Royal Academy proved a commendable accomplishment for the young man from Smallthorne who now went on to follow the traditions of many previous great Potteries' artists and designers. And he took to London with him his mental sketch pad containing the memories of his home town from which he slowly deciphered the codes until they began to emerge into his early work.

In the beginning, Berry's pictures were insubstantial and he often found difficulty in identity and reliability in recall. His restraint of application and self-criticism accompanied him and his skills hardly ever impressed his own self-estimation; his influence upon others was slow in coming. Although he believed he was a talented artist, he feared that the measure of his success was having to be set by the standards of the classroom and that his own capabilities would be lost in the corridors of teaching. When he, much later, discovered his writing talents, Berry used words to reach a wider audience, un-shackled from the imprisonment of the dual dimension of visual art. It was as though being a great painter was never going to be enough. He felt that he needed to have a touching relationship with his audience and not simply by exhibition in the less-frequented enclaves of the galleries. Words were an outreach of his paintbox, they provided him with the third and fourth dimensions which allowed him to sit among his audience and share the experience of intimate of communication.

The debt he repaid to others for their interest and their encouragement to him in becoming an artist was never reflected in his paintings, but his fidelity to his art could be measured by the effect it had on his health. Berry was born with a deformed right arm which was useless to him for any passion he might have held in the physical template of life. A large framed man, he often suffered the illnesses of weakness of body, palled even more by his predilection for alcohol. But it was largely because of his labourious professional progression, and the unease of his relentless and frustrated search for inspiration and identity, that he was to succumb to his phobias. And the regularity in which he lost his muse hurt him as much as his anxiety to make a living out of selling his pictures. That fame only came in his last years when he ultimately owned-up to the consequences of the self-inflicted wounds which had frequently hurt him and cursed his canvas characters. Writing helped. And he discovered in his stories the therapy which enabled him to spasmodically come to terms with his angst.

As a playwright, Berry's characterisations were more pliant - he became a juggler with situations, a potter who was able to mould his canvas characters into fantasies of realism. His invention was extremely successful - Berry found that he was able to cross the divide between the creativity of art and the craft of performance. On the stage the dark pictures he painted came alive and theatre-goers saw what he saw inside his public houses: men and women - ugly and crude yet beautifully romantic - hideous and stunning, all in one go. People who never went to galleries were introduced to the stylish whims of the Spanish Dancer of Pinnox Street, the surprising ordinariness of St George of Scotia Road and the 'wickedness' of the Weston Coyney Cowboy - beer-drinking, life-wrestling, comics of pathos.

To some art critics, Berry was an artist who had forsaken his art, he was a painter turned writer, an artist who had abandoned the solitary dedication to his art for the pleasures of popularity in a mundane craft. Some have said that he'd disengaged from the reporting of life's chronicles and had attached himself to the less valued responsibilities of recording oral history. But the question of balance was no longer Berry's prerogative, it had become a matter for others - his new audience. Nevertheless, before he became a writer he was a painter, and this should never be forgotten.

Berry's hard won diploma brought him home to Biddulph and enabled him to find a teaching job in Manchester where he submitted to a life of being the reluctant instructor who taught life classes trammelled by the grind of daily travel by train from Congleton. Strange people passed in and out of his life now. He chose a wife and took her back to the farmhouse in Biddulph. But, both marriage and city life proved to be too big for him to cope with. He was besieged with agoraphobia which was often accompanied with serious bouts of hypochondria. The breakdown of his marriage was the consequent predictability of the pairing of two independent minds. Out of the clutter and congestion in his life, driven by artistic isolation within a job he resented, came his outright fear of space and his accord with the minutiae of habit.

A failed marriage did not exempt Berry from the fascination he had for women. He courted them with naivety and wooed them with stealth. He explored the opposite sex microscopically. Love for women always provided the adventure of amazement, caution, a mixture of fear and excitement as well as romantic fractiousness. Despite his unrefined facial features and a deep voice oddly affected by an unnatural feminine timbre - he never failed to attract women, and it was women students who were the most attracted to him. Like Arnold Bennett, who also had a failed marriage, neither man found a capacity to solve the disciplines of shared housekeeping. Both loved female companionship, and both carried around with them the life-long burdens of physical disability which they berated as its host, though always in the privacy of the mind, yet with the attendant pruriency of morbid self-diagnosis.

Arthur Berry was at home in Burslem. He was inescapably drawn to its dirty streets, its buildings, its public houses and the characters that lived here. As a writer he was a natural successor to Bennett but his influences were drawn from the sarcastic beauty of Dylan Thomas and the obstinate criticisms of James Joyce. In his monologue Sweet Mystery of Life, Berry notices the townsfolk passing across Market Place into Cock's Entry:

> '..."and one by one and everyone, all different and yet all the same. Them with a bit of egg on their chin and them with none."

The legions of the nondescript drawing their next breath and unthinkingly, blinkingly as they work through the days of their lives. Vacant-looking gas men in green overalls, bus conductors and tidy little wives with push-chairs looking in the cake-shop windows at the pretty little cakes. And mothers of poverty with their crammed-jam-full-prams. And fancy women dressed to kill in their imitation musquash and Indian lamb. And fancy-men wearing mohair coats and signet rings. And the girl who's been up Ticklebelly Entry once too often and is up-the-spout. And floods of bingo-women squashing their bootees flat. And fourteen-year-old lad-mad wenches new to their charms who wobble past on platform heels linking arms, pursued by gangs of hooligans with their little bitten fingernails who roar back at the wind

> "Richy-Tichy bitter and crud
>
> who live on a diet of chewing-gum and blood."

And honest clerks from the building society offices in knitted cardigans. And plausible rogues and mumblers and oddballs, psychos and nuts, addle-heads, pin-heads, nitwits, non-wits, the soaked, the half-soaked, and everyone of them with eyebrows and eyelashes, nostrils and a nose. And blue black-men and green black-men, brown black-men, full-black black-men each with a hundred teeth. And there are others. Great boozers high in the full flush of their lives. The poker-faced professional gamblers and those with crazy betting-shop-madness hoping to make a fortune out of a midday sun. Head-road cods and lesser-road cods. Head-bummers and lesser-bummers. Schoolteachers ambitious for Grade B. Schoolteachers ambitious for Grade C. And zip-zap-zonkers followed by pigeon-arsed local Sabbathers. Stylish smokers of pot and old men coughing their guts up with silicosis. All of them have no hair and all of them have bad teeth and all of them have stomachs. And some of them are as game as tip-cats. And there are those poor buggers who have to draw fourteen breaths to take the next step. Rake Hells and innocence. The good and the mindless good. And them that have just come to fetch the birdseed.

> "And some fancy belly-pork and some fancy chops.
>
> And some fancy knuckle-bones and some live on slops."

And some live exclusively on tripe chitterlings and hodge. And beside these are the chip-reared legions and all that lot. And all them and all the families of them and all them that live next door to them and them that live next door-but-one to them and them that live in the next street. All this procession of forked-legged, nipple-damp creatures. And all those and endless more go backward and forwards under the entry of Cock Yard about their daily business of their various lives.'

Even without the lure of this environment Berry could never have remained in Biddulph or Smallthorne painting scenes of bucolic reverence, for, in a theme he often touched on in his written work - it was an idle man's preference to becoming nothing more than a handicapped labourer. The die had been long cast, before he could have anything to do to influence the result. Instead of becoming a declared great and potent artist, he became instead influential among his peers - and that very much included the characters and ordinary people of Burslem's public houses - and he was iconic to his students who were quite simply enraptured to be counted among his companions. And he stayed in Burslem where he became the complete self-analyst and communicator, community judge and municipal advocate most expressed through his paintings his plays and stories reflecting his own life and life-style.

Berry's autobiography, **'A Three And Sevenpence Halfpenny Man'**, published in 1986, is a glum compendium of the state of a mind often at the end of its tether. It tells of illness and sudden death; of the anguish of failure, the departure of identity, the fear of loneliness and worse, much worse - the inevitability of disappearance. It makes grim reading and has a difficult style which presents the reader with a semantic challenge in order to worm-out the personality from the prosaic form.

The story is un-illuminated with Berry's high achievements - it is what the author in him would have called, 'an ordinary life'. As a biographical acclamation it says little about the genius behind the pen and brush. It is, in the most basic format, a documentary portrait of himself as observer - like one of his black paintings - ordinariness encapsulated. The writing craft and style of this autobiography obviously fascinates Berry the chronicler, more than the writing of his own life. It is as fragile as a painted egg in its design, and he has used all his simplistic devices and materials to paint a most complex picture of himself. Bleak nakedness, bare of the big event, a disappointment for the reader looking for explanations or the harmony of a life with its times. It is a book that literally drowns in sulky resentment in the final pages. It is the story of a life and nothing more.

In the book's structural style, Berry often wallows in surges of pointless recollection, like the time he was sick on a train, putting his head out of the window as a passing train fills his face and lungs with smoke and steam. The shock of it, makes him sick even more, **'the spew'** coming from him **'like a pipe, streaming'**. And his temporary passion for a young London prostitute while he simultaneously hopes for the unreturned love of an artistic colleague. And page after page of blank remorse over the drunken death of his friend Copey, resulting in his own personal descent into phantom sicknesses culminating in a prurient interest, and later fear, in the imagined ailments of his lower intestines. His move to a new house, and his irrational conflict with a bunch of local youths late in his life, pestered by them, believing they were conspiring against him. His health was deteriorating, his depressions were deep as he looked dissolutely for symptoms of rare and unknown illnesses peculiar to himself, obscure diagnoses found in medical dictionaries. He blamed society, youth, their mothers and fathers and the inadequacy of the law. The autobiography ends amid the low horizon of a black sky over the broken fence of some long deserted field, an allotment and a broken shed.

As with all Berry's stories and his pictures, the bits and pieces of the book are little more than instant snapshots taken in a hurry, during a crisis, quickly before the unreasonable mind erodes them. The backdrop is the forgotten years of austerity, the 1930's, '40's and 50's. These long drab years that were the dark ages of the 20th century. Berry's pictures are reflective of this. Berry was, it seems, unable to talk of happiness. He could only tell the truth.

Here is a society driven by that bleakest of Potteries' colloquialisms, 'scrimping!' It's a word that lived in the bug-filled 'pegged-rugs' on the cold hearths of a thousand terraced houses. Scrimping and saving, an essential factor of those times, an age which permitted few meagre pleasures, other than those found on the hard seats in cold chapels, in draughty flea-pit cinemas and in the sparsely furnished bars of the public houses. It was a society that was held together by thrift and hand-me-down values, and Berry reported on this, these dismal brittle connections, these threads of choking industry. He saw his town through the imagination of broken house-women - 'mothers of poverty' - wearing head-scarves and age-stained tatty raincoats drawn over pinafores, clutching children about their black skirts, waiting for some tragic news at the pit-head and the factory gate. Time will look back one day to record that the stories and the paintings of Arthur Berry told the bitter truth of a people that held together when it would have been easier to give-in, and the Three And Sevenpence Halfpenny Man told the bitter truth of the artist who was worth, at the very least, ten-shillings!

Arthur Berry died on 4th July 1994. His remains lie in an un-notable part of the cemetery in High Lane, a restful place that also watches over the ashes of Arnold Bennett, in the shadow of the Dirty Hill, below the extinguished flames of Sneyd Colliery. The memorial inscribed on Arthur Berry's gravestone does not say enough for the artist or the man. And yet, in its ambiguity, perhaps it does:

**'Whisper to the silent earth - I'm flowing.
To the flashing water Say - I am.'**

Berry was a successor to a fabulous ancestry. From the time of Josiah Wedgwood great artists have provided their talents to fashion and embellished the manufacture of that most basic of form of craftsmanship - pottery. Wedgwood himself employed world renowned artists knowing that he required the best to eliminate his competitors. Academicians such as John Flaxman and M. Jean Voyez brought their talents to North Staffordshire working under Wedgwood's direction. The employment of acknowledged artists was an approach that was found practical and preferable to the master potters and pottery manufacturers of the late 18th - early 19th centuries, for their designs and decorations were greatly sought after by the rich and noble to whom the names of Adams, Wedgwood and Wood of Burslem conveyed only that they were dedicated enough to employ such artists as George Stubbs, Joshua Reynolds, Angelini and Roubiliac. And in those times, the potters were possessive creatures who worked in secret and protected their designs and inventions from all who would covet their 'curious' trades. Teaching the crafts was one thing, allowing an apprentice the knowledge of design and decoration was taboo for he may one day take his master's art to copy, steal and brutalise.

Perhaps the earliest form of art education in the pottery industry came under the instigation of Herbert Minton and Colin Minton-Campbell who respectively employed, Leon Arnoux and Louis Solon at their Stoke company which was to become Minton Hollins. These Renaissance and Classical artists not only were uniquely creative - Solon introducing the pate-sur-pate process to the industry - they encouraged their local assistants to experiment in their own right and taught them practical and theoretic style and traditional artistic principles during the middle of the 19th century.

Only to a minority of far-sighted potters did it become apparent that art training was fundamental to creativity and therefore to necessary to create a sounder and stronger foundation on which to build a reliable and reliant economy. But for the majority of manufacturers the fear of training an artist and then to have him abscond to their competitors, with his 'deviously' acquired talent, would result in nothing less than perfidy and sabotage. Education? Training? Out of the question! The answer for the employer, largely ignored by the employer, lay in rewarded trust and payment for skilled production. One such forward-looking manufacturer was Henry Doulton.

Henry Doulton came to Burslem in 1877 having at first gone into partnership with Shadford Pinder of the then Pinder, Bourne and Hope, Nile Street works. Pinder's were producers of basic tableware under the management of the last in the line, Shadford Pinder, who was seeking to improve the quality of his produce, and to succeed he employed John Slater of Minton-Hollins who had been trained by M. Arnoux. Design work improved but it was Henry Doulton who saw the true potential in the Burslem company and directed Slater in his own personal preferences, his individual company plans, in which used new specifications in the manufacture of bone china as well as in both ephemeral and enduring design. In 1882, Doulton's took over the sole running of the potbank. Henry Doulton was an inspiration to his workforce at whatever level and his zeal demanded the most intense energy for them to keep up with his visionary pace. What Doulton acquired in return for his enthusiasm was a town full of craftsmen who were born into the making of pottery. All he had to do was provide them with innovative passion and, most importantly, in-house training in art. Doulton found in John Slater the ideal man to deliver his mission.

John Slater was the grandson of William Slater of Derby (1784-1864) who was a self-taught artist and pottery painter and who instructed all his family in his artistic methods and styles. Winning the district's ceramic painting first prize in 1863 and 1864, whilst at Minton's, John Slater was considered among the leading artists of his time and his talents were much sought after. Born in 1877, Slater exemplified master teaching pupil but on a wider scale. A decorator himself, he established in-house seminars of brainstorming sessions bringing his individual craftsmen together to overview each departmental side of productivity so that the end product could be examined and amended before completion. This was unique in the pottery industry controlled by a system of individual trades and tempered by the necessity of having such a wide and varied output diversified across the region. John Slater led a team of modellers, designers, engravers and painters of such talent that it became the goal for every artist to work for Doulton and the postulation of pride in reaching that goal.

Nor were Doulton's restricted to choosing from local artists. Famous modeller Charles Noke trained at Royal Worcester where the development of ceramic form had reached the highest degree of international recognition and appreciation. He came to the Burslem pottery at a time when Henry Doulton had no qualms about what, in the 1980's, was known as 'head-hunting'; Noke was an artist who had great influence on the development of glaze, rouge flambe and lapis lazuli surfacing, and Henry Doulton was his boss. Another Worcester man was Edward Raby who possessed the properties of unique imagery and used wide expression in floral painting, whose use of deep reds gave prominence to a range of exceptional brindled ware that even world-wide could easily be identified as classical Doulton. Specialists were employed, such as David Dewsbury, a Burslem man trained at the Hill Pottery in the Samuel Alcock school, was employed at Doulton's to perfect his interpretation of orchid reproduction by the gift of freehand, while John Hugh Plant, having trained at Coalport, came as a landscape artist. Pupils of these artists found their own styles by studying in-house production; great names such as floral artist Percy Curnock and gilder William Skinner, who produced some of the finest gilding ever seen in the ceramic arts. Artists were employed individually to paint landscapes, seascapes, fish and fruit; animals and the fine plumage of exotic birds, while men such as Charles Vyse took the art of engraving to such a high level that Doulton's, along with Heath and Baddeley, became the leading engravers in the district, comparable with the nation's greatest. All of these artists were proud to be retained by Doulton and all of them passed on their skills to their apprentices down to recent times when a number of modern artists received their formal training at the Royal Doulton School of Sculpture before it closed. Recognisable street art and statues are prominent in a number of North Staffordshire locations, the work of Steve Whyte and Mike Talbot, both artists having passed through Doulton's school.

Many leading pottery manufacturers were, by the middle of the 19th century, engaging their own teachers, while centralised schools of art education were beginning to make some ground in training local men and women to become freelance and actually financially aided by the possessive and exploitative manufacturers. The 1860's saw some of the most spectacular changes in artistic and practical developments in ceramics since Wedgwood. And it was planned to initiate a central school for art education, under which roof would contain a central ceramic museum and library. Manufacturers in Burslem had already decided that the ceramic art of the district and indeed of the nation, would be placed in the Mother Town. Where else!

William Woodall was born in Shrewsbury in 1832 and lived his younger life in Liverpool where his industrial management training took him to work for the pioneering and experimental Liverpool Gas Company. At the age of twenty-five, he was recruited to manage the newly formed Burslem Gas Company which was based in the Holehouse off Nile Street. Although in its infancy as a public service, Woodall immediately revolutionised gas production to the extent of a 300% increase in consumption in factory lighting bringing high returns for the shareholders who consented to his supervision of the Burslem Gas Company's move to Longport in order to accommodate its growth and to take over the responsibilities also for lighting the streets of Tunstall. The Mother Town was made for Woodall and she duly provided un-met opportunities as reward for the energy of the young aspiring and enterprising Salopian. At the time of his arrival, voice had already been given to the building of a central school of art in the town and within two years Woodall had been seconded to its steering committee. Almost from the first day of his arrival, Woodall was taken under the wing of Scotsman James Macintyre who was one of the most successful pottery manufacturers in Burslem at the time. Woodall's career began reflecting that of Macintyre's for both men had been educated in business in Liverpool, although Macintyre's route had been through shipping and canal freight transportation. By the time Woodall arrived in the Mother Town, the Macintyre's had been well settled for twenty-five years and had formed the Anderton Carrying Company of Liverpool with important offices at Longport serving canal freight.

In 1854. James Macintyre, looking for local diversity, took over the pottery business of his brother in law, William Sadler Kennedy who was in partnership with William Maddock at the Washington Works in Waterloo Road making ceramic door handles and other fittings. Macintyre, a potent businessman, improved trading a hundred fold in all descriptions of domestic porcelain specialities. The degree to which his business expanded was reflected in a workforce of some 600 operatives and, in 1862, he took a new chief of staff and manager, Thomas Hulme. During that same period William Woodall married Macintyre's daughter Evelyn, a union which was accompanied by a dowry in the shape of a partnership in the great Washington Works as it was called. In that same year, these three men laid out the ground which enabled them to become the most important businessmen and public benefactors that Burslem has ever seen - Macintyre was 51, Hulme 24 and Woodall 22. Captains Courageous!

Whilst they were building their company they began to formalise their own programme of civic involvement at the pinnacle of power of three other important Burslem families, the Alcocks' of Brownhills and Sytch, The Davenports' of Longport and the mighty Wood family of Burslem. These were the principal movers behind the erection of a new town hall in the central market place which opened in 1857, inside which was placed the pottery museum based upon the entire Wood collection. The great architectural council house was designed for exhibition and choral performance with a large civic function room, a small council meeting place, a police station and a few committee and administrative offices. Opening to huge civic celebration, the town hall offered nothing in the way of education for art which was seen as the role of the manufacturers and individual teachers such as William Muckley, a talented art teacher who had promoted the idea of a school of design in 1852 but was told, in no uncertain terms, that because of the refusal of central financial investment he must continue to make-do with his existing classes which he held in rooms above the stables in the Legs Of Man public house in Market Place. Muckley promptly left and took a post in Wolverhampton - he had decided that the Burslem managers were simply not interested in art education. The three entrepreneurs from the Washington Works were planning to change this.

In the sparse loft spaces above the town, over the Legs Of Man and across the way above the New Inn, where John Lockwood Kipling was teaching poor pupils for pennies, the great talents of the ceramic trades were given the basics of art tuition. One of Muckley's students, Joseph Walker, son of a Burslem surgeon of Church Street, became despondent over inadequate facilities in a town which, by the manufacturer's claims, purported to be the world's centre of ceramic design. It was the young Walker that approached William Woodall, at a time when the latter was beginning to make a name in local politics and civic guardianship, and proposed to him that he should come behind a movement that was growing strength among pottery artists to establish a permanent school of art in the Mother Town. But as yet Woodall was not in any position to entirely fund such a long term project. However, the proposition remained close to his heart until 1859 when Walker, Woodall and Hulme, attempting to take advantage of the new Public Libraries Act, stimulated the Burslem Board of Health to petition the Liberal government for public funds to be made available for a free library to be initiated in the town.

But Woodall's overall view was much larger than providing reading books for people. Through the offices of his father-in-law, who by then had become an influential member of the Burslem Board of Health, Woodall pressed for the erection of a combined library, school of art and museum. That year the Wedgwood Memorial Institute Committee was inaugurated with Macintyre as its secretary and included honorary committee members the Earl of Carlisle and his great niece, Millicent, Duchess of Sutherland. There was land in Queen Street which was owned by Cork and Edge and which had been the site of the Brick House Works of John Adams and Josiah Wedgwood. This land was not readily available even in 1860 until, with its amalgamation with Sydney Malkin, the company moved to Middleport leaving their potworks and the old potworks opposite, available for re-development but the scheme was not as plain sailing as at first thought. The land, though tied, was in the end released in 1863 when the committee purchased it for fifteen-hundred pounds raised by the sale of premiums. Woodall took over the position of secretary from his father-in-law in an attempt to move the project on and work was commenced to clear the old factory ruins. A competition was organised for the best architectural design which was very much influenced by government stipulation as it was required to pay the cost of the bulk of the construction work. This didn't pass without its own problems for it took a second competition to award the first prize to Mr G B Nichols an architect from West Bromwich, endorsed by central government. And then, in the closing weeks of the approval of contract, much of the front pediment was altered from the purity of Italian Renaissance to incorporate the inclusion of terra-cotta panels in Roman style designed and made by Rowland Morris and William Wright, two local sculptors who were taught at South Kensington School of Art at the same time as J L Kipling, whose own first successful competition entry in collaboration with Robert Edgar, was also side-stepped by the Nichol's contract.

On 26th October 1863 the site was presentable enough for the Chancellor of the Exchequer, W E Gladstone, to come to Burslem to lay the foundation stone, a ceremony which he performed using an exquisite silver trowel manufactured with a ceramic handle made in fine china and enamelled in gold by James Macintyre. The speeches took some two hours to complete and were followed by a banquet at the Marquis of Granby Inn which lasted throughout the day. And that was it! The following day Burslem got back to normal in its industry, grime and smoke. And in the days following nothing happened for the project, almost as soon as it was begun, ran out of money and it needed all the efforts of persuasion of William Woodall to undertake even the commencement of work on the site which lay derelict behind boards for five years!

Woodall commissioned an important fine-art exhibition of national and local contributions shown at Alton Towers which raised some two-thousand pounds towards the total cost estimated five years previously at 5,800. Meanwhile, the site was subjected to the elements behind boarding until the spring of 1868 when construction work finally started. On April 21st 1869 the building was officially opened by Earl Grey of Rippon as an education centre even though substantial debts carried-over prevented the building from being opened as an art school until October that year when it admitted its first 150 students. The facade was magnificent! The frontage was like a classical tableau and the breathtaking detail was a unique example of Italian classical design crafted by the finest representations of Victorian industry with typical attention to elaborate and ornate construction. The Mother Town had been in danger of trailing behind Stoke and

Hanley in contemporary architectural design and production - not any more, for the Wedgwood Institute stands today as a monument to great Victorian enterprise.

At the instigation of a board of governors which included such prominent names as Davenport, Woodall, Maddock, Hulme, the first art principal was appointed, Mr W Theaker, a graduate from the South Kensington school, who set the standards of pottery design lecturing from a centrally positioned teaching balcony dictating art form by parrot-repetition. Under Theaker semi-nude model classes were modified from clothed classical poses, a daring step under a Victorian civic administration. Over the next twenty years the Wedgwood Institute played a leading part in the town's education; it housed the free library of 2000 books - mainly collected by donation - (Burslem was in fact the second library in the country to adopt the Free Library's legislation) - and the Endowed School for Boys existed here until it moved to Longport Hall in 1880 - it was in the Wedgwood Institute and Longport Hall that Arnold Bennett received his educational preparation before moving to his alma-mater, the Middle School in Wolstanton.

Theaker died in 1902 at a time when popularized art tuition had become appreciated and accepted by the manufacturers. This in turn encouraged the student into clay experimentation in design and fashion. Parents also no longer perceived the social difference of extended classical education for their offspring, seeing now the consequences of the developing trades which had been all the time on their doorstep. Theaker was seen as a man who provided variation in art as well as pottery crafts; his trained students were instantly sought after by pottery manufacturer once they had completed their courses.

The new success of art education saw the Wedgwood Institute outgrow itself and, in becoming home to the Stoke on Trent ceramic technical college in 1892, the building was enlarged at the rear to accommodate some fourteen extra classroom and studios. The redeveloped Wedgwood Institute was officially opened by Queen Victoria's daughter, Princess Louise in 1894 and immediately the pottery scientific and technical studios were filled. The Endowed School had already moved to Longport Hall and it was obvious that the school of art needed a new home, a separate building altogether.

William Woodall, tired from his civic exertions - he had been Member of Parliament for Hanley for 15 years holding a ministerial position, chief bailiff and mayor of Burslem where he was a member of the Board of health and chairman of most spending committees, a writer of books and newspaper articles - retired to the home of his nephew in Llandudno where he died, as Theaker had, in 1902 at the age of sixty-nine. His great friend, pottery manufacturer, mayor and confirmed bachelor Thomas Hulme, was determined to see the completion of their combined endeavour for the benefit of the education of Burslem citizens, and in doing so to leave their names etched in stone in permanent recognition. Both men had been making financial preparation for a separate school of art and in the year of Hulme's own death, 1905, while serving his second term in the office of mayor, he gave the land opposite to the Wedgwood Institute in Queen Street, which he owned, to the Mother Town for the purpose of erecting an art school there. Hulme died in August, but within six months, the foundation stone of Burslem's art school was laid by the Earl of Dartmouth. These great Victorian benefactors had done their bit!

The first art principal at the new college when it opened in 1906 was George Thorogood, another classical student from South Kensington School who promoted his style in accordance to the traditions expected by the ceramic manufacturers. These were times of new technical innovations and scientific advances, some would say to art's detriment because of the over-use of lithography to push the bounds of trade and economic wealth and speed of production, rather than to pursue the internal ethics of social purity of art. There were indeed but a limited number of artist who dared to challenge the manufacturer; very few artists with confidence in their own talents to stand against the economics of the trades. No one was more prominent as a courageous artist who believed in his own skills than William Moorcroft, an ironic product of the schools that Macintyre and Hulme had instigated.

Moorcroft was born in Burslem in 1872 and five years the junior of Arnold Bennett, he followed Bennett through the classes of the Wedgwood Institute and Longport Hall before taking an art diploma at South Kensigton Art School. In 1897 at the age of twenty-five, William Moorcroft was invited to work at James Macintyre's Washington Works where he experimented with colour and developed a style call Florian Ware which involved lining a plain biscuit pot with tubed slip and 'dripping' colour into the contours. While Macintyre's potworks prospered in ceramic electrical and constructional furniture, Moorcroft was securing fame for them under his own creativity. By 1911 he had elevated his department at Macintyre's into one of the most respected art studios in the world. Among his most honoured clients were Liberty of London who urged him personally on to create bolder designs and patterns. Moorcroft's success led to jealousy among other department heads at the Washington Works and in 1912 he was given a twelve-month notice to quit.

He very soon entered into a partnership with Liberty and took over some land occupied by a brick manufacturer in Sandbach Road. Macintyre's closed down Moorcroft's studio which had been extended to a former public house across Waterloo Road known as Washington Stores and connected by a tunnel to the main factory. At the same time Macintyre sacked Moorcroft's 34 pottery operatives. Happily for the ceramic industry, the great potter set them all on the following day, walking them in a line to his new potbank.

An un-restricted experimenter in colour, Moorcroft gave himself a free hand in designing patterns of fruit and flowers, while at the same time, through in-house technology, he developed high-temperature flambe glazes. He veered away from trends and was tempted only by the Art Nouveau Movement which featured in his younger years, and he dabbled briefly with Art Deco. And though a secretive man who specifically oversaw all his flambe firing which he conducted privately, William Moorcroft firmly believed in education and gave every encouragement to his employees to attend Burslem School of Art cautioning them not to divulge his own practices whilst they were there. But his workers had little need to fear the consequences of the transmission of Moorcroft's secrets for, from 1918, the school was presided over by the empathetic educational skills of an extraordinary teacher who needed no other style than his own.

In the year Enoch Bennett found success as a solicitor, 1879, moving his growing family to the middle-class district of Cobridge to occupy his first 'owned' house at 198 Waterloo Road, Gordon Mitchell Forsyth was born in Fraserburgh Scotland. His education guided him to art, and his secondary education success in Aberdeen won him a place at the South Kensington School of Art, soon to be re-designated as the Royal College of Art, where he studied design. Here he was taught calligraphy and illumination by the master Edward Johnstone, and stained-glass design and craft by Christopher Whall. This artistic media was favoured by Forsyth throughout his life and was representative and characterised much of his work. At the age of twenty-three, Forsyth came to the Potteries to work and was successful in securing the position of Art Director at Minton's in 1903, following the famous footsteps of M. J F L Arnoux. At Mintons', his classical designs in tile manufacturing won Forsyth praise and brought him to the attention of a number of Minton's competitors among whom were the international tile maker's Pilkinton. Forsyth moved to Pilkintons and it was a company that he worked for as a consultant until his retirement at the age of sixty-five. And it was while working in the design rooms of Pilkington's that he was engaged to design the bathroom suite tiling for RMS Titanic.

It is said, and largely acknowledged, that many lives meet their destiny unplanned. We say, do we not, 'Cometh the hour - cometh the man', and in many cases this statement has proved portentous. Indeed, it is often the case where the person precedes and actually provokes the hour. In such cases destiny is fulfilled for the benefit of many others and not just the individual.

This was the case with Forsyth and Burslem School of Art.

In December 1918, a letter appeared in the local newspaper, the Staffordshire Sentinel, under the title, **'The Need For Better Design'**. Its theme was the promotion of better artistic design in the pottery industry which the writer of the letter condemned as restrictive in a vitriolic attack against manufacturers for ignoring the challenge of the artist and for importance of good design for public consumption. The letter slammed the 1918 pottery exhibitions at the British Industries Fair and went on to accuse the manufacturers of being party to 'a conglomeration of hideousness'. The author of the letter was Gordon Mitchell Forsyth. Although Forsyth's letter left the pottery owners with a startled sourness, the message was meritoriously considered for, within twelve months, Gordon Forsyth was appointed as principal superintendent for the instruction of art and design for Stoke on Trent based at Burslem School of Art. He was the new principal, taking over from George Thorogood.

It was apparent that many potters resented Forsyth's remarks, but there were those, important members of the Ceramic Society, a group established to impose finer art into the crafts of design, who no doubt saw in Forsyth an opportunity for the school to break from the traditions of having a headteacher of art whose interests were to serve the manufacturer and not the pupil. So far as Forsyth was concerned, he had made his attack upon the men who had seen themselves as the best designers in the industry, it was up to him now to take them ahead of themselves and to show them that his accusations had foundations. The difficult part was to prove it, and the only way to do that was in the classroom and what came out of it; to provide tuition and education resulting in such merit to produce at least a generation of design artists that would not only satisfy the home executive but to take the art abroad and to demonstrate that the Staffordshire Potteries was indeed the true centre of the world ceramic industry wherein the greatest exponents of the art of the potter lived and worked. The consequences of Forsyth's claim and of those who courageously supported him, was established in the fact that he held his esteemed position for forty-five years

- head of art and design - it is a statement that simply presents in the passage of years a chronological summary of his unembellished achievements. He taught the width and depth of art in its many forms: he permitted his pupils to experiment, and they loved him for it.

It cannot be emphasised enough, and should not be understated, that ceramic design had rested much upon the laurels earned by the great Victorian family potters and whose creative craftsmanship by 1918 had begun to lose its direction in the lure of the insidious monotony of lithographic copy. It was a dearth of repetition which had been tolerated, even though Burslem had the finest school of art anywhere, a deficiency, manifested by copy, that stood still and festered throughout the years of the Great War. After the war a degree of aimlessness entered the design rooms of the potbanks relying much upon the same lithographic heritage in a seemingly un-urgent replenishment of 'as we were'. Many artists had been killed as were many sons of the manufacturers who were expected to take the reins to lead in new production. Forsyth's message was directed to all the manufacturers - the point of his verbal spear was very sharp - it insisted upon the freedom of art to allow it to become an endless loop of creativity and experimentation - there were no limits, no bounds to what the student wanted in the responsibility which had been thrust upon them echoing mournfully from the trenches of Belgium.

Within two years Forsyth had won the respect of the manufacturers who had appointed him, and in 1921, he became Art Advisor to the British Manufacturer's Federation. From this point in ceramic history, the artistic education of the potter knew no boundaries. Forsyth's pupils took away the skills learned in the classroom and presented them on the factory floor and in the pottery design studios. Every student was made to feel individual, as indeed as artists they were, although now the future of ceramic design became the policy of self-appraisal and not that decided by the manufacturer. And the un-compromised rewards were gathered up by the manufacturer who benefited as much as the purchaser of his ware did from this freshly discovered source of talent.

Forsyth was not without his detractors among whom was George Wade. Born in 1864, Wade began a business making ceramic shuttles for the Lancashire cotton industry and electrical porcelain. He soon branched out into the artistic manufacture of figures and, upon the take-over of the Hallen Pottery, Wade erected and developed a new factory which was called the Manchester Works. The potbank today overlooks the Sytch and Brownhills and from these early times the community thereabouts was at first colloquially, then officially known as 'Lancashire'. In the early part of the 20th century Wade was the chairman of Burslem School Board and was personally instrumental in establishing the outlines of art specialisation in elementary school education. Art education in the schools of Stoke on Trent owes much to George Wade.

It was while Frank Wedgwood, initiator of the progressive Design Industries Association forum group, was praising Forsyth that George Wade took his opportunity of criticising Forsyth's methods of teaching claiming that, despite encouraging individuality, Forsyth lowered standards in artistic business by producing, as the V&A art historian Ann Eatwell reports Wade's words, **'uniform students who did not have the range of ability to introduce improvements'** in the pottery trades. Wade was proved wrong, as Eatwell diversely continues with her own assertions, **'...Forsyth was all too guilty of having inculcated in his** *students a certain uniformity. That is the uniformity of a high standard of work, great enthusiasm, and the confidence to claim good design as a necessity for the industry. These are the hallmarks of the "little Forsyths" that Major Wade would have recognised'.*

Gordon Forsyth had a dynamic personality. He was an artist who was a born teacher - a born art teacher. By 1925 he had instituted a Junior Art Department which began taking pupils from the age of thirteen. Over the years, these 'stars' had come recommended to him by art teachers in elementary schools, his own disciples whom he had himself taught progressing through his earlier classes. These were artistic pyramids known as 'Forsyth's people' - 'Little Forsyths' of Burslem School of Art. It seemed that he turned no one away whether they had come seeded or otherwise from recommendations or heresay. He supervised day to day tuition; he oversaw the agendas of his adult evening classes, nothing was too much trouble for him in his encouragement and the promotion of his beloved pupils, for it was those urchins who came from the backs and terraces of working-class Burslem and Smallthorne or Biddulph, or even further afield, who came first. It was a wonder that he had time for his own designs and projects. And yet somehow he found that time.

Well known for his technical approaches in industry and in art education, Forsyth is lesser known for his painting and church designs in sculpture and particularly stained glass. Through this medium he found a passion in illuminated lettering and heraldry. The impressive windows in St Joseph's RC Church in Hall Street were designed by him, as were the side alter's painted panels, murals and metal work, all laid-out by his pupils under his direction. The Tunstall Sacred Heart Church contains some of his most imaginative work in stained-glass and wood carving, as does the glass in Etruria Parish Church. Decorative metal work on the drawn railings at the Hartshill Orthopaedic Hospital; a bronze of a lion's head at the Haywood Hospital. Windows and paintings in the town halls of Stoke on Trent all bear Forsyth's trade marks; it seemed that nothing was too great or small for him to become involved with whether it be the simple calligraphy of a friend's privately published book on inn signs or huge memorial church glass. He retired from his post as art master in 1944, but that did not stop him from working.

At an exhibition at the City Museum and Art Gallery in Pall Mall, Hanley, as it was then known, some seventy-four of his collected works were shown revealing a wide versatility in watercolours, oils and pottery. He wrote books and gave lectures all over. His output and industry parallelled that of Arnold Bennett and William Woodall; it was as if living in the Potteries influenced the urgency of these men as they ran ahead of their contemporaries before the Devils of art caught them up and put a stop to their impudent inventiveness. But the dark hounds of hard work began to wear Forsyth down.

In 1952 Forsyth took ill and in a recuperative holiday in Holland, he took succour in a visit to Rembrandt's studio where the atmospheric past brought ghosts to pleasantly haunt him. Shortly after his return to his home in Newcastle under Lyme, he passed away in hospital in December 1952 aged seventy-three. In that decade it was said that some 90 percent of industrial designers and artists working in the Potteries had passed through his schools or had in various critical methods been exceptionally influenced by Forsyth. A modest tribute to a man who had the appearance of a cockney spiv; a rodent face with a trimmed moustache, always to be seen wearing a felt wide-brimmed trilby, a bespoke double-breasted suit and a bow tie.

One artist who had passed through Forsyth's school, who was feted by Stoke on Trent and the world of ceramic art in 1992, was Susie Cooper. At the age of 90, this famous artist was publicly acknowledged for the work she had done and the influence she had made upon ceramic design a generation previously. She was, perhaps, Gordon Forsyth's most famous pupil, and a true child of the Potteries. Born in Burslem in 1902, Susan Cooper was the youngest of seven children; and was the smallest, but like so many 'runts', she was a fighter. The family all worked within her father's retail business, he a greengrocer who died when Susie was 12. The family continued making a small living by 'keeping the business going', until she decided, at the age of 17, that there were more important things to do with her life. Having found the pedestrian work of office secretary unsuitable, Susie Cooper began to study art at the time Forsyth began his long tenure at Burslem School of Art. Influenced and encouraged by Forsyth, Cooper won a scholarship and found employment at the pottery of A E Gray in Hanley who himself was like-minded and stylishly in accord with the Burslem art master, specifically in hand painting. Even at this early stage, Forsyth seemed to have spotted Cooper's potential for he was no doubt influential in guiding her to Gray's.

But the little woman with big talent was equally modest about her own beginnings. In an interview before her death in 1995 with journalist Madeleine Marsh of the Independent on Sunday, Cooper describes her start as a world famous artist as, '...it was all chance, really. I never took pottery at art school and I intended to be a fashion designer. The only reason I went into ceramics was that I wanted to go to the Royal College and I couldn't get a scholarship unless I was employed in the decorative arts. Pottery was simply the local industry.' To Forsyth's disappointment, Cooper never made it to the Royal College of Art for her private designs were instantly successful and she straight away began making her own ware. By 1924, at the age of twenty-two, Susie Cooper became the first woman to have her own name back-stamped on her ware in the Potteries district. Her progress at Gray's was however limited because Gray did not actually make his own pottery, merely buying biscuit shapes and decorating them. In 1929 Susie Cooper left Gray's and with her brother-in-law, Jack Beeson, she started her own production. It was a bad start for the landlord of the potworks was bankrupted in his other businesses and Susie was forced to move, opening the Chelsea Works in Moorland Road with a single oven - the smallest in the town.

Susie was instantly successful and she was encouraged in her progress by a move to Wood's Crown Works in Burslem where she developed some of her most notable designs. During this period Susie Cooper pottery and designs were famously popular through the selling ability of Jack Beeson who coined the phrase, **'No home is complete without Susie Cooper Pottery'**, particularly her geometric patterns contributing to the vogue for Art Deco and emulating the art style of Cubism. At this point of her artistic development she only had one real competitor - by chance another woman producing ware in the Mother Town who, in design, style and production couldn't be more further from the fluid decorations then propounded throughout the district known as Cooper's three 'f's' - Form Following Function.

Clarice Cliff was as different as chalk is to cheese in character to Susie Cooper. Academically they were poles apart; as artists their training was incompatible and in their produce there was nothing to illustrate similarity. As competitors they were uncommunicative, though it is known that they thought little of each other's work: *'I didn't admire her work'*, Cooper said in her late life of Cliff's work, *'It was not what I thought of as being the epitome of good design.'* And yet both women were for their time. They brought in a breath of fresh air at a time when the industrial western world was entering a period of damned depression, and they left behind them recognisable styles in a period identifiable in ceramics by their own names.

Clarice Cliff was born in the most northern of the Potteries' towns of Tunstall in 1899, and like Cooper she came from a large family which contained also seven children, though unlike her counterpart, the Cliffs were of less substantive financial accents. As most local girls did, Clarice Cliff entered the factory floor of a potbank receiving training as an enameller and a lithographer. When she was seventeen she went to work at A J Wilkinson's in the Burslem district of Middleport continuing to attend Tunstall Art School evening classes learning design and hand-painting. Wilkinson's was a leading manufacturer of tableware and it would have been easy for Cliff to have become lost on the free-hand painting benches amid the hundreds of chirrupy girls who were content to perform their days work and to get off home to their families or nights-out at theatre, the pubs or the new picture palaces. It was her overseer, Jack Walker who noticed her talents in brash decoration as she would often apply her own designs to faulted biscuit cups and plates. Walker drew the attention of art manager and part owner Colley Shorter to his happy and brusque intuitive paintress, and Shorter was impressed sufficiently to let Cliff carry on her own experiments in design. Brightly coloured diamonds, oblongs and squares appeared on Wilkinson's beakers and mugs readily identified with the recklessness of the Jazz Age. This sundry ware was an instant success and soon a range of tableware was brought out which was given the name 'Bizarre' and it set the pattern for future generations of Wilkinson's design and for Midwinter's which followed them into the last half of the 20th century, even Midwinter's last range meditated upon the moods set by Clarice Cliff, called 'Earth, Moon and Fire'.

When Forsyth retired, it was clearly going to be very hard to replace him, even though, by the outbreak of WWII the industry was slowing down in pottery production. Hard times were being weathered and the depressions and slumps of the 1930's had adversely affected the industry throughout the Potteries. Art education for the student was relegated below the sciences and regulated to the needs of the employer. And there was an emptiness in new development - a lack of unique and inspired innovation. The war years again exposed the raw strife of the ceramic trades as all industry turned to the efforts of war. In 1944, Gordon Forsyth was sixty-five, and he retired as principal art master although he remained as an active member of a number of advisory committees and kept his position as president of the Society of Staffordshire Artists over which he had presided since its inception in 1933.

The replacement of Forsyth proved immensely difficult especially with the introduction of a new Education Act which made juvenile attendance at school compulsory for children from 5 to 15 years. The responsibility for its administration, finance and curricula was placed heavily within the arena of local government, and the recruitment of headteachers was handed over to elected representatives. It became a matter for local councillors, and often their nominees, without experience in art, to select the district's principal educators. In many authorities it was much a matter of who the applicant knew or how strong were their paper qualifications, or how empathetic they were in the district's indigenous art and craft. From this time the supply of artists from the local art schools into the studios of the manufacturer began to dry up. All the most promising artists wished to leave the district to practice and ply their own trades.

Forsyth's replacement was a Hertfordshire man, another Royal Academician, Reginald Marlow. An outgoing homosexual, he brought with him a casual approach but nevertheless adherent to the principles of the education authority, particularly in examination study. Under Marlow exam pass-rate grew, more students developed a wider artistic interest in accord with the rest of the country and 'experimental' art, though some grieved, was excessively propounded.

A physically large man, Marlow's relaxed attitude pleased most students and this reflected inside the community spirit of the Mother Town which, throughout the late 1950's reflected an anxious determination by the youth to break moulds. The old town appeared to be populated by duffle-coated extroverts who inhabited the local pubs throughout the day and, once each year, took over the Queen's Hall, and therewith the town, for their annual Art's Ball. It was these students that influenced most aspects of the social life of youth - the age of the popularity of 'Traditional Jazz' emerged here in Burslem with regular performances of the Ceramic City Stompers at the Embassy Club in Waterloo Road. Reggie Marlow, a believer in the freedom of expression, presided over these potboiling times with many of his students finding the call to go outside the Potteries for work with few remaining to feed the pottery art studios as asserted by Forsyth. Marlow's retirement in 1967 brought a local artist to prominence.

Colin Melbourne was locally taught and was given the job as Principal of Burslem School of Art on his return from the Royal Academy. He was to be the last principal of Burslem's Art School for, in 1974, the responsibility of education was devolved once again, this time into the larger pool of the County Council which funded education on a pro-rata basis to his county divisions. The Queen Street school was relegated to an annex for sculpture while the main school of art became a 'department' and was transferred to Stoke under the general umbrella of polytechnic.

Melbourne himself was a masterful sculptor and there are a number of his works, publicly commissioned, situated in prominence throughout the district, his life-size statue of Henry Doulton stands in pride of place in the Market Place of Burslem. Perhaps Melbourne's most famous local sculpture is that of the Steelman sited in front of the Potteries' Museum in Hanley.

Amid the variety of art training in the polytechnic, Colin Melbourne became designated as principal of fine art. It was a position he saw out along with his counterpart in the same department, Jack Skinner - principal of art and craft - before the word 'principal' was finally omitted. In 1984, another fine tuning of education legislation saw the position re-titled again to 'Head of Fine Art'. Arthur Berry was the first to hold this position, followed by George Mallellieu and finally by Terry Shave whose position today, (2000) is that of 'Professor of Fine Art'.

A full circle has failed to join. Although art is still initiated in elementary schooling, it is now inside the colleges and adult-learning departments where post-school art is developed and where diplomas and occupational qualifications are quested. It is in the universities that degrees are pursued and, the poly's have now become those universities. Many pottery manufacturers still recruit from these ranks and from these ranks pupils are taught on the shop floor to aim their brushes, not in the direction of the freehand of their designers, but in the copy of the computer keyboard.

It is said that, when William Moorcroft left Macintyre's to set-up on his own, a large number of finished pots were found hidden away, all of which would have been found suitable in any saleroom of the times. It was just that William Moorcroft, a simple Burslem boy, educated in the Mother Town to become an artist and who rose to become a great potter, just didn't think they were good enough to bear his name on the backstamp.

NOTE IN FRED HUGHES JOURNAL

I first met Arthur Berry in 1958. I hadn't a clue who he was - a big man, one arm, a dirty mac and a flat cloth cap which appeared stuck to his head - irremovable by wit or whim. It was in a public house called the Durham Ox that we met, a corner beer-house in Nile Street opposite Parker's Brewery. Two decades earlier there were four other pubs in the same street including the Nile Hotel, flagship of the brewery's huge fleet, standing proudly, tall in all its Victorian architectural splendour. Just why Parker's retained the little beer-house in preference to the demolition of the great Nile Hotel, which they shut down in 1948, and even in proclivity to its many other great halls about the district which were discharged in 1948, was odd. I can only thing that it was because the Durham Ox was less prominent, unobtrusive, with a concealed back-way that was extremely conducive for comings and goings to after hours' sessions and 'lock-ins'.

I had returned to Burslem from travelling abroad and it had been my first visit to the eponymous Durham Ox in over two years - a pub always known by its full name, never scowled at with the use of the diminutive 'OX', nor elevated to the pretentiousness of a nickname after the licencee's surname as was often the affectionate practice of those times; never 'the corner house' nor even the 'local' - so far as I remember the little beerhouse had always been always afforded the dignity of its full name by my father and my father's father.

Inside the gloomy back room I was introduced to the landlord and his wife, Sam Packet and Minnie, a couple who had lived in the house for well over a decade. It was apparent from their alcohol-wrecked faces that they had been in the trade all their lives, long before they had taken up the tenancy of their present pub, for in those days (do you remember?) all publicans looked as old as if they had been born with that leathery straight-faced guise, gained in a long lifetime that stretched symbolically between 'opening' and 'closing'.

*It was half past two and pubs by the rule of law closed for the afternoon's 'rest' period until 5.30.pm. The Durham Ox was not the exception, in fact there were no exceptions, for the local police were very, very sharp on such matters as drinking out of time. And it was without exception that the doors of the Durham Ox that day were unceremoniously locked and bolted, and those who were **in** would remain **in** for as long as the licencee gave his permission.*

Customers who were **in** *stopped being customers at half-past two when, at a stroke, they became 'guests of the licencee'. They were no longer in the taproom, they were suddenly symbolically transported, without movement, into the private quarters of the innkeeper where all the drinks were supplied free of charge. Of course in reality this was not the case as all the drink was paid for in advance or taken on tab to be settled later when 'time' became lawful again. Perhaps now and then the landlord's wife might put on a bit of food, pig-pudding, cheese and pickles, maybe a sausage-roll or pork-pie if times were good. And it was in these times between 2 and 6, and in the long dark hours after ten o'clock at night that the landlord of the back-street pub made his money.*

The two rooms of the Durham Ox served as a taproom (bar) and a parlour (smoke-room). On this day both rooms were well occupied - Sam loaded the fires sensing a session! The parlour, the back-room, was filled with the smoke of a dozen cigarettes as the tips burned through the foggy gloam, intermittently brightening with a suddenness as the fags were stoked by asthmatic inhalation.

Beauty strikes at the given moment of a lock-in, descending as a abruptly as a winter's night; curtains are closed and the whole atmosphere churns quietly as at the end of a storm when a balmy breeze wafts away the cross clouds which break apart so that day and night appear as one. Moody figures settle, and faces light-up as pinpoints; hunting ancestors hunched around some distant fireside. Here and there, and every now and then, the scene becomes altered by a dim glimpse of daylight straying through narrow gaps in the heavily brocaded curtains splayed by a draft of a fugitive movement. These pallid splashes reveal clusters of grey faces, crouched and lounging figures seated with coats removed, collars undone, shirt sleeves rolled-up; stuff bagged-up and piled around the hiss of shuffled playing cards - knaves, queens, kings and jokers. Muted conversation comes and goes and erupts sometimes into coarse laughter accompanied by an occasional barrack-room oath. Old topers know these sounds and sights well - these are forbidden times - what they are doing is devilish.

My eye was affected by a narrow shank of daylight from the window of the back room which joined with a similar shaft from the window in the front room as they arrived at a single spot together, like theatrical searchlights high in the wings as they plunge their beams into the middle of a stage. And here, in the middle of the dividing passage, the light became raddled beneath a single naked light bulb. This epicentre of mysterious life created a central fracture in the arc of overall illumination in the passage and provided the outdoor hatch area with the deception of false daylight as it tantalised diverse and beautiful pools of tumbling silver dust and curling parodies of sprites and spirits made from cigarette smoke. In the front room, more dark figures moved about amid the laughter of female voices and the threat of uttered male assertion. Glasses tinkled, copper coins thudded into a collection. Two tables, drawn together were occupied by a group of young men and women, babbling and gibbering in melodic conversation like water running over pebbles and discussed by excited apes. And among this flurry of speech were the deeper voices of adults through which I heard the rise and fall of a voice of authority, insistence, dogma; masculine and charged up with a feminine timbre.

I discovered that the card-players of the back room were the out-going end of the early-turn police shift from the local station, incarcerated inside the pub for a few pints and a few games of brag before going home to tea and wives. Among these were the shift sergeant and a police woman, one of only ten in the entire county at the time. Such selective representation was to be marvelled at. A dozen coppers at tables which were littered with pint glasses of Parker's bitter. And the police station but 200 yards away, and the brewery just fifty paces across the road! It was as though beer was on tap from its source and approved by the grace of the law! The fag smoke hung above them like a barrage balloon threatening to collapse in its slow rolling motion. Van Gogh would have expressed a masterpiece had he known of these times.

Sam and Minnie paid these likely lads their due tribute by fetching and carrying their drinks on request and responding to the landlord's encouragements when it looked as though the clients were flagging. Meanwhile the party of students, from the College of Art in Queen Street, kept their distance with their impudence and cheek and their alley cat freshness. Here they were in a weekly reunion with their tutors, out for a drink after morning classes. For afternoon classes were dismissed as the students paired off in strumpery. This was Friday POETS day!

In the centre of this group was the man with lumpy features; the flat cap and all. He was going on about the clearance of slum dwellings around St John's Church, and although he was addressing a number of people, he seemed to be talking over them as though he was talking to himself, though rather loudly:

'...You might say that the problem is insolvable - something we've inherited however the council sees it. But, and we all must be aware of this, taking folk out of towns and planting 'em in the countryside is the worst move possible. The towns and the shops will never recover. It's robbery and its rape. It's pillage, and people belong in towns, where shops are, and pubs. And towns can't survive without folk, they can't exist. They're knocking houses down all around, and shops and factories. And one day there'll be no Middleport, there'll be no Cobridge and no Burslem. And the people that are left will go to Hanley and sit at home, stuffed in their high-rise, one bedroom flats with nothing to do except to watch the tele...'

It was almost a sermon. The conjunctives peppered the speech as though they were intentionally inserted to prevent interruption until the breath finally gave up. The theme of urban change ran on with the odd contribution from the other tutors, but the big man continued his diatribe against anyone or any organisation that appeared to hold a view against his principles. There was passion in this voice, a passion built up over many years of a life that had lived in the past and demanded that life and the ways of life remained true to the old values. Principles of paradox that had seen the unremittent consequences of poverty trying to be resolved and conquered with only community strength to hand while the artillery of deception was brought up to defend the existing state of affairs. Judging by the obstinacy of his address there was no doubt that here was a man whose source of self protection and topical preservation lay at the other end of his life. I felt that the man could see no future in change yet unsurprisingly, and he must have known, his future held for him that thing he most feared and despised - change! That's what he saw.

Others made small contributions to the conversation, and the theme of urban regeneration ran on for some 30 minutes until, by the end, it had developed into a long lecture about traditional values during which the big man had lost the attention of many of his pupils who began making diverse conversations and sweeter plots in each other's ears. Amid descriptions of temples of public houses, libraries and civic piles, there were fondlings above and beneath the tables as students furtively demonstrated romantic ownerships. Eventually the big man ran out of steam, no doubt appreciating that his themes were running thin. He heaved himself to his full height of over six feet and made his way to the men's lavatory at the bottom of a high blue-bricked back yard. I stood beside him inside a whitewashed stall looking into the flowing gutter at my feet as the man contemplated the wall ahead.

'That was a nice speech,' I said, 'I suppose you were talking about the demolition of St John's.' He glanced at me with indifference, clearly not wishing to speak to a stranger, and looked back at the whitewashed wall. I felt a bit uncomfortable noting that it would better if I'd said nothing and carried on with my ablutions. But the man with one arm fascinated me and I foolishly persisted. 'It's a lively crowd you're with. Art students, are they? Are you regulars?' He shook himself with his good hand and turned to leave. And then icily he said, 'Are you with those coppers? No don't tell me, I don't want to know.' He countered himself quickly and finally. 'You keep yourself to yourself or whoever you're with. We stay in the front room and nobody gets bothered.' He walked out and I followed him into the yard at a decimal interval, rather offended by his snub. I breathed what fresh air there was. In the sky the sun was hidden by black clouds of smoking chimneys. A sleeping cat idly eyed me from its interrupted rest on top of a shed. There wasn't a bird in sight nor any sound to be heard except the dull roar of factory machinery. I felt as though I was at the end of the world.

And the afternoon wore on as both parties in the lock-in grew steadily intoxicated, until, at five o'clock, as though by some unobserved signal, the back door suddenly flew open as a crowd of white overall-clad potters with hard clay clinging to their faces, came flooding into the bar having been emptied-out from the back gates of Royal Doultons. Minnie Packet drew- open the curtains, the policemen folded their cards into their boxes as new decks were unwrapped for use by the newcomers. Such a noise that heralded the change of shifts, the opening of 'time', the closing of the lock-in. I glanced across the front room to see the big man leading his followers up to the town.

Young ladies were clinging to young men; there was laughter as promises were made for promises to be kept or to be broken. Steam buzzers from a multitude of potbanks echoed across the Mother Town. People were coming and going.

I worked in Burslem for the next twenty years and during that period I got to know the big art teacher quite well. We found that we had things in common with each other, none least than the preservation of the social structures of Burslem. Our main shared interest however was drinking and the enjoyment of public houses. And I found that being a social type who liked a drink, many others joined me, men and women of similar attractions and diversions: the battalions of the bars and those lovely folk who had a story of the past to tell and who insisted on being heard.

During those years I engaged in many debates about the merits of where we lived, how we lived and why we lived; captured, enraptured in long forbidden afternoons in the men-only taproom of the Swan and the Red Lion. The plush pumps of the George and the Duke and the Marquis, and the drinking galleries of the Leopard, the New Inn and the Star with men who carried on with the attitudes and the balls of Frankie Beech, Joe Poulson and Albert Murphy; the Jocks and the Paddies, the Snowies, the Tich's and the Lofty's, and all those other giants that left much more of their character than their names. There were students and colleagues of Arthur Berry as well; George Mallelieu, Stan the dustbin man and Tony Wild and many,

many others who left behind more than their fame in their contribution to the old town. All these people who made time stand still and caught the world's interests and digested them and carefully dissembled the carcasses in the taverns of the town. Inns and vaults, most of which have been demolished and long gone like the people who haunted them. Those people - who lived in those houses that disappeared as though they had never existed. Those very special people.

Chapter Eight

DRUNKENNESS AND SOBRIETY

'...There were in the parish of Burslem, in the year commencing Michaelmas 1838, 38 inns and public houses, and no less than 90 Retail Beer-Houses, to the scandal and grief of the sober and moral part of the community, but to the benefit of the revenue, and the glory of our free-trade policy...'

(Ward, pg 272)

On 4th August 1914, the day after bank holiday Monday, Horace Pepper of Longport wrote to his brother, Jack, a seaman on board the destroyer HMS Pathfinder, sailing with the British fleet out of the Channel into the North Sea:

'...You have never seen anything like it dear brother. Every pub and tavern in the town was filled, many had run out of beer and stout and they were even drinking in the streets out of bottles and any other container they could put their hands on, jumping on and off the trams as they tried to whiz past. A bunch of the Irish lads from the Sytch had taken long poles out and were lifting the hot-beams off the wires - all the electricity had gone out and the tramcars were stranded in the street. Not that the conductors gave a d**n, they just gave up and joined in the merry-making. Me and 'Snowy' Procter went up in the town as soon as the pubs in Station Street closed their cellars. Our kid, you wouldn't believe that the landlords just shut-up shop when the taps had run dry..they left their doors wide open - everybody ran up Newcastle Street shouting and singing! I've never seen such crowds! Burslem was filled with men and women, and children half drunk were tippling over on the setts. People were passing out jars of beer from the beershops and taverns..everybody, 'cats and dogs', seemed to have a drink in their hands, singing and dancing, climbing street columns, chasing up and down the lanes and entries. Kid, I'll tell you, there'll be some headaches tomorrow...'

Towards midnight that bank holiday Monday, two drunken young men were making their way along the unlit passage known as the Jawnels, walking out from the town centre, passing by the squealing abattoir and into High Street. Here, in an atmosphere a little quieter, the men staggered towards the Dolphin Inn near the entrance of the 'Road to Lancashire', along which un-lit lane they were temporarily residing in digs. They had not a penny between them, yet they were blind drunk, their inebriated condition no doubt aided by the spending of the combined income, resulting from tatting, they had scrambled together and the dependency on friendly gratuity; for neither were men to miss an opportunity when it came their way.

Attempting to make their way home, they were unable to resist the beckoning lights and music of the little public house where they hoped to take a 'flyer', a glass consumed in one swallow, before the landlord had time to ask for his payment which they knew they would be unable to make. However, the licencee

Thomas Shaw, was already alert to them. Having had to quell a number of fights on his premises that evening, he was on the look-out for potential trouble and saw the two men approaching as he glanced through his taproom window. Together with his brother in law, Alf Mason, the landlord stood on the cobbled pavement and barred the front entrance of his pub. The two drunks straightened up as best they could, the smaller one beginning his greeting in slurred speech:

"Are ye O rate Tummy? It's on'y us, don't yer know? Arrs abite a drink er two fer a couple o men bind fer th' war?"

"Yer con bugger of Riley, ern tak that drunken mate er thine wi'thee. Yerl 'av no ale in 'ere ter nate."

The statement was final and the two men knew better than to argue.

"Ay, ern thats o rate then, fer when we'an dun wi th' Kaiser wane bee back. Ern then yerl want ter know us. Then yern be sayin' ar pride thee at ter call us mates, ern theyt want give us a drink then - yer owd bastard!"

"War? Yown see no bloody war, yer drunken sod. The on'y war yown say erl bay th' ceilin' er th' guard room. - Goo fetch off 'em Toss!"

At this point, Alf Mason's bull terrier did the rest of the talking, responding to the urging of its master as it tore into the legs of the two scurrying men. Falling over each other in their rush to escape the canine teeth, young Vincent Riley and his mate tumbled into the hedgerows that lined the lane along Back Sytch to that oddly named locality, 'Lancashire', where his mother lived. Out of breath, bitten and bedraggled, and not quite making the distance to home, the two men settled for the night under the hedge behind the Royal Oak Inn, an out of the way hostelry kept peaceably by an ex collier, Joe Boulton. They knew better than to ask him for a drink, so they slept in the damp grass, their bodies kept alive in the warm stupor of drink.

Above the level of the Sytch, up in Burslem's town centre, celebrations continued all through the night, and that meant drinking. In a town which was serviced by one-hundred and forty-seven public houses, no one, man, woman or child appeared to be sober. Drink flowed like nothing seen in living memory; indeed not since the peace celebrations of 1815, or perhaps the implementation of the Beer House Act of 1830 had so much drunken revelry taken place, repeated in all the Potteries towns and everywhere that communities gathered across the length and breadth of Britain that summer's night. Days of waiting anxiously for the declaration of war had at last given way to reality and the falsity of that waiting had released a nationalistic fervour so intense that it affected all the classes as one; the bulldog roared. And all through that hot Bacchanalian night, in every town in Europe universal cries rang out - 'Before the leaves fall', and, 'home for Christmas' - yelling and echoing along avenues and alleys; in fields, farms and factories, hurrahs resounding. It was the night when everyone got drunk for they knew that tomorrow they'd be sober - very sober.

Several days later, Vincent Riley, walked from his mother's house up the Sytch and over to the Navy recruiting office in Hanley to become a seaman in the war. Born in Hanley in 1891, Riley had so far had a rough passage in his upbringing; addicted to stealing, having at first been driven to it out of poverty, he had served several periods in reform schools culminating in an attempt at permanent correction when he was ultimately sent to an industrial school at Stockport for four years. Towards the end of this period the young Vincent joined a naval training ship anchored in the Mersey where he was taught naval trades and seamanship. Later he was transferred to the naval barracks at Chatham and travelled abroad a number of times as a cargo-minder, a position of some trust.

At the age of twenty-two, having served his time, he returned to Burslem, the town that the recently widowed Mrs Riley had turned to for the companionship of her own family, where Vincent took up occupation as a pony attendant at one of the Bycars collieries. It was during this time that the young man discovered the pleasures of the far flung fame of the notoriety of the beer houses of the Mother Town. But now, after the grand drinking spree of August 4th, the smartly dressed young man stood before the recruiting panel in Old Hall Street Hanley. To his horror, his shock and shattering disappointment, Vincent, a sea-man trained for the sea, was rejected. Either because of his poor physical condition caused by early-life drinking bouts, or by the consideration of the prior knowledge of his juvenile delinquency that the recruiters had. In any event his Liverpool and Chatham naval training was disregarded and he was advised to join the army. Wracked with the self-pity of rejection, he turned around in the street where the recruiting office temporarily stood, and shuffled into the nearest pub, the Woodman, where he got gloriously drunk.

Exactly one month after the declaration of war, the British Destroyer, HMS Pathfinder, pulled out of the Firth of Forth into the North Sea. On September 5th, the German submarine U21 took a sounding of it and propelled a torpedo at its bow. The destroyer's forward magazine hold was struck and the ship exploded with the loss of 250 crew. Days later a war office telegram was delivered to a little cottage in Clarence Street Longport. Horace Pepper was having a pint around the corner in the Milton's Head when a neighbour dashed into the taproom and told him to come home to comfort his weeping mam. Now, at nineteen, he had tragically become the eldest, and consequently the head, of a family of five. No one knew the whereabouts of the father for he had deserted his family some three years previous. The absent father would never know of the death of his eldest son and heir: but that was nothing strange for these times for life was cheap and responsibility was either accepted or rejected out of hand.

Horace, having comforted his mother and put his tearful siblings to bed, returned to the Milton's Head and quietly got drunk. In this way two very different young men sought solace in the only way on offer to them. It was the way folk had always behaved in times of grief and in times of celebration. Sense and emotion dictated the route into the fermentation that lay through to the bottom of an empty glass - narcosis in alcohol - it was the best way, it was the way it would always be.

The public house is as old as man himself. By definition, it is exactly what its says, and it reaches as far back to when cave dwellers met beside a fire to discuss social events and exchange grunted reports in expressions of unity, rifts and gifts. Alcohol was not to be the dominant factor of the public house until the time of the Romans. The first public houses in Great Britain came with the Romans. They were not much more than huts where Mediterranean wine was served to the passing legions. Although the wine was at first brought into the country already fermented, demand quickly surpassed the supply and vineyards began to sprout all over the south-east districts of England where the weather was more conducive to the fruiting of the grape.

From the early years of subjugation, the local Celtic tribes - already noted brewers of a honey based intoxicating drink favoured by the Romans who gave it the name **kourmi** - started to fashion their own versions of the Legion's wine huts into identifiable structures. In a typical Roman style of early signage, the wine-maker placed a vine branch over the door of his premises to announce a brew was ready: the shoemaker used a piece of shaped leather, the tailor a roll of cloth; thus it was clear to the traveller what the trader dealt in. The Roman legionary called his drinking huts, **tabernae**, from which expression the word **tavern** has evolved.

In Northern Europe, during the Roman occupations, a richer intoxicating drink had been refined from the malting of crushed barley. Finding that the grain grew prolifically in the wetter northern hemisphere, the Romans abroad acquired its taste, but nowhere was it consumed in such quantity than in the low countries of the Franks and in Saxony. To the Angles and the Saxons, the drinking of the liquid from mashed grain was a religion. The Saxon's called it **ol**, or **eal** and they introduced it to Britain after the Romans had been recalled to their homeland. Today we call it ale, but very few of us have drunk it.

By 500AD, a happy exchange of drink produced a mixture of ethnic variety; wine was commonly being drunk by the lords and earls, while ale was scrumptiously consumed by the Anglo-Saxon peasant. But in the south-west and Wales, honey-mead and apple cider hung on as the daily drink as the Britons and Celts continued to fight off the Germanic raiders with the aid of their natural mountainous barriers .

Between 600AD and 1066AD, as a result of the Christian conversions of the Anglo-Saxons initiated by Pope Gregory the Great, a number of hostels were established up and down the country and were administered by papal monks. They were little more than barns set aside and adjacent to the monasteries wherein pilgrim travellers would be provided with accommodation, food and drink to aid their journey. The word **inn** is Saxon in origin, and began to make its appearance towards the end of the 12th century. The early use of the word was to provide a meaning for a room or chamber. Our modern abbreviation, **in**, deriving from **within**, is an associated domestic verb. Inns were also referred to the town residences of important people who had their grand principal homes in their country estates. When they were in London, the Lords Gray and the Earl of Lincoln were known to be 'in' when they occupied their chambers. Over a period of time, scholars were invited to use the chambers as temporary lodgings and they soon became the educational bases for students of the Law. Between the hostel (hostelry) and the inn, the two names commonly used for public houses in the latter part of the twentieth-century, we have a picture of a roadside rest-house which has today fallen into common use to describe the local licenced public house.

The most popular drinking establishment for the common people emerging out of Anglo-Saxon Britain is the English alehouse. It's name deriving from **al-hutte**, these small houses could be found in most towns managed by the wife of the farmer, or a trader occupying it for a secondary wage. The sickly-sweet product resulting from the mash of malt, was brewed in open vats in the most unhygienic conditions. The simplicity of its methods of production provided the necessary encouragement for the ale-wife to brew it. Little could be said for it, except that it was intoxicating. Because of the impurity of drinking water, every house had its brewing vat, but by the 13th century, the professional calling of ale-sellers and brewsters was fairly common throughout the land.

In a census of 1577 set to apply taxes on alehouses for the repair of Dover harbour, it was assumed that the number of designated houses in the Realm dealing in the supply and sale of alcohol, of which ale was by far the most frequent intoxicant consumed, was 19,759. Most of these premises were to be found in the south-east of England and in the large townships of London, Norwich and St Albans and Canterbury; while in the Midlands and the north-west, ale was still much of a home brew practice with a communal brew allowed for festivals and wakes. But alehouses had continued to roll north where, in a census set to specifically identify alehouses in 1621, it was discovered that there were 13,000 licenced alehouses to a population of under 4 million. Every community had its local!

By the early 17th century, Burslem had become known as a centre of pottery making undergoing a slow transition from self-sustaining tenant farmers involved in crop cultivation, into a base of more dedicated market trading. This situation had been projected and helped on by the Hulton Abbey monks who developed the system of producing goods for sale on the Grange lands in Rushton. The monks had introduced a common practice of selling vegetables, home brewed wine and monk's ale to their neighbours, who were at that time the tenant farmers, woodmen, coopers and fletchers of adjacent Burslem. It is most likely that the early settlement of a place of worship on the flat shelf at St Johns, included a hostelry for itinerant travellers where bread and ale were provided to accompany a nights lodgings. In the brewing of church-ales up to the early 16th century, the clergy would brew great vats of ale to give to the communities served by the church in exchange for gifts and repairs of the various buildings. By such devices the church became forever associated with intoxication and its clergy were often tolerated for their drunken priests.

The early map of Burslem, 1720, lists 19 alehouses, of which 8 had expressed names.

Jolly Potters, Bear, Court House, Talbot, Shoulder of Mutton, George and Dragon, Red Lion and Packhorse.

Each of these houses existed well into the 20th century, but today only the sites of the George Hotel, the Red Lion and the Bull's Head (formerly BEAR) remain as licenced premises. Of the other eleven un-named alehouses in 1720, most came through to the 20th century but only two, Lloyds Tavern, formerly the Millstone, and Duke William remain as public houses.

Of the two 18th century similar maps that exist of Burslem, one is entitled **'A Map of Burslem, About the Year 1720'**, it was drawn by Thomas Ryles born in 1725; and the other map entitled, **'The Town of Burslem About AD 1750'**, was drawn by Enoch Wood, born in 1759. Both men were historians, Ryles a printer and publisher, Wood, a famous potter, a collector of antiquities and curator of Burslem's first museum and archive office. The main differences of the two maps are illusive:

> Ryles' map appears with a nomenclature of occupants at the foot of the map,
>
> Wood's map has a separate key to the occupiers,

Ryles' map is drawn in three dimensional perspective,

Wood's map is flat,

Ryles' map has an absence of a windmill on a field known as Jenkins,

Wood's map depicts the windmill which was built by James Brindley in 1757,

Ryles' map refers at number 101 to Madame Egerton - incorrect for her name in 1720 wasBourne, the second of her three husbands,

Wood's map correctly shows the name Egerton, her name in 1750.

Ryles' map refers to number 107 as 'school house' - incorrect as the foundation of the school did to take place until 1748,

Wood's map correctly places the school house in accordance with its date.

Accuracy appears therefore to favour Woods' map. Other maps have emerged, dated 1740 (known as the Heaton Map) and 1760, but they both appear to have been influenced by either one or both of the other two. Indeed, there is also a popular copy of Wood's map - undated - with the names of the householders printed alongside the premises. This seems to be the map that most researchers prefer and is reproduced in Frank Falkner's The Wood Family of Burslem, published in 1912 by Chapman and Hall Ltd London. The Enoch Wood collection of documents and pottery is unchallengeably the finest in the potteries, although, kept safe in the safe vaults of the Potteries Museum, the full collection of Wood documents assembled together is rarely seen because of its age.

Enoch Wood was the youngest son of the master potter and pottery experimenter Aaron Wood. Enoch became the resulting celebrity of the phenomena of the great potting family. He was trained as a classical artist and was employed as an artist/modeler by Josiah Wedgwood. His independent career began in partnership with his cousin Ralph Wood but, from 1790 to 1818, a successful partnership with James Caldwell who provided most of the finance and remained a sleeping partner, gave production to one of Enoch Wood's most fertile periods as an artist. Caldwell was extremely rich by the standards of his location who married a daughter of the landowner Thomas Stamford. He lived at Linley in Talke and became a deputy to the Lord Lieutenant of Staffordshire as well as being the recorder for Newcastle under Lyme and was the solicitor who provided for the execution of the will of Josiah Wedgwood .

Enoch Wood raised the largest ever potbank in Burslem stretching across the whole of the eastern flank of the Hill Top. Known as the Fountain Works, its frontages emulated the architecture of crusading fortifications with high castellated walls bearing subdued pediments in Romanesque classical style. In the centre of his factory, Wood erected a large mansion with laid-out gardens reaching across land occupied by St Paul's church and as far out as the Brindley canal. Inside his mansion, Enoch Wood set aside rooms in which he displayed his collection of early artifacts, pottery treasure and the results of ceramic scientific experimentation. It is said that he had the finest collection of Wedgwood in the Kingdom, including that held in the museum of Wedgwood itself.

Wood was everything in Burslem and rightly considered as the 'Father of Burslem' because of his civic input at a time when the town was making the transfer from frontiers' town to one with civic responsibility. He was its Chief Constable, President of an association to prevent crime and promote good order, and it principal church warden with influence in all matters civil.

In 1788, the Wedgwood's were anxious to relinquish civic power, or rather, reluctant to accept it after Josiah had moved out to Etruria. It was apparent that to take on the responsibilities of commanding law and order and the preservation of the Peace, coupled with that of running a business and creating a strong base on which to build a future town, required the services of a unique person. Enoch Wood was that man!

Burslem's population was growing week to week. The opening of the Trent and Mersey canal had brought many men and their families into the town with specialist trades to hand. The Irish and Welsh came in droves to provide regiments for necessary labouring needs. Roads were being built and repaired under the turnpike legislation, the canals were being extended to cut into to the town centres at Middleport and Newport and segregated housing and religious conceptions were being manufactured here there and everywhere. And the poor people took their pleasures where they could. Alehouses sprung up all over: ale was taken into the potbanks and whenever the annual hirings had been made, the remainder of the unemployed scratched around for a scavenger's living on which to spend it on alcohol. The meadows and the furlong down Beeches Row were filled nightly with drunken revelry and debauchery where men and women crawled under the hedges to sleep off their worldly aches and pains.

In July 1788 Enoch Wood put his signature, as principal churchwarden, alongside that of 31 other Burslem residents who had become terrified to pass out of their own homes for fear of being accosted and even molested by beggars and drunken vagabonds:

> **...observing with great uneasiness and concern the may irregularities and disorders that prevail in this parish...**

promising to take what law there existed and apply it to its full force in order to stop and prevent the scandalous behaviour from being committed at least on a Sunday. Wood drew up a list which included the payment of wages on a Saturday at 4.pm which would see the most drunken and orgiastic performances curtailed before the Lord's Day commenced. The order also instructed that all shops and market stalls should be closed on Sunday and that no hairdresser (where much ale was consumed) should shave or dress hair after 12 noon on Sunday. The most severe regulation was applied to public house keepers and victuallers who were prohibited to sell any intoxicating liquor after 10.pm on Saturday, and if the ale seller sold any alcohol on a Sunday, the full punishment of the law would be applied.

> **'Every person found tippling in a public house, or drunk in the open street on the Sabbath day shall be punished as the law directs.'**

These were harsh measures indeed and could only be enforced by the most determined of forces. To carry his instructions, Wood recruited the Association For The Prosecution Of Felons, a strong body of manufacturers, who employed constables to watch and call curfew and to bring before magistrates any offenders caught in the act or on information being presented.

Among fine archives of social and industrial documents are lists of petitions and records of births and deaths of early inhabitants, these were supplemented by the inclusion of tythe terriers and details of messuage houses, rotas of church wardens, dating from the first manorial transcriptions. Wood was the first person to underwrite the Burslem and Pottery Bank which became the towns first national bank in Market Place at the side of which Cock's Entry runs. He also inaugurated Burslem Sunday School to which he provided pottery ink wells and ceramic handled pens. He feared the rise of trades unions and predicted the Chartists riots which occurred two years after he had died. He provided a public fountain outside his potbank at the top of Liverpool Road and invented and installed a steam engine to provide air to the tunnels of his coal mine on the Bicars Fields. He provided money to develop Newcastle Street and build a terrace of brick houses in Newport Lane, though he simultaneously stopped-up the old Packhorse Lane to incorporate it into his huge Fountain Works. Enoch Wood could have become MP for the district but he loved his town too much to leave it and preferred the position of power broker which he carried out effectively in the case of William Davenport. But he was unable to permanently resolve the plague of drunkenness which no amount of local legislation was able to eradicate.

Some of this invaluable material was later lost in time as the collections were removed by transfer, first to the Museum of the Old Town Hall, secondly to the Wedgwood Institute; then returned to the Old Town Hall; after which some of it was transferred to Hanley Museum in Pall Mall, and lastly, in the 1970s, to the Potteries Museum in Bethesda Street. In 1835, many irreplaceable finds of palaeontology and ancient rock were acquired by the then National Geology Museum in London; some went to Edinburgh and a fine collection of early English ware went to the Porcelain Museum of Dresden, Germany. Today, it is possible that many valuable archives and artifacts of the Wood Collection will never be recovered.

The preparation of Wood's map for inclusion in Shaw's history, was commenced in 1820 at a time when the master potter was in semi-retirement, much of his business being conducted by his son, Enoch Jnr, in association with his other sons. In Ward's history the author uses many of Wood's papers including an edited list of messuages copied second hand from Wood's collection and dated 1657, the only copy of which was known to have been owned by Enoch Wood. The list refers to properties which were called upon to provide churchwardens for the Burslem parish and included the names of some of the great pioneering potters in the level above that of the producers of butter-pots: John Turner, William Colclough, members of the Daniel family, Thomas Bourne, Thomas Mitchell and John Adams. Linking these names to his own times, John Ward lists in an appendix of comparative dwellings in the town known to have been passed on in the continuity of family habitation. Enoch Wood, it has been established, had also used these early names and locations to place the families alongside their dwellings, probably using a method of superimposition viewed from his own time and placed within the layout of the streets and lanes he knew so well. The result is a 1720s list of householders placed upon a contemporary town plan of 1750 which even in the 1820's was changing on a weekly basis.

In 1838 when Wood's map was first introduced to the public, he refers to property number 2, 'Jolly Potters Alehouse' which, according to the Churchwarden's rota, in 1742 was a house occupied by John Marsh, and earlier, in 1657, by Thomas Bourne. At number 57, the George and Dragon, occupied by William

Barlow in 1838, was a house owned by Richard Cartwright in 1742 and by Thomas Daniel in 1657 - although there is no doubt that it was an inn on both these earlier occasions. At number 24, Wood names the Court House alehouse - the reference to the messuage on the same site states 'Croft House - (near the Star)' - that is in 1838. In 1742 it was a house owned by Samuel Hyde and in 1657, by potter John Lee or Leigh.

Wood's intention was to define the layout of the town he knew by using the lanes and the meadows, which were fast disappearing under industrialisation, as templates. He saw his town and its current community fabric rapidly changing as a consequence of the great surge forward brought about by the beginnings of the Industrial Revolution. Being born at the height of important changes in mechanical development and social adaptation, Enoch Wood was to witness the end of the House of Hanover as it gave way to the great trading and social democracies begun under the new reign of Victoria. He was the town's last great Georgian. His own great age and his long life spent in one single town pursuing and participating in the indigenous arts and crafts of the region, within the comforts of a life of one born into family wealth, afforded Wood the tribute of being praised as the patriarch of the Mother Town. No other person, before or since, has worn those garments of civic references better than he.

His map of Burslem not only gives a visual antecedents of families of potters, but allows a cumulative view of its preparation for status in an ongoing design; as well it provides a snapshot of a village life metamorphosing into an industrial township covering but a hundred years. Wood managed to compress all of this information onto a single sheet of paper.

Wherever he could, in his gazetteer, Wood uses the names of alehouses which were current in his time and which had doubtless been used for at least two generations before his own birth. Because of this, many of the alehouses known to exist prior to 1720 were only referred to by the trade of its tenant. It is very likely that no names were given to these premises as they were probably used as a secondary business - a shed at the rear of a workshop, a barn at the side of a potter's oven.

Here is a list of alehouses which were known to have existed in Burslem in 1801. The first 19 are included in Wood's map and are therefore presumed to have been established by 1720.

NAMED HOUSES

1. **Jolly Potters** - situated on the southern side of Market Place. The building on this site remained a public house and by 1801 was known as the Legs of Man - demolished in 1958. The site is today occupied by the Britannia Building Society. (Wood ref. No 2)

2. **Bear - (Bull's Head 1801)** situated on the south-westside of St John's Square. The earliest deeds to the alehouse date to 1698. The premises were modernised with a mock Georgian town-house frontage in 1939. (Ref. 21)

3. **Court House - (Star or Star of Bethlehem 1801)** situated on the south-east side of St John's Square at the south end of Queen Street. In 1740 it was also known as Croft House, as it was prominently overlooking the farming croft land. Demolished in 1967, The site is today occupied by a craft shop. (Ref. 24)

4. **Talbot - (Black Lion 1801)** situated in Queen Street. Demolished in 1967 and occupied today by Boots Chemists. (Ref. 27)

5. **Shoulder of Mutton - (Blue Ball 1801)** situated on the north side of the head of Nile St. The alehouse ceased trading in 1933 and was converted to commercial use. Its site was occupied by Playland, a company providing nursery requisites until 1989 when it was demolished, the site being incorporated into the George Hotel. (Ref. 56)

6. **George and Dragon** - The premises kept its name until it became a hotel in 1929.(Ref. 57)

7. **Red Lion** - In 1720, the building, like the majority in the town, had a thatched roof and half timbered walls with cross beams. It underwent redevelopment in 1675 and in 1875, the latter resulting in a fine example of a mock Tudor house. In 1963 the old inn was demolished and a new modern purpose built public house has been erected on the site. (Ref. 72)

8. **Packhorse** - The building was situated at the head of Packhorse Lane but was incorporated within Enoch Wood's Fountain Works when the potter stopped-up Packhorse Lane in 1825. (Ref. 120)

UN-NAMED HOUSES

9. (Ref. 13) Alehouse owned by Isaac Noden **(Cock Inn 1801) Later Wedgwood Inn.** Closed 1946. Demolished in 1992 after a fire) Brickhouse Street.

10. (Ref. 22) Alehouse owned by Joseph Adams **(Freemason's Arms 1801)** Demolished 1965. Now a video rental shop. St John's Square.

11. (Ref. 34) Alehouse owned by Thomas Harvey. (Un-named in 1801. Became **Victoria Inn circa 1830**) Demolished 1946). Bourne's Bank.

12. (Ref. 37) Alehouse owned by Elizabeth Harvey. (Un-named in 1801. **Became Royal Express circa 1824 - aka the Jig Post 1930 - 1955 - became the Unity Club 1965 - 1973 - became the Summerhouse Club 1979 - 1995.** The building is today derelict but still standing) Bourne's Bank.

13. (Ref. 103) Alehouse owned by Paul Sheldon. (Un-named 1801. **Became New Vaults in 1840)** Demolished in 1956 and is now part of a private forecourt to James Sadler's potworks. Market Place.

14. (Ref. 104) Alehouse owned by Timothy Lockett. (Un-named 1801) **Became the Millstone circa 1830 - renamed Lloyds Tavern in 1985)** Market Place.

15. (Ref. 125) Alehouse owned by John Hurd. (Un-known in 1801 as an alehouse - possibly reverted to a dwelling. Situated in Packhorse Lane and is part of the rear of the former Burslem Co-operative Offices)

16. (Ref. 128) Alehouse owned by William Allen. **(Duke William in 1801)** St John's Square.

17. (Ref. 137) Alehouse owned by Stephen Cartlich. **(Became known as the Bowling Green by 1801)** and stood in a meadow near today's Furlong Lane). The site today is derelict. Nearby stood John Ward's house before demolition in 1870's.

18. (Ref. 140) Alehouse owned by Mary Marsh. **(Known as the Bluebell in 1801)** It was demolished in 1835. Market Place.

19. (Ref, 144) Alehouse owned by Jane Bagguley. **(Known in 1801 as the Turk's Head)** It was demolished in 1835. Market Place.

NAMED HOUSES NOT REFERRED TO IN WOOD'S MAP BUT EXISTING IN 1801.

Albion, Navigation Street

Black Boy, Cobridge Road

Blacksmith' Arms, Station Street Longport.

Britannia Inn, Grange Street

Dog and Partridge, Hot Lane

Foaming Quart, Greenhead Street.

Globe, Hot Lane

Highgate Inn, Brownhills Road

Leopard, Market Place

New Inn, Market Place

Mitre, Pitt Street

Old Bull's Head, Sneyd Street

Old King and Queen, Sneyd Street

Packhorse, Station Street Longport

Rams Head, Market Place

Raven, Elder Road

Ship Inn, Hot lane

Talbot, Westport rd

Travellers Rest, Newcastle Street

Village Tavern, Lower Hadderidge

Wayside Inn, Sytch

Westport Inn

White Horse, Brownhills

White Horse, Elder Road

White Swan, Elder Road

It is more than likely that many of these alehouses were established by 1720 in one form or another, probably as ancillary businesses, thus making a total of 43 houses where the labourer could get a drink and spend time in the company of their peers. But of this number, by using the nationwide precedence of naming inns, only the houses which carried names can be reliably said to have been alehouses a generation before, in the latter part of the 17th century. To the eight named in the firsts list above, The Mitre in Pitt Street should be added, for it is possibly the only example of a former hostel set aside by the monks to accommodate travellers.

Of all the houses in Burslem that carry the appurtenance 'inn', the Mitre is probably the only one with the credentials of authenticity to display it. It was certainly a well established property being referred to in 1865 by Eliza Mettyard as an old inn used by packhorse drovers and known as the Crown. It has also been referred to in a map dated 1801 as the Crown and Mitre. A former administration employee of Parker's Brewery has related that his records show that at the time of its acquisition by the brewery in 1865, the house was called the Crown but the acquired deeds report the property as being formerly named Mitre, therefore the brewery officers reverted back to what they saw as its proper name.

In the religious purges following the Dissolution of the Monasteries commencing in 1536, the keepers of many inns which bore connotations to religious or Papal affiliation or allegiance, were either compelled or volunteered to change their names to suit the new regime. It is entirely credible that in this manner the hostelry known as the Mitre near to the Church of St John, simply became known as the Crown in deference to Henry VIII. By these benchmarks, it is reasonable to propound the theory that the Mitre in Pitt Street is the oldest site of an alehouse in the town. If the Mitre existed in Tudor times - and the community of Burslem surrounding St John's Church certainly did - its location would have stood on the important crossroad of the lane which ran from Sneyd Green connecting Hanley, and including the lane which led from the Grange, converging at this point as they together traversed below the hill on its western side to the head of Packhorse Lane before descending through the common lands (later Furlongs) to the long-bridge over the Fowl Brook, through Bradwell Wood into Dimsdale and on to the market of Newcastle under Lyme.

The important junctions within the boundaries of Burslem lying along the single track lane connecting Hanley, Burslem and Newcastle under Lyme, lay, and still lie, on the ridge at Sneyd Green, which by a series of terraces, falls to the flat land at Elder Road, on down to the flat land at St John's Church, and even further on down into the flat wetland in the Longport valley. It so happens that on each of these junctions there is at least one alehouse as you would expect, the site of each one being of considerable age - in descent: Sneyd Arms, Raven, White Horse, Mitre, Westport Inn. Only the last named has disappeared but only because the community's centre shifted from the east to the west side of the canal.

Naming of premises which brewed and sold alcoholic drink, as we know, can be traced to the Romans. For as few people were taught to read, visual signs depicting the house's commodities were placed over the doorway. This practice stayed in England during the Anglo Saxon period and was prominent during the Norman Conquest where another example of picture-reading was introduced, that of armorial illustration on the field of battle in order for the infantry to identify the standard bearers. From this source the heraldic arms of families became a feature in the names of public houses; none were held higher than the King's Arms.

Nothing has more impact upon our lives than the imposition of legislation. Beginning with local rules which have become law in order to raise taxes, to keeping the peace, to protecting the person and his property, and to providing penalty and sanction against the individual who breaks the law. In England and Wales there are two kinds of law, Common Law and Statute Law. Custom of conduct, following the departure of the Romans, has directed that many outrages were dealt with both by the local king and the governors of townships at variant levels. Common Law was said to include all those breaches of customs and their penalties which had been laid down from Time Immemorial, which means before the royal controls and covenants brought by the introduction of the Statutes of Edward I.

Returning from the Crusades upon the death of his father in 1272, Edward issued a long series of central reforms which were agreed in baronial consultation through his parliament. These mandates were issued as royal statements and were re-enforced with a list of prescribed punishments. Edward was merely cementing the programme of Assize legislation that his father Henry III had initiated, by providing the power of enforcement through a central channel. One of the first laws Edward tackled was his father's Assize of Bread and Ale of 1267, a set of rules which established a method of standardising the purity of the drink and bread, preventing its adulteration and regularising the price of both commodities. At first this assize proved unenforceable in the far reaches of the kingdom and it took a written statute by Edward, contained within the Tumbril and Pillory Statute, allowing punishmentfor the brewster, whether man or woman, by a public flogging. By these methods the standard of ale and bread was brought to some control and the quality was improved. Ale-tasters, or conners as they were known, were employed to travel from town to town testing the quality of ale and they were considered and feared as important officials.

In 1393, Richard II, a great grandson of Edward I and the last of the law making Plantagenets of the House of Anjou, made it compulsory for brewsters to identify their premises with a sign making so as to make it easy for the government official, the ale conner, to locate them. By this time most drinking establishments served the traveller, and the common term of inn was then in use. Richard compelled the innkeeper to state on their signboards that their premises were used to provided sanctuary as well as board and lodgings. He was well aware that the innkeeper's profits were largely made from the drink he provided and so he made the penalty of forfeiture of ale to any landlord who breached the signage regulations.

From this point inn signs began to reflect the associations and relationships with the district, armorial insignia, trades and religion. These names indicated topical themes throughout the country and were copied from town to town. Every town and village had a Kings Head, or Kings Arms. The Royal Oak said all there was to be claimed about Englishness, while the Bush and the Vine recalled the message behind the first signs. The Cross Keys and the Mitre respected religion; the Miner or Bricklayer's Arms, or the Jolly Sailor or Potter, attracted tradesmen.

A traveller's inn at Canterbury, the Fountain, was said to have been in continuous use longer than any other. And in the same town the Pilgrim's Rest was built in the second decade of the 15th century. Certainly one of the oldest names is the Trip To Jerusalem, formerly known as Pilgrim, in Nottingham, cut into the castle walls and used by the crusaders as a recruiting and assembly point in 1189. Ostrich in Buckingham, Ancient and Royal in Grantham, are very old inns, while the Taberd in the London township of Southwark was the starting point for Geoffrey Chaucer's Canterbury pilgrims. Angel at Grantham, King's Arms at Dorchester, King's Head at Shrewsbury, Turk's Head at Exeter, all have great claims to antiquity. Royal Standard at Forty Green, Ye Olde Fighting Cocks at St Albans, and the famous Prospect of Whitby all hold the privilege of age. The smallest is said to Smith's Arms in Dorset, and the highest, as recalled by near neighbour Arnold Bennett on the first page of Old Wives' Tale, is the Cat and Fiddle in the Peak District near to Buxton.

As the industrial towns of the Midlands, the North, North West and East grew, the compulsion to name the inn and alehouse remained; if a licence was in force there is little doubt that the inn had a name. Those innkeepers who didn't wish to pay revenue simply operated without a licence and, consequently, without a name! But the penalties when caught out were unremitting as publicans were run out of town and their houses pulled down or conflagrated.

The eight named public houses listed in Burslem between 1650 and 1720 can be said to have been the original licenced premises of the town - its inns. They provided lodgings, food and toa lesser degree, religious comfort. The remaining eleven were known as common alehouses and were favoured by the growing urban working classes. The pattern of the growth of public houses was to be affected dramatically by three pieces of corrective legislation reflecting the social issues that led up to their implementation. Two of the measures procured changes in drinking habits and the other one forced social change as a result of the direct restrictions resulting from the implementation of the other two.

Around the year 1400 the hop plant, known and used in most European countries in brewing, was introduced by Dutch and Flemish traders into Kent. While ale was sweet and heavy, beer, with the addition of hops as a preservative, gave the barley taste a bitter flavour and leant a pleasant and distinctive aroma to its frothy brew. At first the introduction of hops was considered as an adulterant, its use was regarded an offence and therefore it was slow to take-off. But by 1529, both hop growing and beer drinking, to give it its Germanic name, (bier) had flourished and was popular with soldiers serving in Europe. By the end of the century beer was preferred in most south-east parts of England so that traditional ale had almost come to its commercial end in those regions. The alehouse however continued brewing liquor without hops in the north, a habit which persisted until the uniformity houses in 1830.

In Holland in the early part of the 17th century, a Dutch chemist, Franciscus de la Boe, invented a medicine designed to ease tropical diseases suffered by traders and soldiers in the Dutch East Indies. His concoction of barley and rye was distilled with juniper berries and given the name, essence de Genievre, from the juniper plant grown in Switzerland. It's medicinal secret (if there was one) lay in the alcoholic strength of its distilled liquid and it became the customary drink for soldiers going into battle who were quickly unrestrained by a mere mouthful of 'Geneva' as the British infantryman came to call it: charging into the field of battle their spirits were re-enforced by a quick swig of 'Dutch Courage!'

Legislation banned the drinking of French brandy in 1688 when William of Orange, then on the English throne, pushed his adoptive country into the Prussian war against France, while at the same time he encouraged large scale distilling and consumption of Dutch gin - he being a Dutchman he no doubt benefited from his Dutch resources so that he was enabled to finance the conflict by raising taxes in the enforcement of excise duty on import and consumption.

Gin overnight became the common man's drink instantly superceding the consumption of both ale and beer. In fact, along with illegally imported French brandy, beer was surprisingly only found on the table of the merchant classes as these men had no reason to become drunk and often welcomed a refreshing pint with their roast beef. The dram of gin - a large mouthful - was left to the poor.

By 1730 gin had become the staple drink in London with whole streets dedicated to gin shops. It has been recorded that one in four of all houses in London was a 'dram-shop' causing one eminent commentator to note that it seemed that **'one half of the town was set to poison the other half.'** It was commonplace to see window signs regaling the pleasures of gin drinking: **'Drunk for a penny, dead drunk for two-pence. Clean straw for sleeping - Free'!** Huge numbers of whole communities were attacked by liver disease, shaking-delirium and madness as poor people, in order to forget the pain of work or the lack of work or the horrors of extreme poverty, drank themselves to death, men, women and children alike.

Between 1690 and 1736, the annual production and consumption of gin climbed from half a million to eleven millions of gallons as the whole fabric of civilised living deteriorated alarmingly. So worrying was this trend that in 1736, magistrates in the administration of the London courts presented a petition to King George II in which they stated that gin drinking was:

'...destroying thousands of His Majesty's subjects, and that great numbers of others were, by its use, rendered unfit for useful labour, debauched in morals, and drawn into all manner of vice and wickedness'.

The pressured king responded to this petition by the implementation of the Prohibition Act of 9 Geo II, cap. 23, commonly known as the Gin Act 1736. The purpose of the act was to reduce the production of gin by making it unlawful to sell less than two gallons unless the seller was licenced at a cost of fifty-pounds, with a duty levied at twenty-shilling for each gallon brewed. This was an attempt to stop the home distiller by not making it worth his while to make small amounts for local sale. The act was severe in its penalties directed to any person selling spirits without a licence who was made liable to a fine of one hundred-pounds. In a further exacting measure the licence to distil could only be granted to victuallers, innkeepers or other public house keepers who carried on no other ancillary business or trade. This of course was designed to curtail the practice of the ordinary shopkeeper and tradesman from supplementing his income with a gin factory as a side-line.

At first the Gin Act caused a swift decrease in gin production and consumption, but soon manufacture of the 'bad stuff' and its trading practices was simply adjusted to fit the manipulable legislation and an illicit trade broke out resulting in an increase in gin drinking more serious than it was before the act was brought in. Illegal distillers took out wine licences to produce an easily concocted mixture made of spices and sugar into which they boiled gin sold under that most ambiguously named drinks, 'sweets' and of course fortified wine. Pharmacists put gin in medicine-labelled bottles and prescribed it for cholic, or mixed it up as gripe waters with directions to administer it by drinking, **'three or four spoonfuls four or five times a day, or as often as the malady persists'**! Gin was sold everywhere under other names - bootlegging was rife! Under the Gin Act, introduced to curb gin excess, consumption of gin rose from 11 million gallons in 1736 to 20 millions by 1740!

An act of 1743 repealed this infamous piece of legislation when it appeared that the government had surrendered to gin and abandoned any form of alcohol control. The new Gin Act was ironically introduced in order to clean-up the quality of gin. It reduced the distilling fee to twenty-shillings and abolished the duty on the gallon. As a result conditions throughout the country became even worse. These foolish attempts to crush the power of the back street gin distiller failed utterly, but the legitimate wholesale distiller remained untouched by the legislation and continued to make good quality drink by standardising their own stock by producing it in greater quantities by the vat. Gin was now being favoured in the withdrawing rooms of the rich who discovered that the better consequences of drinking purer gin resulted in less severe hangovers and less torment from the gout. This was mirrored in the rise of decent professional businesses. The London family distillers of Booth's, Gordon's and Gilbey's attracted good customers by building classy establishments in the town centres known as 'Gin Palaces' on account of their well designed and plush interiors. Their gin also began to find its way to the growing colonies where it was mixed with quinine to ward off tropical ailments.

Throughout the 18th century beer quality was continually being improved. The unappetising cloudiness and the yeast deposits were rectified by the use of an element found in the bladder of the sturgeon called isinglass. And there were a growing number of texts advising on how to improve the brewing of beer paying regards to its temperature, the cleanliness of its containers, and its storage and stillage. The ratio of ingredients and the quality of water were constantly under review. But gin, for the time being remained king. How far it was a problem outside London and the great ports is difficult to assess. The message of gin was introduced by travellers and returning soldiers to the growing factory towns: there is no doubt that the message was heard in Burslem

A meeting between John Tellwright and Ralph Leigh, two old potters reviewing their youth spent in the Burslem potbanks at the time when gin drinking was irrepressible, throws but a narrow shaft of light upon the times. Meeting in Burslem market place in 1810, Tellwright invites Leigh to join him in the Turk's Head to reminisce over a drink or two. They talk of their youth in the 1750s:

T: Wal, bu oi'l ston trayts; so cum, let's goos to th' Turk's Yed an ka' some o Georgy Moore's draps whoile we' tawken oud matters o'er.

(They go to the Turk's Head tavern where Tellwright orders half a pint of gin and two glasses)

T: Coom, sup it Rafy; heres to thee.

L: It's meety noice and verry strung, Mester Terrick.

And the conversation continues about the waste of ware as the potters of the times took to drinking in the alehouses waiting for the kilns to harden the crocks and finish the batch. The conversational piece (re-printed in Ward) says more for the dialect than the quality of the drink, but it shows that even in the first decade of the 19th century gin still appeared to be the popular drink in the town. The common brewers and the scientist however continued to make improvement to beer, but in places such as Burslem, beer remained very much a home brew out of barns for at least another fifty years until Burslem's first common brewer set down his business in Regent Street/ Pitt Street.

One hundred and twenty years earlier in 1685, Doctor Robert Plott found the local beer in and around the Potteries more organic:

> *'About Shenston, as I was informed by the worthy Mr Frith of Thorns, they frequently used the ERICA VULGARIS heath, or Ling, instead of hops to preserve their beer, which he also told me gave it no ill-taste. And that they sometimes here make a malt of oats which, mixed with that of barley is called Dredge Malt of which they make an excellent quick sort of drink.'*

And even after the administrative successes of the common brewers, 150 years after Tellwright and Leigh's discussions, Burslem topers drinking brewery beer still looked back with some affection on the times of the old potters as testified by William Scarratt in 1903:

> *'Home-Brewed was in vogue, and I should think the product very wholesome although done in a primitive fashion, and now and again, not too over clear and not too ripe. If anyone desired to sell beer, either 'on' or 'off' all he had to do was to go to the supervisor (excise man) and pay a sum for his licence and commence business.'*

An early Burslem victualler, was John Mollart (Wood's map ref. 41). On Wood's map he is described as a farmer but from documented transactions including the purchase of yeast from a nearby baker, it seems quite possible that his secondary business was brewing beer. Mollart's farm was situated at the top of Bourne's Bank as it enters the town from the lane to the church. Today the site of Mollart's farm is occupied by the Queen's Head Hotel and is likely to have its prototype in Mollarts barn. Mollart's wife was a typical ale-wife providing bread and ale to pottery workers and brewing for wakes. It was her class who comforted the crude worker during his break. Tellwright and Leigh again, this time in a more literate continuity:

T: *If you remember Ralph, those old potters couldn't find two ha'pennies to rub together to make a start in their trades.*

L: *Yes, that's very true, Although they pretended they were the best and could make the best, the result was that in the end they achieved nothing. And even before they could begin they were beaten by their bad habits.*

T: *The old master potter was a companionable man. Very much one of the boys and part of the crew; men who liked a good time.*

L: *They were that, Mr Tellwright. Just as soon as they had placed the ware in the ovens, off they'd go and make straight for alehouse on*

Swan Bank. And there they'd drink and drink until the ware would be ready to be taken out, or so they thought, relying on guesswork and the state of intoxication they found themselves in. The master potters always took their labourers with them to the alehouse, and when they were all half drunk, many a row and fight would break out, each man taking his turn in the arena, arguing over whose turn it was to pay. And when they eventually returned to their oven with sore heads, all their pots would be spoiled.

T: Of course the masters are much more sober and industrious these days.

L: Yes we never see them drunk during the day beating their wives and spoiling their work as they used to do. They think a great deal more of themselves and their families now.

T: Do you remember how we used to see them tied up to the stocks in front of the Red Lion until they became sober and repented?

It's hard to imagine Josiah Wedgwood lying drunk in a hedge while the load in his oven burned and cracked. Of course the Wedgwoods and their peers weren't of this class. Tellwright and Leigh were conversing about the men they themselves worked for, the second tier masters who might have learned under Adams, Wood and Wedgwood but were not taught by them. And, because of the free market, saw an opportunity to make money: semi-skilled men who had neither the artistic nor the business skills to thrive and prosper.

And yet there were many good and popular innkeepers in the Wedgwood family: Doctor Thomas Wedgwood (1655-1717) who lived at the Red Lion, grandson of Gilbert the patriarch, owned all the land on the east of Market Place to the open fields of the Jenkins. He acquired and improved the old inn in 1675 passing the land on to John and Thomas great-grandsons of Gilbert who erected the famed Big House next door to the Red Lion, while his own grandson, Carlos, became the licencee of the Duke William; and so popular was he that his eminence earned him the nickname, 'Duke Carlos'! Imagine the growing town in these times. The rich potter living in sturdy houses at the top of the hill with their potbanks adjacent; the new so-called 'master potters' packed tight on the hill slopes living beside their kilns and hovels while their workers literally existed from day to day, living in camps in the low-lying fields in houses made of broken saggars.

Arnold Bennett knew this part of the town as well as his own Cobridge, a place in which he set the Clayhanger Prin the 1870s - a corner where Mollart's Farm still stood in the author's time with its alehouse at the side of the barns. He was able to see what his town had inherited from those rough people - his own grandfather among them. A town which, **'bursts forth out of a damp jungle of careless habit and negligence... ragged brickwork, walls finished anyhow with saggars and slag; narrow uneven alleys leading to higgledy-piggeldy workshops and kilns; cottages transformed into factories and factories into cottages, clumsily, hastily because nothing matters as long as "it will be made to do"'**. And as he climbed up Bourne's Bank, the old lane, he noted the George and Dragon Inn, and the Swan Inn in Swan Bank, **'surviving all revolutions by the mighty virtue and attraction of ale'**. Emerging as Edwin Clayhanger out of the lane and into the street, he saw **'cocks and hens scurrying, with necks horizontal, from all quarters, and were even flying to the call of a little old woman who threw grain from the top step of her porch.'**

While, **'On the level of the narrow pavement stood an immense constable, clad in white trousers, with a gun under his arm for the killing of mad dogs.'**

At 'wakes' all work stopped and a number of brews of ale and beer would be made ready. Barns and trestles would be set aside with the whole family taking part - children would run about calling aloud that there was ale to sell, and they ran to neighbour's cottages delivering orders in jugs. These were drinking sessions that would last a week in and out of the market where jugglers, fools, actors and acrobats would arrive from the surrounding villages bringing bears and bulls for bating by local terriers. Wagers were made on dog-fights and cock fights while the men and youths would engage in day-long battles of 'prison bars'.

It was in 1790 that the improvements in brewing beer had finally caused it to supercede the production of ale, even though gin remained the common man's drinks. Bad water - someting to be avoided - was a contributory factor to the increased use of beer for it was found that beer could be brewed again from the spent mash so that children could be given it safely. This was called 'small beer' and it was by far cleaner than the so-called fresh well water which was too unwholesome to boil. What's more, small-beer was both invigorating and narcotising for little boys required to work and babies needing to sleep.

Beer was drunk domestically by all with all meals as a necessity; ale and gin was drunk publicly for recreation. Within thirty years many purpose-built drinking houses appeared, at first in London and the in large towns. But the public houses were soon spreading to the major new manufacturing conurbations. In these first two decades of the 19th century many new buildings were erected on chosen sites in the new towns and on the new road junctions. The term alehouse gave way to the new public house. In Burslem as elsewhere, the old alehouse disappeared or was re-developed into improved or larger premises. By the late 1820's a number of old alehouses such as the Legs of Man, George and Dragon, Royal Express, Leopard, Foaming Quart and American, were being improved to become staging houses providing accommodation or stabling for the Stage Coaches and the Royal Mails. It is from this time that the names of Burslem's first alehouses and inns have been lost forever, although a number were simply given new names.

Also in the 1820's it was possible to notice that spirit drinking had somewhat given way to beer consumption as the excise duty on spirits and gin continued to push the ceiling out of the price range of the common drinker. Gin had become professional, almost decent. And even though the excise of beer often rose in dizzying leaps, beer remained cheaper than spirits. But in 1826, when a series of quirky excise laws resulted in spirits falling from twenty shillings to seven shillings against a gallon, it was no surprise to see a gin revival taking it into the golden age of the Gin Palace and making fortunes for the distillers. By this time success of the East Indian Trading Company brought about the relaxation of import duty on tea - the great hot beverage which was coming to replace beer on the meal tables of the working man's house. Clean drinking water was still scarce and still very dangerous to consume so the common practice was to warm it with milk which gave it a blue appearance, hence its name, 'blue milk' or 'skimmer'. It was an insipid drink although it provided a small meal when bread was soaked into giving the name to it of 'pudding-brew', or in the Potteries shortened version 'pobs'.

Now that gin drinking was freed again beer drinking declined and the new public houses were fully occupied by gin drinkers. These houses were tied by the spirit tax and were owned by influential business men who used their money to buy a number of houses and to tenant them to managers. An earlier example of tying was the purchase of a number of licenced houses throughout the land by John Manners, the Marquis of Granby, (1721-1770) who handed them to many of his disabled non-commissioned officers who were wounded in the Seven Years War; each public house being named after the title of the hearty general. The public however remained averse to paying through the nose for the privilege of drinking in these tied 'public houses' and therefore returned to the practice of home-brew. But the loudest voice in opposition to 'tax and tying' came from the 'Free-Traders', former licensees who formed the Free Trade Movement who called for the opening up of the beer trade and removal of the franchise from the restrictions of tied owners: out of the hands of the victualler and into the pocket of the brewer.

Free Trade for public drinking houses was principally supported by the Prime Minister, the first administration of the Duke of Wellington, who with his chancellor, attempted to strike a balance between direct revenue taxation and free enterprise. By this method, in addition to the tax at the public bar being reduced on the sale of beer to the consumer, its was planned that the ring of tied houses owned by gin barons would be broken. The public generally were right behind these measures particularly the growing temperance movements who saw that free-trading in beer would rid the communities of the evils of gin drinking. And so the government prepared to bring in legislation to move the balance to favour the consumer.

As with many other remedial instruments of legislation, the government lurched from the frying pan into the fire. The Beer House Act 1830, in its attempt to beat gin drinking, allowed for three principles which ought to have balanced out the franchises:

a) **a payment of two guineas enabled a local householder whose name appeared in the rate book, to sell beer and only beer from his house;**

b) **a licence could be obtained from the new local excise officer, where previously it had to be obtained from a locally appointed licensing justice;**

c) **hours of opening were restricted to the exclusion of the period between 10pm and 4am.**

Any person therefore need only to apply to the excise man and prove he owned his own house or shop and was of previous good character by bringing with him two other rate-payers to vouch to his credentials.

The Act became operative from 6am on 1st October 1830 and by 31st December the country had no fewer than 24,342 new public houses! Beershops were opened in cellars, in parlours, in front rooms of terraced houses and in converted retail shops. The majority of these places were totally unfit as public houses; some were unable to accommodate more than half a dozen customers at a time, but it was if the drinkers of the world had suddenly been released into Paradise - indeed one of the commonest names for the new beerhouse from these times was 'Paradise Inn' - and men and women were unable to pass along a town's pavement without encountering loud advertisements from the vocal licensees extolling the merits of their special brews.

For most people it was like going home, stepping straight from their own front door and into the doorway of their neighbours' to settle down in *his* parlour instead of their own. In Liverpool it was the case that *fifty new beer shops were being opened each day* until the great port reached saturation point on 31st October - just one month after the Act had become law - when it was reported that *every house in Scotland Road sold beer!* In its comparative size, Burslem was no exception as houses were converted in back streets, lanes and alleys giving substance to the still commonplace motto that Burslem was the 'best drinking town in the potteries'.

New names appeared by which these houses became known. Altered town centre shops were called 'beer stores'. Comparisons with regular public houses as against beer houses were topical as the public referred to the beer houses as 'Tom and Jerries' and 'Kidleywinks'. Knowledgeable observers sneered at these new publicans as being 'men without capital and without character'. The former 'hush shops' and the secret drinking 'dram shops' suddenly came out into the open and sold beer under the legitimacy of the new regime, while many workers supplemented their income by obtaining the cheap licence and letting their wives manage them. In Burslem in the middle of the day, men and women were drunkenly rolling around in public places often incapable of taking care of themselves. In the ensuing six months, the increased number of places where the potter could drink was both astonishing and alarming. A census taken a year after the Act came into force recorded a list of 190 beersellers in the Mother Town, which were distinct and separate from the established 47 public houses which had themselves been increased by some further 50 on account of the 'tax and tying' regulations, giving Burslem's townsfolk a choice of around three-hundred establishments in which to consume alcohol - in catering terms, 156 persons to each public house!

The majority of Burslem's beerhouses now remained without name and bore absolutely no resemblance to the established public house either in comfort, decor or quality of beer. It was found that the new landlords, for that is what they liked to be called and from where the popular term came from - as it were, owning their little plots of land - had no knowledge of how to brew beer. In the main they turned out weak beers which were commonly bad and sour, or they brewed collectively in groups which gave the whole batch a bad name. The better beers were purchased from the emerging common brewer, the most famous Burslem one being Parkers Brewery.

For some seventy-odd years between 1790 and 1860, access to alcohol for the working classes had flourished setting the common recreational base for those who worked hard and played equally as hard. And it was commonplace for all categories and levels of the poorer quarters to indulge themselves each day. Beer was taken into the workplace where men and women remained after their hours of work to take part in Bacchanalian orgies in which children were participants or at least corrupted onlookers. Wages were paid out in lump and shared-out in public houses resulting in a landlord's profit and workers went home to their families with much less in their pockets and angry with themselves for being easily parted with their hard earned wage; an anger which was released into the worker's home with the consequence of many violent interludes. Children of large families were sent to work as young as seven to supplement the household income and in their turn they became as their fathers were, remaining in the same locations for life and going in the same direction.

Legislation was introduced to protect children by the 1860s but drunkenness had by then become a fact of life, an unbroken chain that succoured the new Victorian masses. Yet even by 1908 it was still common for children to accompany adults in the bars of the public houses; indeed, the best attempt at remedy only occurred on 1872 when the problems found in public houses and the vexations caused by drink outside of them, were eventually tackled. The Licencing Act 1872 addressed the specific problems of drunkenness in a public place and introduce law to curb the effects to the public at large. Offences were created that made it a crime to be found drunk on a highway; being incapable of taking care of oneself through drink; of riotous and disorderly behaviour; drunk in charge of a horse, cattle, pigs and sheep; of a loaded firearm; of a vehicle. And yet being drunk in charge of a child under the age of seven was not created an offence until 1902!

Temperance was introduced to Burslem in 1850. During the Chartist Riots of 1842, the numerous beerhouses were used as meeting places by any group lingering with subversive intent. But this included how the employer viewed his worker who, with no harmful intent other than gathering together for domestic conversation and comfort, were perceived a recidivist drunks. It is fair to describe the sociological and environmental situation in Burslem during the 1840's as pretty basic. The standing of the townsfolk had much in common with their brothers and sisters in the rest of the growing civilized world as they struggled to break free from agrarian fiefdom into a commonly shared enterprise arena, a utopian world which offered the opportunities of industrialisation and greater earning capacity. Any man, with eagerness and financial providence, was able to prosecute his own life and thereby consolidate his family strengths by making independent excursions into domains from which he was hitherto debarred. All he needed to do was to take advantage in one of the growing educational outlets, remain teetotal, and, attend the prescribed chapel. It was still a hard road up, but by the end of the 1860s, many had successfully taken it.

Drunkenness was viewed as an element in and part of the overall pattern of poverty. It was expected of the working classes who knew no better than to take up the baton of the lives of those who had gone before them, their fathers and their grandfathers. A temperance leader wrote that these working drunkards made themselves idle in *'...**the utter contempt the worker has for common decency in his crude and unresisting degeneration through the poisoned tankard and the foulness of beer and spirituous liquor.**'* It was the pledge of these temperance men to purge drink from the public house and the home. And for a time it was partially successful by the creation of associations known as the Band of Hope which set about in public houses reforming hardened drinkers by urging them to sign-up to the contract of abstinence. In the Potteries these sober and righteous men published a magazine entitled the **Beacon**, which they sold on the factory floor and in the pubs wherein lists of reformed drunkards were displayed in order to encourage others to protect hearth and home against the evil booze.

Burslem was **'the busiest and wickedest drinking town'**, and was for those very same reasons the strongest centre in the Potteries for the **Temperance**

Alliance under its leadership and editorship of J E Keates. And it was in Burslem that the local association had its closest relationship with the principal **United Kingdom Alliance Against Drink.** James Edward Keates, a draper and tailor of St John's Square, was a total abstainer. He came to Burslem in 1840 when he was twenty-three observing first hand the consequences of the Chartist Riots, deploring the results of the town's tolerance to the mis-use of alcohol which he noted was causative to the insurrection. His closest rival in business was Robert Longson, a grandfather of Arnold Bennett, whose own draper's shop was just across the road. Both Keates and Longson placed great store on family values and were impeccable in their domestic management. But in kindred and commercial relationships, that is as far as their likenesses extended.

A very active member of the Swan Bank Wesleyan Methodists, Keates wrote compulsively for all the national temperance journals, preaching his messages of zeal wherever he went in business or pleasure, travelling frequently to America studying the origins of the Movement and its potential for the recovery from drink of the United Kingdom. He was also keenly interested in progressing the Tonic-sol-fa system of music-reading in support of his friend Joseph Wolstancroft Powell, the town clerk and director of a number of choirs. The single-minded Keates had, in his later life, little good to say about the famed music teacher, Madame Reymond, whose achievements he sought to belittle; nor had Keates much praise for her protégé John Cope, the founder and conductor of the North Staffordshire Symphony Orchestra. But the protection of people from the evils of drink was his particular cause; in this he carried the banner Excelsior while he led from the front.

James Edward Keates' younger brother, John Keates, was the publisher of the North Staffordshire local information books, Keates' Almanacs, Gazetteers and Directories. As a young technician he became the first printer of the Staffordshire Sentinel and was a rival of Joseph Dawson, the printer and publisher of the Staffordshire Knot and friend of Arnold Bennett. (To add to the irony of intimacy, another of Bennett's good friends was Harold Keates Hales - the Card - who was the grandson of James Edward Keates.)

During the 1850s, by and large, the Temperance Movement in Burslem was reasonably successful although it may be argued that drunkenness and alcoholism had reached its nadir at the end of the 1840s and there really was no further depth for the potter's social descent as he had already reached the rock bottom of debauchery. Although non-alcoholic drinks were a novelty, a number of temperance hotels were established and thrived and there was growing patronage for tea-shops and cafes which were largely passed-by however by the in-work potter. A big stumbling block for total temperance presented itself in the continued impurity of drinking water, and as a consequence, clean-water drinking fountains were erected in places of public open space such as the squares. This was carried on and grew more passionate in the late 1880s when fountains were placed in the pleasure parks in Moorland Road and in Cobridge. But in the short term, the temperance societies were quite successful.

Keates published many articles in the Beacon which were sentimentally unrestrained. In 1853, 'yours truly, "INQUISITIVE"' wrote that he had walked through the Mother Town at half-past eleven in the evening observing that all the shops were closed except for the liquor shops which were all open for business. **'In one I entered at twelve o'clock, I found a room containing about 60 or**

70 young persons, most of them, under 20 years of age; some were sitting on one another's knees, many were under the influence of drink, they were all in the act of singing a chorus to a song by which... I knew was not of the purest kind - a fiddle assisted their harmony...'. In his nocturnal wanderings, "INQUISITIVE" encountered a known woman of **'ill-fame'** who attempted to cajole a glass of spirits from him. In other public houses he was witness to **'abominable dealings'**, swearing, cursing and even more singing. Another report in the Beacon listed statistics from the Post Office directory in fanciful comparison:

Burslem has... ***'14 places of worship, which we know are not too well supported; and according to the rate book 121 spirit vaults, inns and beerhouses - it thus appears that while Burslem dedicates 14 buildings to the worship of God it has 121 to the worship of Bacchus and his midnight orgies... 7 bakers..7 shops for the Staff of Life and 121 for the Spirit of Death... five public schools to teach ignorant youth, while there are 121 'schools' to educate in vice and immorality..'***

The Sentinel's editor in 1857 - its first editor - Mr Thomas Phillips, himself a teetotaller, became alarmed at the aggressive language used by his temperance correspondents, nevertheless permitted reams of letters to be published attacking the drunken morals of the Burslem inebriants. In his Leader he was able to declare that, **'Burslem has most decidedly taken the lead in the Potteries with reference to the Maine-Law Movement'** - ie. the United Kingdom Temperance Alliance, a union to which, irrespective of his own alcoholic restraint, he was personally opposed. Indeed temperance meetings had become somewhat frenzied in their own inner transactions. A local builder, William Ford, member of the Burslem Board of Health, made a personal verbal attack on the moralising of Alliance leader, Dr Lees, at a meeting held at the newly opened Old Town Hall. He accused Lees of 'stumping' (ie illegally promoting) Ford's election candidate, Lord Ingestre, and using the temperance meeting for political gain. In the resulting argument Ford insulted the assembly by turning his back to the crowd and posturing his backside on the orchestra platform. Someone shouted out that he was drunk and that if he were a working man he would be thrown out, which is what happened, **but only after it was put to the vote!**

Temperance continued in many quarters aided by public meetings, prayer congress and religious programmes, but by the late 1870s much of the unrestrained drunkenness was receding by virtue of the strong pro-active Licencing Act 1872 which was reinforced by supportive legislation in the prevention of crime, forgery and coinage and offences against persons. Nevertheless drunkenness persisted, it was most difficult, if not impossible to put down completely and forever. In an attempt to distance themselves from the motley of beerhouses the large breweries began a programme of regeneration and rebuilding which reached its height in the 1890s. During this decade many superb examples of Victorian architecture were structured in the large town centres. The Leopard was given a new extended frontage with an antique Georgian design, as were the New Inn and the George Hotel. But the best example of Gothic Victorian conversion was the rebuilding of the Queen's Head, on the site of the old farm and alehouse of William Mollart.

Undertaken in 1898, it is still possible to see part of the former farm house on the left side, set back from the forward curtilages of the new building. It was built with two main rooms with an additional 'snug', and a seated 'outdoor' with an entrance in Bourne's bank, was provided for private preferences. The original long taproom bar-counter was made of solid mahogany and the high moulded ceiling was supported by two fine leaf scrolled cast-iron pillars. The room was lined with green leather pumps and the whole premises was adorned by gas-lit glass chandeliers. A wide passage directly leading from the street, passed between the two main rooms to accommodate customers who were wandering the town and stopping only for a brief drink, which was a fashionable custom of the middle-class Victorians, a ritual - gathering in pub passage-ways - which has been carried down into modern times given to 'open-planning'. The Queen's Head was all that was modern in Burslem and its ambience represented a middle-class fellowship, men of substance, customers with money in their pockets.

Other pubs too reflected Victorian confidence; the Star with its high windows, its wealth of ground space that fitted the shape of the corner of Queen Street and Church Street, and its swinging barrel sign: The Victoria Hotel, later named the White Hart Music Hall and even later, the Huntsman; each had their decor improved in the styles which moderately copied the grand Victorian public houses of London and the large cities where the breweries attempted to outdo each other in grand and luxurious accommodation.

As the country entered Edwardian times the differentials between status in class and its acceptability of interactive classes who demanded public entertainment, for a short time grew wider. Now the up-town centre pubs belonged to the businessman where trade was negotiated, deals undertaken, success celebrated and failures commiserated. Rooms in the Leopard, the Marquis of Granby, the Duke William and the George Hotel were set aside, and bell-pushes driven by electric accumulators were conveniently provided to call the waiter, while bar fronts were made with sliding casements enabling a section of the room to be closed for instant privacy. And the working classes kept themselves to themselves in other rooms, usually the taproom or bar, and in the beerhouses, unwilling to dress-up and pay the extra coppers for the same brew. These beerhouses stood wherever their was a community - Middleport had eight, Longport eight; Waterloo Road eighteen, Nile Street nine. In all places where a man needed comfort and respite there was a beerhouse. Many men were lucky enough to have one next door, some poor souls had to walk up to a hundred yards to reach one! But through all the bad times and the good, it was the public house that stood-out more importantly and more valued even than the worker's own terraced cottage or slum; it was in these establishments that he spent all his valued time, prime time, his special times.

When Horace Pepper walked into Burslem from Longport on the eve of World War I, he and his fellows were able to drink from four in the morning until well after ten at night. Workmen finishing their shifts at 6.am, at 2.pm and at 10.pm would make their way from the factory gate stumbling into the pub that invariably stood at the factory entrance and 'barred' their direct route to home. As they walked into the pub, their colleagues just starting their shift - their replacements - were leaving. The Potters Arms, the Moon and Stars and the Royal Oak stood near the entrance to Wilkinson's Potbank; outside the gates of Rogers, Dunn-Bennetts, Davenports, standing side by side were the Staff of Life, Great Eastern, the Great Britain and the Travellers Rest. The railway workers, canal workers, gas workers of Longport all supped at Miltons Head, Blacksmiths Arms, Packhorse, Railway and the Duke of Bridgewater. The thousands who lived in Burslem and worked in Middleport were compelled to pass the Navigation Inn, the Three Tuns, the Albion, Britannia, Lamb Inn, Rose Shamrock and Thistle even before they arrived in Queen Street! There was no way around the public houses whichever way the workers went! On the doorstep of Royal Doultons were the Blue Ball, British Flag, Crown and Anchor, White Lion, Nile Hotel and the Durham Ox. The potbanks of Alcock's, Sadler's, Steventon's, Wade's and Wood, physically stood inside the town centre and their workers were serviced by the Millstone, Roebuck, New Vaults, Rams Head, Olde Crown, Talbot, Royal Hotel, Dolphin; there was hardly a location where a public house didn't stand and there was barely fifty yards between each public house.

Pubs were the life-blood of all; men like Horace Pepper and Vincent Riley had good reasons to patronise them. After his brother was killed on HMS Pathfinder, Horace attempted to enlist in the Army but was rejected on the grounds that he was the main supporter of a young family and was needed at home and so he drank away his idle time. In the days that Vincent Riley suffered rejection at the hands of the Royal Navy's recruiters, his mam saw little of him as he went from pub to pub, drinking, begging for drink and tatting for scrap to provide for his alcoholic sustenance. During those bad times, both men anaesthetised their pain with drink. But, after the long binge, Vincent eventually went to the Hanley army recruitment centre in Canon Street where he enlisted in the 5th Battalion North Staffordshire Regiment.

During his service on the Western Front, Vincent Riley was wounded twice, shrapnel that showered him in battle permanently disabled his arm, and at some stage he was awarded the Military Medal for gallant service. To the proud soldier this would have been sufficient compensation for all his earlier set-backs in life, to return home in rewarded courage, marching up the street to his waiting mother, to settle to a steady job and to enjoy his due leisure, perhaps with a young woman, a wife, and children. But two occurrences came to influence his future. The first he gave little consideration to for it was well outside the jurisdiction of his influence and that of all his fighting comrades, but it was to come to have a great effect upon his leisure time after he became demobbed.

In 1909 David Lloyd George was Chancellor of the Exchequer in the reforming Liberal Government. That year again saw an upturn in the activities of the Temperance Movement, once again brought about by lax restrictions on drinking regulations and alcohol influences upon child prostitution and crime in the large towns and cities. Lloyd George, himself a teetotaller and sympathiser of temperance, attempted to reduce the hours of public drinking and threatened once again to curb its excesses by increasing the duty on the production and sale of beer. These measures were dismissed summarily in the Conservative controlled House of Lords. But, in 1915, as Minister for Munitions, the Welsh Wizard brought to statute the Defence of the Realm Act which curtailed the permitted hours of public drinking. It was a second best law after considering and rejecting the wholesale banning of the sale of alcohol for the duration of the war. Apart from a limited number of relaxations in post war England and Wales, Lloyd George's wartime restrictions on hours continued until 1921 when they were officially confirmed by law to eight hours per day, not earlier than 11am and not later than 10pm. On Sundays, Christmas Day and Good Friday, the permitted hours were cut to five. For alcoholics, these hours were insufficient - drink had now to be taken elsewhere which meant drink of a different quality. The Second World War in 1939, prevented any realistic amendment to an anti-social law which eventually lasted until 1988 when the Conservative Government of Margaret Thatcher allowed public houses to open for 12 hours each day. Only the times of opening and closing are today controlled by law. This law - DORA - has had an adverse effect on the life-style of the poor and working classes which has echoes today in street drunkenness and vagrancy purely by its failure to compromise for the men and women who simply can't live without a drink.

The second occurrence that turned Vincent Riley's life was his discovery that he was addicted to alcohol. Having no job at the end of the war, Vincent at first spent all his back pay and war injury pension treating his mates and generally going from pub to pub. It was one long glorious binge which only ended when his money ran out. When this happened the wounded warrior turned to scissor sharpening gaining work by posing as an out of work Sheffield steel worker. He begged and gambled and stole, and what payment for work he did was all spent on his habit. Had the old uninterrupted licensing hours prior to 1915 still been in force, he like many drinkers may have paced himself better, but from this time forward, Vincent Riley spent the rest of his life enjoying his favourite pastime of lying in meadows, under hedges wonderfully drunk in comatose bliss.

Like many of his kind he was an 'open' alcoholic, public drinkers passing through the years of Depression and another world war drinking and begging, taking opportunities as they presented themselves. And he never hid away from life which continuously brought him to the attention of the police. In his life of drink, Vincent Riley received two-hundred and forty-four prison sentences. It was after a release from Strangeways Prison in Manchester when he was thirty years old that Vincent had his first drink of 'MOJO', a mixture of methylated spirit with any other diluting drink, often cold tea, beer and more dangerously cider.

His return to Burslem brought him further experimentation with meths and he very soon gained a reputation for its purchase with local pharmacists. Almost every bout brought him to the gutter from where he was arrested and as a rule sent to prison. He had by this time made such a nuisance of himself in the Mother Town that chemists refused to sell him meths over the counter. His ruse of sending a proxy for him was quickly rumbled and he began to travel, at first to the other Potteries towns and later to towns outside the district. Even as far as Glasgow his convictions for drunkenness were recorded, spending time in the infamous Barlinny Prison . His absences caused by his incarcerations were jovially referred to by him as attendance at 'college'. But afterwards he would always be drawn back to Burslem to find kip in his favourite 'hotel', lying with his mates beside the warmth of the brick kilns of Sneyd Brickworks in Nile Street.

At some stage Vincent Riley married. It was short lived and it is not known who the woman was or if there were any children of the union. The women in his life were prostitutes and sister drunks, but he was never known to complain of the company he kept. Martin Welsh was a particular companion and they could often be seen emerging from the magistrates court rubbing their red eyes against the morning sunlight after a night in the dark damp police cells, smiling together and laughing out loud having succeeded in winning a fine, which they could never pay, instead of being sent to prison.

Day after day, interminably, Vincent Riley got drunk on mojo, until one day in 1951 he was missing from his usual haunts. It was easy to find him though, 'asleep' at his favourite hotel in Nile Street. He was buried, having reached the undeserved age of sixty, in Burslem cemetery beneath the dirty hill in a field that hosts the last remains of Arnold Bennett, overlooking the redundant Sneyd Colliery and Sneyd Brickworks. Two fine artists.

THE WRAITH WAS A DRUNK

From the High Street down Furlong's lane,
Along by terraces, on cobblestone all strewn with ash,
By an old brick wall on the right hand side,
With some double-gates, all rotten and wide,
Where I once took my fancy Elaine, where we tried
To make babies one Sunday when the sun had died,

It was here I met a spirit, a tramp and he stank,
His name was Vincent and he smelled, oh so rank.
And his eyes were wild with memories past,
And his face was all soiled by Mojo and waste.
But it wasn't from cowardice, no was it from funk,
And I didn't know then, but the wraith was a drunk.

From cobbles to tarmac and old broken stones,
Where allotments stood empty and crops overgrown.
Bottom-enders were laughing and chuckin' their crack
At this old man who stood givin' it back
In oaths and prophesies so loud and so black.
So we top-enders beat the bottom lot back.

It left us wi' th bloke, this tramp, an' he stank,
His name was Vincent and he stank oh so rank.
And his eyes, they were wild with memories past,
And his face was all soiled with Mojo and waste.
But it wasn't from cowardice, and it was from funk
That made this poor soldier a wraith that was drunk.

He shouted so fierce tha' sound laid-by paled.
And top-enders turned from the phantom in th' field.
I couldn't fast skip, nor hop it me sen,
So I stood and I stared at yon Furpo agen.
And he grabbed at my jersey, pullin', and then,
He scufted my neck to teach me for sense.

I was close to this bloke, this tramp who so stank.
And he said, 'I'm Riley and I stink some'at rank.'
His eyes they were wild with sad memories past.
His face black and soiled with Mojo and waste.
Though it wasn't from cowardice, nor was it from funk.
It avoided me then why this wraith was so drunk.

Said he, 'Do yer know young man, what ter do for me?
Here's threppence fer chemist that's at top of th' way.
Tell him its fer stains in yer mother's wash.
Three penn'orth of jollop - that's a bottle o meth.
Now, off yer go and dunna be nesh.
You've heard what I've said - here a penny for th' dash.'

I walked from this tramp, this bloke that so stank,
That said he was Riley and smelled oh so rank.
Whose eyes were so wild with memories past,
With face hurt and soiled with Mojo and waste.
It wasn't with cowardice, it wasn't with from funk,
But I had to obey this wraith who was drunk.

I nervously stood at the counter so full
Of pills and bottles of 'pecaque and squill.
'Mis'r Stanyer, me mother says I've gone and spilled ink
O'er me best school trousers she's got in the sink.
Cost let her have three penn'orth of summat to blink
It all off. Me mother says meth's would do't in a wink!'

Old Stanyer looked with suspicious eye
And measured my question to see through the lie.
And then he just turned and came back with a jar
Of purple-blue liquid that he handed o'er.
'I'll want th' bottle back. So tell thee ma.'
And I scarpered out with that precious star.

I passed it on to the tramp who so stank
Who was singing sweet songs though smelling so rank.
His eyes, they grew wilder with memories past,
And his face became soilder with mojo and waste.
He wasn't a coward, he wasn't no funk,
He was just so grateful, that wraith that was drunk.

He mixed 'blue' with cider he kept in a flask,
And together we sat in the hedgerows' green cask.
And he sang me some ballads and told me some tales
Of a place called Somme and cruel Paschendale;
And a bullet in th' arm that he could still feel.
And as day turned to dusk, came a friend for his kale.

Together they walked down lanes Burslem way,
Vincent and Martin shouldering arms over lea.
Singing laments about times long ago
About 'warmers' and cider and favourite Mojo.
About sleeping in cinders by Sneyd's ovens' glow.
Martin and Vincent and times long ago.

And when I got home and took cursing from mam
Who sent me to bed with no bread and no jam.
I saw at the door a black grimy card.
And written in writing so crooked and hard,
A message from Vincent. I wept at the word
That he'd left for me, a memories' shard:

      "IF YOU BUY THIS CARD
YOU WILL HELP AN EX-SERVICEMAN
      WHO IS DOWN ON HIS LUCK:

> **Just a simple story**
> **I want to tell to you**
> **In spite of its simplicity**
> **It is alas too true.**
>
> **I'm a poor disabled soldier**
> **Who answered duties call**
> **Forgotten by my country**
> **To wither and to fall.**
>
> **I've tramped along the highway**
> **And searched each city through**
> **Good luck will never come my way**
> **I have no work to do.**
>
> **NB - If you do not purchase this card, it will**
> **be collected later with civility and thanks)**
>
> **That's the last I saw of the tramp who so stank,**
> **Whose name was Vincent, who smelled putrid and rank.**
> **Whose eyes were so wild with sad memories past,**
> **Whose face was so soiled with Mojo and waste.**
> **He was never a coward. In him was no funk.**
> **In a poisoned glass lies the wraith who was drunk**

In 1915, in response to Kitcheners call, at last and with secretive haste hidden from his distraught mother, Horace Pepper joined the army and was sent to the Western Front where he joined up with the 1st - 5th North Staffords as they prepared to enter the battle of Loos, and later at the Hohenzollern Redoubt where they lost 500 out of 700 men.

In a trench off the Menin Road Horace was billeted with a platoon containing some regulars including Private Riley. Air fire was exploding all around them and, after one close call, the sergeant ordered them into a nearby bomb crater for shelter, where they rested.

"Where yer from lad?". Riley leaned over and passed a glowing Woodbine to the young Horace.

"From Burslem; the pots", he replied drawing on the fag. "Bloody 'ell yer are. Where d'yer drink?"

"Oh, Longport mainly - Railway, Milton's Head and the Blacksmiths".

"Eh lad, I was in the Blacksmiths th' night war broke out. Drunk 'em dry that night, dust know? I'll never forget it. Never".

"Yes, I remember it", responded Horace. "We went up 't town and couldn't get in a pub anywhere. Finished up in the Jig Post on Bourne's Bank".

"Ay, those were the days owd youth, wine, women and song. Its the only thing that keps me goin'". Vincent quietly began humming a music hall song.

The message came from the sergeant:

"Right boys. It's over the top for us. Straight into the field and Bobs yer uncle".

"Ay, an' Fanny's yer aunt!" came the returning chorus.

"God's luck lad. See yer in th' Foaming Quart", shouted Vincent.

"Never", Horace shouted back. "It'll have ter be the Leopard after this lot."

"Right lad. Yer on!"

The two comrades walked into the smoke and hail of German machine gun bullets. 'Potter's forever!', they all shouted, like a choir. Within the hour Private Riley was carried back on a stretcher on his way to Poperinghe hospital. Any remains of Horace Pepper were never found.

In a nearby echelon that same day, September 27, platoon commander Lieutenant John Kipling was urging his own troops on. Amid the stinking fog of death, the pain of shrapnel and explosion came to claim the young subaltern's life and hid his mortal remains from the eyeless world, mixed in macabre confusion along with the bits of Horace Pepper and the hundreds of other khaki-clad men who were never seen again as they walked into the field of steel rain and drowned in a soup of gas.

Two soldiers anonymous and unknown to each other. One born in the Mother Town, and the other born because Burslem was where his grandmother met his grandfather, on another glorious summer's day at a picnic beside a nearby placid lake. At Rudyard, near Leek.

Chapter Nine

A DEATH A DAY

'Of deaths, the church registers contain, in 1838, 355, and the Registrar's book the same number; so that it is pretty clear that the office of District Registrar, for the parish of Burslem, is not a very arduous one...'

(Ward, pg 221)

This is not a very nice story.

In some regions of the British isles, in the middle of the 19th century, death was more common place than birth. A table of statistics for a government health survey in the middle of the 19th century showed that, of regions in England and Wales, the death rate in the Potteries was 5% higher than the average for the rest of the country:

<u>Stoke on Trent</u>	<u>England and Wales</u>
per 1000 of av population:	
1841 - 26%	21.8%
1861 - 25.7%	21.9%
1871 - 25.7%	22.%
1881 - 23.5%	19.9%

Perspective needs to be considered:

Population in 1871 to the nearest 1000:

London	3,900,000
Liverpool	493,000
Manchester	351,000
Bolton	153,000
Norwich	80,000
The Potteries' Borough of Stoke on Trent	102,000
Burslem	22,000

At its highest, in 1925, the population of Stoke on Trent reached a ceiling of 278,900 of which 48,000 lived in Burslem, which was also the Mother Town's highest recorded population census. Stoke on Trent in area - then as it does today - comprised 11,139 acres of which Burslem stretched to 1,862 acres. Manchester covers an area of 140 sq miles, while Bolton has an area covering just less than 10,000 acres. Demographic figures released for the Potteries in 1898 reported that 31 people lived to each acre in Hanley while in Burslem there were 27 to each acre.

These correlations mean that in Burslem, between 1870 and 1900, roughly 12 people lived to each acre. This could be considered socially equitable until toll is taken of actual land ownership. The largest land owners in Burslem were, in order of size in descent:

1) the corporation owning land for industrial and social development including open space,

2) private land for residential and occupational purposes of which the biggest portions were owned by farmers,

3) colliery owners and iron masters,

4) pottery factories and other industrial locations,

5) land owned by employers and private landlords for domestic housing.

Considering that the greatest concentration of potbanks were in the centre of the towns most people either chose or were compelled to live close to their work therefore it follows that the vast majority of people would have to live in, and be collected around, the close environs of the centre of the township, blighted land which had been first occupied by indigenous industry. In Burslem this town centre plot is an area which covers not much more than some 25 acres of land. In the value of these proportional statistics it would seem then that some 880 persons lived and worked within or close to *each acre of central land!* That so much this land was used by heavy industry and commercial premises, housing was an afterthought. A similar status existed in the cotton towns of the north-west - Accrington, Bolton, Bury, Burnley, Blackburn, Oldham, Preston, Rochdale, Wigan. The centre of this huge conurbation was Manchester in view of its drawing power of commerce, communication and centralisation of local government. While Manchester took advantage of its full authority beginning in 1835, it took Stoke on Trent until 1910 to develop the same dominion and a further ten years of boundary annexations before it qualified as a city with modern guild responsibilities. In galactic terms Stoke on Trent is a new born star compared with a matured glowing sun of Manchester - both were born out of the same Big Bang - Stoke on Trent was a little further away from the epicentre.

As with the majority of towns that came from the Industrial Revolution, Burslem town centre was primarily used for commercial transactions and as a recreation and an accommodation base. All the potbanks and workplaces had their front gates facing the high street shops (it has to be considered that Queen Street in 1851 was the home of two huge potbanks, the Brickhouse and Messrs Cork and Edge, the Independent Methodist Chapel and a jumble of cottages and inns - the principal shopping centre was Market Place). All the workers had their houses at the back gates. And as the population grew due to the insistence of the growth of industry and its support services, what domestic housing there was simply extended by a spreading distance further outwards and backwards. These houses were grouped in 'squares' and many workers lived on the potbanks in rear sheds or in cellars and attics above the shops.

For the immediate outlying districts of St Johns, Brownhills (Sytch), and Nile Street/Hot Lane, the town centre provided all the needs for living, working and recreation that their inhabitants required. The concentration of slum dwellings in the middle of Bolton and Manchester were therefore proportionate when stood against the slums of Burslem. In each of these three centres, Bolton - a wool spinning town, Manchester - textile factory manufacture, and Burslem - ceramics; industrial death stalked the inhabitants in their dwellings as well as at their workplace.

Illness and disease in the Mother Town was sometimes worse than that of its pottery neighbours and its neighbouring industrial districts because of the concentration of collieries within its precincts. Throughout the two centuries of clustered and cluttered industry and heavy manufacturing from 1750 to 1950, the primary causes of death in the Potteries were in line with national statistics, pertinent that is to:

a) overpopulation of towns due to industrial manufacture,

b) rapid increase in population in towns due to indifferent morals and lack of education,

c) non-existence, ignorance and restricted availability of efficient and appropriate health care.

In other words, two-hundred years of gross overwork, bad living conditions and poor nutrition, a combination which stunted the physical development of the majority of the people who inhabited the richest nation in the world. It wasn't until the consequences of the London cholera epidemic of 1854 were realised, and the seriousness of the statistics of death caused by typhus in London in 1869, that town managers took notice of public health and embarked on sanitary treatment which triggered dramatic improvements beginning in 1868. That year an officer of the Burslem Medical Board of Health reported that smallpox and scarlatina were the principal causes of death of young children in Burslem. Of the old, and old was considered above forty years, fatalities in the workplace together with chest and lung illnesses were among the common causes. Measles and fever were attributed to the deaths of 43 children that same year and a curious illness simply recorded as 'convulsions' did for 36. Consulting physician to the North Staffordshire Royal Infirmary, Dr J T Arlidge, recorded in his book, the Hygiene Diseases and Mortality of Occupations published in 1892, lists of no less than 81 trades and professions in Great Britain from which activity in the pursuit of occupation caused or hastened the death of the employee. Even the consequences of the most unassuming of jobs seemed to have some effect on the lives of those working in it. Arlidge's notes reported the case of a tea-taster employed at the Eley Tea Warehouse, number 1 Queen Street, who had tasted tea for many years with the result that she 'had lost her sense to taste and suffered depressing flatulence before meals accompanied by a strong feeling of hunger. A peculiar nervousness, faintness, inability to sleep [with a] red and congested throat, cracked tongue, enlarged cervical glands, weakness and lassitude.'

Epidemics of fevers frequently broke out in the Mother Town's claustrophobic working districts for which the only public health remedy was the free issue of lime to make whitewash which was painted inside and outside the houses over and over. It was later discovered that hot bitumen poured into open ditches and drains in order to provide a lining helped to prevent flowing excrement and polluted soil from becoming snagged or trapped or filtered into the earth.

Housing and proper domestic arrangements were as foul as the surroundings. What went behind the walls were subjects rarely talked about. Full family incest was commonplace. Abuse of children was accepted. Children were left un-counselled in the ways of life and hygiene wearing open sores exposed on filthy bodies with heads full of lice; ignorance and poverty were the norm. Private toiletry was not an option and bodily evacuations were made in pots which were deposited in a central bin to be collected by night-soil operators; old men pulling swill carts and taking the contents to tips and ditches called cesspools where it was loosely covered with quicklime and clay to be left to the clouds of flies until the whole mass eventually degraded into nature. Even thirty years on (in 1914) there were still only 1,138 flushing water cisterns in Burslem, the majority of its population of 35,000 had to make do with slop-water closets which frequently became blocked and clogged in the most foul of stinks - *figures for a township that supplied most of the civilised world with ceramic water closets!* In his book, When I Was A Child, Christopher Shaw, 'an old potter' described the area of Nile Street/Hole House as being **'In squalor, in wretchedness, in dilapidation of cottages, in half-starved and half-dressed women and children, in the number of idle, drunken men it was as terribly dismal as its name would suggest.'** HELL HOLE! Shaw named it. In the middle of the 19th century Burslem owned the biggest slums in the Potteries and quite comparable with those that stagnated in the docks of Liverpool and the east-end of London.

Medical aid was not for the poor, general practitioners were for those who could afford to pay for medicines and remedies. Hospitals were not available generally, the first in Burslem being opened in 1887 in the open fields in Moorland Road as a result of the benefit of a legacy bequeathed for that purpose by the tile-making Haywood brothers of Brownhills. The poor sick were to receive treatment here and it was a daily sight to see a horse-drawn ambulance slowly climbing the steep bank with an *emergency case* on board where, under the supervision of Miss Moore, the hospital's first matron, respite and warm, clean clothing and bedding was often the best prescription for the patient before he or she died.

Cholera reached Burslem in 1865. The afflicted were virtually condemned to death. They were isolated inside the slum districts while the affected areas were bypassed by the rest of the town's population, ghettoised as in medieval times. There was little to be done for the victims; the disease ran its course before severe or cold winter weather came to turn it when the bodies of the dead were buried anonymously in pauper's graves or by the families of the deceased - somewhere in parts of the churchyard set aside, or in the distanced grave plots at the workhouses.

Rickets was known as an ancient disease yet it was virtually unknown outside of towns. In the late 19th century it was as tolerated as the common cold within the industrial cities and was caused entirely by dietary deficiencies with the lack of vitamins the prime catalyst. And it was aided by the unfulfilled exposure to sunlight begun at birth, and at such an early age when children started work to enter into the long hours spent in dark, damp workplaces. Little mites with twisted joints with the identifiable carriage of bowed legs which was the stigmata of rickets and malnutrition.

Although hands-on health care for town dwellers was largely ignored, medical experimentation had been tackled in order to combat epidemics evolving from air-borne, water-borne and food-borne diseases, although it wasn't until 1888 that immunisation programmes were begun on the European mainland in order to counter rabies and agricultural based illnesses such as anthrax. Such luminaries as Louis Pasteur (1822-1895), experimenting with germ infection and the isolation of bacteria, and Robert Koch (1843-1910) identifying micro organism in such severe ailments as tuberculosis, were among the forerunners of later public health care; and yet little could be done until 1928 for the killing diseases of gangrene, blood poisoning, diphtheria and scarlet fever and many other environmental ailments that are today eliminated and largely forgotten. The experiments of Scotsman Alexander Fleming (1888-1955) brought the ultimate breakthrough in modern medical science.

Fleming found that penicillin strongly affected positive-stained micro-organisms in the bacteria staphylococci, streptococci, gonococci, meningococci and defeated the diphtheria bacillus and assailed the spore-like bacteria, pneumococci. It was discovered that treatment with penicillin had no toxic effects on healthy tissues and did not impede the body's white cell defence functions; however, the 'wonder drug' was unable to combat negative-stained micro-organisms which brought on cholera and plague, endemic diseases that often seemed to have been halted by restrictive immigration barriers that lay across the European continent between the Ottoman and Hapsburg Empires - the east and west frontier. Penicillin was made to take on the fight against diseases of the transmittable types caused by overcrowding and local contact contamination, until the routes to infection were finally isolated by improved public health means. It wasn't until the 1950's that widespread vaccination became practised and regulated. Until then TB, polio, typhoid fever, rubella, diphtheria, tetanus, whooping cough and measles - illnesses caused by protein deficiency - pellagra, dermatitis, diarrhoea and dementia, were rife, and they were all killer diseases.

Poverty was the accepted lot of the working classes. The reverse cover of the Sentinel Yearbook of the Potteries and North Staffordshire for 1928 carried an advertisement for the established chemist and druggist T C Cornwell of Hanley for the administration of 'Cornwell's Bactericide' in the prevention of influenza. It proclaimed -

INFLUENZA
'Like the Poor - is always with us.'
CORNWELL'S BACTERICIDE
'Is the safest adjunct, and will quickly conquer in the fight against this hardy annual of winter.'

The advertisement's statement, 'Like the poor - is always with us', was a doom-laden proclamation, but accurate, an attestation which insinuated that the poor would *always be with us*, for the poor were always the main sufferers when epidemics arrived. They were, needless to say, in the frontline of the majority of sufferers when the influenza pandemic that charged through the world like the stinking wind of death came to celebrate the ending of the Great War in 1918. Between August and October that year, 228,000 died in Britain as a result of a disease that left as quickly as it came. These are figures accepted, though not revealed, at the time for fear of causing public dismay following the battlefield deaths of the war. Among many experts today there is general acknowledgement that the figures were much higher and that many deaths at the time were attributed to illnesses and diseases that were recorded under other post mortem classification.

The American soldiers were at the battlefront in Europe in the spring of 1918. Because of their fresh and high presence the war was turning. Coinciding with their arrival, the army of 'doughboys' (soldiers with money), at the front began complaining of a fever which manifested itself in a sore throat, headache and loss of appetite which laid the individual low for three days, then passed off leaving very little consequence other than tiredness. Distinct from 'trench fever' which was often a prolonged illness and often fatal, 'three day fever', as the American fever was known, passed without long term results. But it was the infectious nature of the illness that concerned the army doctors for, although it was short-lived, nearly every soldier in these new companies were incapacitated by it. After a few weeks, medical officers at the hospital bases were able to diagnose the fever as a new virulent strain of influenza and it was dubbed 'Spanish Flu', though no one knows why.

The virus became rampant on the Western Front at first among the Americans. But as soon as other national troops became infected it seemed that their resistance, weakened and easily fatigued by long years on the battlefield, simply gave in. By summertime many of the men were dying of the flu's attendant diseases of bronchial pneumonia and septicaemia. These of course were common illnesses in the trenches, but medical officers began to identify symtoms of Spanish Flu by the bluish colour of the skin immediately prior to death. The death rate of all men who displayed this heliotrope cyanosis was a startling 95%. The double-edged sword of Spanish Flu then flashed its blade in a return cut as it swept across the western front in a second wave to infect the Americans once again who succumbed without resistance like corn being scythed in an Oklahoma cornfield. In one sector of the front alone, in one calendar month, 23,500 American died of the flu.

French, English, Belgians and very many colonial allies from all parts of the world also became infected until, in late September 1918, it was known by the army commanders that the flu virus was killing the German Army faster than the opposing forces were. Meanwhile the returning German soldiers brought the flu home with them and as a consequence, within two weeks after first contact, some 400,000 German civilians died. The poor districts of the industrial cities at once became the sore-beds for the flu. Home-coming Scottish soldiers on leave in the Glasgow Gorbals were among the first to pass it to their families although, as with the first Americans, it wasn't as instantly noted as influenza and drew no outside attention.

All through the summer Spanish Flu quickly spread across the rest of Britain. The Potteries were not to be excluded. Suspiciously the first cases reported in July occurred in the Holehouse district of Burslem, that foul cauldron of alcoholism and prostitution that lay in the hollow opposite the George Hotel and Royal Doulton, a location that always seemed to be the place where evil started.

On Monday 1st July 1918, a man and his wife died almost at the same time in Princes Street in the Hole House. Their eldest daughter looked after them for just a few days as they sweated their fever out in the attic of their ramshackle cottage. Thinking her parents were over the worst, the 15 year old daughter went to the shops to buy a meal. An hour later she found her mother supine on the bedroom floor with clots of blood heaved from her chest floating in foul-smelling green mucus that swilled about her head. The woman was clearly dead and where the flesh wasn't splashed with blood, the blue pigment of Spanish Flu covered the whole of her body. The girl's father was also lying on the floor as he had tried to struggle to his wife and failed. He was breathless and a wracking cough had gripped him as he thrashed about the newspaper covered floorboards. As the girl helped him back to his bed she noticed that his breath stank of sewerage and his face and upper body were turning blue. Later that day the girl's father died in the midst of a coughing fit as he threw up bloody clots. The father was 37 and the mother 33. Four girls suddenly became orphans.

By that weekend eleven more Burslem potters had joined them, and on the week ending 13th July another 30 died of flu. During the whole of that month 223 in the Potteries had succumbed. Then it stopped and the panic in the streets subsided. Little attention was paid to the brief report in the Sentinel at the end of July as the people of Burslem were cheered by other headlines in Staffordshire's main newspaper which reported daily the allied progress as it looked at long last that the Great War was finally coming to the end. Although the Potteries thought themselves rid of the flu pandemic deaths were still being reported elsewhere. Elsewhere? The whole world was being blighted but the war news kept the whole world from knowing how serious the plague was.

Before the end of 1918 a further 100,000 civilians died in Germany, poor people from poor districts made poorer by the fatal consequences of defeat and facing irresponsibly applied reparations. In America the flu returned to the Republic to claim some 450,000 people over the whole of the states although communities on the east coast were particularly hit badly. In India, during three months - August to October - it has been estimated that more people died of influenza than the combined dead of all the participating countries on battlefields throughout the Great War - the highest estimate being over 25,000,000 deaths attributed to Spanish Flu! Even remote communities did not escape - a quarter of the population of Samoa in the South Seas perished with flu. Countries as far apart as Sierra Leone and Alaska were all affected and it all happened so swiftly that mankind and its doctors were unable to do anything at all to stop it. It was feared at the time, and considered by many of today's medical scientists, that the most likely consequence of the flu, had the pandemic not mysteriously and suddenly halted itself, was that mankind on Earth would have been extinguished. The emphasis of this statement needs to be repeated - man and his physicians had no control over the outcome - at the close of 1918 mankind's tenancy of the Earth was about to come to an end!

In October Spanish Flu returned to the Potteries with more fatal results. In the two weeks from 12th to the 26th October 1918, a further 100 people were struck down and at once the whole of Burslem began to fear that God had dispatched Apocalypse as men were sent into the streets spraying the gutters and sewers with heavy-smelling chemicals. Workmen selected for their old age, wore nose masks and were clothed with fustian overalls tied tight at the neck to be destroyed after each day's use. The Medical Officer of Health for Stoke on Trent, Dr G Palgrave-Johnson, was called upon to issue warning notices which listed a series of advice instruction to be recommended by all GP's which described the flu as:

> **'...being present in epidemic form in the Borough. The disease is very infectious and spreads rapidly... The disease usually shows itself by sudden onset with headache, aching in the limbs and back, catarrh and fever.'**

Palgrave-Johnson insisted upon immediate isolation with all **'human discharges** [being] **carefully dealt with.'** Spraying all rooms with a mixture of permanganate of potash or izal was strongly insisted upon and religiously carried out. Home remedies came to the fore with potions made from nettles, dandelion, docks, roots, herbs - almost anything of a natural function found growing in the hedgerows was tested. Cigarette smoking to ease the removal of phlegm and catarrh was highly considered as a potion and many concoctions were ground from spices and mixed with liquorice; concoctions which sprang from these home experiments and were carried on to become household names: Venos linctus, Liquafruta, Pulmo-Bailey's, concoctions of ginger root, Sanategans, rubs and vapours, Vick, Zam-Buk, mentol inhalers and pills that were said would prevent and cure anything from chest ailment to 'boiling blood'; boils and festering's. Carter's liver pills came into their own as did Bile Beans, suppositories of phosphates and any curative medicine that was available. OXO, Bovril and large quantities salty porridge were particularly recommended. Opium, the drug of the rich, overnight became the salvation of the poor and was made available in diluted form for babies under the comforting name of Mother's Friend. It was common to use coco-leaves, Indian hemp and morphine and cocaine based medicines which were prescribed in 'household' quantities by doctors, dentists and veterinaries. Until 1920 poisons were defined under the Pharmacy regulations brought into enactment only when a need was considered, usually after the outbreak of a series of homicides whereby death was induced by poison. But these restriction were only placed upon pharmacists who were compelled to label the bottle 'POISON' and to make sure that the purchaser sign his registration book. The Dangerous Drugs and Poison's Act 1923 made it an offence to

> *'...sell certain poisons including (aconite, arsenic, atropine, belladonna, cantharides, coco, corrosive substances, sublimate, prussic acid, diamorphine, barbituric acid, ecgonine, ergot, lead, strychnine, morphine and tartar emetic (unless introduced by a person known by both parties) without making the prescribed entry in the Poison's Book by the purchaser and the person who has introduced him.'*

This is a way of saying that no person shall be sold poison unless issued with a written letter by their doctor - an example of the prototype prescription.

It seemed that prior to 1920 whole populations of poor communities were high on drugs! And drug taking was indeed common; like alcohol it eased the pain of living. Yet there is no doubt that it caused many deaths by itself for only the most obvious cases of drug use were recorded as the cause of death. (My maternal grandmother's first partner was killed in 1919 when he fell onto a hearth fire in an opium drugged state - cause of death on the death certificate BURNING!)

A popular remedy which persisted into the 1950's, until it was formally abolished and removed as a medicine, was the infusion of chloroform by nasal emetic, rubbing into the skin and by drinking it. It became the practice to drink it in liquid form available over the chemist counter if asked for as 'half an ounce of glycerine mixed with six-pennyworth of chlordane' - it was said to work wonders for the relief of indigestion! Many men carried bottles of the stuff with them down the pits and into the potbanks and mixed the same with alcohol at night before bedtime, the consequences of which resulted in many deaths caused by slow poisoning. And of course there was always alcohol which now had to be purchased from off-licences inside the public house as a consequence of the

Defence of the Realm Act which severely restricted permitted hours as to when the pub could be opened.

Governments and health authorities simply didn't know how to tackle epidemics, and as in the case of the pandemic of Spanish Flu, much information was kept from the general public. So carefully employed was the secrecy over public health that many communities believed that epidemics were localised to them, they had no knowledge how widespread epidemic diseases were and how far-flung they had become. The Sentinel spoke of it just once in October when it briefly reported that the flu had returned from July and August commenting that *'...several schools had been closed'*, and, *'...the corporation was endeavouring to obtain the services of extra nurses to assist the district nurses.'* Many military doctors were also being removed from active service to be brought home to attend to flu victims. Then at the end of October, as it had in August, the flu went away. The last recorded death attributed to it in the Potteries was once again in the Hole House district of Burslem. Weeks passed into months as governments across the world waited its return with worried anticipation, but the flu had gone; the world had been saved.

But there were many other causes of death to keep the doctors employed. In Burslem it had become accepted that there would be a death a day from work related illness. The act of burial for the poor town dweller was gruesome; most died as paupers and were committed to earth in thin boxes that often fell apart as they were lowered into the ground. Or the bodies were simply wrapped in canvas shrouds before burial behind the parish church or in the grounds of the workhouse, in unconsecrated fields, and then forgotten. Between 1801 and 1900, as populations continued to increase daily in the industrialised towns, early death became accepted and expected. The perceptions and fundamentals of the burial mechanics became countenanced by a submissive society with the results that churchyards were overfilled and became nothing more than neglected enclosed meadows - death tips!

Village churchyards that had once accommodated all the serenity of the yeoman force; a serenity that the Common Man should expect, became replete with the anonymous relics of a worn-out, faceless and valueless force. Add the numbers of family graves in situ in St John's churchyard with those named-graves in the High Lane Burslem Cemetery, those buried between 1750 and 1950, then remove those graves from the numbers of the actual death toll to see what is left. (It would be a fair estimate to concede that 160,000 people lived in Burslem during the 20th century as a base from which to begin.) So, where have all the bodies gone? Just how many tons of bones of our ancestors lie under the Tilewright's Acre - bones without identity, relics of the hundreds of thousands who once lived in Burslem and contributed to its growth and fame. Where are their graves, their portals to death?

Governments were slow to observe the problems of burying the dead brought about by the massive increase and the overpopulation of towns. Where to put the growing number of deceased became a vexatious matter as churchyards, asylums and poor houses ran out of space. The 1847 Burials Act was implemented to enforce and empower local authorities to provided appropriate land for the interment of its citizens and for the ongoing maintenance of these new approved cemeteries. Imagine trying to find sufficient land space in Burslem when most of its was occupied by industry!

Amended legislation was later introduced to curb the practice of reusing graves so as to prevent the exposure and defilement of human remains which had become commonplace throughout the country. A curious case was brought to Burslem magistrates in 1879 when constables had arrested a number of youths for playing football in St John's churchyard contravening a section of the Ecclesiastical Courts Jurisdiction Act 1860 - the offending part of the game, the constables reported, was that the youths were found to be using a disinterred skull as the football! Under the same piece of legislation a young man and his girlfriend were convicted of **'performing the act brawling in a churchyard'** when they were discovered by a constable on top of Molly Leigh's tomb in the act of sexual intercourse! In 1852 the Staffordshire Advertiser reported on the general state of church burials in the north of its county where it described scenes of abomination wherein bodies were removed to make way for others:

> *'We see the connection clearly only when the exposure of putrescent remain, or the escape of effluvia from an opened grave immediately produces horrid varieties of disease, sometimes like fever, and sometimes like the plague....'*

Graveyards often looked like sewage bogs and hung with a pall of gruesome stench caught in earth-hugging early morning hazy clouds, or hanging as a foul-smelling ground mist in an autumn evening..

At the end of 1866 instructions from the Home Office were circulated concerning the overcrowding of churchyards; it insisted that local authorities provide more burial land for its deceased citizens. In 1879 the High Lane Cemetery at Burslem was taken into use and interments in the churchyards were prohibited. Two years later, in October 1881, burial instructions for St John's and St Paul's were restricted to accept the deposit of remains only into vaults or walled graves or existing graves where relatives were buried, and only then if a depth of five feet could be reached. Officially the last burial in St John's took place in 1870. St Paul's Church, which had opened in 1831 when at the same time its graveyard was taken into use, received the remains of its last citizen in 1881; the church was demolished in 1970 and the burial ground laid-out as lawns. There were also graveyards attached to the churches at Norton and Smallthorne, but they continue to make burials supervised by the council reflecting the arbitrary stipulations made in 1881.

A number of Anglican vicars continued to carry out unlawful interments in order to benefit from the payment made by their more well-to-do parishioners resulting in a personal lucrative business. One such self-seeker was the rector of St John's and St Paul's, Alfred Watton, who in 1882 was caught-out having made a profit from a number of burials after the council's prohibition order had come into force. Watton was the heavy drinking friend of criminals and was at this time over his head in debt as was the parish administration under his dubious stewardship. Although Watton was prosecuted for the burial offences he was not convicted and, rumour has it that he continued to make money from illegal burials until his suicide in 1886.

History is written in these graveyards attached to churches and in public cemeteries.

One-hundred yards south of the Nettlebank entrance of Burslem Cemetery lies the grave of Lily Prince. The tall headstone is shaped to the life-size figure of an angel in bowed prayer holding the Christian book of God. Insignificant though the shrine is, the memorial is notable among the adjacent obelisks, vaults and decorated tombs only for the fact that at all times a bunch of poesies is often to this day placed near the centre pot, or in the actual hands of the angel. No one knows who places the flowers; no one will ever know I suspect.

Lily Prince was once a nationally acclaimed athlete. She was born at her father's newsagent's shop at 148 Newcastle Street, Burslem opposite Newport Lane in 1893. Here Lily grew up with her three sisters and brother. She was drawn to water, as they say, like a duck is and was swimming in school championships at the age of seven, among the pioneers of the then popular sport. As soon she reached her teens Lily was already an important member of the Stoke on Trent ladies' fast swimming team and she trained daily at Burslem Baths in Moorland Road where she was well respected by the male major competitors of the day. Burslem at this time had the strongest water polo team in the district with many notables in the town such as the Stockton's, the Westlake's, Littlehales' and Duros's. Swimming ran in families and Burslem baths was a focal point for the sport.

In 1905, at the age of 13, Lily became the English Schools' Girls' Championship winner, a title she retained in 1906 and 1907. She was champion of Staffordshire ladies each year from 1909 to 1912; ladies northern champion in 1908 and was recipient of the English gold medal also in 1908.

In Edwardian Britain swimming had never been more popular both as a sport and a pastime. Every weekend charabancs of families and friends would take the slow journey to the new coastal resorts while trains in the Stoke Wakes week would carry whole communities daily to the Welsh resorts of Rhyl and Llandudno where folk would take to the sea emerging from swimming machines and beach huts in the new styles of costume as fashionable and as daring as were their wearers in their gaily coloured horizontal stripes.

Swimming had really come into its own as a sport after the first competition was held in Australia in 1846 when eight men swam 440 yards to decide who was the fastest in the world. From the outpost colony the sport soon spread to the mother country where water competitions became popular among the rich whose sons took up swimming at their colleges. By the 1860's the common people had taken to water when, in 1869, a group of club members, sponsoring different teams, organised the Metropolitan Swimming Clubs of London which sub-divided into leagues to emerge as the Amateur Swimming Association which remains the governing body of British amateur swimming. In 1896 the sport was admitted to the Olympic Games and in 1912 it was decided to include a women's competition. Those in the know nationally had already decided that Lily Prince was destined to take one of the world's most prestigious gold medals in the Games of 1916 - war cancelled those Games. But in the event Lily died on 31st January 1914 at the age of twenty-one. She 'fell asleep' the lead letters of the white stone memorial sigh. At the funeral hundreds turned out to mourn her passing and give praise to the merits she already had achieved and those she would have won for Burslem. Ask in Burslem today who remembers Lily Prince, none will respond. Do not go in search of an appraisal of Lily Prince's achievements, there are none to be given. She died before her famous destiny could embrace her and before the emancipation of women would have let her in.

And just ten years later another daughter of the Mother Town was buried nearby, a poor soul whose name would never have been remembered except for the circumstances of her death. But, I wonder, do I have a right to tell her story? For now I struggle with the conscience of the historian advocating a sense of duty while flinching from a sense of shame. Integrity? What place has integrity in this contest? These are ordinary lives and ordinary lives also make history as well. But these ordinary people do not seek the medals of the rostrum; their place in history is assured in anonymous perpetuity: 'taking part' suffices. The difficulty for the historian will always be - 'how near is history - how close dare historians approach?'

Are they prying into lives where memory still lives? How long is it to be before it is 'safe' to tell their stories? A journalist reports history - exonerated from hurtful intent because he deals in contemporaneous record. Not so the historian who is often criticised for controversy, charged with 'opening up old wounds' and confounded by the machinery that tells him to be *gentle with truth* - appease the causal agent - do not cause offence: consideration, conciliation are his mottos. It is a difficult choice to be made when times call to be analysed for the sake of historical record. And so I do battle with conscience constantly, not only mine but with yours, for you, the reader, have to play your part as well. And we will laugh and weep together.

I tell this story not because it is unique for its times, it is not. Although it tells of a murder, homicide is not its theme. It tells of confinement, oppression and self-harm; furtiveness, secrecy, dispossession and above all segregation and disaffection. And importantly it recalls the universal picture of an aimless society that was going nowhere. The poor were becoming poorer, the rich were becoming more detached and it took a second world war to smash it and to fill in those stagnant ponds of depression forever. And because it still hurts to recall those times, for they are so near, I choose not to reveal identity. Instead I use the style of faction to tell this story - personal names and locations are changed - the detail is true. Here are occurrences that happened so often in Burslem that I owe the memories to all those shipwrecked souls who stood by the banks of the Macaloney and contemplated their fate and their place in history.

Maybe if Nellie Faulkner hadn't been so beautiful her short life need not have been suddenly and violently curtailed. From Alpha to Omega in the lexicon of language of love, throughout the channels of living and forgotten etymology, no words come so shocking as those that represent the quandary of the man and of the woman - love and jealousy reciprocated. Oh how to begin to define them! How to isolate the pieces that plague all lovers in the strains of love as it passes into the destructiveness of envy and covetousness! The honesty of love; the dishonesty of passion. That coarse thing that we align with the beauty of nature in order to curse and crush it with the cruelest device devised by the spirit of man; that very element which provides one with the ability to love and hate simultaneously - **self interest**. Such is the power in the destruction of beauty that it can be made to scorch the earth leaving shadows as a pile of dust. Love. That thing of beauty that is an everlasting joy, that we watch joylessly as it dies at the hand of the animator, he who loves it most. Oh wise words, oh poets of love and of death!

Doctor Francis Shayler of Hanley received a letter at the beginning of August 1925 from the Burslem Mutual Assurance Society asking him to examine a life insurance applicant living at Eaves Lane Bucknall. He noted the name, the sex and the age of the client and he decided to make his visit on a Sunday. Upon his arrival, Doctor Shayler was greeted at the front door of the terraced house by an extremely attractive 19 year old girl, full of figure and bearing a glowing demeanour. It was obvious to the medical practitioner that there was little physically out of order with the young woman whom he was surprised to find was married with two young babies. Introductions completed, Shayler was invited into the neat and tidy front room facing the busy road overlooking a brook that feeds the River Trent where the recently developed isolation hospital had been opened. This was the rented house of the young woman, Nellie Faulkner and her husband, Leonard - Lennie - whom, the doctor had presumed was not at his home that day. On the side of one wall was a cot in which a new born baby was sleeping, recently laid from engorging at his mother's bosom. An elder child, perhaps one years old, was sleeping on a sofa completely unaware of the presence of the medicine man.

The doctor began by asking a number of questions of Nellie, the answers to which he wrote on the insurance form. Then he said that he would have to give her a physical examination which would require her to remove some of her clothing. Perhaps Nellie was surprised at the request for her to take off all the clothes covering the top half of her body, she was without doubt taken by a display of nerves which, in the doctor's eyes, rendered her countenance to become even more virtuous and deliciously coy. But after all, she reasoned, this man was a doctor, what he was about to see he had seen many times before, and in any case her husband was upstairs where she had bid him earlier to be hidden, not wishing to discuss her intimate matters in front of him.

Nellie stripped laying her cardigan, her buttoned blouse and her vest on the settee next to the sleeping child, uncovering completely the still fruiting but maturely fulfilled ivory whiteness of the female torso. Doctor Shayler walked across the room towards her. Investigative hands explored the nakedness of the woman - 'Oh physic, heal thyself'. Just then, the door leading to the stairs flew open and in strode the aggressive figure of Nellie's husband.

'Right. What's all this then, Eh? What's going on here then?'

Nellie was speechless, she stood petrified in the middle of the room with her hands held high as the doctor continued to complete his examination totally ignoring the intrusion.

'Well, what's this? Are you the doctor?'

Shayler turned and simply and quietly said, 'Yes.'

The moment was ended. The wonder had ended. The fire that burns deep in all men and women from the beginning of time had flared and had passed. That occasion - a moment in a millennium, could never be repeated, and, it would never be erased.

There was a stillness. No one spoke for a while. Nellie let her arms drop cupped together to cover her breasts; the doctor turned to his writing; Lennie went to the corner of the room and picked up two Indian Clubs which he started to swing about his head in an intimidating manner, and the doctor turned once more to resume the physical examination of Nellie.

'Right, that's enough of this. You've seen enough of her so get on with your business and leave.'

At this Lennie stepped forward and took hold of his wife's arm and pulled her away from the doctor.

'Get dressed.' he commanded.

The sweet pale girl looked embarrassedly at the doctor as she took up her cardigan, slipping her arms into the sleeves, her chestnut hair falling across her face to hide her shame.

'It's quite alright my dear, I've done a sufficient examination to warrant you a certificate of physical fitness which I will send to the insurance company. Oh, and don't worry about your husband's behaviour; there'll be no report on that.'

He glowered at Lennie and, collecting his bag, made to the door followed by Nellie who thanked him for his consideration and comments. The doctor walked out into the warm afternoon. He was to reflect some two years later how different the outcome could have been had he taken an alternative course of action - perhaps, he wondered, if the husband hadn't been at home.

Leonard Faulkner, aged 18, and Eleanor Prudence Watts, aged 17, were married on 23rd November 1923 at Sneyd Church in Nile Street; that huge black Gothic pile that literally stood at the gates of Royal Doulton potbank facing the Hole House. Nellie's father had been killed in the Great War and she and her sister Elsie had been brought up by their mother, Elizabeth, in a comfortable terraced house in Mellor Street, the new part of Burslem called the Park Estate. Apart from the domestic personal pain of wartime home-front Britain, the sisters had a relatively comfortable upbringing attending Park Road School in the next street and having the magnificent Burslem pleasure park for their back garden. On the other hand, Lennie, who had a twin brother, was brought up in totally different circumstances, among the workmen's houses and factories of Middleport. How Faulkner and Nellie met must remain an irrelevant riddle; perhaps a walk in the park, part of the Sunday 'monkey-run' which involved a tour around the town centre and into Moorland Road and back; but as special youngsters they had both borne striking looks - a physical attraction that took them both to special places in the realm of love.

To marry at eighteen was not uncommon in those times - man and woman, both working, could live as cheaply as one unless either were required to keep up the parental household. But as a rule, these young marriages were as a consequence of an unwanted pregnancy - this was not the case with Lennie and Nellie, it appears they were intensely in love. It was as simple, and as dangerous, as that.

After a short period in lodgings, the young couple rented the terraced house at Bucknall. Leonard was a jobbing-joiner on a potbank and Nellie decorated ware. Very soon though, Nellie became pregnant with their eldest child, a boy they named after his father. And almost at once after young Leonard was born, Nellie fell with child again. It may be reasoned that the poor woman looked into her future and saw a bleakness in poverty and a smothering life in and out of the child-bed - ever-wet nipples and the sickly smell of sour milk. Her disenchantment can be well understood by those who lived in those gloomy times.

As soon as she was able, after the birth of her second child, Nellie started back to work, more in the projects of helping out with the domestic finances than in the enjoyment of other female company; and yet there is no doubt that she was at her happiest at this time among her female friends singing afternoon choruses on the potbank piece-line. Lennie by now had begun to reveal the darker side to his personality. His long depressions manifested themselves in violent rage in which his anger, taken out against his wife, subsided into periods of tearful self-remorse and woe. His twin brother was often the only person who was able to ease the pain that visited Lennie's mind in increasingly frequent visits following occasions of the billowing rage caused by the frustrations of his poor circumstances.

Lennie and Nellie were poor; this was bad enough, but yet more sinisterly stirred the anger in his over-protection of his wife and his jealousy of every man who came into contact with her. He thought, as others historically have, she was too good for him - she would leave him. If he could have his way, Leonard Faulkner would have tied his succumbing wife to the counterpane of pregnancy for the rest of her life so that he alone would possess her every waking minutes as she waited to her master's will. This was how Lennie showed his infinite love to the only person he had ever loved in his life. His love and desire for her were so strong and so powerful that he would accumulate and preserve its energy for both of them. He would share it with no one. To him his love was so divine, so special. And such a love as he could give she should not be able to resist.

Nellie remembers her father and realises her foolishness in believing that all men are father's to their daughters and all men are like their fathers:

'I would wait for him to come home from work. The brass-latch would click and I would run into his arms:

'Hey hey, here's my little girl then. Here she is jumping into the black arms of her dad. Oh, now be careful. Look at how she clutches the waistcoat, and look how all the workdust has gone up her nose - a-tissue, a-tissue - Oh we all fall down!'

And he would roll us both onto the sofa while my mother shouted to my father to behave;

'You'll get her dirty again - oh now look, I'll have to get you both into the bath'.

And there was laughter all through the house.

The kitchen was steaming with pots and pans of water bubbling out of spouts into the galvanised long-bath as it swilled with the body movements of this beautiful dark man, his sinews straining and glistening and shivering sensually; his muscles strong and set against his back as my mother - his wife - swilled the water over his buttocks and into the scummy reservoir as the man stepped onto the pegged rug before the warmth of the crackling coal fire wrapped him in the comfort of home; hearth and home within a warm grey flannel towel. I would sit at his shoulder, and I would watch him closely as he meditated over thick crusts of bread and bacon, and bacon fat and cheese, slurping and laughing as he did so, slurping from a mug of hot tea, telling of some occurrence he'd had at work. And I would trace my fingers along the lines of the blue scars on his face, concerned for the pain he had endured in collecting them. And smell his body in the masculinity of the sweat of hard work purified by carbolic soap. And he would let me sip from his saucer, and hand me a plug of bread dipped in fat, and let me suck on a piece of bristly bacon rind. And when he was dry and had done with his supper, scraping the tin of his plate with his knife, he would lift me onto his knee and light a pipe of billowing sweet aromas; and he would talk to my mother and make promises of better times in which seaside holidays were always talked about. And he would stroke my hair with his black leathery hands, hard with the callouses of work - for I never saw my father's hands clean, no matter how much he scrubbed - and yet his touch was as tender as a flower-cup as he stroked my neck, as he smiled into my face, as I fell asleep while I distantly tried to listen to the comforting unintelligible drone of far away sentences of two people who loved each other, as I nightly lay in the comfort and protection of this man's arms'.

One night the rage of Leonard Faulkner was so extreme that neighbours sent for a constable under whose wrath Lennie cowered and promised never again to hurt his wife or subject her to his fit-like rages. But even as the constable made his way back to his beat, Lennie was at it again, plaguing Nellie with accusations of indiscretion even to suggest that she had looked at the constable in a 'certain way' so as to allure the officer of law, for they were 'all the same with only one thing on their mind.' But Nellie, deprived of her father's protection, the one person that ever knew her, had suffered enough. The next day she went home to her mother and her sister and took her two boys along with her.

Nellie had made the break. She knew it was the only thing she could do to free herself, and probably her boys, from a life of miserable possession and imprisonment. This was confirmed by the intense pressure and the stalking behaviour the husband then embarked upon. He followed her everywhere; whenever she went to the pictures with her sister, he was there. At the shops, he waited outside. On her way to work and coming home, he pestered her. Nellie was so afraid of going out alone that she was always accompanied by her sister or her mother. And even when they had been separated for some two months and a legal separation order had been taken out by Nellie, Lennie continued to haunt the back alleys of Park Estate, wailing at the back door for Nellie to come home with his children.

The court had ordered Leonard to pay his wife twenty-five shilling each week for maintenance, a gratuity the handing-over of which enabled him to visit the house. But this caused so much trouble that she arranged through the court for the money to be deposited with Mr Shipley, the clerk to the justices at Hanley. Meanwhile Leonard Faulkner had taken a job in Longport purposely so that he could be in the locality. Here, in June 1927, he took up lodgings with George Mountford in his cottage in Davenport Street, a dirty man who let beds at a shilling a night.

Working on the same contract as Lennie was a young apprentice, Harry Jackson. Faulkner found out that Jackson lived in Hamil Road just a short distance away from the Watts' house in Mellor Street. He hit upon the idea that in order to maintain a watchful surveillance of his wife he would pay young Jackson five-pounds to keep a look-out for Nellie and to report to him he ever saw her with another man. Lennie was prepared to go to any lengths to get his wife back and he would prowl around all night to see if Nellie went out, and if she did he followed her and was always hanging around in the back alley to see if she was accompanied by any men.

One evening, in late June, the Watts' neighbour's 18 year old daughter Janet Jones, disturbed Faulkner as he climbed over the back gate and into the yard of the Watts's:

'Oy!' she cried, startled by the sight of Faulkner creeping up to the back window. 'What are you doing there?' Lennie stood up flustered. 'It's not what you think, I'm just calling to see my wife.'

'Oh no you're not,' exclaimed Janet bravely, 'You're bloody well separated you are. You'd better get off quick or I'll fetch my father to you!'

Faulkner made to escape and started to scramble over the gate.

'That's right', shouted Janet becoming more confident, 'You want to leave them poor kids alone. You're bloody daft you are!'

A dog close by started to bark at the disturbance which was echoed by another dog further along the alley. Then dogs all over the neighbourhood started to bark at the occurrence which they knew nothing of nor cared one fig for, continuing to make their canine threats and yelps at each other until they were individually called to cease by their masters. But Lennie was long gone scampering into the park and across Moorland Road towards Ticklebelly Entry. Someone said they had seen him later hanging about the old colliery behind Lorne Street but Nellie and her sister had been out all the time and knew nothing of the unwelcome prowler until Janet told them the next day.

Over the following week, Leonard Faulkner left his wife in relative peace. He was only seen on one occasion by Elsie walking up Hamil Road. She had reason to warn him about his presence in the proximity of her house, and cautioned him as to his conduct, to which he said that he wasn't about to cause any trouble and he slunk away quietly. Some relations of the Faulkner's said they had seen him around Burslem town pubs, but Nellie thought this unlikely as Lennie didn't drink very often.

Lennie sat in a corner of the Duke William and stared into his half-empty glass thinking of his desperate past:

> **The parlour had been closed off for some weeks. Neither me nor my twin brother were now allowed to enter this room, it was a forbidden part of the house. Over the door that stood between the room and the rest of the back of the small house, a woollen blanket had been fastened down by nails hammered in by my father a few days before, this was to deaden some of the sounds that had been getting louder; screams, and awful gurglings and splutterings,. And yet the sounds still managed to push through the cracks under the doors where newspapers had been threaded and stuffed. Old coats and rags had been hung over the top of it all; but the terrible noises would not be deadened, and so my brother and me just clung to each other for safety's sake, even closer in chilling fear. Now and then my father came out, his face in agony and flecked with blood and oral froth. He would pass us and never look at us, he went without speaking and disappeared to the lavatory in the**

back yard where he emptied the foul-smelling contents of the bucket he'd removed. Now and then, Mrs Woolley would come to help father in whatever he was doing in the parlour, and then the screaming would become louder. Bumps and crashes we could hear all the time and adult oaths and curses we heard exchanged. But worse, much worse, was the never ending muffled sounds of a single anguished voice, the groaning, the mewling, the whining, the whimpering, all liquidised into an endless unintelligible oral paste; a wall of unconfirmed apprehension - of childish thoughts left to the horrors of our imagination.

One morning, there was more activity than usual. Strange men in brown jackets came and went without bidding through the parlour and into the street. I watched on my own from the window of father's bedroom, and I saw that a crowd had gathered outside the house. Some women stood at a doorway nearby, huddled in secret conversation. Net curtains were shuffled in terraced houses and anonymous eyes looked across to see me, trying to pierce me through the walls. Shortly a green petrol-engine van drew up outside and another man with a brown coat came into the house. Suddenly there was the most devilish of screams penetrating the whole of the house and into the street:

'NOOOoooooooooooooooooooogggghhhh!'

On and on it went reaching to the furthest of the Devil's witch's covern, a banshee's howl, until a sickening thud suddenly silenced it. Within a few minutes three brown-coated men left by the front door carrying between them a stretcher on which lay a pile of clothes and blankets. This was hurriedly placed into the back of the green van and the driver resumed his place. Father was in the street crying and being helped back into the house by Mrs Woolley. In a cloud of smoke and noise, the van clanked away and people came from their houses and gathered in groups:

'Shame! Oh what a shame! Poor man! Oh what a great tragedy! What's to become of them? What's to become of the boys?'

Later, at supper time, my brother and I were called to come down stairs. Father was hunched in his chair in the corner, Mrs Woolley fussed over a pot of stew. I then noticed that all the blankets and covers over the parlour door had been removed; though the door was shut the brass knob shone at the same time inviting and forbidding.

After we boys had eaten and the plates had been cleared away, Mrs Woolley left, whispering a farewell into father's ear, so quiet, so urgent - encouraging, meant only for the comprehension of this man. An hour seemed to pass in total silence until father shifted.

'Right boys', he exclaimed cheerily, 'time for bed. You can both sleep with me in the big bed tonight. Oh, and your sister's gone now. She won't be coming home!'

That was the only explanation me and my brother ever received. We'd once had a sister.

The events of the parlour were never discussed again; it became a room that was set apart from the rest of the house. That night, in a secret corner of the big bed, I learned that the furtiveness of self-love was the only thing I had left, and, it induced sleep. In sleep, ghosts never haunted real houses; only the waking hours brought the phantoms..

At six o'clock on Thursday 30th June, Nellie and Elsie were preparing themselves to walk to work across the Bycars Fields to the potbank at which they worked in Tunstall. Having cut sandwiches and left the two children sleeping in the care of their grandmother, they set out across the street at about seven o'clock to travel the half hour journey to the Woodland Pottery.

As the sisters entered the meadow, Nellie look round and gasped, "Oh, no Else, he's following us again. Lennie's coming!"

"Come on," cried Elsie, "lets walk a little faster. He won't keep up".

The young women began to hurry but Faulkner, seeing their haste, cut across the paths and began to bear down on the fleeing women from alongside the embankment of the Loop Line, by the allotments and pigeon lofts. Near to Caulton Street he stopped the two women.

"Nellie; I've got to talk to you!"

"No Len, there's no use talking. It's all over now. I don't want to see you again!"

"But just listen a minute, just listen. I don't want to cause any trouble. It's about the kids. Nellie, you can't take them away from me. They're all I've got. Just let me take them out for a bit. Just let me see them now and again." he begged.

At this Elsie accused him of being a bad father and a dangerous man.

"You're not fit to have any kids you aren't!" she shouted. "Just get away from her and let her get on with her own life. It's all over. You know it is."

Lennie glared at his sister in law.

"Look, just let's talk on our own for a bit". He stared at Elsie and said, "I've got some money for her, for the kids. Maintenance money".

"If you've got money you should take it to Mr Shipley in Hanley. That's what the order says. You've no right's to keep contact with her."

"You just shut up you!", Lennie shouted at Elsie in a scornful voice, "You're don't know what you're talking about, you interfering bitch!"

Elsie reeled upon him but Nellie leapt between them and with fiery eyes wide open said to her sister, "It's OK Else. I'll just be a moment".

She turned to Faulkner and nodded, walking a few steps away from her sister. By now Scotia Road was filled with men and women on their way to work and several passengers had turned to witness the commotion.

"It's over Lennie", Nellie whispered, trying to keep calm and to quieten her husband down. "I aren't coming back and that's all there is to say. I'm not stopping you from seeing your children but I'm not having you causing trouble for them with your shouting and bellowing. Now please go, we've got to be at work for half-past".

Leonard Faulkner wore the look of insanity. His face glowered and broke down all at the same time. Tears shone in his eyes. Nellie was appalled at what she suddenly saw.

"Nellie I love you. I have no life without you dearest. If you don't come back I might as well be dead. And you as well, my dearest will have to die with me".

From a short distance Elsie saw only the blankness in her brother-in-law's face. Shocked at his mad demeanour she made to get between the two but Lennie pushed her away and she stumbled to stop herself from falling to the ground. And as she looked up at the man she saw the madness of a lunatic as he grabbed her sister around the neck. A stroke of his right hand, like the gentle touch of a lover, embellished by a quick flourish high in the morning sky; and the glint of the pale sun on the flashing razor dripping red.

"I'm going to do it!" he screamed as Nellie collapsed onto the pavement of Scotia Road. But she rose almost at once and began to run away as her raging husband caught her again. He only swung the razor for a second before the wife fell dying at his feet.

Elsie saw that her sister lay seriously injured and that her brother-in-law also was cut across his throat. He sat down helplessly upon the kerb edge of the pavement.

"Oh dear! Oh dear! The poor girl is dying, and she is my wife. Don't let her die!" he cried to the gathering crowd of workers from the potbank at the top of the road.

"Oh, my girl, my girl! Oh, my girl! I've killed her. Oh don't let her die, please save her. Don't let her die".

A constable came upon the scene and decided that Nellie was already dead having lost the amounts of blood necessary to keep her alive. He turned to Lennie who was sobbing with his hands about his head; "Look after Nellie. Don't let her die. Let me die!"

Both Nellie and Lennie were taken side by side in an ambulance to the Haywood Hospital. Lennie survived with a superficial wound which required six stitches. Later he was arrested and remanded to Strangeways prison. Charged with murdering his wife, he appeared before a jury at Stafford Assizes in November 1927 and was found guilty of murder but insane. He was therefore detained during His Majesty's pleasure. Leonard Faulkner was afterwards taken to St Edward's Hospital, Cheddleton near Leek where he remained for the rest of his life. He was never heard of again. Two days after Faulkner had appeared at his remand court in Burslem town hall a week after he had killed his wife, the Staffordshire Sentinel reported the following:

Large Gathering At Burslem Funeral

Between six-thousand and seven-thousand people witnessed the funeral at Burslem Cemetery this Tuesday afternoon of Mrs Eleanor Prudence Faulkner of Mellor Street Burslem, whose death occurred in tragic circumstances on Thursday morning.

Sometime before the cortege was due to leave the house at Mellor Street, many hundreds of people gathered in the vicinity and many more sympathisers lined the route of the procession which was along Hamil Road and High Lane to the cemetery. A crowd of several thousand waited to greet the cortege at the cemetery. The procession was headed by a number of workpeople from the Woodland Pottery, some of whom carried a small hand bier on which rested a globe of artificial flowers bearing the inscription - 'A Token Of Respect And Esteem From The Workpeople Of Woodland Pottery'.

A pathetic little figure among the mourners was the three year old son of the late Mrs Faulkner dressed in a suit of black velvet. Other mourners included the brother of the deceased's husband who was considerably affected by the ceremony at the grave-side and had to be assisted away by a friend. The interment was proceeded by a service in the cemetery church conducted by the reverend J B Wilson, vicar of Sneyd, who also officiated at the grave-side where a rope barrier had been placed to keep the huge crowds under control.

At the conclusion of the committal ceremony, workmates of the deceased filed past the grave and dropped flowers onto the coffin. The ceremony was most impressive. There were a large number of wreathes, including one bearing the inscription, 'With The Deepest Sympathy Of Friends And Neighbours At Bucknall', and another with the inscription - 'With The Deepest Respect And Sympathy Of The Neighbours of the Park Estate.' A large number of police were in attendance to regulate the crowd. The floral tributes included a wreath from the relatives of the deceased's husband.

In November the Staffordshire Sentinel reported in its late edition:

Burslem Wife - Murder Charge - Husband Found Guilty But Insane

The public accommodation at Stafford Assize Court was crowded today when Mr Justice Sankey sat to hear the case against Leonard Faulkner on the capital charge of murdering his wife. The accused was dressed in a navy-blue suit and black bow to his collar. He looked very pale as he gazed around the court as the clerk read over the charge to which he replied, 'Not Guilty'. The defending council was Mr MacGreggor Clarkson who gave a review of the committal proceedings.

Question of motive of so grave a charge was hard to ascertain, or indeed of any motive. The only thing referred to was a medical examination incident for an insurance policy two years before the murder.

The father of the accused gave evidence that the accused had had a sister who had died when she was fourteen years of age. Her death had taken place at the Burntwood Asylum. Doctor Menzies, a medical practitioner at

Cheddleton, said the accused was suffering from a disease from birth. He said that this disease had sometimes had an effect on the mind with the general result being one of instability and want of self control, the victim being likely to act on impulse.

The jury was absent for forty-minutes and then delivered its verdict of guilty but insane. Faulkner was sentenced to be detained during His Majesty's pleasure.

Walking around the High lane cemetery one summer's morning, I met the superintendent of cemeteries at the Nettlebank gate of Burslem Cemetery. We walked together along the tarmacked path that led to the newest part of the grounds which bordered on Leek New Road. The superintendent pointed out to me something I had never before considered during my meanderings around the precincts of burial grounds.

"See the old part, that which surrounds the chapel?". I followed her pointing finger as my gaze found its way between the trees to the central chapel where Arnold Bennett's ashes lie.

"All the tombstones there were purchased and laid-out by the rich Victorians throughout the 1870's, and all through the Edwardian times up to 1914. On the level above this are the plots which were developed from the 1960's through the 1970's and into the 1980's. At the lowest level, by the wall of Leek new Road, are the most recent interments, graves which were laid in the 1990's. Looking objectively, and considering what I have just told you, what do you notice instantly about the dimensions of the cemetery?'

I gazed over all these acres of termination; trees waved in a warm breeze, beckoning. And I saw at once what the superintendent wished me to see, how thickly populated were the Victorian plots and those tracts which belonged to the reign of the second Elizabeth, terracing into formal arrangements. It then dawned on me how desolate were the lower echelons, the vagueness of design and the sparseness of the lawned meadows that lay in the middle of the cemetery. Beneath this fallow land were the final resting places of those who had died in the 1920's and the 1930's. I was bewildered by the emptiness. Here were relics unremembered; no less prominent than the rest of Burslem's dead but unremembered individually and forgotten by time. Here lay human beings who'd lived in those misplaced times of poverty and austerity. Times we well remember but whose people we easily forget. Those who left a future for their living relations, children who had neither the energy nor the resources to keep-up their parent's final resting places besieged as they became by the second world war.

In the middle of all this half an acre of meadow, tastefully attended by a gardener straddling a mechanical mower, the superintendent pointed to an empty patch of grass and said, 'That's the ground you were looking for. Plot number 11/23-27 - the eleventh grave in the twenty-third row referring to 1927.' Here buttercups were still pushing through grass valiantly avoiding the next slice of the mower. And amid all the towering tombs erected in tribute to the lives of the famous and wealthy, I saw that this plot of land was the freshest and purest and the most fertile in the cemetery. Peace here was perfect.

Later that day, I made a phone call, half expecting and fearing the response.

'Oh no you don't; I'm saying nothing to you or anybody about that business. You don't realise how my life had been affected by all of this. I've spent seventy years, all my life living with it, trying to forget what happened and wishing it hadn't. I will say nothing while I'm alive, and all my memories will die with me. And that will be the end'

The phone clicked to silence. I guessed it had been slammed down, and I can't say I blamed the old man for preserving his silent memories. I despised myself for making the call. Should I be writing this at all?

And later still. A few years after my phone call, the family of Leonard Faulkner laid to rest their beloved father and grandfather. AT REST, the tombstone accurately states.

As the last decade of the 20th century drew to a close, it could be seen that the land in the cemetery was almost full and the most recent graves have been settled to push against those empty spaces where people still lie from the troublesome years of the 1920's and 1930's. How strange to find that poor little boy, once dressed in his velvet suit, lying here for the want of burial space in a cramped cemetery *just twenty yards away from his mother, lying in her own anonymous grave.* How perfect. How perfect. I'm sure that their spirits know.

When I visit the cemeteries, I am reminded of the death of Willie Price who suffered under his love for Anna Tellwright. Her sacrifice to him as he still lies at the bottom of the blackest hole in another unmarked grave somewhere in Burslem. I am reminded of the man who was shot in 1842 in front of the Big House at the height of the Chartist Riots and wonder who he was and what he came to represent. For we are told, and still hold true to the myths and legends of history; that he was a young hero who became martyr to his cause. So should I disturb the memory of Josiah Heapy? Have I the right, and will I be cursed or praised for truth?

At the inquest of Heapy, held at the Swan in Hanley, evidence was given that when the body was recovered by a constable it was found that his skull had been shattered by a ball and his brains were protruding. A bludgeon was discovered lying between his legs and it was presumed that it belonged to him and that he had come to Burslem to make mischief. In his pocket was found cash amounting to three-shillings and five-pence-ha'penny in silver and copper. Major Trench, giving evidence stated that a young girl was brought into the town hall room where the body had been taken and there she identified her dead cousin.

Sarah Heapy of Leek told the inquest that she had last seen her cousin the day before his death when they had family breakfast after which Josiah left for work with her own three brothers, as far as she knew to go to work as a shoemaker at Mr Rigby's It was on their way to work that Josiah Heapy departed from his cousins and took up with a mob which was bound for the Chartist's meeting in Burslem - although Sarah Heapy insisted that her cousin was 'compelled by the mob to go with them.' She also told the court that Josiah was 19 years old and had recently become a widower having buried his wife only two weeks previously. He was the father of three children!

The witness then startled the court by announcing that she had seen her cousin place twenty sovereigns in his pocket as he left, ten pounds in money which he had told her had resulted from an insurance policy paid out on the death of his wife, and a similar amount paid to him by a Rechabite society. This caused the investigating magistrates to call to court the constable who carried the body to the town hall. His evidence concluded that the only money he had found on the deceased's person was that change which had already been described to the court. The magistrate had no alternative than to pronounce that the twenty sovereigns had been removed from the pockets of Heapy by persons unknown between the time he had left home and the time his body was searched in the town hall. The authorities, naturally, were completely exonerated from suspicion. "It was a mystery," said the magistrate, "That would have to remain a mystery". He then went on to in bring the verdict of 'justifiable homicide by an unknown member of the defending troops.'

Presumably Heapy was taken back to Leek where his body was interred in some unknown plot of moorland. Nothing of his children is recalled, the name is forgotten in Leek. And yet myth- makers still, by design or otherwise, confuse the identity of the 'poor man from Leek who was shot to death in front of Wedgwood's Big House standing up for worker's rights and union representations - a hero', with that of Nathaniel Johnson who died by some unknown means on 12th July 1837.

> **Under this stone the body lies**
> **Of a good and faithful child.**
> **His father's hope and his mother's pride,**
> **His life was hasked but God denyed.**
> **I went up to town a sight to see,**
> **And met with a shot which did kill me.**
> **No mourn for me, I beg you make,**
> **But love my sister for my sake.**

To make some sense of this epitaph it must first be divided into two sections. The first four lines - two couplets - are of a style quite common in the late Georgian age of epigram and epitaph memorials. Similar examples can be found in a number of country churchyards in a time between the middle of the 17th century and the commencement of the Victorian period. The aitch that precedes asked was a form generally used as an emphasis often by rhyme-makers and broadsheet writers of the times. The 'y' in the word 'denyed' was well used as a vowel in the style of writing known as 'inkhorn' (in which much ink is used to write the flowery words of antiquity.) Throughout the times of Elizabeth I, there was a long running debate about the betterment of plain English and, as a consequence, fewer 'foreign words' were borrowed and there was a literary review of the commonly used Old English. The words of Geoffrey Chaucer are peppered with ,,,onyons, drynken, wyn, latyn, a peep into the Celtic use of the letter crossed between 'u' and 'w' used by the Welsh today. It was custom to use the letter 'y' as the perfect vowel from latyn influences in place of the later 'i' which was used in conjunction with 'e' either to extend a word to affection or render it as a diminutive - merrie, prettie,,, et al.

William Caxton, the inventor of the printing press (1422-1491) was completely confused by the spoken English as he set about the task of standardising word construction for repetitive printing; here he came across the idiosyncrasies of the written English and the interpretation of sounds and expressions; accent and colloquialism. Samuel Johnson (1709-1784) overhauled the language in his English Dictionary in his accomplishment in **"setting the orthography, displaying the analogy, regulating the structures and ascertaining the significations of English words'**. Thus we find his influence in Josiah Wedgwood's letters to see how the modern form has done away with the vowel 'y' while he still writes in the slovenly English of abbreviation - '***...By the proof in D, you'l perceive...***' he writes to his partner Bentley continuing with the prolific use of the popular sentence shortener - etc, etc! And amateurs in the practice of convolution, Simeon Shaw and John Ward writing to fill the spaces with unnecessary words to make their point, reliant upon the pleasuring of the educated who were the only class who were supposed to know what the writer's were talking about. But neither of these two, writing in the 1820-1840's - in the times of Nathaniel Johnson - at any point use the 'y' as a vowel nor prefer abbreviation. The language was being cleaned-up!

It is reasonable, I suggest, to separate the first four lines of Johnson's memorial, those being typical of the tombstone epitaph style from the fourteenth century to the middle nineteenth. The puzzle lies in the last four lines which continue to confuse. One thing is clear - it is not a poem nor has it been excerpted from verse or essay. It implies to give information of an actual event but there are no reports of any incident involving a fatal shooting either in Burslem or Hanley at that particular time.

Cemeteries and churchyards are full of mystery. Epitaphs and epigrams are often designed to confuse, so much so that books have been written extolling their grim humour and articles have been prepared attempting to decipher many of the codes left to conceal some hidden reason or warning. I am reliably told that a warning epigram was carved into one tombstone in the High Lane Cemetery which read:

> **'Chewing gum, chewing gum,**
> **I loved chewing gum**
> **But chewing gum took me to my grave.'**

I have not seen this myself but my sources are immaculate. It tell's the cause of death of a young girl who fatally choked on a piece of gum far more realistically than the death certificate's 'pulmonary infarction following asphyxiation due to a foreign body accidentally admitted through the trachea.'

Here we also find J W Powell's memorial is carved in tonic-sol-fa notation, while the couplet on Arthur Berry's grave is as enigmatic as his life. But perhaps the most unusual memorial is that of Arnold Bennett.

Report has it that his ashes were being carried in a casket on a train from London when the courier errantly missed his stop and travelled on to Manchester passing by a number of noted guests and relatives waiting at Stoke station on a day full of drizzle and smoke. Another version is that the train wasn't due to stop at Stoke and expressed through the station in clouds of steam before it finally halted at Manchester. Once again myth and legend enters the story for some reporter opined that the courier in fact alighted at Stoke but forgot to remove the casket from the luggage rack after which the irate and upset relatives had to travel to Manchester to recover the grisly package from the LMS lost property office. Amusing and delightful stories such as these are still the bread and butter of news hounds - I do not believe that we are any the worse off for believing their content for many myths have passed into history as fact, just as long as we do not make them representative of academic history, or interpret the personality of a subject in order to win an audience. It becomes the task of the researcher, biographer and historian to seek out the real truth. But, it may be fair to say that truth lies in a life, and we may if minded search for it; but if we search we must do so with all the dignity and decency the subject deserves. I continue to ask myself - am I wrong to interfere and prod and probe into another's life - into the lives of the children so that I may tell the story of the Mother?

And so to end with the great author himself. The most unusual written component on the tomb of Arnold Bennett is more of an unfortunate error than that of leaving a dust-filled box on a train. And it goes a long way in explaining why one of the greatest writers in the English language is so unevenly observed by his townsfolk. (How can anyone not love his books!)

Arnold Bennett died 27th March 1931. Simultaneous memorial services were held at St Clement Dane Church London and at the side of the Longson family grave in High Lane Burslem Cemetery, at which only family mourners were permitted to attend. The author's mischievous ashes were placed in the tomb by younger brother Frank Bennett. After the service was ended and all the relations and friends had gone home, the public were eventually allowed to see the marble tribute and there saw the most curious sentence in the last chapter in the bizarre death of Arnold Bennett. In a simple statement the memorial noted:

'Here lie
The ashes of
Enoch
Arnold Bennett
Author
Son of
Enoch & Sarah Anne
Bennett
Born 27th May 1867
Died 29th March 1931'

How strangely humorous the author, I'm sure, would have found the mistake in the date of his death - two days later than it actually occurred! And how much is he still chuckling in the great bookshop in the sky when, even after seventy years, the unfortunate error on his last resting place still hasn't been corrected!

END PIECE

(with a nod to Lewis Carroll)

The Goose and the Falcon were pretty much bored with everything. Here they were, at the end, with nothing else to do but to look at the water or fly around. Mind you, the Goose didn't do much flying these days on account of the arthritis in her wing joints, so most days she just sat at the edge of the lake dangling her legs, making ripples, dreaming of aquamarine eggs. The Falcon hovered aimlessly in the gold of the lowering sky looking for quarry that had long disappeared.

The Falcon looked puzzled as he wheeled in long circles bringing himslef to hover above the Goose.
    "Hey!" he squarked, "Are we really the last?"
    "I think so," replied the Goose as she fluffed her feathers and sighed, "We seem to be alone."
    "Well, are we starting it or ending it", queried the Falcon, becoming tired of hovering in one spot.
    "We're ending it, I think. Although it might have been a Dove."
    "Or a Raven," interrupted the Falcon.
    "Hmm," thought the Goose, "Water!"
    "What-er?". asked the Falcon.
    "Shall we have another story?" the Goose prompted hopefully.
The Falcon dropped beside the Goose like a stone.
    "Why not," he declared, "While we wait."

Something disappeared down a hole close by.

    "This way; this way!" called the Mouse, excitedly. "If we all gather around this pond we shall have a better view of the arrival."

    "Someone coming?" yawned the Lory, as he pulled himself out of the hole, closely followed by Duck who made sure that a long cloud passed over his head before he shook the dust of the tree roots from his grey feathers.

    "Of course, of course, this is what I've been telling you about over the last hundred years. I just knew you hadn't been listening, not to one word I've said."

Somewhat dazed by the sudden light, Alice hauled herself out by hanging onto the cowslip and woodbine that the Lory had pushed towards her. And as the mouse ran about in circles, trying to focus on the best position for the arrival, Alice was followed from the widening hole by their new companions scrambling in turn to the edge of the pond. First came the Norman, William, pushed from behind with a helping hand by Edwin and Morcar who preceded the old Pope and the Archbishop of Canterbury. And finally, Edgar Atheling who joined everyone as they tumbled out onto the grass.

    "Where's Alfred?" asked the Mouse in a matter of fact tone.

    "Oh," replied the Archbishop looking over his shoulder at the mouth of the hole, "He's decided to stay down the hole with John and Elizabeth."

"Well it's their loss." determined the Mouse. "Let's get on."

"At least I'm dry now," winced Alice as she prised a pebble from her shoe. And then she looked around at her new surroundings.

"Where are we?" she said with tears welling in her eyes.

"Oh, for goodness sake, let's not have another flood!" cried the Mouse, assuming his stance as leader. "Once is more than enough, and what's more, another deluge would cast us all back to the beginning, and that would never do. Floods, floods and floods. What trouble they have caused!"

"Indeed not," said the Duck with a sort of deep growl as he remembered the flight from the ingurgitated sanctuary. The Lory shuddered as well, for well he was reminded of his own personal escape from the canary-besieged aviary in the Well of the Catalyst. Of course, that was very personal, and a long, long time ago; so far back that he thought he had forgotten it completely. He was shocked that he had recalled it to his mind.

"Oh dear!" he thought to himself. "Oh dear, oh dear."

Alice, who was sitting between William and Edgar, suddenly saw the Falcon and the Goose on the other side of the pond.

"Look," she pointed to the shrouded birds.

"It's rude to point," said William the Conqueror.

"Indeed it is," joined Edgar Atheling; "Desist at once dear girl, if you please."

Alice then indicated with her eyes, her gaze being picked-up instantly by the Mouse.

"That's better." said William. And Edgar agreed nodding silently.

"Oh yes." said the Mouse. "So I see. Now, leave this to me. I say, you two." He called across the water. "What are you doing here?"

Over the far side, the Goose continued dangling her feet in the pond making ripples and checking the width of their swell with her yellow beak.

"He's talking to you." The Falcon nudged his neighbour and nodded towards the newly arrived group. The Goose looked across and glared severely at the Mouse who was standing on his tiptoes.

"I don't think so." she commented haughtily, and splashed the water once more sending out more liquid serries towards the centre.

"He is you know." judged the Falcon, "Listen."

The Mouse shouted at the top of his voice, "Can you hear me. I'm talking to you."

"Are you?" asked the Goose. "I thought you were shouting to someone else. What do you want?"

"How long have you been here?" the Mouse called in a high pitched squeak.

"What did he say?" the Goose asked the Falcon.

"He's asking us how long we have been here."

"Tell him then."

"Well I'm sure I don't know," said the Falcon, "And in any case, he's talking to you."

The Goose pondered this last statement for some minutes, and then resignedly she said,

"Hm, I'd better answer him then".

She scrutinized the far side of the pond. There was something about the group that was vaguely familiar, but try as she might, she was unable to remember where she had seen this itinerant party before. Her eyes settled on the Duck. She sighed and then she turned to squint the Mouse.

"Do you know any stories?"

"Well, yes, I do as a matter of fact" replied the Mouse, taking the question as a request. "Shall we come across and I'll tell you one while we're all waiting?"

"Oh yes please" cooed the Falcon, "I've used all mine up".

Both the Duck and the Lory groaned. William and his party, not being able to stand another history story, wandered off looking for inviting holes. And Alice began to cry.

Just then another group wandered into the scene led by a portly man in a dinner suit with tails.

"Oooh look," said Elsie Watts, "That mouse is going to tell a story. Shall we sit down by the water's edge and listen?"

"Ugh!" cringed Arnold Bennett, "We'll find somewhere else to wait."

"Why can't we wait here?" demanded The Card.

"Because, w-w-water kill's me!" he replied as he led his party away.

SOURCES AND ACKNOWLEDGEMENTS

Wherever appropriate, full acknowledgements to specific publications have been made within the text. Much of the reference to official documents and files together with news cuttings have been made with the cooperation of the staff of Stoke on Trent City Libraries Archive Department for whose assistance I am grateful.

I thank Madame Virginia Eldin, daughter of Arnold Bennett and administrator of his estate, for permission to quote many passages from the author's works.

I am particularly grateful to Faber and Faber the publishers of The Whitsun Weddings by Philip Larkin for their permission to reproduce in full MCMXIV. And to Macmillan & Co Ltd for permission to reproduce When You Are Old from the Collected Poems of W B Yeats (1933).

I am also grateful for the permission to print from the recordings of Arthur Berry and thank Tony Wild and Cynthia Berry for their interest and permission where appropriate.

The following is a list of books I have referred to which the genuine researcher and the casual reader will find indispensable in their own references.

    Baker, Diane. The Industrial Architecture of Staffordshire pub. by the Royal Commission on the Historical Monuments of England. (1991)

    Briggs, J. Newcastle under Lyme 1173-1973

    Burchill F & Ross R, A History of The Potter's Union pub. by CATU (1977)

    Christianson, Rex & R W Miller. The North Staffordshire Railway, David & Charles

    Clark, Peter. The English Alehouse (Longman 1883)

    Dimond, Francis and Roger Taylor. Crown and Camera Pub. Penguin

    Fielding, Steve. The Hangman's Record Vol. one 1868-1899 (Chancery House Press 1994)

    Glen, Fred. Vincent Riley, (The Story of a Methylated Spirit) L Orridge Newcastle, Staffs

    Havergal Brian On Music, ed. by Malcolm MacDonald, Pub. by Toccata Press

    Mantoux, Paul. The Industrial Revolution in the Eighteenth Century, pub. by OUP

    Meteyard, E. The Life of Josiah Wedgwood (1865)

    Moriarty's Police Law 1929 Edition. Pub. by Butterworths

    Music in The Potteries by Reginald Nettell pub. by

    Owen, Harold. The Staffordshire Potter Redwood Press Ltd.

    Plott, R. The Natural History of Staffordshire (1886)

    Presidential Address by H J Steele, pub. by North Staffordshire Field Club Transaction 1943.

Rendevous With The Past - Pub. by Staffordshire Sentinel Newspapers Ltd. 1954

Rhead, GW & EA. Staffordshire Pots and Potters, pub. by Hutchinson & Co

Scarratt, William. Old Times in The Potteries privately published by the author (1905)

Scriven, H. The Education of Children in The Potteries. (1843)

Stuart, Denis. People of the Potteries Vol. 1 pub. by Dept. of Adult Education of the University of Keele. (1985)

Talbot, Richard The Church and Ancient Parish of Stoke on Trent, Webberley's Ltd.

The Sentinel Story pub. by James Heap (Hanley 1925) Ltd.

Thomas, J. Rise of the Staffordshire Potteries (Bath 1971)

Thompson, WJ. Industrial Archaeology of North Staffordshire pub. by Moorland Publishing Co, Buxton, Derbyshire.

Victoria County History of Staffordshire Vol. 2 and 8

Ward John, History of the Borough of Stoke on Trent by John Ward, pub. by W Lewis & Son London (1843)

Warrillow, Ernest JD, A Sociological History of the City of Stoke on Trent, pub. by Etruscan Press (1977)

Wedgwood, Henry. Romance of The Potteries

I would like to thank the board and members of Burslem Community Development Trust, and in particular Anthony Tabbinor M.S.F.A, A.L.I.A (dip), F.L.I.A and Chris Nocetti for their individual support in bringing this book to publication.

Fred Hughes is very much a believer in the adage 'try everything once'. A professional soldier at the time of the Suez Crisis, then a policeman stationed at Burslem. When he retired from Staffordshire Police, having 'seen-off' two careers, he turned to local politics working as agent and secretary to a Stoke on Trent MP. About this time his own political career was maturing and he was elected as a councillor representing Burslem both with Stoke on Trent City Council and with Staffordshire County Council. His strong links with the Mother Town and his passion for history, document collecting and photography presented him with yet another career move when he began sharing his experiences by giving popular history talks and walks. Often to be heard on BBC Radio Stoke, and in articles published by the Sentinel, he has become a consultative authority on Burslem's historical background. His published history works include contributions to Radio Stoke's Biography of Arnold Bennett, The Sentinel's The Way We Were Millennium, A History Of Cobridge, published by Cobridge Community Renewal (The Voice), and the history script for the SRB Final Report. He is currently writing the history of the Burslem Association for the Prosecution of Felons.